OXFORD SHAKESPEARE CONCORDANCES

OXFORD SHAKESPEARE CONCORDANCES

THE TAMING OF THE SHREW

A CONCORDANCE TO THE TEXT
OF THE FIRST FOLIO

OXFORD
AT THE CLARENDON PRESS
1969

Oxford University Press, Ely House, London W. 1

GLASGOW NEW YORK TORONTO MELBOURNE WELLINGTON
CAPE TOWN SALISBURY IBADAN NAIROBI LUSAKA ADDIS ABABA
BOMBAY CALCUTTA MADRAS KARACHI LAHORE DACCA
KUALA LUMPUR SINGAPORE HONG KONG TOKYO JOHANNESBURG

FILMSET BY COMPUTAPRINT LIMITED
AND PRINTED IN GREAT BRITAIN
AT THE UNIVERSITY PRESS, OXFORD
BY VIVIAN RIDLER
PRINTER TO THE UNIVERSITY

GENERAL INTRODUCTION

IN this series of Oxford Shakespeare Concordances, a separate volume is devoted to each of the plays. The text for each concordance is the one chosen as copy-text by Dr. Alice Walker for the Oxford Old Spelling Shakespeare now in preparation.

Each concordance takes account of every word in the text, and represents their occurrence by frequency counts, line numbers, and reference lines, or a selection of these according to the interest of the particular word. The number of words which have frequency counts only has been kept as low as possible. The introduction to each volume records the facsimile copy of the text from which the concordance was prepared, a table of Folio through line numbers and Globe edition act and scene numbers, a list of the misprints corrected in the text, and an account of the order of printing, and the proof-reading, abstracted from Professor Charlton Hinman's *The Printing and Proof-Reading of the First Folio of Shakespeare* (Oxford, 1963).

The following notes on the main features of the concordances may be helpful.[1]

A. *The Text*

The most obvious misprints have been corrected, on conservative principles, and have been listed for each play in the introduction to the corresponding concordance. Wrong-fount letters have been silently corrected.

Obvious irregularities on the part of the original compositor—for example the anomalous absence of full stops after speech prefixes—have been normalized and noted. Colons, semicolons, exclamation and interrogation marks after italicized words have been modernized to roman fount after current practice, since this aspect of

---

[1] An account of the principles and methods by which the concordances were edited appears in *Studies in Bibliography*, vol. 22, 1969.

compositorial practice would not normally be studied from a concordance. The spacing of words in the original printed texts, particu-
larly in 'justified' lines, is extremely variable; spacing has been
normalized on the basis of the compositor's practice as revealed in
the particular column or page.

For ease of reference, the contractions *S.*, *L.*, *M.*, and forms such
as *Mist.* and tildes, have been expanded when the compositor's own
preferred practice is clear, and the expansion has been noted in the
text. For Mʳ, the superior character has been lowered silently.
Superior characters like the circumflex in *baâ* and those in y̒, y̦, y̒, and
w̧, have been ignored. The reader should find little difficulty in dis-
tinguishing the original form of the pronominal contractions when
they are encountered in the text. They are listed under Y and W
respectively.

B. *Arrangement of entries*

The words in the text are arranged alphabetically, with numerals
and & and &c listed at the end. Words starting with I and J, and U
and V, will be found together under I and V respectively. The reader
should note that the use of U for the medial V (and I for J) leads in
some cases to an unfamiliar order of entry. For example, ADUISED is
listed before ADULTERY. The reader will usually find the word he
wants if he starts his inquiry at the modern spelling, for when the old
spelling differs considerably from the modern spelling, a reference
such as 'ENFORCE *see* inforce' will direct the reader to the entry in the
concordance.

In hyphenated compounds where the hyphen is the second or third
character of the heading-word (as in A-BOORD), the hyphenated form
may be listed some distance from other occurrences of the same word
in un-hyphenated form. In significant cases, references are given to
alert the user.

Under the heading-word, the line numbers or lines of context are
in the order of the text. The heading-word is followed by a frequency
count of the words in short and long (that is, marked with an
asterisk) lines, and the reference lines. When a word has been treated
as one to have a frequency count only, or a list of the line numbers

and count, any further count which follows will refer to the reference lines listed under the same heading. Where there are two counts but no reference lines (as with AN), the first count refers to the speech prefix.

C. *Special Forms*

(*a*) The following words have not been given context lines and line references but are dealt with only by the counting of their frequency:

A AM AND ARE AT BE BY HE I IN IS IT OF ON SHE THE THEY TO WAS WE WITH YOU

These forms occur so often in most texts that the reader can locate them more easily by examining the text of the play than he could by referring to an extensive listing in the concordance.

Homographs of these words (for example I = *ay*) have been listed in full and are given separate counts under the same heading-word.

(*b*) A larger number of words, consisting mainly of variant spellings, have been given line references as well as frequency counts.

These words are: ACTUS AN AR ART ATT AU BEE BEEING BEEN BEENE BEING BENE BIN BUT CAN CANST CE COULD COULDST DE DECIMA DES DID DIDD DIDDEST DIDDST DO DOE DOES DOEST DOETH DONE DOO DOOE DOOES DOOEST DOOING DOON DOONE DOOS DOOST DOOTH DOS DOST DOTH DU E EN EST ET ETC FINIS FOR FROM HA HAD HADST HAH HAS HAST HATH HAUE HEE HEEL HEELE HEL HELL HER HIM HIR HIS IE IF IL ILL ILLE INTO LA LE LES MA MAIE MAIEST MAIST MAY ME MEE MIGHT MIGHTEST MIGHTST MINE MOI MOY MY NE NO NOE NON NONA NOR NOT O OCTAUA OFF OH OR OU OUR OUT PRIMA PRIMUS QUARTA QUARTUS QUE QUINTA QUINTUS SCAENA SCENA SCOENA SECUNDA SECUNDUS SEPTIMA SEPTIMUS SEXTA SHAL SHALL SHALT SHEE SHOLD SHOLDE SHOLDST SHOULD SHOULDE SHOULDST SIR SO SOE TE TERTIA TERTIUS THAT THEE THEIR THEIRE THEM THEN THER THERE THESE THEYR THIS THOSE THOU THY TIS TU VN VNE VOS VOSTRE VOUS VS WAST WEE WER WERE WERT WHAT WHEN WHER WHERE WHICH WHO WHOM WHOME WHY WIL WILL WILT WILTE WOLD WOLDE WOLDST WOULD WOULDE WOULDEST WOULDST YE YEE YF YOUE YOUR YT & &C 1 2 3 4.

Homographs of words on this list (e.g. *bee* = n.) have been listed in full, and also have separate counts.

(*c*) All speech prefixes, other than *All.*, *Both.*, and those which represent the names of actors, have been treated as count-only words. In some cases, however, where a speech prefix corresponds to a form already on the count-only list (e.g. *Is.*), a full entry has been given. In some other cases, when two counts are given for the same heading-word for no apparent reason, the count which does not correspond to the following full references or to the list of line references is that of the speech prefix form (for example AN in *The Tempest*).

(*d*) Hyphenated compounds such as *all-building-law* have been listed under the full form, and also under each main constituent after the first. In this example there are entries under ALL-BUILDING-LAW, BUILDING, and LAW. When, however, one of the constituents of the compound is a word on the count- or location-only list ((*a*) or (*b*) above), it is dealt with in whichever of these two lists applies. References such as 'AT *see also* bemock't-at-stabs' are given to assist the reader in such cases.

Simple or non-hyphenated compounds such as *o'th'King* have been listed only under the constituent parts—in this example under OTH and KING.

(*e*) 'Justified' lines where the spellings *may* have been affected by the compositor's need to fit the text to his measure are distinguished by an asterisk at the beginning of the reference line. If only location is being given, the asterisk occurs before the line reference. If only frequency counts are being given, the number *after* the asterisk records the frequency of forms occurring in 'justified' lines. Lines which do not extend to the full width of the compositor's measure have not been distinguished as 'justified' lines, even though in many cases the shorter line may have affected the spelling.

D. *Line Numbers*

The lines in each text have been numbered from the first *Actus Primus* or stage direction and thereafter in normal reading order, including all stage directions and act and scene divisions. Each typographical line has been counted as a unit when it contains matter for inclusion in the concordance. Catchwords are not included in the count. The only general exception is that turn-overs are regarded as belonging to their base-lines; where a turn-over occurs on a line by itself, it has been reckoned as part of the base-line, and the line containing only the turn-over has not been counted as a separate line. Turn-overs may readily be distinguished by vertical stroke and single bracket after the last word of the base-line; for example *brought with* | (*child*,.

When two or more lines have been joined in order to provide a fuller context, the line-endings are indicated by a vertical stroke |, and the line reference applies to that part of the line before the vertical stroke. For the true line-numbers of words in the following part of the context line, the stated line-number should be increased by one each time a vertical stroke occurs, save when the next word is a turn-over.

The numbering of the quarto texts has been fitted to that of the corresponding Folio texts; lines in the Quarto which do not occur in the Folio are prefixed by $+$. The line references are similarly specified. The line references of these concordances therefore provide a consistent permanent numbering of each typographical line of text, based on the First Folio.

PROGRAM CHANGES

Preparation of concordances to the first few texts, and the especial complexity of *Wiv.*, have enabled some improvements to be made to the main concordance program. For texts other than *Tmp.*, *TGV*, *MM*, and *Err.*, the concordances have been prepared with the improved program.

Speech-prefixes now have separate entries under the appropriate heading-word and follow any other entry under the same heading-word. Entries under AN in *Wiv.*, AND and TO in *TN*, and AD in *AYL* offer examples. This alteration provides a clearer record of the total number of occurrences of words which occur both as speech-prefixes and also as forms on the 'count only' or 'locations only' lists.

Another modification supplies a more precise reference to the location of words such as BEENE for which line numbers but no full lines are given. When a 'location only' word is encountered to the right of the 'end-of-line' bar (which shows that lines of text have been joined together in order to provide a sufficient context), the line number is now adjusted to supply the exact reference. In the concordances to the texts listed above, users will find that in some instances the particular occurrence of a 'location only' word which they wish to consult in the text is to be found in the line after the one specified in the concordance; this depends on whether lines have been joined in the computer-readable version of the text from which the concordance was made. It is not expected that readers will be seriously inconvenienced by this. Should a concordance to the First Folio be published, it will, of course, incorporate all improvements.

THE TAMING OF THE SHREW

Lee's facsimile of the First Folio (Oxford, 1902), which provided the copy for the concordance to *Shr.*, shows the corrected states of formes S2:5^v and V1:6^v but the variants do not affect the text (Hinman, *Printing and Proof-Reading*. Oxford, 1963. V. 1, p. 262–3). The order of printing which he gives for this section of the Folio (v. 2, p. 515) runs as follows:

| By By | By By | By By | By By | ‖ | By By | By By | By By | By By |
| S3^v:4 | S3:4^v | S2^v:5 | S2:5^v | ‖ | S1^v:6 | S1:6^v | T3^v:4 | T3:4^v |

| Cy Ax | Cy Ax | Cy Ax | Cy Ax | Ax Cy | Ax Cy | ‖ | [At this point |
| T2^v:5 | T2:5^v | T1^v:6 | T1:6^v | V3^v:4 | V3:4^v | ‖ | |

| a major interruption.] | By By | By By | By By | By By |
| | V2:5^v | V2^v:5 | V1^v:6 | V1:6^v |

TABLE OF LINE AND ACT/SCENE NUMBERS

Page	Col.	Comp.	F line nos.	Globe act/scene nos.
S2^v	a	B	1–48	Ind.1.1–Ind.1.44
	b	B	49–96	Ind.1.86
S3	a	B	97–161	Ind.2.9
	b	B	162–227	Ind.2.77
S3^v	a	B	228–91	Ind.2.140
	b	B	292–354	1.1.52
S4	a	B	355–420	1.1.119
	b	B	421–86	1.1.188
S4^v	a	B	487–551	1.1.248
	b	B	552–616	1.2.50
S5	a	B	617–82	1.2.117
	b	B	683–747	1.2.182
S5^v	a	B	748–812	1.2.240
	b	B	813–76	2.1.22
S6	a	B	877–941	2.1.78
	b	B	942–1007	2.1.142
S6^v	a	B	1008–73	2.1.200
	b	B	1074–139	2.1.262
T1	a	C	1140–203	2.1.325
	b	C	1204–69	2.1.389
T1^v	a	C	1270–330	3.1.37
	b	C	1331–95	3.2.7
T2	a	C	1396–461	3.2.78
	b	C	1462–526	3.2.145

Page	Col.	Comp.	F line nos.	Globe act/scene nos.
T2v	a	C	1527–88	3.2.203
	b	C	1589–653	4.1.15
T3	a	B	1654–719	4.1.93
	b	B	1720–84	4.1.158
T3v	a	B	1785–850	4.2.4
	b	B	1851–916	4.2.63
T4	a	B	1917–978	4.3.SD
	b	B	1979–2043	4.3.60
T4v	a	B	2044–109	4.3.123
	b	B	2110–75	4.3.194
T5	a	A	2176–238	4.4.56
	b	A	2239–302	4.5.6
T5v	a	A	2303–67	4.5.68
	b	A	2368–431	5.1.55
T6	a	A	2432–96	5.1.118
	b	A	2497–557	5.2.19
T6v	a	A	2558–623	5.2.76
	b	A	2624–88	5.2.131
V1	a	B	2689–719	5.2.161
	b	B	2720–2751 (Finis)	5.2.189

Alterations to the text were made at these points:

S3	171	Sies		1943	you
S3v	244	3.*man.*		1965	you
	295	a a	T4v	2061	If
	313	brough		2126	*Tai*:
	351	resolu∧d		2171	Aud
S4	394	resould:	T5	2190	,Twere
	441	too∧t		2206	*Ped*∧
	466	*Luc*∧		2281	fot,
S4v	513	Conlord	T5v	2314	theu
	552	you		2315	in
	612	twixr		2379	*Bianea*,
S5	703	*disgused.*		2422	brough
S5v	803	streers		2431	*Vincentio*?
	824	*Baptistæs*	T6	2444	doubtlet,
S6	1000	yet		2502	*Bnp.*
S6v	1134	rhen		2520	doug,hbut
T1v	1322	*hie*		2526	Mo
T2v	1640	*Gru*:		2532	ueuer,
T3	1784	you	T6v	2624	Igoe.
T3v	1857	ptoue	VI	2694	thretaning
T4	1918	eountenance		2743	weee'le

Three conversion errors have been noted in the course of checking the film of the concordance. Because they are textually unimportant and because attempts to correct them by altering the film from which the concordance is printed might lead to the inadvertent loss of a character or line during printing, I have decided to let them stand. If a concordance to the Folio should be published, it will not contain these blemishes.

In lines 1456 and 1672 under the headings of the main words comprising the lines, 'z' has failed to convert to &; these lines are, however, properly recorded under the & heading. Further, readers will observe that where line 8 is printed the end-of-line bar in *Pau-|cas* is improperly rendered.

December, 1968   **T. H. H.**

THE TAMING OF THE SHREW

ABOUE *cont.*
And slept aboue some fifteene yeare or more. 267
Exeunt. The Presenters aboue speakes. 557
ABOUT = 5*3
*Master, master, looke about you: Who goes there? ha. 706
I promist to enquire carefully | About a schoolemaster for the faire
Bianca, 731
Shee hung about my necke, and kisse on kisse 1188
*Bride about the necke, and kist her lips with such a cla- | morous 1559
Ile finde about the making of the bed, 1834
You might haue heard it else proclaim'd about. 1943
Luc. And what of all this. | *Bion.* I cannot tell, expect they are busied
about a 2276
Hap what hap may, Ile roundly goe about her: 2292
ABROAD = 1
And so am come abroad to see the world. 624
ABSENT = 1
That I should yet absent me from your bed: 277
ABUSD = *1
Vin. Thus strangers may be haild and abusd: oh mon- | strous villaine. 2486
ACCEPT = 4*1
2.Player. So please your Lordshippe to accept our | dutie. 91
Accept of him, or else you do me wrong. 920
His name is *Cambio*: pray accept his seruice. 946
If you accept them, then their worth is great: 964
If this be court'sie sir, accept of it. 1967
ACCESSE = 4*1
*we may yet againe haue accesse to our faire Mistris, and 420
That none shal haue accesse vnto *Bianca*, 692
Her father keepes from all accesse of sutors, 833
For our accesse, whose hap shall be to haue her, 841
And free accesse and fauour as the rest. 960
ACCOMPANIE = 1
Vnlesse you wil accompanie me thither. 672
ACCOMPLISHED = 1
Vnto their Lords, by them accomplished, 123
ACCORD = 1
Bian. Gamouth I am, the ground of all accord: 1366
ACCORDING = 1
According to the fashion, and the time. 2080
ACCOUNTEDST = 1
If thou accountedst it shame, lay it on me, 2164
ACCOUTREMENTS = 1
As I can change these poore accoutrements, 1502
ACHIEUE *see* atcheeue, atchieue
ACQUAINTED = 2
One *Kate* you must kisse, and be acquainted with. 1781
Made me acquainted with a waighty cause 2208
ACQUAINTAINCE = 1
Balke Lodgicke with acquaintaince that you haue, 333
ACTION = 3
He beare himselfe with honourable action, 121
Voice, gate, and action of a Gentlewoman: 144
Ile bring mine action on the proudest he 1620
ACTUS *I.*1 1294 1977 2533 = 4
AD = *1
preuilegio ad Impremendum solem, to th' Church take the 2279

2

ADAM = 1
There were none fine, but *Adam*, *Rafe*, and *Gregory*,   1763
ADDE = 2
Tra. But sir, Loue concerneth vs to adde   1511
The wager thou hast won, and I will adde   2667
ADDER = 1
Or is the Adder better then the Eele,   2160
ADEW = *1
*stuffe a Rabit, and so may you sir: and so adew sir, my   2286
ADIEU = 2
Pet. Father, and wife, and gentlemen adieu,   1201
Gre. Adieu good neighbour: now I feare thee not: 1281
ADMIRE = 1
Onely (good master) while we do admire | This vertue, and this morall
discipline,   328
ADOE = *1
Kate. Husband let's follow, to see the end of this adoe.   2522
ADONIS = 1
Adonis painted by a running brooke,   202
ADRIATICKE = 1
Affections edge in me. Were she is as rough | As are the swelling
Adriaticke seas.   639
ADUANTAGE *see* vantage
ADUERSARIES = 1
And do as aduersaries do in law,   850
ADUICE = *1
*parle, know now vpon aduice, it toucheth vs both: that   419
ADUISD = 1
But art thou not aduis'd, he tooke some care   489
ADUISE = 4*1
Luc. Gramercies *Tranio*, well dost thou aduise,   340
*But sirra, not for my sake, but your masters, I ad-|uise   549
Petr. Sirra be gone, or talke not I aduise you.   610
This wil I do, and this I wil aduise you.   1948
Now doe your dutie throughlie I aduise you: 2192
AEACIDES = 1
Bian. Mistrust it not, for sure *Aeacides*   1345
AFEARD = 1
I meane *Hortentio* is afeard of you.   2557
AFFABILITY = 1
Her affability and bashfull modestie: 910
AFFABLE = 2
An affable and courteous Gentleman,   664
With gentle conference, soft, and affable.   1130
AFFEARD = 1
Wid. Then neuer trust me if I be affeard.   2554
AFFECT = 2
In briefe sir, studie what you most affect.   339
Bian. If you affect him sister, heere I sweare   869
AFFECTED = 1
I am in all affected as your selfe,   325
AFFECTION = 3
Affection is not rated from the heart: 463
Cfavt, that loues with all affection: 1369
Tra. Signior *Hortensio*, I haue often heard | Of your entire affection to
Bianca,   1870

3

AFFECTIONS = 2

Affections edge in me. Were she is as rough | As are the swelling *Adriaticke* seas.   639

Or both dissemble deepely their affections: 2224

AFFIED = 1

We be affied and such assurance tane,   2231

AFFOORDS = 1

Let them want nothing that my house affoords. | *Exit one with the Players*.   114

AFFORDS = 2

Bap. Padua affords this kindnesse, sonne *Petruchio*.   2550

Petr. Padua affords nothing but what is kinde.   2551

AFFRAID = 1

Hor. I am affraid sir, doe what you can   2640

AFRESH = *1

*yongest free for a husband, and then haue too't afresh: 441

AFTER = 7*5

Tra. So could I 'faith boy, to haue the next wish af-|ter,   547

And then I know after who comes by the worst.   580

Kate. Her silence flouts me, and Ile be reueng'd. | *Flies after Bianca*   886

Bap. After my death, the one halfe of my Lands,   986

Was it not to refresh the minde of man | After his studies, or his vsuall paine?   1306

Bap. Ile after him, and see the euent of this. *Exit*.   1510

*swore, as if the Vicar meant to cozen him: but after ma-|ny   1552

*he, as if he had beene aboord carowsing to his Mates af-|ter   1554

*after mee I know the rout is comming, such a mad mar-|ryage   1562

Tra. Let vs intreat you stay till after dinner.   1580

*make a fire, and they are comming after to warme them: 1643

After our great good cheere: praie you sit downe,   2547

AFTERNOONE = 1*1

Please ye we may contriue this afternoone,   848

*afternoone as shee went to the Garden for Parseley to   2285·

AGAINE = 8*5

To morrow I intend to hunt againe. | *Hunts*. I will my Lord.   32

And once againe a pot o'th smallest Ale.   227

*But I would be loth to fall into my dreames againe: I   280

*we may yet againe haue accesse to our faire Mistris, and   420

Nay, come againe, good *Kate*, I am a Gentleman,   1095

Pet. I sweare Ile cuffe you, if you strike againe.   1097

Luc. Spit in the hole man, and tune againe.   1333

And as he stoop'd againe to take it vp,   1546

Tra. What said the wench when he rose againe?   1550

*the sleeues should be cut out, and sow'd vp againe, and   2129

Goe on, and fetch our horses backe againe,   2305

Petr. Why then let's home againe: Come Sirra let's | awaie.   2527

Bian. I, but not frighted me, therefore Ile sleepe a-|gaine.   2585

AGAINST *see also* 'gainst = 3*1

To giue my hand oppos'd against my heart   1397

Ile buckler thee against a Million. *Exeunt. P. Ka.*   1625

*the Priest be readie to come against you come with your | appendix. *Exit*.   2288

And not vnluckily against the Bias: 2322

AGE = 4

Then any woman in this waining age.   215

Skipper stand backe, 'tis age that nourisheth.   1221

To giue thee all, and in his wayning age   1283

AGE *cont.*
And now by Law, as well as reuerent age,   2359
AGENOR = 1
Such as the daughter of *Agenor* had,   471
AGLET = *1
*to a Puppet or an Aglet babie, or an old trot with ne're a   645
AGOE *see also* goe = 1
Bian. Why, I am past my gamouth long agoe.   1364
AGREE = 2
Luc. At last, though long, our iarring notes agree,   2538
Should well agree with our externall parts?   2726
AGREED *see also* greed = *1
**Grem.* I am agreed, and would I had giuen him the   444
AGREEMENT = 3
Vpon agreement from vs to his liking,   748
No worse then I, vpon some agreement   2215
As shall with either parts agreement stand.   2232
AH = 1
Luc. Ah *Tranio*, what a cruell Fathers he: 488
AIAX = 1
Was *Aiax* cald so from his grandfather.   1346
AIMD *see also* aym'd = 1
This bird you aim'd at, though you hit her not,   2593
AIRE *see* ayre
ALARUMS *see also* larums = *1
*mine to endure her lowd alarums, why man there bee   431
ALAS = 2
Pet. Alas good *Kate*, I will not burthen thee,   1076
Ped. Alas sir, it is worse for me then so,   1944
ALCE = 1
Beg. Alce Madam, or *Ione* Madam?   264
ALCIDES = 1
And let it be more then *Alcides* twelue.   830
ALE = 3*1
with Ale, this were a bed but cold to sleep so soundly.   37
Beg. For Gods sake a pot of small Ale.   153
*sheere Ale, score me vp for the lyingst knaue in Christen|dome. What
I am not bestraught: here's---   176
And once againe a pot o'th smallest Ale.   227
ALEWIFE = *1
*Aske *Marrian Hacket* the fat Alewife of Wincot, if shee   174
ALIGHTED = *1
**Gre.* E'ne at hand, alighted by this: and therefore be   1744
ALIUE = 1
Bianca. Beleeue me sister, of all the men aliue,   865
ALL *see also* withall = 100*17
But sup them well, and looke vnto them all,   31
And hang it round with all my wanton pictures: 51
Lord. With all my heart. This fellow I remember,   93
And see him drest in all suites like a Ladie: 117
See this dispatch'd with all the hast thou canst,   140
Their harnesse studded all with Gold and Pearle.   194
And Citherea all in sedges hid,   203
But did I neuer speake of all that time.   235
Beg. Now Lord be thanked for my good amends. | *All.* Amen.   250
I am your wife in all obedience.   261
Being all this time abandon'd from your bed.   269

THE TAMING OF THE SHREW

ALL *cont.*

My trustie seruant well approu'd in all,	306
It shall become to serue all hopes conceiu'd	314
I am in all affected as your selfe,	325
Hor. From all such diuels, good Lord deliuer vs.	*Gre.* And me too,	
good Lord.	369
*them, would take her with all faults, and mony enough.	433
Perhaps you mark'd not what's the pith of all.	469
Sacred and sweet was all I saw in her.	479
*you vse your manners discreetly in all kind of com-|panies:	550
*When I am alone, why then I am *Tranio*: but in | all places else, your	
master *Lucentio*.	551
To see my friends in *Padua*; but of all	567
Grumio, and my good friend *Petruchio*? How do you all | at *Verona*?	589
And shrow'd, and froward, so beyond all measure,	656
Gru. Katherine the curst, | A title for a maide, of all titles the worst.	694
All bookes of Loue, see that at any hand,	712
Hortensio, haue you told him all her faults?	752
If that be all Masters, I heare no harme.	754
You shal haue me assisting you in all.	761
To whom my Father is not all vnknowne,	813
Gre. What, this Gentleman will out-talke vs all.	820
Petr. Hortensio, to what end are all these words?	822
Her father keepes from all accesse of sutors,	833
Must steed vs all, and me amongst the rest:	838
To whom we all rest generally beholding.	846
Yea all my raiment, to my petticoate,	860
Kate. Of all thy sutors heere I charge tel	863
Bianca. Beleeue me sister, of all the men aliue,	865
You haue but iested with me all this while:	875
Ka. If that be iest, then all the rest was so. *Strikes her*	877
A man well knowne throughout all Italy.	930
This liberty is all that I request,	957
And so I pray you all to thinke your selues.	978
Left solie heire to all his Lands and goods,	982
In all my Lands and Leases whatsoeuer,	990
That is her loue: for that is all in all.	994
Yet extreme gusts will blow out fire and all:	1000
For dainties are all *Kates*, and therefore *Kate*	1060
Kate. Where did you study all this goodly speech?	1141
And therefore setting all this chat aside,	1147
Pet. Father, 'tis thus, your selfe and all the world	1170
My hangings all of *tirian* tapestry:	1231
Pewter and brasse, and all things that belongs	1237
And all things answerable to this portion.	1241
Of fruitfull land, all which shall be her ioynter.	1252
My Land amounts not to so much in all:	1255
Gre. Nay, I haue offred all, I haue no more,	1263
And she can haue no more then all I haue,	1264
Tra. Why then the maid is mine from all the world	1266
To giue thee all, and in his wayning age	1283
And to cut off all strife: heere sit we downe,	1316
Luc. All but the base.	1339
Bian. Gamouth I am, the ground of all accord:	1366
Cfavt, that loues with all affection:	1369
Bion. Oh sir, his Lackey, for all the world Capari-|son'd	1451
Bap. Why that's all one.	1465

6

ALL *cont.*

Hath all so long detain'd you from your wife,	1486
As you shall well be satisfied with all.	1492
Which once perform'd, let all the world say no,	1524
Ile keepe mine owne despite of all the world.	1525
All for my Masters sake *Lucentio.*	1531
That all amaz'd the Priest let fall the booke,	1545
*all in the Sextons face: hauing no other reason, but that	1556
*smacke, that at the parting all the Church did	1560
And honest company, I thanke you all,	1575
For I must hence, and farewell to you all.	1579
Tra. Of all mad matches neuer was the like.	1628
Gru. Fie, fie on all tired Iades, on all mad Masters, z	1640
*all foule waies: was euer man so beaten? was euer man	1641
Cur. All readie: and therefore I pray thee newes.	1687
Gru. I, and that thou and the proudest of you all shall	1716
they kisse their hands. Are they all readie?	1723
companions, is all readie, and all things neate?	1742
Nat. All things is readie, how neere is our master?	1743
All ser. Heere, heere sir, heere sir.	1750
And *Gabrels* pumpes were all vnpinkt i'thheele:	1760
Pet. 'Tis burnt, and so is all the meate:	1793
There, take it to you, trenchers, cups, and all:	1797
That all is done in reuerend care of her,	1838
And in conclusion, she shal watch all night,	1839
As one vnworthie all the former fauours	1878
Hor. Would all the world but he had quite forsworn	1883
Bion. As much as an apple doth an oyster, & all one.	1957
And thinke it not the worst of all your fortunes,	1960
In all these circumstances Ile instruct you,	1975
And that which spights me more then all these wants,	1989
Sorrow on thee, and all the packe of you	2012
Petr. How fares my Kate, what sweeting all a-mort?	2016
And all my paines is sorted to no proofe.	2024
Petr. Eate it vp all *Hortensio*, if thou louest mee:	2032
With Amber Bracelets, Beades, and all this knau'ry.	2040
The match is made, and all is done,	2228
Bio. The old Priest at Saint *Lukes* Church is at your | command at all houres.	2274
Luc. And what of all this. | *Bion.* I cannot tell, expect they are busied about a	2276
Gre. I maruaile *Cambio* comes not all this while.	2386
And by all likelihood some cheere is toward. *Knock.*	2394
I neuer saw you before in all my life.	2429
*at home, my sonne and my seruant spend all at the vni- | uersitie.	2447
forsweare him, or else we are all vndone.	2489
Gre. Here's packing with a witnesse to deceiue vs all.	2499
Out of hope of all, but my share of the feast.	2521
You are welcome all. *Exit Bianca.*	2591
Therefore a health to all that shot and mist.	2594
I thinke thou hast the veriest shrew of all.	2607
Luc. Ile haue no halues: Ile beare it all my selfe.	2626

ALLA = *1

Hor. Alla nostra casa bene venuto multo honorata signi-|or mio Petruchio.	593

ALLEGES *see* leges

ALLOTS *see* lots
ALMES = 1
   Vpon intreatie haue a present almes,   1983
ALMOST = 2
   Master and mistris are almost frozen to death.   1674
   Kate. I dare assure you sir, 'tis almost two,   2172
ALOFT = *1
   Enter aloft the drunkard with attendants, some with apparel, | Bason and
   Ewer, & other appurtenances, & Lord.   151
ALONE = 6*1
   Beg. 'Tis much, seruants leaue me and her alone: 270
   *When I am alone, why then I am *Tranio*: but in | all places else, your
   master *Lucentio*.   551
   Though *Paris* came, in hope to speed alone.   819
   'Tis bargain'd twixt vs twaine being alone,   1184
   How tame when men and women are alone,   1192
   Par. Take me your loue, and then let me alone.   1924
   You are still crossing it, sirs let't alone,   2176
ALONG = 3
   And bring along these rascal knaues with thee?   1758
   Which way thou trauellest, if along with vs,   2349
   Petr. Come goe along and see the truth hereof,   2374
ALTHOUGH = 1
   Although I thinke 'twas in another sense,   521
AM = 63*17
AMASDE = 1
   That with your strange encounter much amasde me: 2352
AMAZD = 1
   That all amaz'd the Priest let fall the booke,   1545
AMAZED = 1
   And there I stood amazed for a while,   1023
AMBER = 1
   With Amber Bracelets, Beades, and all this knau'ry.   2040
AMBO = 1
   Exeunt ambo. Manet Tranio and Lucentio   448
AMEN = 2
   Beg. Now Lord be thanked for my good amends. | *All*. Amen. 250
   Gre. Tra. Amen say we, we will be witnesses.   1200
AMENDMENT = *1
   Mes. Your Honors Players hearing your amendment,   283
AMENDS = 1
   Beg. Now Lord be thanked for my good amends. | *All*. Amen. 250
AMIABLE = 1
   And in no sence is meete or amiable.   2699
AMID = 1
   I, and amid this hurlie I intend,   1837
AMISSE = 2*1
   *two and fiftie horses. Why nothing comes amisse, so | monie comes
   withall.   647
   It were impossible I should speed amisse.   1163
   That talk'd of her, haue talk'd amisse of her: 1171
AMONG = 2*1
   *To make one among these wooers: if thou ask me why, 555
   Tra. Among them know you one *Vincentio*?   1952
   Gre. My cake is dough, but Ile in among the rest,   2520
AMONGST *see also* 'mongst = 2
   To make a stale of me amongst these mates?   360

8

AMONGST *cont.*
    Must steed vs all, and me amongst the rest: 838
AMOROUS = 3
    Grumio. A proper stripling, and an amorous.   709
    Our fine Musitian groweth amorous.   1356
    The quaint Musician, amorous *Litio,*   1530
AMORT *see* a-mort
AMOUNTS = 1
    My Land amounts not to so much in all: 1255
AN *l.**16 137 332 *645 664 709 726 753 769 915 1256 1258 1285 1302 1417
    *1432 *1434 *1436 *1454 1484 *1720 1913 *1957 2074 *2284 *2469 2578
    2582 2632 2652 2664 = 21*12
ANCIENT = 3*1
    Call home thy ancient thoughts from banishment,   183
    Your ancient trustie pleasant seruant *Grumio*:   613
    An ancient Angel comming downe the hill, | Wil serue the turne.   1913
    **Tra.* Sir, you seeme a sober ancient Gentleman by   2451
AND *see also* & = 598*119, 7*5
    And if the boy haue not a womans guift   135
    **Kate.* A pretty peate, it is best put finger in the eye, | and she knew
    why.   381
    *good fellowes in the world, and a man could light on   432
    Petr. Will it not be? | 'Faith sirrah, and you'l not knocke, Ile ring it,   581
    *A my word, and she knew him as wel as I do, she would   674
    *that's nothing; and he begin once, hee'l raile in his rope   677
    *trickes. Ile tell you what sir, and she stand him but a li-|tle,   678
    Bian. God giue him ioy. | *Tra.* I, and hee'l tame her.   1902
    **Tail.* This is true that I say, and I had thee in place   2132
    Tra. Then at my lodging, and it like you,   2237
    Bian. Head, and but an hastie witted bodie,   2582
    Would say your Head and But were head and horne.   2583
ANGEL = 1
    An ancient Angel comming downe the hill, | Wil serue the turne.   1913
ANGER = 2
    For it engenders choller, planteth anger,   1804
    My tongue will tell the anger of my heart,   2062
ANGRIE = 1
    **Pet.* Come, come you Waspe, y'faith you are too | angrie.   1084
ANGRY = 4
    Rage like an angry Boare, chafed with sweat?   769
    Nor bite the lip, as angry wenches will,   1127
    Pet. O *Kate* content thee, prethee be not angry.   1601
    Kat. I will be angry, what hast thou to doe?   1602
ANNA = 1
    As *Anna* to the Queene of Carthage was: 457
ANNE = *1
    **Beg.* Yes by Saint Anne do I, a good matter surely: 560
ANNOYD = 1
    Because she will not be annoy'd with suters.   487
ANON = 1
    Anon Ile giue thee more instructions. | *Exit a seruingman.*   141
ANOTHER = 9*1
    Another beare the Ewer: the third a Diaper,   61
    Another tell him of his Hounds and Horse,   65
    Although I thinke 'twas in another sense,   521
    Hath promist me to helpe one to another,   738
    *another lac'd: an olde rusty sword tane out of the   1434

ANOTHER *cont.*

Another way I haue to man my Haggard,	1827
This way the Couerlet, another way the sheets:	1836
to take vpon you another mans name.	2416
Another dowrie to another daughter,	2669

ANSWER = 1

Thy hounds shall make the Welkin answer them	197

ANSWERABLE = 1

And all things answerable to this portion.	1241

ANSWERE = 2*1

*Beg. Third, or fourth, or fift Borough, Ile answere	15
*Petr. How? she's busie, and she cannot come: is that | an answere?	2631
Hor. I know her answere. | Pet. What? | Hor. She will not.	2649

ANT = 1

Ser. An't please your Honor, Players | That offer seruice to your Lordship.	84

ANTICKE = 1

Were he the veriest anticke in the world.	111

ANTONIO = 1

Antonio my father is deceast,	620

ANTONIOS *see also Butonios* = 1

Pet. Petruchio is my name, Antonio's sonne,	929

ANY = 21*3

*me any Conserues, giue me conserues of Beefe: nere ask	160
Then any woman in this waining age.	215
There, there Hortensio, will you any Wife?	358
Or signior Gremio you know any such,	400
*I can by any meanes light on a fit man to teach her that	415
*her father be verie rich, any man is so verie a foole to be | married to hell?	428
We haue not yet bin seene in any house,	505
Comes there any more of it?	561
any man ha's rebus'd your worship?	572
All bookes of Loue, see that at any hand,	712
Petr. Not her that chides sir, at any hand I pray.	795
Tra. And if I be sir, is it any offence?	800
And will not promise her to any man,	834
Which I could fancie, more then any other.	867
More kindely beholding to you then any:	941
Within rich Pisa walls, as any one | Old Signior Gremio has in Padua,	1249
Then hath beene taught by any of my trade,	1362
Now take them vp quoth he, if any list.	1549
My horse, my oxe, my asse, my any thing,	1618
Doth fancie any other but Lucentio,	1848
Tra. 'Tis death for any one in Mantua	1937
Kate. Then both or one, or any thing thou wilt.	2007
Tis well, and hold your owne in any case	2186
Beside, so qualified, as may beseeme | The Spouse of any noble Gentleman:	2365

ANYTHING *see* thing

APACE = 2

I will to Venice, sonday comes apace,	1202
Kate eate apace; and now my honie Loue,	2034

APEERETH *see* peereth

APES = 1

And for your loue to her, leade Apes in hell.	892

APOLLO = 1*1
   *Wilt thou haue Musicke? Harke Apollo plaies, *Musick*   187
   And at that sight shal sad Apollo weepe,   211
APPAREL = *1
   Enter aloft the drunkard with attendants, some with apparel, | Bason and
   Ewer, & other appurtenances, & Lord.   151
APPARELD = 1
   Yet oftentimes he goes but meane apparel'd.   1458
APPARELL = 2*1
   To buy apparell 'gainst the wedding day;   1195
   Costly apparell, tents, and Canopies,   1234
   *in't for a feather: a monster, a very monster in apparell,   1455
APPARELLD = 1
   Tra. Not so well apparell'd as I wish you were.   1473
APPARREL = 1
   And aske him what apparrel he will weare: 64
APPARRELL = 2
   Puts my apparrell, and my count'nance on,   536
   I know not what, but formall in apparrell,   1917
APPEARS = *1
   Ka. The more my wrong, the more his spite appears.   1980
APPENDIX = 1
   the Priest be readie to come against you come with your | appendix.
   Exit.   2288
APPLE = 1*1
   Bion. As much as an apple doth an oyster, & all one.   1957
   What, vp and downe caru'd like an apple Tart?   2074
APPLES = *1
   *apples: but come, since this bar in law makes vs friends,   438
APPLIE = 1
   Vertue and that part of Philosophie | Will I applie, that treats of
   happinesse,   317
APPOINTED = 1*1
   What shall I be appointed houres, as though   407
   *Master hath appointed me to goe to Saint *Lukes* to bid   2287
APPROUD = 1
   My trustie seruant well approu'd in all,   306
APPROUED = 1
   My best beloued and approued friend | *Hortensio*: & I trow this is his
   house: 568
APPURTENANCES = 1
   Enter aloft the drunkard with attendants, some with apparel, | Bason and
   Ewer, & other appurtenances, & Lord.   151
APT = 1
   She's apt to learne, and thankefull for good turnes: 1033
APTLY = 1
   Was aptly fitted, and naturally perform'd.   97
ARE *see also* they're, y'are, your = 67*18, 1
   Are, to plead *Hortensio's* passion: 1367
ARGOSIE = 2
   That she shall haue, besides an Argosie   1256
   What, haue I choakt you with an Argosie?   1258
ARGOSIES = 1
   Then three great Argosies, besides two Galliasses   1260
ARGUING = 1
   I should be arguing still vpon that doubt,   1348

ARISTOTLES = 1
Or so deuote to *Aristotles* checkes   331
ARMD = 2
And by my fathers loue and leaue am arm'd   304
But be thou arm'd for some vnhappie words.   1004
ARMED = *1
*that Ile proue vpon thee, though thy little finger be ar-|med in a
thimble.   2130
ARMES = 2
Kate. So may you loose your armes,   1098
And if no Gentleman, why then no armes.   1100
ARMORY = *1
*Towne Armory, with a broken hilt, and chapelesse: with   1435
ARRAS = 1
In Cypres chests my arras counterpoints,   1233
ARRAY = 2
We will haue rings, and things, and fine array,   1203
For this poore furniture, and meane array.   2163
ARRIUALL = 1
Who will of thy arriuall be full ioyous.   2369
ARRIUD = 2
I am arriu'd for fruitfull *Lumbardie*,   302
Grem. Hortensio hearke: | This Gentleman is happily arriu'd,   779
ARRIUED = 2
Lucentios Father is arriued in *Padua*,   2248
And happilie I haue arriued at the last | Vnto the wished hauen of my
blisse: 2507
ARROGANCE = 1
Pet. Oh monstrous arrogance: 2092
ART *see also* th'art *l*.29 213 456 489 1124 2162 *2340 2346 2413 2525 =
9*1, 3
I must begin with rudiments of Art,   1359
Hor. I reade, that I professe the Art to loue.   1855
Bian. And may you proue sir Master of your Art.   1856
ARTILLERIE = 1
And heauens Artillerie thunder in the skies?   771
ARTS = 1
To see faire *Padua*, nurserie of Arts,   301
AS = 161*24
Hunts. Why *Belman* is as good as he my Lord,   25
Lord. Thou art a Foole, if *Eccho* were as fleete,   29
Lord. Euen as a flatt'ring dreame, or worthles fancie.   48
As he shall thinke by our true diligence   74
Tell him from me (as he will win my loue)   120
Such as he hath obseru'd in noble Ladies   122
Bid him shed teares, as being ouer-ioyed   131
*shooes, or such shooes as my toes looke through the o-|uer-leather. 164
As beaten hence by your strange Lunacie.   181
*1.*Man*. Say thou wilt course, thy gray-hounds are as | (swift   199
As breathed Stags: I fleeter then the Roe.   200
Euen as the wauing sedges play with winde.   205
Lord. Wee'l shew thee *Io*, as she was a Maid,   206
As liuelie painted, as the deede was done.   208
Or when you wak'd, so wak'd as if you slept.   233
Nor no such men as you haue reckon'd vp,   245
As *Stephen Slie*, and old *Iohn Naps* of Greece, | And *Peter Turph*, and
Henry Pimpernell,   246

AS *cont.*

And twentie more such names and men as these, | Which neuer were, nor no man euer saw.	248
And am to *Padua* come, as he that leaues	321
I am in all affected as your selfe,	325
As *Ouid*; be an out-cast quite abiur'd:	332
Fall to them as you finde your stomacke serues you:	337
Such friends (as time) in *Padua* shall beget.	344
What shall I be appointed houres, as though	407
Gre. I cannot tell: but I had as lief take her dowrie	434
Hor. Faith (as you say) there's small choise in rotten	437
That art to me as secret and as deere	456
As *Anna* to the Queene of Carthage was:	457
Such as the daughter of *Agenor* had,	471
Keepe house, and port, and seruants, as I should,	509
Waite you on him, I charge you, as becomes:	540
Petr. Such wind as scatters yongmen throgh y world,	616
Happily to wiue and thriue, as best I may:	622
Petr. Signior *Hortensio*, 'twixt such friends as wee,	631
(As wealth is burthen of my woing dance)	634
Be she as foule as was *Florentius* Loue,	635
As old as *Sibell*, and as curst and shrow'd	636
As *Socrates Zentippe*, or a worse:	637
Affections edge in me. Were she is as rough | As are the swelling *Adriaticke* seas.	639
*tooth in her head, though she haue as manie diseases as	646
Brought vp as best becomes a Gentlewoman.	653
For I will boord her, though she chide as loud	661
As thunder, when the clouds in Autumne cracke.	662
*A my word, and she knew him as wel as I do, she would	674
To old *Baptista* as a schoole-master	698
As for my patron, stand you so assur'd,	721
As firmely as your selfe were still in place,	722
As wil a Chesse-nut in a Farmers fire.	776
Gru. I would I were as sure of a good dinner.	785
Tra. Why sir, I pray are not the streets as free | For me, as for you?	803
Hor. Sir, let me be so bold as aske you,	823
The one, as famous for a scolding tongue,	826
As is the other, for beauteous modestie.	827
You must as we do, gratifie this Gentleman,	845
And do as aduersaries do in law,	850
Striue mightily, but eate and drinke as friends.	851
Bap. Was euer Gentleman thus greeu'd as I? | But who comes heere.	895
Bap. Mistake me not, I speake but as I finde,	927
Beene long studying at *Rhemes*, as cunning	943
As the other in Musicke and Mathematickes:	945
And free accesse and fauour as the rest.	960
I am as peremptorie as she proud minded:	996
Pet. I to the proofe, as Mountaines are for windes,	1005
As on a Pillorie, looking through the Lute,	1024
As had she studied to misvse me so.	1027
She sings as sweetly as a Nightinghale:	1040
Say that she frowne, Ile say she lookes as cleere	1041
As morning Roses newly washt with dew:	1042
As though she bid me stay by her a weeke:	1047
Yet not so deepely as to thee belongs,	1064
Kate. No such Iade as you, if me you meane.	1075

AS *cont.*

Kate. Too light for such a swaine as you to catch,	1078
And yet as heauie as my waight should be.	1079
Kat. I for a Turtle, as he takes a buzard.	1083
But slow in speech: yet sweet as spring-time flowers.	1125
Nor bite the lip, as angry wenches will,	1127
Is straight, and slender, and as browne in hue	1133
As hazle nuts, and sweeter then the kernels:	1134
As *Kate* this chamber with her princely gate:	1138
And bring you from a wilde *Kate* to a *Kate* | Conformable as other	
houshold *Kates*:	1157
For shee's not froward, but modest as the Doue,	1173
Shee is not hot, but temperate as the morne,	1174
Gre. Yongling thou canst not loue so deare as I.	1218
Gre. First, as you know, my house within the City	1228
Ile leaue her houses three or foure as good	1248
Within rich *Pisa* walls, as any one | Old Signior *Gremio* has in *Padua*,	1249
And twice as much ere thou offrest next.	1262
Gre. And may not yong men die as well as old?	1273
Your Lecture shall haue leisure for as much.	1303
But learne my Lessons as I please my selfe,	1315
*Luc. Hic Ibat, as I told you before, *Simois*, I am Lu-|centio,	1325
Methinkes he lookes as though he were in loue:	1382
*Bion. Master, master, newes, and such newes as you | neuer heard of,	1420
Tra. Not so well apparell'd as I wish you were.	1473
As if they saw some wondrous monument, | Some Commet, or vnusuall	
prodigie?	1478
As you shall well be satisfied with all.	1492
As I can change these poore accoutrements,	1502
As before imparted to your worship,	1513
Gre. As willingly as ere I came from schoole.	1534
And as he stoop'd againe to take it vp,	1546
**swore, as if the Vicar meant to cozen him: but after ma-|ny	1552
**he, as if he had beene aboord carowsing to his Mates af-|ter	1554
**him sops as hee was drinking: This done, hee tooke the	1558
Cur. Is she so hot a shrew as she's reported.	1659
*Gru. Why Iacke boy, ho boy, and as much newes as | wilt thou.	1677
Gru. Heere sir, as foolish as I was before.	1755
Yet as they are, heere are they come to meete you.	1765
As he forth walked on his way.	1774
**to speake, and sits as one new risen from a dreame: A-|way, away, for	
he is comming hither.	1819
That is, to watch her, as we watch these Kites,	1829
As with the meate, some vndeserued fault	1833
Lou'd me in the World so wel as *Lucentio*.	1861
Nor a Musitian as I seeme to bee,	1865
For such a one as leaues a Gentleman,	1867
As vnworthie all the former fauours	1878
Ere three dayes passe, which hath as long lou'd me,	1886
As I haue lou'd this proud disdainful Haggard,	1887
In resolution, as I swore before.	1891
As longeth to a Louers blessed case:	1893
As if he were the right *Vincentio*.	1923
But then vp farther, and as farre as Rome,	1930
*Bion. As much as an apple doth an oyster, & all one.	1957
Looke that you take vpon you as you should,	1964
Go with me to cloath you as becomes you. *Exeunt*.	1976

14

AS *cont.*

As who should say, if I should sleepe or eate	1991
Hor. Mistris, what cheere?	*Kate.* Faith as cold as can be.	2017
And reuell it as brauely as the best,	2036
And Gentlewomen weare such caps as these.	2054
Euen to the vttermost as I please in words.	2065
As thou shalt thinke on prating whil'st thou liu'st:	2099
Iust as my master had direction:	2102
And as the Sunne breakes through the darkest clouds,	2156
With such austeritie as longeth to a father.	2187
As shall with either parts agreement stand.	2232
*afternoone as shee went to the Garden for Parseley to	2285
Hort. Say as he saies, or we shall neuer goe.	2307
And the Moone changes euen as your minde:	2317
As those two eyes become that heauenly face?	2330
And not a Maiden, as thou saist he is.	2342
And now by Law, as well as reuerent age,	2359
Beside, so qualified, as may beseeme	The Spouse of any noble	
Gentleman:	2365
and then come backe to my mistris as soone as I can.	2385
Ped. What's he that knockes as he would beat downe	the gate?	2398
shall neede none so long as I liue.	2405
Vin. His name, as if I knew not his name: I haue	2459
Exit Biondello, Tranio and Pedant as fast as may be.	2490
For now we sit to chat as well as eate.	2548
And then pursue me as you draw your Bow.	2590
And as the Iest did glaunce awaie from me,	2604
For she is chang'd as she had neuer bin.	2670
As prisoners to her womanlie perswasion:	2676
Luc. I would your dutie were as foolish too:	2682
It blots thy beautie, as frosts doe bite the Meads,	2697
*Confounds thy fame, as whirlwinds shake faire budds,	2698
Such dutie as the subiect owes the Prince,	2713
My minde hath bin as bigge as one of yours,	2728
My heart as great, my reason haplie more,	2729
Our strength as weake, our weakenesse past compare,	2732

ASCONCE *see* sconce

ASHAMD = 3

Petr. What art thou asham'd of me?	2525
Kate. No sir, God forbid, but asham'd to kisse.	2526
I am asham'd that women are so simple,	2719

ASHORE *see also* a-shore = 1

If *Biondello* thou wert come ashore,	341

ASIDE = 2*1

Bianca stand aside, poore gyrle she weepes:	881
And therefore setting all this chat aside,	1147
Petr. Preethe *Kate* let's stand aside and see the end of	this	
controuersie.	2438

ASK = *2

*me any Conserues, giue me conserues of Beefe: nere ask	160
*To make one among these wooers: if thou ask me why,	555

ASKE = 4*2

And aske him what apparrel he will weare:	64
*Aske *Marrian Hacket* the fat Alewife of Wincot, if shee	174
Hor. Sir, let me be so bold as aske you,	823
When I shall aske the banes, and when be married.	1049
Should aske if *Katherine* should be his wife,	1543

ASKE *cont.*
  *his beard grew thinne and hungerly, and seem'd to aske   1557
ASKETH = 1
  Pet. Signior *Baptista*, my businesse asketh haste,   979
ASKING = 1
  daughter without asking my good will?   2514
ASLEEPE = 1
  *him by Law. Ile not budge an inch boy: Let him come, | and kindly.
  Falles asleepe.   16
ASSE = 3*1
  Gru. Oh this Woodcocke, what an Asse it is. | *Petru.* Peace sirra.   726
  Luc. Preposterous Asse that neuer read so farre,   1304
  My horse, my oxe, my asse, my any thing,   1618
  Ped. Awaie, awaie mad asse, his name is *Lucentio*, and   2462
ASSES = 1
  Kate. Asses are made to beare, and so are you.   1073
ASSIST = 2
  Wherein your cunning can assist me much.   102
  Assist me *Tranio*, for I know thou wilt.   461
ASSISTING = 1
  You shal haue me assisting you in all.   761
ASSURANCE = 7*2
  And let your father make her the assurance,   1269
  Be Bride to you, if you make this assurance: | If not, to Signior *Gremio*:   1278
  And make assurance heere in *Padua*   1517
  And giue assurance to *Baptista Minola*.   1922
  To passe assurance of a dowre in marriage   1973
  We be affied and such assurance tane,   2231
  *counterfeit assurance: take you assurance of her, *Cum*   2278
  Petr. Well, I say no: and therefore sir assurance,   2608
ASSURD = 1
  As for my patron, stand you so assur'd,   721
ASSURE = 6
  Pet. And for that dowrie, Ile assure her of   988
  That can assure my daughter greatest dower, | Shall haue my *Biancas*
  loue.   1225
  Say signior *Gremio*, what can you assure her?   1227
  And twelue tite Gallies, these I will assure her,   1261
  Kate. I dare assure you sir, 'tis almost two,   2172
  Hort. I doe assure thee father so it is.   2373
AT = 53*16
ATCHEEUE = *1
  *Bend thoughts and wits to atcheeue her. Thus it stands: 482
ATCHIEUD = 1
  By vertue specially to be atchieu'd.   319
ATCHIEUE = 3
  If I atchieue not this yong modest gyrle: 459
  And let me be a slaue, t'atchieue that maide,   525
  Atchieue the elder: set the yonger free,   840
ATTEND = 4
  Let one attend him with a siluer Bason   59
  Looke how thy seruants do attend on thee,   185
  Pet. I pray you do. Ile attend her heere,   1037
  Obey the Bride you that attend on her.   1609
ATTENDANCE = 1
  What? no attendance? no regard? no dutie?   1753

ATTENDANTS = 4*1
And braue attendants neere him when he wakes,   44
*Enter aloft the drunkard with attendants, some with apparel, | Bason and
Ewer, & other appurtenances, & Lord.   151
Enter Lady with Attendants.   252
*Enter Baptista, Gremio, Tranio, Katherine, Bianca, and o-|thers,
attendants.   1387
Enter Petruchio, Kate, Vincentio, Grumio | with Attendants.   2387
ATTENDS = 1
To want the Bride-groome when the Priest attends   1393
ATTIRE = 1
Tra. He hath some meaning in his mad attire,   1507
AUGHT see ought
AUSTERITIE = 1
With such austeritie as longeth to a father.   2187
AUTUMNE = 1
As thunder, when the clouds in Autumne cracke.   662
AWAIE = 3*2
*Ped. Awaie, awaie mad asse, his name is Lucentio, and   2462
Bap. Awaie with the dotard, to the Iaile with him.   2484
*Petr. Why then let's home againe: Come Sirra let's | awaie.   2527
And as the Iest did glaunce awaie from me,   2604
AWAKE = 2
I pray awake sir: if you loue the Maide,   481
And with the clamor keepe her stil awake: 1841
AWAKENED = 1
Vin. I Mistris Bride, hath that awakened you?   2584
AWAY = 14*2
Tranio. I loue no chiders sir: Biondello, let's away.   796
Bap. Is't possible you will away to night?   1571
Pet. I must away to day before night come,   1572
That haue beheld me giue away my selfe   1576
Gru. Away you three inch foole, I am no beast.   1664
*how I cried, how the horses ranne away, how her   1711
Pet. I tell thee Kate, 'twas burnt and dried away,   1802
*to speake, and sits as one new risen from a dreame: A-|way, away, for
he is comming hither.   1819
Heere take away this dish. | Kate. I pray you let it stand.   2025
Away with it, come let me haue a bigger.   2052
Away thou Ragge, thou quantitie, thou remnant,   2097
Away I say, commend me to thy master. Exit Tail.   2151
Good morrow gentle Mistris, where away: 2325
Whether away, or whether is thy aboade?   2336
Away I say, and bring them hither straight.   2660
AWFULL = 1
An awfull rule, and right supremicie: 2664
AWRIE = 1
Out you rogue, you plucke my foote awrie,   1775
AY see I
AYMD = 1
Kate. Well aym'd of such a yong one.   1114
AYRE = 1
And with her breath she did perfume the ayre,   478
A-MORT = *1
*Petr. How fares my Kate, what sweeting all a-mort?   2016
A-SHORE = 1
For in a quarrell since I came a-shore,   538

BABE = 2

For I am rough, and woo not like a babe.   1002
And speake I will. I am no childe, no babe,   2059

BABIE = *1

*to a Puppet or an Aglet babie, or an old trot with ne're a   645

BABIES = 1

A knacke, a toy, a tricke, a babies cap: 2051

BABLE = 1

Off with that bable, throw it vnderfoote.   2678

BACARE = *1

*poore petitioners speake too? *Bacare*, you are meruay-|lous forward.   933

BACKE = 4*2

Skipper stand backe, 'tis age that nourisheth.   1221
*Staggers, begnawne with the Bots, Waid in the backe,   1442
*Bion. No sir, I say his horse comes with him on his | (backe.   1464
Goe on, and fetch our horses backe againe,   2305
*Biond. Nay faith, Ile see the Church a your backe,   2384
and then come backe to my mistris as soone as I can.   2385

BACKES = *1

*then backes: no more stockings then legges: nor   162

BAD = 1

I bad the rascall knocke vpon your gate,   604

BADE *see* bad

BAGGAGE = *1

*Beg. Y'are a baggage, the *Slies* are no   6

BAGS = 1

Gru. And that his bags shal proue.   743

BAIE = 1

'Tis thought your Deere does hold you at a baie.   2599

BAITE = 1

That baite, and beate, and will not be obedient: 1830

BALKE = 1

Balke Lodgicke with acquaintaince that you haue,   333

BALME = 1

Balme his foule head in warme distilled waters,   52

BANDIE = 1

To bandie word for word, and frowne for frowne;   2730

BANES = 2

When I shall aske the banes, and when be married.   1049
Make friends, inuite, and proclaime the banes,   1404

BANISH = 1

And banish hence these abiect lowlie dreames: 184

BANISHMENT = 1

Call home thy ancient thoughts from banishment,   183

BANKET = 1

My Banket is to close our stomakes vp   2546

BANQUET = 3

A most delicious banquet by his bed,   43
Visit his Countrimen, and banquet them?   503
The Seruingmen with Tranio bringing | in a Banquet.   2536

BAP = 50*17

BAPT = 1

BAPTISTA *see also Bap., Bapt.* = 25*7

Enter Baptista with his two daughters, Katerina & Bianca,   347
Hor. Signior *Baptista*, will you be so strange,   388
Gre. Why will you mew her vp | (Signior *Baptista*) for this fiend of hell,   391
Hor. Her father is *Baptista Minola*,   663

BAPTISTA cont.

Therefore this order hath *Baptista* tane,	691
To old *Baptista* as a schoole-master	698
Trow you whither I am going? To *Baptista Minola,*	730
To the house of Signior *Baptista Minola?*	789
Baptista is a noble Gentleman,	812
Enter Baptista.	878
Gre. Good morrow neighbour *Baptista.*	900
Pet. Signior *Baptista,* my businesse asketh haste,	979
Enter Baptista, Gremio, Trayno.	1155
But now *Baptista,* to your yonger daughter,	1213
*Enter Baptista, Gremio, Tranio, Katherine, Bianca, and o-│thers, attendants.	1387
Tra. Patience good *Katherine* and *Baptista* too,	1409
Enter Petruchio, Kate, Bianca, Hortensio, Baptista.	1565
And giue assurance to *Baptista Minola.*	1922
Signior *Baptista* may remember me │ Neere twentie yeares a goe in Genoa.	2183
Tra. But hast thou done thy errand to *Baptista.*	2195
Here comes *Baptista:* set your countenance sir.	2199
Enter Baptista and Lucentio: Pedant booted │ and bare headed.	2200
Tra. Signior *Baptista* you are happilie met:	2202
Signior *Baptista,* of whom I heare so well.	2219
Signior *Baptista,* shall I leade the way,	2254
*Biond. Then thus: *Baptista* is safe talking with the	2268
Pedan. Helpe, sonne, helpe signior *Baptista.*	2437
Enter Pedant with seruants, Baptista, Tranio.	2440
*the Iaile: father Baptista, I charge you see that hee be │ forth comming.	2470
*Gre. Take heede signior *Baptista,* least you be coni-│catcht	2476
*Vin. Feare not *Baptista,* we will content you, goe to:	2515
*Enter Baptista, Vincentio, Gremio, the Pedant, Lucentio, and	2534

BAPTISTAS = 4*2

*Baptistas eldest daughter to a husband, wee set his	440
*that Lucentio indeede had *Baptistas* yongest daugh-│ter.	548
For in *Baptistas* keepe my treasure is:	683
You vnderstand me. Ouer and beside │ Signior *Baptistas* liberalitie,	714
Did you yet euer see *Baptistas* daughter? │ *Tra.* No sir, but heare I do that he hath two:	824
'Twixt me, and one *Baptistas* daughter heere:	1974

BAR = *1

**apples: but come, since this bar in law makes vs friends,	438

BARBERS = 1

Like to a Censor in a barbers shoppe:	2076

BARE = 1

Enter Baptista and Lucentio: Pedant booted │ and bare headed.	2200

BARE-FOOT = 1

I must dance bare-foot on her wedding day,	891

BARGAIND = 1

'Tis bargain'd twixt vs twaine being alone,	1184

BARNE = 1

My houshold-stuffe, my field, my barne,	1617

BARRES = 1

Which barres a thousand harmes, and lengthens life.	290

BARTHOLMEW = 1

Sirra go you to Bartholmew my Page,	116

BASE = 1*2

Luc. All but the base.	1339

BASE *cont.*

Hort. The base is right, 'tis the base knaue that iars.   1340
BASHFULL = 1
Her affability and bashfull modestie: 910
BASON = 2
Let one attend him with a siluer Bason   59
*Enter aloft the drunkard with attendants, some with apparel, | Bason and
Ewer, & other appurtenances, & Lord.*   151
BASONS = 1
Basons and ewers to laue her dainty hands: 1230
BASTA = 1
Luc. Basta, content thee: for I haue it full.   504
BATTELL = 1
Haue I not in a pitched battell heard   772
BAUBLE = 1
A custard coffen, a bauble, a silken pie,   2067
BE *see also* shalbe = 170*28
BEADES = 1
With Amber Bracelets, Beades, and all this knau'ry.   2040
BEARD = 2*1
Tra. Gray-beard thy loue doth freeze. | *Gre.* But thine doth frie,   1219
Wee'll ouer-reach the grey-beard *Gremio*,   1528
*his beard grew thinne and hungerly, and seem'd to aske   1557
BEARE = 11*1
Another beare the Ewer: the third a Diaper,   61
He beare himselfe with honourable action,   121
And make her beare the pennance of her tongue.   393
*Farewell: yet for the loue I beare my sweet *Bianca*, if   414
Tra. Not possible: for who shall beare your part,   500
And beare his charge of wooing whatsoere.   783
Kate. Asses are made to beare, and so are you.   1073
Pet. Women are made to beare, and so are you.   1074
Hort. Sirra, I will not beare these braues of thine.   1310
Come Mistris Kate, Ile beare you companie.   2031
While he did beare my countenance in the towne,   2506
Luc. Ile haue no halues: Ile beare it all my selfe.   2626
BEARES = 2
I tel you sir, she beares me faire in hand.   1849
My Fathers beares more toward the Market-place,   2390
BEARETH = 1
And for the loue he beareth to your daughter,   2211
BEARE-HEARD = *1
*Beare-heard, and now by present profession a Tinker.   173
BEARING = 1*1
Petruchio with Tranio, with his boy | bearing a Lute and Bookes.   898
regia, bearing my port, *celsa senis* that we might be-|guile the old
Pantalowne.   1329
BEAST = 1*2
Lord. Oh monstrous beast, how like a swine he lyes.   38
*know'st winter tames man, woman, and beast: for it   1661
Gru. Away you three inch foole, I am no beast.   1664
BEASTLY = 1
Fie on her, see how beastly she doth court him.   1882
BEAT = *2
*horse vpon her, how he beat me because her horse stum-|bled,   1708
Ped. What's he that knockes as he would beat downe | the gate?   2398

BEATE = 1*2
That baite, and beate, and will not be obedient: 1830
*me in the skirts of it, and beate me to death with a bot-|tome of
browne thred: I said a gowne. 2119
*Tra. Sir, what are you that offer to beate my ser-|uant? 2441
BEATEN = 2*1
As beaten hence by your strange Lunacie. 181
Yet would you say, ye were beaten out of doore, 238
*all foule waies: was euer man so beaten? was euer man 1641
BEATES = 1
Vin. Ist so indeede. He beates Biondello. 2434
BEATS = 1
Kate. Go get thee gone, thou false deluding slaue, | Beats him. 2009
BEAUTEOUS = 2
As is the other, for beauteous modestie. 827
Kindnesse in women, not their beauteous lookes 1889
BEAUTIE = 6
Luc. Oh yes, I saw sweet beautie in her face, 470
That hearing of her beautie, and her wit, 909
Thy vertues spoke of, and thy beautie sounded, 1063
What stars do spangle heauen with such beautie, 2329
It blots thy beautie, as frosts doe bite the Meads, 2697
Muddie, ill seeming, thicke, bereft of beautie, 2701
BEAUTIES = 1
Sweete Kate embrace her for her beauties sake. 2332
BEAUTIFUL = 1
His yongest daughter, beautiful Bianca, 685
BEAUTIFULL = 2
Thou hast a Ladie farre more Beautifull, 214
Because his feathers are more beautifull. 2159
BEAUTIOUS = 1
With wealth enough, and yong and beautious, 652
BEAUTY = 2
For by this light, whereby I see thy beauty, 1152
Thy beauty that doth make me like thee well, 1153
BECAUSE = 7*1
Because she brought stone-Iugs, and no seal'd quarts: 241
Because I know you well, and loue you well, 355
Because she will not be annoy'd with suters. 487
Because so well I loue Lucentio. 523
Luc. Tranio be so, because Lucentio loues, 524
*horse vpon her, how he beat me because her horse stum-|bled, 1708
Because his feathers are more beautifull. 2159
Because his painted skin contents the eye. 2161
BECKE = 1
Each in his office readie at thy becke. 186
BECOME = 3
It shall become to serue all hopes conceiu'd 314
Pet. Did euer Dian so become a Groue 1137
As those two eyes become that heauenly face? 2330
BECOMES = 4
Waite you on him, I charge you, as becomes: 540
Brought vp as best becomes a Gentlewoman. 653
Go with me to cloath you as becomes you. Exeunt. 1976
Katerine, that Cap of yours becomes you not, 2677

BED = 12*1

*Beg. No, not a deniere: go by S.(aint) *Ieronimie*, goe to thy | cold bed,
and warme thee.   11
with Ale, this were a bed but cold to sleep so soundly.   37
What thinke you, if he were conuey'd to bed,   41
A most delicious banquet by his bed,   43
Lord. Take him vp gently, and to bed with him,   76
Softer and sweeter then the lustfull bed   190
Being all this time abandon'd from your bed.   269
Madam vndresse you, and come now to bed.   271
That I should yet absent me from your bed: 277
*woe her, wed her, and bed her, and ridde the | house of her. Come on.   446
Pet. Marry so I meane sweet *Katherine* in thy bed: 1146
Ile finde about the making of the bed,   1834
Pet. Come *Kate*, wee'le to bed,   2743
BEDAZLED = 1

That haue bin so bedazled with the sunne,   2344
BEDFELLOW = 1

A lots thee for his louely bedfellow.   2339
BEE *l.**431 522 *1719 1865 *2111 = 2*3
BEEFE = 3*2

*me any Conserues, giue me conserues of Beefe: nere ask   160
What say you to a peece of Beefe and Mustard?   2001
Kate. Why then the Beefe, and let the Mustard rest.   2004
Or else you get no beefe of Grumio.   2006
Gru. Why then the Mustard without the beefe.   2008
BEEME = 1

Beeme, Bianca take him for thy Lord   1368
BEEN *l.**1445 = *1, 1

Petruchio, I shal be your *Been venuto. Exeunt.*   854
BEENE *see also* bin *l.**529 940 943 1351 1362 *1433 *1554 1949 = 5*3
BEETLE-HEADED = 1

Pet. A horson beetle-headed flap-ear'd knaue: 1786
BEFALL = 1

Bap. Now faire befall thee good *Petruchio*;   2666
BEFORE = 13*7

Before I haue a husband for the elder: 353
For those defects I haue before rehearst,   689
The yonger then is free, and not before.   836
If you should die before him, where's her dower?   1271
Luc. Hic Ibat, as I told you before, *Simois*, I am Lu- |centio,   1325
Hor. Madam, before you touch the instrument,   1357
*and shoulder-shotten, neere leg'd before, and with a   1443
As before imparted to your worship,   1513
*neuer was before: harke, harke, I heare the min- |strels play. *Musicke
playes.*   1563
Pet. I must away to day before night come,   1572
*so raide? was euer man so weary? I am sent before to   1642
Gru. She was good *Curtis* before this frost: but thou   1660
*me: how he swore, how she prai'd, that neuer prai'd be- |fore: 1710
Where is the foolish knaue I sent before?   1754
Gru. Heere sir, as foolish as I was before.   1755
In resolution, as I swore before.   1891
And so shall mine before you touch the meate.   2028
Enter Biondello, Lucentio and Bianca, Gremio | is out before.   2379
Vin. You shall not choose but drinke before you go,   2392
I neuer saw you before in all my life.   2429

BEG = 13*10
BEGAN = 1
  Began to scold, and raise vp such a storme,   475
BEGET = 1
  Such friends (as time) in *Padua* shall beget.   344
BEGGER see also Beg. = 3
  Enter Begger and Hostes, Christophero Sly.   2
  Would not the begger then forget himselfe?   45
  No better than a poore and loathsome begger: 134
BEGGER = 1
BEGGERLY = 1
  The rest were ragged, old, and beggerly,   1764
BEGGERS = 1
  Beggers that come vnto my fathers doore,   1982
BEGIN = 4*3
  *best horse in *Padua* to begin his woing that would tho-|roughly   445
  *that's nothing; and he begin once, hee'l raile in his rope   677
  I must begin with rudiments of Art,   1359
  *now I begin, Inprimis wee came downe a fowle   1699
  Hor. Who shall begin? | *Luc*. That will I.   2621
  Pet. Come on I say, and first begin with her. | *Wid*. She shall not.   2691
  Pet. I say she shall, and first begin with her.   2693
BEGINS = 1
  Gre. I marry sir, now it begins to worke.   1604
BEGNAWNE = *1
  *Staggers, begnawne with the Bots, Waid in the backe,   1442
BEGUILE = *2
  Gru. Heere's no knauerie. See, to beguile the olde-|folkes,   704
  . *regia*, bearing my port, *celsa senis* that we might be-|guile the old
    Pantalowne.   1329
BEGUILED = 1
  And how she was beguiled and surpriz'd,   207
BEGUN = 3*1
  Lady. My Lord, 'tis but begun.   562
  Luc. Well begun *Tranio*.   797
  Pet. Thus haue I politickely begun my reigne,   1822
  Petr. Nay that you shall not since you haue begun: 2587
BEHAUIOUR = 5
  Least (ouer-eying of his odde behauiour,   105
  Maids milde behauiour and sobrietie. | Peace *Tranio*.   374
  On this yong man: For learning and behauiour   734
  Her wondrous qualities, and milde behauiour,   911
  Hiding his bitter iests in blunt behauiour,   1401
BEHELD = 3
  I neuer yet beheld that speciall face,   866
  That haue beheld me giue away my selfe   1576
  Hast thou beheld a fresher Gentlewoman: 2327
BEHINDE = 2*1
  So shal I no whit be behinde in dutie   740
  hill, my Master riding behinde my Mistris.   1700
  Biond. Faith nothing: but has left mee here behinde   2264
BEHOLDING = 2
  To whom we all rest generally beholding.   846
  More kindely beholding to you then any: 941
BEING *l*.131 138 269 *600 952 1184 *1445 1630 *1668 1669 2568 2746 = 9*3, 1
  Gaue me my being, and my father first   310

BELEEUE = 7*2
*1.*Hun*. Beleeue me Lord, I thinke he cannot choose.   46
Bianca. Beleeue me sister, of all the men aliue,   865
I tell you 'tis incredible to beleeue | How much she loues me: oh the
kindest *Kate*,   1186
In time I may beleeue, yet I mistrust.   1344
Hort. I must beleeue my master, else I promise you,   1347
Pet. Not I, beleeue me, thus Ile visit her.   1497
Ped. I sir, so his mother saies, if I may beleeue her.   2414
Peda. Lay hands on the villaine, I beleeue a meanes   2417
Gre. Beleeue me sir, they But together well.   2581
BELIKE = 4
Belike some Noble Gentleman that meanes   80
(Belike) I knew not what to take, | And what to leaue? Ha. *Exit*   408
Kate. Oh then belike you fancie riches more,   871
Belike you meane to make a puppet of me.   2088
BELLY = *1
*mouth, my heart in my belly, ere I should come by a fire   1646
BELMAN = 1
Hunts. Why *Belman* is as good as he my Lord,   25
BELONGETH *see* longeth
BELONGS = 2
Yet not so deepely as to thee belongs,   1064
Pewter and brasse, and all things that belongs   1237
BELOUED = 3*1
My best beloued and approued friend | *Hortensio*: & I trow this is his
house: 568
To faire *Bianca*, so beloued of me.   741
Gre. Beloued of me, and that my deeds shal proue.   742
Petr. Nay, I told you your sonne was well beloued in   2406
BELOW = 1
And place your hands below your husbands foote: 2735
BEMETE *see* be-mete
BEMOILD = *1
*place, how she was bemoil'd, how hee left her with the   1707
BEN see been
BEND = *1
*Bend thoughts and wits to atcheeue her. Thus it stands: 482
BENE = 1*1
Contutti le core bene trobatto, may I say.   592
*Hor. Alla nostra casa bene venuto multo honorata signi-|or mio
Petruchio*.   593
BENTIUOLIJ = 1
Vincentio's come of the *Bentiuolij*,   312
BEREFT = 1
Muddie, ill seeming, thicke, bereft of beautie,   2701
BERGAMO = 1
Vin. Thy father: oh villaine, he is a Saile-maker in | *Bergamo*.   2455
BESEECH = 2*1
Tell me I beseech you, which is the readiest way   788
Gre. But so is not she. | *Tra*. For what reason I beseech you.   805
*Cuffe was but to knocke at your eare, and beseech list-|ning: 1698
BESEEME = 1
Beside, so qualified, as may beseeme | The Spouse of any noble
Gentleman: 2365
BESET = 1
Draw forth thy weapon, we are beset with theeues,   1622

BESIDE = 2

You vnderstand me. Ouer and beside | Signior *Baptistas* liberalitie,   714
Beside, so qualified, as may beseeme | The Spouse of any noble
Gentleman: 2365

BESIDES = 4*1

Besides, two thousand Duckets by the yeere   1251
That she shall haue, besides an Argosie   1256
Then three great Argosies, besides two Galliasses   · 1260
*saddle, and stirrops of no kindred: besides possest   1437
Besides old *Gremio* is harkning still,   2235

BESPEAKE = 1

Fel. Heere is the cap your Worship did bespeake.   2047

BEST = 11*5

Kate. A pretty peate, it is best put finger in the eye, | and she knew
why.   381
*best horse in *Padua* to begin his woing that would tho- | roughly   445
My best beloued and approued friend | *Hortensio*: & I trow this is his
house: 568
Happily to wiue and thriue, as best I may: 622
Brought vp as best becomes a Gentlewoman.   653
Whom thou lou'st best: see thou dissemble not.   864
Kate. If I be waspish, best beware my sting.   1086
Bap. I must confesse your offer is the best,   1268
Old fashions please me best, I am not so nice   1373
And reuell it as brauely as the best,   2036
And if you cannot, best you stop your eares.   2061
Ile none of it; hence, make your best of it.   2085
Tra. I thanke you sir, where then doe you know best   2230
Grem. They're busie within, you were best knocke | lowder.   2395
Tran. Then thou wert best saie that I am not *Lu-* | *centio*.   2481
Feast with the best, and welcome to my house,   2545

BESTOW = 2

That is, not to bestow my yongest daughter,   352
I heere bestow a simple instrument,   962

BESTOWED = 1

With one consent to haue her so bestowed: 2217

BESTRAUGHT = 1

*sheere Ale, score me vp for the lyingst knaue in Christen | dome. What
I am not bestraught: here's---   176

BESTREWD = 1

Full of Rose-water, and bestrew'd with Flowers,   60

BESTROW = 1

Say thou wilt walke: wee wil bestrow the ground.   192

BETHINKE = 1

Oh Noble Lord, bethinke thee of thy birth,   182

BETTER = 16

Trust me, I take him for the better dogge.   28
No better than a poore and loathsome begger: 134
Bion. The better for him, would I were so too.   546
Pedascule, Ile watch you better yet: 1343
Petr. Were it better I should rush in thus: 1474
'Twere well for *Kate*, and better for my selfe.   1503
To put on better ere he goe to Church.   1509
And better 'twere that both of vs did fast,   1805
He that knowes better how to tame a shrew,   1844
Kate. I neuer saw a better fashion'd gowne,   2086
Or is the Adder better then the Eele,   2160

BETTER *cont.*

Come sir, we will better it in *Pisa*. 2256
Better once then neuer, for neuer to late. *Exeunt*. 2532
Haue at you for a better iest or too. 2588
Praie God sir your wife send you not a worse. | *Petr*. I hope better. 2634
Petr. Nay, I will win my wager better yet, 2671
BETTERED = 1
Which I haue bettered rather then decreast, 983
BETTERS = 1
Your betters haue indur'd me say my minde, 2060
BETWEENE = 2
Let specialties be therefore drawne betweene vs, 991
Of loue betweene your daughter and himselfe: 2209
BETWIXT *see* 'twixt
BEWARE = 1
Kate. If I be waspish, best beware my sting. 1086
BEYOND = 1
And shrow'd, and froward, so beyond all measure, 656
BE-METE = 1
Or I shall so be-mete thee with thy yard, 2098
BIAN = 18*7
BIANC = *1
BIANCA see also Bian., Bianc., Bianeu = 40*5
Enter Baptista with his two daughters, Katerina & Bianca, 347
Gremio a Pantelowne, Hortentio sister to Bianca. | *Lucen. Tranio, stand*
by. 348
What I haue said, *Bianca* get you in, 378
And let it not displease thee good *Bianca*, 379
Bap. Gentlemen content ye: I am resolud: | Go in *Bianca*. 394
For I haue more to commune with *Bianca*. *Exit*. 405
*Farewell: yet for the loue I beare my sweet *Bianca*, if 414
His yongest daughter, beautiful *Bianca*, 685
That none shal haue accesse vnto *Bianca*, 692
Well seene in Musicke, to instruct *Bianca*, 699
I promist to enquire carefully | About a schoolemaster for the faire
Bianca, 731
To faire *Bianca*, so beloued of me. 741
Then well one more may faire *Bianca* haue; 817
Enter Katherina and Bianca. 855
Bianca stand aside, poore gyrle she weepes: 881
Kate. Her silence flouts me, and Ile be reueng'd. | *Flies after Bianca* 886
Bap. What in my sight? *Bianca* get thee in. *Exit*. 888
Vnto *Bianca*, faire and vertuous: 954
Tra. And I am one that loue *Bianca* more 1216
Now on the sonday following, shall *Bianca* 1277
Enter Lucentio, Hortensio, and Bianca. 1295
Beeme, Bianca take him for thy Lord 1368
Yet if thy thoughts *Bianca* be so humble 1383
Enter Baptista, Gremio, Tranio, Katherine, Bianca, and o-|thers,
attendants. 1387
And marry sweet *Bianca* with consent. 1520
Enter Petruchio, Kate, Bianca, Hortensio, Baptista. 1565
And let *Bianca* take her sisters roome. 1636
Tra. Shall sweet *Bianca* practise how to bride it? 1637
Tra. Is't possible friend *Lisio*, that mistris *Bianca* 1847
Enter Bianca. 1852
you that durst sweare that your Mistris *Bianca* 1860

BIANCA cont.

Tra. Signior *Hortensio*, I haue often heard | Of your entire affection to *Bianca*,	1870
Forsweare *Bianca*, and her loue for euer.	1874
Tra. Mistris *Bianca*, blesse you with such grace,	1892
Giue me *Bianca* for my patrimony.	2205
*Cambio hie you home, and bid *Bianca* make her readie | straight:	2245
But bid *Bianca* farewell for euer and a day.	2282
Enter Biondello, Lucentio and Bianca, Gremio | is out before.	2379
Luc. Looke not pale *Bianca*, thy father will not frown. | *Exeunt.*	2518
Bianca. Tranio, Biondello Grumio, and Widdow:	2535
My faire *Bianca* bid my father welcome,	2541
You are welcome all. *Exit Bianca.*	2591
Bap. Sonne, Ile be your halfe, *Bianca* comes.	2625
Enter Kate, Bianca, and Widdow.	2674
The wisdome of your dutie faire *Bianca*,	2683

BIANCA = 2*1

BIANCAS = 4*1

Sorrie am I that our good will effects | *Bianca's* greefe.	389
*be happie riuals in *Bianca's* loue, to labour and effect | one thing specially.	421
That can assure my daughter greatest dower, | Shall haue my *Biancas* loue.	1225
Doth watch *Bianca's* steps so narrowly:	1522
Luc. Loue wrought these miracles. *Biancas* loue	2504

BIANEU = 1

Enter Biondello, Lucentio and Bianeu.	2485

BIAS = 1

And not vnluckily against the Bias:	2322

BID = 16*4

Lord. Bid them come neere:	87
Bid him shed teares, as being ouer-ioyed	131
Petr. Now knocke when I bid you: sirrah villaine	586
*looke you sir: He bid me knocke him, & rap him sound-|ly	598
These are their Tutors, bid them vse them well,	975
If she do bid me packe, Ile giue her thankes,	1046
As though she bid me stay by her a weeke:	1047
Prouide the feast father, and bid the guests,	1196
When I should bid good morrow to my Bride?	1505
Did I not bid thee meete me in the Parke,	1757
And bid my cozen *Ferdinand* come hither:	1780
Tai. You bid me make it orderlie and well,	2079
I did not bid you marre it to the time.	2082
*vnto thee, I bid thy Master cut out the gowne, but I did	2112
not bid him cut it to peeces. Ergo thou liest.	2113
*Cambio hie you home, and bid *Bianca* make her readie | straight:	2245
But bid *Bianca* farewell for euer and a day.	2282
*Master hath appointed me to goe to Saint *Lukes* to bid	2287
My faire *Bianca* bid my father welcome,	2541
Goe *Biondello*, bid your Mistris come to me. | *Bio.* I goe. *Exit.*	2623

BIDS = 1

She will not come: she bids you come to her.	2644

BIG = 1

Nay, looke not big, nor stampe, not stare, nor fret,	1614

BIGGE = 1

My minde hath bin as bigge as one of yours,	2728

BIGGER = 2
    Away with it, come let me haue a bigger.   2052
    Kate. Ile haue no bigger, this doth fit the time,   2053
BILL = *3
    Gru. Error i'th bill sir, error i'th bill? I commanded   2128
    Gru. I am for thee straight: take thou the bill, giue   2134
BILS = 1
    For I haue bils for monie by exchange   1945
BIN *l*.67 232 505 528 1950 2344 2670 2728 = 8
BIO = 3*2
BION = 1
    come to me forthwith. *Exit. Bion.*   2637
BION = 12*15
BIOND = 2*7
BIONDELLO see also Bio., Bion., Biond. = 24*2
    If *Biondello* thou wert come ashore,   341
    When *Biondello* comes, he waites on thee,   514
    Enter Biondello.   527
    Enter Tranio braue, and Biondello.   786
    Tra. Euen he *Biondello*.   792
    Tranio. I loue no chiders sir: *Biondello*, let's away.   796
    Enter Biondello.   1419
    Enter Biondello.   1910
    Tra. What is he *Biondello*? | *Bio*. Master, a Marcantant, or a pedant,   1915
    Enter Biondello.   2188
    Tra. Feare you not him: sirra *Biondello*,   2191
    Enter Lucentio and Biondello.   2258
    Bion. Cambio. | *Luc*. What saist thou *Biondello*.   2259
    Luc. *Biondello*, what of that?   2263
    Luc. Hear'st thou *Biondello*.   2283
    Enter Biondello, Lucentio and Bianca, Gremio | is out before.   2379
    Luc. I flie *Biondello*; but they may chance to neede   2382
    Enter Biondello.   2419
    Vin. Ist so indeede. *He beates Biondello.*   2434
    Enter Biondello, Lucentio and Bianeu.   2485
    Exit Biondello, Tranio and Pedant as fast as may be.   2490
    Bianca. Tranio, Biondello Grumio, and Widdow: 2535
    Goe *Biondello*, bid your Mistris come to me. | *Bio*. I goe. *Exit.*   2623
    Enter Biondello.   2627
    Hor. Sirra *Biondello*, goe and intreate my wife to   2636
    Enter Biondello.   2641
BIRD = 2
    Bian. Am I your Bird, I meane to shift my bush,   2589
    This bird you aim'd at, though you hit her not,   2593
BIRTH *see also* byrth = 2
    Oh Noble Lord, bethinke thee of thy birth,   182
    Her dowrie wealthie, and of worthie birth;   2364
BITE = 2
    Nor bite the lip, as angry wenches will,   1127
    It blots thy beautie, as frosts doe bite the Meads,   2697
BITTE = *1
    *halfe-chekt Bitte, & a headstall of sheepes leather, which   1444
BITTER = 2
    When did she crosse thee with a bitter word?   885
    Hiding his bitter iests in blunt behauiour,   1401
BLAME = 1*1
    Bap. Goe girle, I cannot blame thee now to weepe,   1416

BLAME *cont*.
  Hor. Signior *Petruchio*, fie you are too blame: 2030
BLEEDS = 1
  Scratching her legs, that one shal sweare she bleeds, 210
BLEERD = 1
  While counterfeit supposes bleer'd thine eine. 2498
BLESSE = 1
  Tra. Mistris *Bianca*, blesse you with such grace, 1892
BLESSED = 3
  As longeth to a Louers blessed case: 1893
  Petr. Nay then you lye: it is the blessed Sunne. 2314
  Kate. Then God be blest, it is the blessed sun, 2315
BLEST = 1
  Kate. Then God be blest, it is the blessed sun, 2315
BLEW = *2
  *blew lift; an old hat, & the humor of forty fancies prickt 1454
  *their blew coats brush'd, and their garters of an indiffe- |rent 1720
BLISSE = 1
  And happilie I haue arriued at the last | Vnto the wished hauen of my
  blisse: 2507
BLOOD = 2*1
  So workmanlie the blood and teares are drawne. 212
  *wil therefore tarrie in despight of the flesh & the blood 281
  Seeing too much sadnesse hath congeal'd your blood, 286
BLOTS = 1
  It blots thy beautie, as frosts doe bite the Meads, 2697
BLOW = 3*1
  *so great *Hortensio*, but we may blow our nails together, 412
  That giues not halfe so great a blow to heare, 775
  Yet extreme gusts will blow out fire and all: 1000
  That shakes not, though they blow perpetually. 1006
BLOWES = 1
  Blowes you to *Padua* heere, from old *Verona*? 615
BLOWING = *1
  *to thaw me, but I with blowing the fire shall warme my 1647
BLUNT = 3
  Gre. You are too blunt, go to it orderly. 906
  Hiding his bitter iests in blunt behauiour, 1401
  Though he be blunt, I know him passing wise, 1412
BOADS = 1*1
  Hor. And so it is: I wonder what it boads. 2662
  Petr. Marrie peace it boads, and loue, and quiet life, 2663
BOARE = 1
  Rage like an angry Boare, chafed with sweat? 769
BODIE = 3*1
  To decke thy bodie with his ruffling treasure. 2042
  For 'tis the minde that makes the bodie rich. 2155
  *to cosen some bodie in this Citie vnder my countenance. 2418
  Bian. Head, and but an hastie witted bodie, 2582
BODIED = 1*1
  Tail. Inprimis, a loose bodied gowne. 2117
  Gru. Master, if euer I said loose-bodied gowne, sow 2118
BODIES = 1
  Why are our bodies soft, and weake, and smooth, 2723
BODY = 1
  And for thy maintenance. Commits his body 2706

BOLD = 4*1
And therefore let me be thus bold with you,	670
Tra. Gentlemen God saue you. If I may be bold	787
Hor. Sir, let me be so bold as aske you,	823
Am bold to shew my selfe a forward guest	912
*May I be so bold, to know the cause of your comming?	950

BOLDNESSE = 1
Tra. Pardon me sir, the boldnesse is mine owne,	951

BONDMAIDE = 1
To make a bondmaide and a slaue of mee,	857

BONNY = 1
But for my bonny *Kate*, she must with me:	1613

BONY = 1
And bony *Kate*, and sometimes *Kate* the curst:	1057

BOOKE = 2*2
Keepe house, and ply his booke, welcome his friends,	502
That all amaz'd the Priest let fall the booke,	1545
*That downe fell Priest and booke, and booke and Priest,	1548

BOOKES = 7
My bookes and instruments shall be my companie,	385
All bookes of Loue, see that at any hand,	712
And other bookes, good ones, I warrant ye.	736
Petruchio with Tranio, with his boy | bearing a Lute and Bookes.	898
And this small packet of Greeke and Latine bookes:	963
Take you the Lute, and you the set of bookes,	969
Pet. A Herald *Kate*? Oh put me in thy bookes.	1101

BOOKS = 1
Nicke. Mistresse, your father prayes you leaue your | (books,	1376

BOORD = 1
For I will boord her, though she chide as loud	661

BOOTE = 1
Then vale your stomackes, for it is no boote,	2734

BOOTED = 1
Enter Baptista and Lucentio: Pedant booted | and bare headed.	2200

BOOTES = 1*1
*paire of bootes that haue beene candle-cases, one buck-|led,	1433
You may be iogging whiles your bootes are greene:	1597

BOOTS = 1
Off with my boots, you rogues: you villaines, when?	1772

BOOT-HOSE = *1
*a kersey boot-hose on the other, gartred with a red and	1453

BORNE = 3
Petr. Borne in *Verona*, old *Butonios* sonne:	756
His name is *Litio*, borne in *Mantua*.	921
For I am he am borne to tame you *Kate*,	1156

BOROUGH = 1*1
Host. I know my remedie, I must go fetch the Head-|borough.	13
Beg. Third, or fourth, or fift Borough, Ile answere	15

BORROW = 1
Gru. Why she comes to borrow nothing of them.	1734

BOSOME = 1
And with declining head into his bosome	130

BOST = 1
Fine Linnen, Turky cushions bost with pearle,	1235

BOTH = 12*6
If either of you both loue *Katherina*,	354
*and fast it fairely out. Our cakes dough on both sides.	413

BOTH *cont.*
    *parle, know now vpon aduice, it toucheth vs both: that   419
    Tra. Master, for my hand, | Both our inuentions meet and iumpe in
    one.   493
    *cloathes, or you stolne his, or both? Pray what's the | newes?   531
    Sufficeth my reasons are both good and waighty.   556
    Sirrah, leade these Gentlemen | To my daughters, and tell them both   973
    'Tis deeds must win the prize, and he of both   1224
    And so I take my leaue, and thanke you both. *Exit.*   1280
    That I haue beene thus pleasant with you both.   1351
    Bian. Farewell sweet masters both, I must be gone.   1379
    Cur. Both of one horse?   1701
    And better 'twere that both of vs did fast,   1805
    Bian. Tranio you iest, but haue you both forsworne | mee?   1896
    Kate. Then both or one, or any thing thou wilt.   2007
    Or both dissemble deepely their affections: 2224
    Hor. For both our sakes I would that word were true.   2552
    To painfull labour, both by sea and land: 2707
BOTS = *1
    *Staggers, begnawne with the Bots, Waid in the backe,   1442
BOTTOME = *1
    *me in the skirts of it, and beate me to death with a bot-|tome of
    browne thred: I said a gowne.   2119
BOULSTER = 1
    And heere Ile fling the pillow, there the boulster,   1835
BOUND = 3
    Hearke you sir, Ile haue them verie fairely bound,   711
    And bound I am to *Padua*, there to visite   2354
    When they are bound to serue, loue, and obay.   2722
BOW = 1
    And then pursue me as you draw your Bow.   2590
BOWD = 1
    And bow'd her hand to teach her fingering,   1018
BOWLE = *1
    Petr. Well, forward, forward, thus the bowle should | (run,   2321
BOY = 7*5
    *him by Law. Ile not budge an inch boy: Let him come, | and kindly.
    Falles asleepe.   16
    Saw'st thou not boy how *Siluer* made it good   22
    And if the boy haue not a womans guift   135
    I know the boy will wel vsurpe the grace,   143
    Tra. So could I 'faith boy, to haue the next wish af-|ter,   547
    Petruchio with Tranio, with his boy | bearing a Lute and Bookes.   898
    An olde Italian foxe is not so kinde my boy. *Exit.*   1285
    *z not like a Christian foot-boy, or a gentlemans Lacky.   1456
    Gru. Why Iacke boy, ho boy, and as much newes as | wilt thou.   1677
    Ped. I warrant you: but sir here comes your boy,   2189
    My Boy shall fetch the Scriuener presentlie,   2241
BOYES = 1
    Tush, tush, feare boyes with bugs. | *Gru.* For he feares none.   777
BRACELETS = 1
    With Amber Bracelets, Beades, and all this knau'ry.   2040
BRACH = 2
    Brach *Meriman*, the poore Curre is imbost,   20
    And couple *Clowder* with the deepe-mouth'd brach,   21
BRAIND = *1
    *This mad-brain'd bridegroome tooke him such a cuffe,   1547

BRAINE = 1
Vnto a mad-braine rudesby, full of spleene,   1398
BRASSE = 1
Pewter and brasse, and all things that belongs   1237
BRAUD = 1*2
Brau'd in mine owne house with a skeine of thred: 2096
*Gru. Face not mee: thou hast brau'd manie men,   2110
*braue not me; I will neither bee fac'd nor brau'd. I say   2111
BRAUE = 2*1
And braue attendants neere him when he wakes,   44
Enter Tranio braue, and Biondello.   786
*braue not me; I will neither bee fac'd nor brau'd. I say   2111
BRAUED = 1
That fac'd and braued me in this matter so?   2501
BRAUELY = 1
And reuell it as brauely as the best,   2036
BRAUES = 1
Hort. Sirra, I will not beare these braues of thine.   1310
BRAURY = *1
*With Scarfes, and Fannes, & double change of brau'ry,   2039
BRAWLE = 1
And if she chance to nod, Ile raile and brawle,   1840
BRAWLING = 2
Petr. I know she is an irkesome brawling scold: 753
With oathes kept waking, and with brawling fed,   1988
BREAK = *1
*Bap. Why then thou canst not break her to the Lute?   1015
BREAKE = 4
You breake into some merrie passion,   107
And if you breake the ice, and do this seeke,   839
Or els my heart concealing it wil breake,   2063
Like pleasant trauailors to breake a Iest   2371
BREAKES = 1
And as the Sunne breakes through the darkest clouds,   2156
BREATH = 4
*Lord. What's heere? One dead, or drunke? See doth | he breath?   34
Which seeme to moue and wanton with her breath,   204
Heere let vs breath, and haply institute   307
And with her breath she did perfume the ayre,   478
BREATHED = 1
As breathed Stags: I fleeter then the Roe.   200
BREATHS = *1
*2.Hun. He breath's my Lord. Were he not warm'd   36
BREECHES = *1
*an old ierkin, a paire of old breeches thrice turn'd; a   1432
BREECHING = 1
I am no breeching scholler in the schooles,   1313
BREEFE = 2
In breefe Sir, sith it your pleasure is,   517
Pet. Well sir in breefe the gowne is not for me.   2138
BRIDALL = 2
Kat. Gentlemen, forward to the bridall dinner,   1605
Come I wil bring thee to thy Bridall chamber. Exeunt.   1810
BRIDE = 7*3
Be Bride to you, if you make this assurance: | If not, to Signior Gremio: 1278
But where is Kate? where is my louely Bride?   1475
Tra. See not your Bride in these vnreuerent robes,   1495

BRIDE cont.
<table>
<tr><td>When I should bid good morrow to my Bride?</td><td>1505</td></tr>
<tr><td>*Tra. And is the Bride & Bridegroom coming home?</td><td>1535</td></tr>
<tr><td>*Bride about the necke, and kist her lips with such a cla-|morous</td><td>1559</td></tr>
<tr><td>Obey the Bride you that attend on her.</td><td>1609</td></tr>
<tr><td>*Bap. Neighbours and friends, though Bride & Bride-|(groom wants</td><td>1632</td></tr>
<tr><td>Tra. Shall sweet Bianca practise how to bride it?</td><td>1637</td></tr>
<tr><td>Vin. I Mistris Bride, hath that awakened you?</td><td>2584</td></tr>
</table>

BRIDEGROOM = *2
<table>
<tr><td>*Tra. And is the Bride & Bridegroom coming home?</td><td>1535</td></tr>
<tr><td>*Bap. Neighbours and friends, though Bride & Bride-|(groom wants</td><td>1632</td></tr>
</table>

BRIDEGROOME = *2
<table>
<tr><td>*Gre. A bridegroome say you? 'tis a groome indeed,</td><td>1536</td></tr>
<tr><td>*This mad-brain'd bridegroome tooke him such a cuffe,</td><td>1547</td></tr>
</table>

BRIDEGROOMES = 1
<table>
<tr><td>Lucentio, you shall supply the Bridegroomes place,</td><td>1635</td></tr>
</table>

BRIDE-GROOME = 1
<table>
<tr><td>To want the Bride-groome when the Priest attends</td><td>1393</td></tr>
</table>

BRIDLE = *1
<table>
<tr><td>*bridle was burst: how I lost my crupper, with manie</td><td>1712</td></tr>
</table>

BRIEFE = 1
<table>
<tr><td>In briefe sir, studie what you most affect.</td><td>339</td></tr>
</table>

BRIEFER = 1
<table>
<tr><td>To teach you gamoth in a briefer sort,</td><td>1360</td></tr>
</table>

BRIGHT = 3
<table>
<tr><td>Good Lord how bright and goodly shines the Moone.</td><td>2297</td></tr>
<tr><td>Pet. I say it is the Moone that shines so bright.</td><td>2300</td></tr>
<tr><td>Kate. I know it is the Sunne that shines so bright.</td><td>2301</td></tr>
</table>

BRING = 11*1
<table>
<tr><td>Well, bring our Ladie hither to our sight,</td><td>226</td></tr>
<tr><td>And bring you from a wilde Kate to a Kate | Conformable as other houshold Kates:</td><td>1157</td></tr>
<tr><td>'Twill bring you gaine, or perish on the seas.</td><td>1210</td></tr>
<tr><td>Her fathers liking, which to bring to passe</td><td>1512</td></tr>
<tr><td>Ile bring mine action on the proudest he</td><td>1620</td></tr>
<tr><td>And bring along these rascal knaues with thee?</td><td>1758</td></tr>
<tr><td>How durst you villaines bring it from the dresser</td><td>1795</td></tr>
<tr><td>Come I wil bring thee to thy Bridall chamber. Exeunt.</td><td>1810</td></tr>
<tr><td>To dresse thy meate my selfe, and bring it thee.</td><td>2021</td></tr>
<tr><td>And bring our horses vnto Long-lane end,</td><td>2168</td></tr>
<tr><td>*Vinc. What if a man bring him a hundred pound or | two to make merrie withall.</td><td>2402</td></tr>
<tr><td>Away I say, and bring them hither straight.</td><td>2660</td></tr>
</table>

BRINGING = 2
<table>
<tr><td>To mine owne children, in good bringing vp,</td><td>403</td></tr>
<tr><td>The Seruingmen with Tranio bringing | in a Banquet.</td><td>2536</td></tr>
</table>

BRINGS = 1
<table>
<tr><td>See where she comes, and brings your froward Wiues</td><td>2675</td></tr>
</table>

BROACHD = 1
<table>
<tr><td>I will continue that I broach'd in iest,</td><td>650</td></tr>
</table>

BROKE = 2
<table>
<tr><td>Enter Hortensio with his head broke.</td><td>1007</td></tr>
<tr><td>Hor. Why no, for she hath broke the Lute to me:</td><td>1016</td></tr>
</table>

BROKEN = *2
<table>
<tr><td>*Towne Armory, with a broken hilt, and chapelesse: with</td><td>1435</td></tr>
<tr><td>*two broken points: his horse hip'd with an olde mo-|thy</td><td>1436</td></tr>
</table>

BROOKD = *1
*Though the nature of our quarrell yet neuer brook'd 418
BROOKE = 1
Adonis painted by a running brooke, 202
BROTHER = 1
Brother *Petruchio*, sister *Katerina*, | And thou *Hortentio* with thy louing *Widdow*: 2543
BROUGHT = 5*3
Because she brought stone-Iugs, and no seal'd quarts: 241
Vincentio's sonne, brought vp in *Florence*, 313
Brought vp as best becomes a Gentlewoman. 653
Pet. Who brought it? | *Peter.* I. 1791
Biond. His daughter is to be brought by you to the | supper. | *Luc.* And then. 2271
Vincentio: now wee are vndone and brought to no- | thing. 2422
*brought him vp euer since he was three yeeres old, and 2460
Till I be brought to such a sillie passe. 2680
BROW = *1
Kate. Fie, fie, vnknit that threatning vnkinde brow, 2694
BROWNE = 2
Is straight, and slender, and as browne in hue 1133
*me in the skirts of it, and beate me to death with a bot- | tome of browne thred: I said a gowne. 2119
BROYLD = 1
How say you to a fat Tripe finely broyl'd? 1998
BRUSHD = *1
*their blew coats brush'd, and their garters of an indiffe- | rent 1720
BUCKLED = *1
*paire of bootes that haue beene candle-cases, one buck- | led, 1433
BUCKLER = 1
Ile buckler thee against a Million. *Exeunt. P. Ka.* 1625
BUDDING = *1
Kate. Yong budding Virgin, faire, and fresh, & sweet, 2335
BUDDS = *1
*Confounds thy fame, as whirlewinds shake faire budds, 2698
BUDGE = *1
*him by Law. Ile not budge an inch boy: Let him come, | and kindly. *Falles asleepe.* 16
BUGS = 1
Tush, tush, feare boyes with bugs. | *Gru.* For he feares none. 777
BUILT = 1
Her new built vertue and obedience. 2673
BURNE = 2
And burne sweet Wood to make the Lodging sweete: 53
Tranio I burne, I pine, I perish *Tranio*, 458
BURNT = 2
Pet. 'Tis burnt, and so is all the meate: 1793
Pet. I tell thee *Kate*, 'twas burnt and dried away, 1802
BURST = *3
Host. You will not pay for the glasses you haue burst? 10
*often burst, and now repaired with knots: one girth sixe 1446
*bridle was burst: how I lost my crupper, with manie 1712
BURTHEN = 2
(As wealth is burthen of my woing dance) 634
Pet. Alas good *Kate*, I will not burthen thee, 1076
BURTON-HEATH = *1
Slie, old Slies sonne of Burton-heath, by byrth a 171

BUSH = 1
  Bian. Am I your Bird, I meane to shift my bush,   2589
BUSIE = 1 *2
  Grem. They're busie within, you were best knocke | lowder.   2395
  That she is busie, and she cannot come.   2630
  Petr. How? she's busie, and she cannot come: is that | an answere? 2631
BUSIED = *1
  Luc. And what of all this. | *Bion.* I cannot tell, expect they are busied
  about a   2276
BUSINESSE = 5 *1
  Pet. Signior *Baptista*, my businesse asketh haste,   979
  And watch our vantage in this businesse,   1527
  Make it no wonder: if you knew my businesse,   1573
  Til you haue done your businesse in the Citie: 1966
  Weele passe the businesse priuately and well: 2239
  *in this businesse: I dare sweare this is the right | *Vincentio.*   2477
BUT *l.*31 37 69 96 104 213 231 235 236 *280 345 366 373 *412 *417 *434
  *438 453 464 489 515 *549 *551 562 567 618 627 629 *678 760 762 765
  805 825 851 858 870 875 896 923 927 937 948 1004 1014 1017 1050
  *1053 1058 1077 1125 1129 1154 1162 1173 1174 *1198 1212 1213 1220
  1222 1272 1289 1292 1299 1315 1339 1349 1355 1381 1396 1410 1430
  1458 1475 1493 1498 1504 1511 *1552 *1556 1569 1588 1613 *1647
  *1654 *1660 *1665 *1666 *1672 *1698 *1704 *1717 1763 1848 1866 1877
  *1883 *1896 1912 1917 1930 1942 1953 1985 2003 2081 2105 2107 *2112
  2182 2189 2195 2252 *2264 2282 2306 2316 2323 2370 *2382 *2392 2401
  *2421 *2452 *2513 2516 2520 2521 2526 2549 2551 2582 *2585 2597
  2617 2711 2717 2725 2731 *2742 2744 = 113*33, 2
  Gre. Beleeue me sir, they But together well.   2581
  Would say your Head and But were head and horne.   2583
BUTONIOS = 1
  Petr. Borne in *Verona*, old *Butonios* sonne: 756
BUTT *see* but
BUTTERIE = 1
  Lord. Go sirra, take them to the Butterie,   112
BUY = 1
  To buy apparell 'gainst the wedding day;   1195
BUZARD = 1 *1
  Pet. Oh slow-wing'd Turtle, shal a buzard take thee?   1082
  Kat. I for a Turtle, as he takes a buzard.   1083
BUZZARD = 1
  Kate. Well tane, and like a buzzard.   1081
BUZZE = 1
  Pet. Shold be, should: buzze.   1080
BY *see also* a = 51 *18
BYRTH = *1
  Slie, old Slies sonne of Burton-heath, by byrth a   171
CAGED = 1
  And twentie caged Nightingales do sing.   188
CAKE = 1
  Gre. My cake is dough, but Ile in among the rest,   2520
CAKES = *1
  *and fast it fairely out. Our cakes dough on both sides.   413
CAL = *2
  Beg. Are you my wife, and will not cal me husband?   258
  Lord. Madam, and nothing else, so Lords cal Ladies   265

CALD = 4*1

Pet. And you good sir: pray haue you not a daugh-|ter, cal'd *Katerina*,
faire and vertuous.   903
Bap. I haue a daughter sir, cal'd *Katerina*.   905
Was *Aiax* cald so from his grandfather.   1346
Gru. And therefore 'tis cal'd a sensible tale: and this   1697
Know sir, that I am cal'd *Hortensio*.   1869

CALL = 20*4

And call him Madam, do him obeisance: 119
I long to heare him call the drunkard husband,   145
Beg. I am *Christophero Sly*, call not mee Honour nor   158
Call home thy ancient thoughts from banishment,   183
Sometimes you would call out for Cicely Hacket.   242
My men should call me Lord, I am your good-man.   259
Beg. I know it well, what must I call her? | *Lord*. Madam.   262
*may perhaps call him halfe a score Knaues, or so: Why   676
Whence are you sir? What may I call your name.   928
Frets call you these? (quoth she) Ile fume with them: 1020
While she did call me Rascall, Fidler,   1025
They call me *Katerine*, that do talke of me.   1055
Kat. Call you me daughter? now I promise you   1165
Call you this gamouth? tut I like it not,   1372
But so it is, my haste doth call me hence,   1569
*Call forth *Nathaniel, Ioseph, Nicholas, Phillip, Walter, Su-|gersop* 1718
Cur. They are. | *Gru*. Call them forth.   1724
Cur. I call them forth to credit her.   1732
To make her come, and know her Keepers call: 1828
Go call my men, and let vs straight to him,   2167
Tra. Sirs, this is the house, please it you that I call.   2181
And if you please to call it a rush Candle,   2310
Tra. Call forth an officer: Carrie this mad knaue to   2469
Bian. Fie what a foolish dutie call you this?   2681

CALLD = 3

Pet. You lye infaith, for you are call'd plaine *Kate*,   1056
Must get a father, call'd suppos'd *Vincentio*,   1290
My name is call'd *Vincentio*, my dwelling *Pisa*,   2353

CALLS = 1*1

*ceremonies done, hee calls for wine, a health quoth   1553
Curt. Who is that calls so coldly?   1651

CALS = *1

Gru. Thou it seemes, that cals for company to coun-|tenance her. 1730

CALST = 1

Why what a deuils name Tailor cal'st thou this?   2077

CAMBIO = 7*1

His name is *Cambio*: pray accept his seruice.   946
Welcome good *Cambio*. But gentle sir,   948
Cambio hie you home, and bid *Bianca* make her readie | straight: 2245
Bion. *Cambio*. | *Luc*. What saist thou *Biondello*.   2259
It shall goe hard if *Cambio* goe without her. *Exit*.   2293
Gre. I maruaile *Cambio* comes not all this while.   2386
Bap. Why, tell me is not this my *Cambio*?   2502
Bian. *Cambio* is chang'd into *Lucentio*.   2503

CAME = 8*3

*Rogues. Looke in the Chronicles, we came   7
For in a quarrell since I came a-shore,   538
Petr. Why came I hither, but to that intent?   765
Though *Paris* came, in hope to speed alone.   819

CAME *cont.*
Tra. That only came well in: sir, list to me,	1245
Bion. Who, that *Petruchio* came? | *Bap.* I, that *Petruchio* came.	1462
Signior *Gremio*, came you from the Church?	1533
Gre. As willingly as ere I came from schoole.	1534
*eccho: and I seeing this, came thence for very shame, and	1561
*now I begin, Inprimis wee came downe a fowle	1699

CAN *l.*102 *110 *415 506 583 651 766 894 1193 1217 1225 1227 1264
*1334 1502 1588 2018 2385 2640 = 17*3

CANDLE = 1
And if you please to call it a rush Candle,	2310

CANDLE-CASES = *1
*paire of bootes that haue beene candle-cases, one buck-|led,	1433

CANNON = 1
Whats this? a sleeue? 'tis like demi cannon,	2073

CANNOT = 6*6
*1.*Hun.* Beleeue me Lord, I thinke he cannot choose.	46
Gre. I cannot tell: but I had as lief take her dowrie	434
And euerie day I cannot come to woo,	980
Bap. Goe girle, I cannot blame thee now to weepe,	1416
Pet. It cannot be. | *Kat.* Let me intreat you.	1583
Gru. I cannot tell, I feare 'tis chollericke.	2000
And if you cannot, best you stop your eares.	2061
For curious I cannot be with you	2218
Luc. And what of all this. | *Bion.* I cannot tell, expect they are busied	
about a	2276
Biond. I cannot tarry: I knew a wench maried in an	2284
That she is busie, and she cannot come.	2630
Petr. How? she's busie, and she cannot come: is that | an answere?	2631

CANOPIES = 1
Costly apparell, tents, and Canopies,	1234

CANST *l.*140 460 *1015 1126 1218 1594 = 6*1

CAP = 6*1
A mad-cap ruffian, and a swearing Iacke,	1168
Fel. Heere is the cap your Worship did bespeake.	2047
A knacke, a toy, a tricke, a babies cap:	2051
Pet. Why thou saist true, it is paltrie cap,	2066
Kate. Loue me, or loue me not, I like the cap,	2069
Hor. I see shees like to haue neither cap nor gowne.	2078
Katerine, that Cap of yours becomes you not,	2677

CAPARISOND = *1
Bion. Oh sir, his Lackey, for all the world Capari-|son'd	1451

CAPE = 2
Pet. Proceede. | *Tai.* With a small compast cape.	2121
Gru. I confesse the cape. | *Tai.* With a trunke sleeue.	2123

CAPS = 2
With silken coats and caps, and golden Rings,	2037
And Gentlewomen weare such caps as these.	2054

CAPTAM = 1
Redime te captam quam queas minimo.	465

CARD = 1
Yet I haue fac'd it with a card of ten:	1287

CARDMAKER = *1
*Pedler, by education a Cardmaker, by transmutation a	172

CARE = 6
But if it were, doubt not, her care should be,	366
But art thou not aduis'd, he tooke some care	489

CARE *cont.*
    Pet. 'Tis with cares. | *Kate.* I care not.   1117
    That all is done in reuerend care of her,   1838
    I care not what, so it be holsome foode.   1994
    I am content in a good fathers care   2213
CAREFULLY = 1
    I promist to enquire carefully | About a schoolemaster for the faire
    Bianca,   731
CARELESSE = 1
    And come to Padua carelesse of your life.   1935
CARES = 2
    Pet. 'Tis with cares. | *Kate.* I care not.   1117
    Thy head, thy soueraigne: One that cares for thee,   2705
CAROWSE = 1
    Carowse full measure to her maiden-head,   1611
CAROWSES = 1
    And quaffe carowses to our Mistresse health,   849
CAROWSING = *1
    *he, as if he had beene aboord carowsing to his Mates af- | ter   1554
CARPETS = *1
    *the Gils faire without, the Carpets laide, and euerie | thing in order?   1685
CARRIE = 2*1
    Carrie him gently to my fairest Chamber,   50
    Tra. Call forth an officer: Carrie this mad knaue to   2469
    Vinc. Carrie me to the Iaile?   2472
CART = 1
    Gre. To cart her rather. She's to rough for mee,   357
CARTHAGE = 1
    As *Anna* to the Queene of Carthage was: 457
CARUD = 1
    What, vp and downe caru'd like an apple Tart?   2074
CASA = *1
    Hor. Alla nostra casa bene venuto multo honorata signi- | or mio
    Petruchio.   593
CASE = 3
    Doe get their children: but in this case of woing,   1292
    As longeth to a Louers blessed case: 1893
    Tis well, and hold your owne in any case   2186
CASES = *1
    *paire of bootes that haue beene candle-cases, one buck- | led,   1433
CAST = 2*1
    As *Ouid*; be an out-cast quite abiur'd: 332
    To cast thy wandring eyes on euery stale: 1384
    Gru. Oh I *Curtis* I, and therefore fire, fire, cast on no | water.   1657
CAT = 2
    *with it, that shee shal haue no more eies to see withall | then a Cat:
    you know him not sir.   680
    But will you woo this Wilde-cat? | *Petr.* Will I liue?   762
CATCH = 2
    Kate. Too light for such a swaine as you to catch,   1078
    Gre. No doubt but he hath got a quiet catch: 1212
CATCHES = 1
    Which runs himselfe, and catches for his Master.   2596
CATCHT = 1
    Gre. Take heede signior *Baptista*, least you be coni- | catcht   2476
CAUGHT = *1
    Gru. Why therefore fire, for I haue caught extreme   1680

CAUILL = 1
Tra. That's but a cauill: he is olde, I young.   1272
CAUSE = 6*2
  *If this be not a lawfull cause for me to leaue his seruice,   597
  *May I be so bold, to know the cause of your comming?   950
  To know the cause why musicke was ordain'd: 1305
  Luc. Faith Mistresse then I haue no cause to stay.   1380
  Hor. But I haue cause to pry into this pedant,   1381
  To come to Padua, know you not the cause?   1938
  Made me acquainted with a waighty cause   2208
  Wid. Lord let me neuer haue a cause to sigh,   2679
CEASE = *1
  Lord. Heauen cease this idle humor in your Honor.   166
CELSA = 2*1
  tellus, hic steterat Priami regia Celsa senis.   1323
  regia, bearing my port, *celsa senis* that we might be-|guile the old
  Pantalowne.   1329
  hic staterat priami, take heede he heare vs not, *regia* pre-|sume not,
  Celsa senis, despaire not.   1336
CENSOR = 1
  Like to a Censor in a barbers shoppe: 2076
CEREMONIALL = 1
  To speake the ceremoniall rites of marriage?   1394
CEREMONIES = *1
  *ceremonies done, hee calls for wine, a health quoth   1553
CERNES = *1
  *sir, what cernes it you, if I weare Pearle and gold: I thank   2453
CFAVT = 1
  Cfavt, that loues with all affection: 1369
CHAFE = 1
  Kate. I chafe you if I tarrie. Let me go.   1120
CHAFED = 1
  Rage like an angry Boare, chafed with sweat?   769
CHAMBER = 7*1
  Carrie him gently to my fairest Chamber,   50
  That done, conduct him to the drunkards chamber,   118
  For though you lay heere in this goodlie chamber,   237
  As *Kate* this chamber with her princely gate: 1138
  And helpe to dresse your sisters chamber vp,   1377
  Goe to my chamber, put on clothes of mine.   1496
  Come I wil bring thee to thy Bridall chamber. *Exeunt.*   1810
  Cur. In her chamber, making a sermon of continen-|cie   1816
CHANCE = 4*1
  And if he chance to speake, be readie straight   56
  Why this a heauie chance twixt him and you,   612
  Heere is a Gentleman whom by chance I met   747
  And if she chance to nod, Ile raile and brawle,   1840
  Luc. I flie *Biondello*; but they may chance to neede   2382
CHANGD = 3
  Tranio is chang'd into *Lucentio*.   545
  Bian. Cambio is chang'd into *Lucentio*.   2503
  For she is chang'd as she had neuer bin.   2670
CHANGE = 1*1
  As I can change these poore accoutrements,   1502
  *With Scarfes, and Fannes, & double change of brau'ry,   2039
CHANGES = 1
  And the Moone changes euen as your minde: 2317

CHANGING = 1
   Hortensio will be quit with thee by changing. *Exit.*   1386
CHAPELESSE = *1
   *Towne Armory, with a broken hilt, and chapelesse: with   1435
CHARGD = 2
   For your Physitians haue expressely charg'd,   275
   For so your father charg'd me at our parting: 519
CHARGE = 4*4
   Lo. Huntsman I charge thee, tender wel my hounds,   19
   Waite you on him, I charge you, as becomes: 540
   And beare his charge of wooing whatsoere.   783
   Kate. Of all thy sutors heere I charge tel   863
   To charge true rules for old inuentions,   1374
   *hold on him I charge you in the Dukes name: oh my   2466
   *the Iaile: father *Baptista*, I charge you see that hee be | forth comming.   2470
   Pet. Katherine I charge thee tell these head-strong   2686
CHARITIE = 1
   If not, elsewhere they meete with charitie: 1984
CHARITY = 1
   Now let him speake, 'tis charity to shew. *Exit*   1845
CHARME = 2
   But I will charme him first to keepe his tongue.   515
   To tame a shrew, and charme her chattering tongue.   1909
CHASTE = 1
   And then let *Kate* be chaste, and *Dian* sportfull.   1140
CHASTITIE = 1
   And Romane *Lucrece* for her chastitie: 1176
CHAT = 4
   Oh how I long to haue some chat with her.   1030
   And therefore setting all this chat aside,   1147
   But what a foole am I to chat with you,   1504
   For now we sit to chat as well as eate.   2548
CHATTELS = 1
   Shee is my goods, my chattels, she is my house,   1616
CHATTERING = 1
   To tame a shrew, and charme her chattering tongue.   1909
CHECKES = 1
   Or so deuote to *Aristotles* checkes   331
CHEEKES = 1
   Such warre of white and red within her cheekes: 2328
CHEERE = 6
   Beg. Marrie I fare well, for heere is cheere enough.   255
   And haue prepar'd great store of wedding cheere,   1568
   Hor. Mistris, what cheere? | *Kate.* Faith as cold as can be.   2017
   Welcome, one messe is like to be your cheere,   2255
   And by all likelihood some cheere is toward. *Knock.*   2394
   After our great good cheere: praie you sit downe,   2547
CHEERFULLY = *1
   Pet. Plucke vp thy spirits, looke cheerfully vpon me.   2019
CHEKT = *1
   *halfe-chekt Bitte, & a headstall of sheepes leather, which   1444
CHESSE-NUT = 1
   As wil a Chesse-nut in a Farmers fire.   776
CHESTS = 1
   In Cypres chests my arras counterpoints,   1233
CHIDE = 2
   Tra. Master, it is no time to chide you now,   462

CHIDE *cont.*
For I will boord her, though she chide as loud   661
CHIDERS = 1
   Tranio. I loue no chiders sir: *Biondello*, let's away.   796
CHIDES = 1
   Petr. Not her that chides sir, at any hand I pray.   795
CHILDE = 2*1
   *A childe shall get a sire, if I faile not of my cunning. *Exit.*   1293
And speake I will. I am no childe, no babe,   2059
Happy the Parents of so faire a childe;   2337
CHILDREN = 2*1
To mine owne children, in good bringing vp,   403
Doe get their children: but in this case of woing,   1292
   Vin. Tis a good hearing, when children are toward.   2741
CHINE = *1
   *with the glanders, and like to mose in the chine, trou-|bled   1438
CHOAKT = 1
What, haue I choakt you with an Argosie?   1258
CHOICE = 1
To striue for that which resteth in my choice: 1312
CHOISE = 1*1
   Hor. Faith (as you say) there's small choise in rotten   437
That she's the choise loue of Signior *Gremio*.   808
CHOLLER = 1
For it engenders choller, planteth anger,   1804
CHOLLERICKE = 3
Since of our selues, our selues are chollericke,   1806
Gru. I feare it is too chollericke a meate.   1997
Gru. I cannot tell, I feare 'tis chollericke.   2000
CHOOSE = 1*3
   1.Hun. Beleeue me Lord, I thinke he cannot choose.   46
   Pet. Be patient gentlemen, I choose her for my selfe, 1182
   Vin. You shall not choose but drinke before you go, 2392
Bion. I hope I may choose Sir.   2425
CHOSEN = 1
Hor. That she's the chosen of signior *Hortensio*.   809
CHRISTENDOME = 1*1
   *sheere Ale, score me vp for the lyingst knaue in Christen|dome. What
I am not bestraught: here's---   176
But *Kate*, the prettiest *Kate* in Christendome,   1058
CHRISTIAN = *1
   *z not like a Christian foot-boy, or a gentlemans Lacky. 1456
CHRISTMAS = 1
a Christmas gambold, or a tumbling tricke?   292
CHRISTOPHER = 1*1
   Beg. What would you make me mad? Am not I *Chri-|stopher* 170
And not a Tinker, nor Christopher Slie.   225
CHRISTOPHERO = 1*1
   Enter Begger and Hostes, Christophero Sly.   2
   Beg. I am *Christophero Sly*, call not mee Honour nor 158
CHRONICLES = *1
   Rogues. Looke in the Chronicles, we came   7
CHURCH = 3*5
The morning weares, 'tis time we were at Church.   1494
To put on better ere he goe to Church.   1509
Signior *Gremio*, came you from the Church?   1533
   *smacke, that at the parting all the Church did   1560

CHURCH *cont.*

Bio. The old Priest at Saint *Lukes* Church is at your | command at all hours.	2274
preuilegio ad Impremendum solem, to th' Church take the	2279
Biond. Nay faith, Ile see the Church a your backe,	2384
Bio. I haue seene them in the Church together, God	2420

CICELY = 1

Sometimes you would call out for Cicely Hacket.	242

CIRCUMSTANCES = 1*1

In all these circumstances Ile instruct you,	1975
Padua: doe you heare sir, to leaue friuolous circumstan- |ces,	2407

CITHEREA = 1

And Citherea all in sedges hid,	203

CITIE = 1*1

Til you haue done your businesse in the Citie:	1966
*to cosen some bodie in this Citie vnder my countenance.	2418

CITIZENS = 2

Pisa renowned for graue Citizens	309
Pisa renowned for graue Citizens.	1951

CITTIE = 1

That being a stranger in this Cittie heere,	952

CITY = 1

Gre. First, as you know, my house within the City	1228

CLAMOR = 1

And with the clamor keepe her stil awake:	1841

CLAMOROUS = *1

*Bride about the necke, and kist her lips with such a cla-|morous	1559

CLANGUE = 1

Loud larums, neighing steeds, & trumpets clangue?	773

CLAPT = 1

Gre. Was euer match clapt vp so sodainly?	1206

CLARKE = 1

Priest, Clarke, and some sufficient honest witnesses:	2280

CLEERE = 1

Say that she frowne, Ile say she lookes as cleere	1041

CLIFFE = 1

D sol re, one Cliffe, two notes haue I,	1370

CLOAKE = 1*1

Vncase thee: take my Coulord hat and cloake,	513
*hose, a scarlet cloake, and a copataine hat: oh I am	2445

CLOATH = 1

Go with me to cloath you as becomes you. *Exeunt.*	1976

CLOATHES = 2*1

Wrap'd in sweet cloathes: Rings put vpon his fingers:	42
*cloathes, or you stolne his, or both? Pray what's the | newes?	531
To me she's married, not vnto my cloathes:	1500

CLOCK = 1

It shall be what a clock I say it is.	2178

CLOCKE = 1

Let's see, I thinke 'tis now some seuen a clocke,	2170

CLOSE = 2

Which in a Napkin (being close conuei'd)	138
My Banket is to close our stomakes vp	2546

CLOSELY = 1

And therefore has he closely meu'd her vp,	486

CLOTHES = 1

Goe to my chamber, put on clothes of mine.	1496

42

CLOUDS = 2
　As thunder, when the clouds in Autumne cracke. 662
　And as the Sunne breakes through the darkest clouds, 2156
CLOWDER = 1
　And couple *Clowder* with the deepe-mouth'd brach, 21
COATE = 1
　Grumio. Nathaniels coate sir was not fully made, 1759
COATS = 1*1
　*their blew coats brush'd, and their garters of an indiffe-|rent 1720
　With silken coats and caps, and golden Rings, 2037
COBWEBS = *1
　*trim'd, rushes strew'd, cobwebs swept, the seruingmen 1682
COCKE = 1*1
　Pet. A comblesse Cocke, so *Kate* will be my Hen. 1103
　Kate. No Cocke of mine, you crow too like a crauen 1104
COCKES = 1
　not--- Cockes passion, silence, I heare my master. 1745
COCKLE = 1
　. Why 'tis a cockle or a walnut-shell, 2050
COFERS = 1
　In Iuory cofers I haue stuft my crownes: 1232
COFFEN = 1
　A custard coffen, a bauble, a silken pie, 2067
COLD = 6*2
　Beg. No, not a deniere: go by S.(aint) *Ieronimie*, goe to thy | cold bed,
　and warme thee. 11
　with Ale, this were a bed but cold to sleep so soundly. 37
　will take cold: Holla, hoa *Curtis*. 1649
　cold comfort, for being slow in thy hot office. 1669
　Gru. A cold world *Curtis* in euery office but thine, z 1672
　*cold. Where's the Cooke, is supper ready, the house 1681
　Hor. Mistris, what cheere? | *Kate.* Faith as cold as can be. 2017
　To watch the night in stormes, the day in cold, 2708
COLDEST *see* couldest
COLDLY = 1
　Curt. Who is that calls so coldly? 1651
COLOUR = 1
　There was no Linke to colour *Peters* hat, 1761
COLOURD *see* coulord
COM = *1
　Ped. Soft son: sir by your leaue, hauing com to *Padua* 2206
COMBD = *1
　*and the rest: let their heads bee slickely comb'd, 1719
COMBE = 1
　To combe your noddle with a three-legg'd stoole, 367
COMBLESSE = 1
　Pet. A comblesse Cocke, so *Kate* will be my Hen. 1103
COME = 66*21
　*him by Law. Ile not budge an inch boy: Let him come, | and kindly.
　Falles asleepe. 16
　Lord. Bid them come neere: 87
　Well you are come to me in happie time, 100
　Madam vndresse you, and come now to bed. 271
　Are come to play a pleasant Comedie, 284
　Come Madam wife sit by my side, 297
　Vincentio's come of the *Bentiuolij*, 312
　And am to *Padua* come, as he that leaues 321

COME *cont.*

If *Biondello* thou wert come ashore,	341
*apples: but come, since this bar in law makes vs friends,	438
*woe her, wed her, and bed her, and ridde the | house of her. Come on.	446
Luc. Sirra come hither, 'tis no time to iest,	533
Petr. Signior *Hortensio*, come you to part the fray?	591
then had not *Grumio* come by the worst.	602
come you now with knocking at the gate?	609
And so am come abroad to see the world.	624
Hor. *Petruchio*, shall I then come roundly to thee,	625
I come to wiue it wealthily in *Padua*:	641
And euerie day I cannot come to woo,	980
Pet. Thou hast hit it: come sit on me.	1072
Pet. Come, come you Waspe, y'faith you are too | angrie.	1084
Nay, come againe, good *Kate*, I am a Gentleman,	1095
Pet. Nay come *Kate*, come: you must not looke so | sowre.	1105
If it would please him come and marry her.	1408
Bap. Is he come? | *Bion.* Why no sir.	1424
Bap. I am glad he's come, howsoere he comes.	1459
Pet. Come, where be these gallants? who's at home?	1469
Petr. And yet I come not well. | *Bap.* And yet you halt not.	1471
First were we sad, fearing you would not come,	1481
Now sadder that you come so vnprouided:	1482
Sufficeth I am come to keepe my word,	1489
Pet. I must away to day before night come,	1572
Bap. She shall *Lucentio*: come gentlemen lets goe. | *Exeunt.*	1638
*mouth, my heart in my belly, ere I should come by a fire	1646
Cur. Come, you are so full of conicatching.	1679
And *Walters* dagger was not come from sheathing:	1762
Yet as they are, heere are they come to meete you.	1765
And bid my cozen *Ferdinand* come hither:	1780
Come *Kate* and wash, & welcome heartily:	1783
Come *Kate* sit downe, I know you haue a stomacke,	1787
Come I wil bring thee to thy Bridall chamber. *Exeunt.*	1810
To make her come, and know her Keepers call:	1828
And come to Padua carelesse of your life.	1935
To come to Padua, know you not the cause?	1938
'Tis meruaile, but that you are but newly come,	1942
Beggers that come vnto my fathers doore,	1982
Come Mistris *Kate*, Ile beare you companie.	2031
Come Tailor, let vs see these ornaments.	2044
Away with it, come let me haue a bigger.	2052
Pet. Thy gowne, why I: come Tailor let vs see't.	2071
Pet. Well, come my *Kate*, we will vnto your fathers,	2152
And well we may come there by dinner time.	2171
And 'twill be supper time ere you come there.	2173
Come sir, we will better it in *Pisa*.	2256
*the Priest be readie to come against you come with your | appendix.	
Exit.	2288
Petr. Come on a Gods name, once more toward our | fathers:	2295
Kate. Forward I pray, since we haue come so farre,	2308
Petr. Come goe along and see the truth hereof,	2374
and then come backe to my mistris as soone as I can.	2385
*come from *Pisa*, and is here at the doore to speake with | him.	2409
Ped. Thou liest his Father is come from *Padua*, and	2411
Vin. Come hither crackhempe.	2424
Vin. Come hither you rogue, what haue you forgot | mee?	2426

44

COME *cont.*

Petr. Why then let's home againe: Come Sirra let's | awaie.	2527
Petr. Is not this well? come my sweete *Kate.*	2531
And time it is when raging warre is come,	2539
To come at first when he doth send for her,	2611
Goe *Biondello,* bid your Mistris come to me. | *Bio.* I goe. *Exit.*	2623
That she is busie, and she cannot come.	2630
Petr. How? she's busie, and she cannot come: is that | an answere?	2631
come to me forthwith. *Exit. Bion.*	2637
Pet. Oh ho, intreate her, nay then shee must needes | come.	2638
She will not come: she bids you come to her.	2644
Petr. Worse and worse, she will not come:	2645
Say I command her come to me. *Exit.*	2648
Petr. Goe fetch them hither, if they denie to come,	2658
Wid. Come, come, your mocking: we will haue no | telling.	2689
Pet. Come on I say, and first begin with her. | *Wid.* She shall not.	2691
Come, come, you froward and vnable wormes,	2727
Pet. Why there's a wench: Come on, and kisse mee | *Kate.*	2738
Pet. Come *Kate,* wee'le to bed,	2743

COMEDIE = 1

Are come to play a pleasant Comedie,	284

COMES = 21 *5

Lord. Hence comes it, that your kindred shuns your | (house	180
When *Biondello* comes, he waites on thee,	514
Heere comes the rogue. Sirra, where haue you bin?	528
Comes there any more of it?	561
And then I know after who comes by the worst.	580
*two and fiftie horses. Why nothing comes amisse, so | monie comes withall.	647
Bap. Was euer Gentleman thus greeu'd as I? | But who comes heere.	895
And woo her with some spirit when she comes,	1038
But heere she comes, and now *Petruchio* speake.	1050
Heere comes your father, neuer make deniall,	1159
I will to *Venice,* sonday comes apace,	1202
Lucentio that comes a wooing, *priami,* is my man Tra-|nio,	1328
Bap. Who comes with him?	1450
Bap. I am glad he's come, howsoere he comes.	1459
Bion. Why sir, he comes not. | *Bap.* Didst thou not say hee comes?	1460
Bion. No sir, I say his horse comes with him on his | (backe.	1464
*finde when he comes home. But what talke I of this?	1717
Gru. Why she comes to borrow nothing of them.	1734
Ped. I warrant you: but sir here comes your boy,	2189
Here comes *Baptista:* set your countenance sir.	2199
Gre. I maruaile *Cambio* comes not all this while.	2386
Bap. Sonne, Ile be your halfe, *Bianca* comes.	2625
Bap. Now by my hollidam here comes *Katerina.*	2654
See where she comes, and brings your froward Wiues	2675

COMFORT = 2

The rest wil comfort, for thy counsels sound.	467
cold comfort, for being slow in thy hot office.	1669

COMING = *1

Tra. And is the Bride & Bridegroom coming home?	1535

COMMAND = 8 *1

Say, what is it your Honor wil command:	58
And say: What is't your Honor will command,	126
Or what you will command me, wil I do,	861
Kate. Go foole, and whom thou keep'st command.	1136

COMMAND *cont.*

Pet. They shall goe forward *Kate* at thy command,	1608
Hor. Why so this gallant will command the sunne.	2179
Bio. The old Priest at Saint *Lukes* Church is at your | command at all houres.	2274
I thinke I shall command your welcome here;	2393
Say I command her come to me. *Exit.*	2648

COMMANDED = 1*1

To raine a shower of commanded teares,	136
Gru. Error i'th bill sir, error i'th bill? I commanded	2128

COMMEND = 2

Then Ile commend her volubility,	1044
Away I say, commend me to thy master. *Exit Tail.*	2151

COMMENDABLE = 1

More queint, more pleasing, nor more commendable:	2087

COMMET = 1

As if they saw some wondrous monument, | Some Commet, or vnusuall prodigie?	1478

COMMING = 7*4

*May I be so bold, to know the cause of your comming?	950
Bion. Why, is it not newes to heard of *Petruchio's* | (comming?	1423
Bap. What then? | *Bion.* He is comming.	1426
Bion. Why *Petruchio* is comming, in a new hat and	1431
*after mee I know the rout is comming, such a mad mar-|ryage	1562
*make a fire, and they are comming after to warme them:	1643
Cur. Is my master and his wife comming *Grumio*?	1656
*to speake, and sits as one new risen from a dreame: A-|way, away, for he is comming hither.	1819
An ancient Angel comming downe the hill, | Wil serue the turne.	1913
But soft, Company is comming here.	2323
*the Iaile: father *Baptista*, I charge you see that hee be | forth comming.	2470

COMMITS = 1

And for thy maintenance. Commits his body	2706

COMMODITY = 1

Tra. Twas a commodity lay fretting by you,	1209

COMMON = 1

And practise Rhetoricke in your common talke,	334

COMMONLY = 1

And that's a wonder: fathers commonly	1291

COMMUNE = 1

For I haue more to commune with *Bianca*. *Exit.*	405

COMONTIE = *1

Beg. Marrie I will let them play, it is not a Comon-|tie,	291

COMPANIE = 8

With his good will, and thy good companie.	305
But stay a while, what companie is this?	345
My bookes and instruments shall be my companie,	385
Or else you like not of my companie.	926
And for this night we'l fast for companie.	1809
Come Mistris Kate, Ile beare you companie.	2031
We shall be ioyfull of thy companie.	2350
Vpon the companie you ouertake?	2372

COMPANIES = *1

*you vse your manners discreetly in all kind of com-|panies:	550

COMPANIONS = 1

companions, is all readie, and all things neate?	1742

COMPANY = 4*1
That she shall still be curst in company. 1185
And wherefore gaze this goodly company, 1477
And honest company, I thanke you all, 1575
*Gru. Thou it seemes, that cals for company to coun- | tenance her. 1730
But soft, Company is comming here. 2323
COMPARE = 1
Our strength as weake, our weakenesse past compare, 2732
COMPAST = 1
Pet. Proceede. | Tai. With a small compast cape. 2121
COMPLAINE = *1
*or shall I complaine on thee to our mistris, whose hand 1667
COMPOUND = 1*1
Rise Grumio rise, we will compound this quarrell. 595
*Bap. Content you gentlemen, I wil co(m)pound this strife 1223
CONCEALING = 1
Or els my heart concealing it wil breake, 2063
CONCEIT = 1*1
Pet. Why sir, what's your conceit in that? 2143
*Gru. Oh sir, the conceit is deeper then you think for: 2144
CONCEIUD = 1
It shall become to serue all hopes conceiu'd 314
CONCEIUE = 2
Hor. Sir you say wel, and wel you do conceiue, 843
Kat. Mistris, how meane you that? | Wid. Thus I conceiue by him. 2560
CONCEIUES = 2
Petr. Conceiues by me, how likes Hortentio that? 2562
Hor. My Widdow saies, thus she conceiues her tale. 2563
CONCERNES see cernes
CONCERNETH = 1
Tra. But sir, Loue concerneth vs to adde 1511
CONCLUDE = 1
And to conclude, we haue greed so well together, 1177
CONCLUSION = 1
And in conclusion, she shal watch all night, 1839
CONDITION = *1
*with this condition; To be whipt at the hie crosse euerie | morning. 435
CONDITIONS = 1
But that our soft conditions, and our harts, 2725
CONDUCT = 1
That done, conduct him to the drunkards chamber, 118
CONFERENCE = 1
With gentle conference, soft, and affable. 1130
CONFERRING = 1
Kate. They sit conferring by the Parler fire. 2657
CONFESSE = 8
And now in plainnesse do confesse to thee 455
My selfe am strooke in yeeres I must confesse, 1242
Bap. I must confesse your offer is the best, 1268
Gru. I confesse the cape. | Tai. With a trunke sleeue. 2123
Gru. I confesse two sleeues. | Tai. The sleeues curiously cut. 2125
Hor. Confesse, confesse, hath he not hit you here? 2602
Petr. A has a little gald me I confesse: 2603
CONFORMABLE = 1
And bring you from a wilde Kate to a Kate | Conformable as other
houshold Kates: 1157

47

CONFOUNDS = *1
*Confounds thy fame, as whirlewinds shake faire budds,   2698
CONGEALD = 1
 Seeing too much sadnesse hath congeal'd your blood,   286
CONI = 1
 *Gre. Take heede signior *Baptista*, least you be coni-|catcht   2476
CONICATCHING = 1
 Cur. Come, you are so full of conicatching.   1679
CONQUEROR = *1
 *in with *Richard Conqueror*: therefore *Pau-!cas pallabris*, let the world
 slide: Sessa.   8
CONSENT = 3
 And marry sweet *Bianca* with consent.   1520
 With one consent to haue her so bestowed: 2217
 Your sonne shall haue my daughter with consent.   2229
CONSENTED = 1
 Thus in plaine termes: your father hath consented   1148
CONSERUES = *3
 *2.*Ser.* Wilt please your Honor taste of these Con-|serues?   155
 *me any Conserues, giue me conserues of Beefe: nere ask   160
CONSIDERING = *1
 *selfe: for considering the weather, a taller man then I   1648
CONSOLATION = 1
 Take this of me, *Kate* of my consolation,   1061
CONSTER = 1*1
 Bian. Conster them.   1324
 Bian. Now let mee see if I can conster it. *Hic ibat si-|mois*,   1334
CONSUME = 1
 They do consume the thing that feedes their furie.   998
CONTAIN = *1
 Plai. Feare not my Lord, we can contain our selues,   110
CONTENDING = 1
 What is she but a foule contending Rebell,   2717
CONTENT = 11*2
 Bian. Sister content you, in my discontent.   383
 Bap. Gentlemen content ye: I am resolud: | Go in *Bianca*.   394
 Luc. Basta, content thee: for I haue it full.   504
 I am content to bee *Lucentio*,   522
 Bap. Content you gentlemen, I wil co(m)pound this strife   1223
 Pet. I am content. | *Kat.* Are you content to stay?   1585
 Pet. I am content you shall entreat me stay,   1587
 Pet. O *Kate* content thee, prethee be not angry.   1601
 I am content in a good fathers care   2213
 Vin. Feare not *Baptista*, we will content you, goe to: 2515
 Hort. Content, what's the wager? | *Luc.* Twentie crownes.   2613
 Luc. A hundred then. | *Hor.* Content.   2618
CONTENTED = 3
 The meate was well, if you were so contented.   1801
 I wil with you, if you be so contented,   1873
 Luc. I may and will, if she be so contented: 2290
CONTENTS = 2
 Luc. Gramercies Lad: Go forward, this contents,   466
 Because his painted skin contents the eye.   2161
CONTINENCIE = *1
 Cur. In her chamber, making a sermon of continen-|cie   1816
CONTINUE = 2
 Glad that you thus continue your resolue,   326

CONTINUE *cont.*
  I will continue that I broach'd in iest,   650
CONTRIBUTORS = 1
  Hor. I promist we would be Contributors,   782
CONTRIUE = 1
  Please ye we may contriue this afternoone,   848
CONTROUERSIE = 1
  *Petr. Preethe *Kate* let's stand aside and see the end of | this
  controuersie.   2438
CONTUTTI = 1
  Contutti le core bene trobatto, may I say.   592
CONUEID = 1
  Which in a Napkin (being close conuei'd)   138
CONUEYD = 1
  What thinke you, if he were conuey'd to bed,   41
COOKE = 1*1
  *cold. Where's the Cooke, is supper ready, the house   1681
  What dogges are these? Where is the rascall Cooke?   1794
COOLE = 1
  And say wilt please your Lordship coole your hands.   62
COPATAINE = *1
  *hose, a scarlet cloake, and a copataine hat: oh I am   2445
CORE = 1
  Contutti le core bene trobatto, may I say.   592
CORNER = 1
  At the hedge corner, in the couldest fault,   23
CORRALL = 1
  Luc. Tranio, I saw her corrall lips to moue,   477
COSEN = *1
  *to cosen some bodie in this Citie vnder my countenance.   2418
COST = 1
  Hath cost me fiue hundred crownes since supper time.   2684
COSTLY = 2
  Some one be readie with a costly suite,   63
  Costly apparell, tents, and Canopies,   1234
COUCH = 1
  Or wilt thou sleepe? Wee'l haue thee to a Couch,   189
COUENANTS = 1
  That couenants may be kept on either hand.   992
COUERLET = 1
  This way the Couerlet, another way the sheets: 1836
COULD *l.*342 *432 *547 605 867 1088 1501 *2428 = 5*3
COULDEST = 1
  At the hedge corner, in the couldest fault,   23
COULORD = 1
  Vncase thee: take my Coulord hat and cloake,   513
COUNSAILE = 1
  Counsaile me *Tranio,* for I know thou canst: 460
COUNSELL = 2
  Ile in to counsell them: haply my presence   148
  Thou'dst thanke me but a little for my counsell: 627
COUNSELS = 1
  The rest wil comfort, for thy counsels sound.   467
COUNTENANCE = 4*2
  *Cur. Do you heare ho? you must meete my maister | to countenance
  my mistris.   1726
  *Gru. Thou it seemes, that cals for company to coun-|tenance her.   1730

49

COUNTENANCE *cont.*

In gate and countenance surely like a Father.   1918

Here comes *Baptista*: set your countenance sir.   2199

*to cosen some bodie in this Citie vnder my countenance.   2418

While he did beare my countenance in the towne,   2506

COUNTERFEIT = 1*1

*counterfeit assurance: take you assurance of her, *Cum*   2278

While counterfeit supposes bleer'd thine eine.   2498

COUNTERPOINTS = 1

In Cypres chests my arras counterpoints,   1233

COUNTNANCE = 2

Puts my apparrell, and my count'nance on,   536

In count'nance somewhat doth resemble you.   1956

COUNTREYMAN = 2

Gre. No, sayst me so, friend? What Countreyman?   755

Tra. What Countreyman I pray? | *Ped.* Of *Mantua.*   1932

COUNTRIMEN = 1

Visit his Countrimen, and banquet them?   503

COUPLE = 2

And couple *Clowder* with the deepe-mouth'd brach,   21

Bap. Nay, let them goe, a couple of quiet ones.   1626

COURSE = 1*1

*1.*Man.* Say thou wilt course, thy gray-hounds are as | (swift   199

A course of Learning, and ingenious studies.   308

COURT = 4*1

Leaue shall you haue to court her at your pleasure.   356

And vnsuspected court her by her selfe.   702

Now for my life the knaue doth court my loue,   1342

Hor. See how they kisse and court: Signior *Lucentio*,   1875

Fie on her, see how beastly she doth court him.   1882

COURTEOUS = 2

An affable and courteous Gentleman,   664

For thou art pleasant, gamesome, passing courteous,   1124

COURTESIE = 1

Tra. Wel sir, to do you courtesie,   1947

COURTSIE = 1

If this be court'sie sir, accept of it.   1967

COXCOMBE = 1

Kate. What is your Crest, a Coxcombe?   1102

COY = 1

'Twas told me you were rough, and coy, and sullen,   1122

COZEN = 1*1

*swore, as if the Vicar meant to cozen him: but after ma-|ny   1552

And bid my cozen *Ferdinand* come hither: 1780

CRAB = 1*1

Kate. It is my fashion when I see a Crab.   1107

Pet. Why heere's no crab, and therefore looke not | sowre.   1108

CRACKE = 1

As thunder, when the clouds in Autumne cracke.   662

CRACKHEMPE = 1

Vin. Come hither crackhempe.   2424

CRAFTY = 1

Tra. A vengeance on your crafty withered hide,   1286

CRAUE = 1

If she denie to wed, Ile craue the day   1048

CRAUEN = *1

Kate. No Cocke of mine, you crow too like a crauen   1104

CRAUES = 1
And craues no other tribute at thy hands,   2710
CREATURE = 1
She was the fairest creature in the world,   218
CREDIT = 1
Cur. I call them forth to credit her.   1732
CREDITE = 1
His name and credite shal you vndertake,   1962
CREDULOUS = 1
Tra. If he be credulous, and trust my tale,   1920
CREST = 1
Kate. What is your Crest, a Coxcombe?   1102
CRETAN = 1
When with his knees he kist the Cretan strond.   473
CRICKET = 1
Thou Flea, thou Nit, thou winter cricket thou: 2095
CRIED = 1*1
He cried vpon it at the meerest losse,   26
*how I cried, how the horses ranne away, how her   1711
CROSSE = 2*1
*with this condition; To be whipt at the hie crosse euerie | morning.   435
When did she crosse thee with a bitter word?   885
Nor hast thou pleasure to be crosse in talke: 1128
CROSSING = 1
You are still crossing it, sirs let't alone,   2176
CROST = 3*1
Gru. Tell thou the tale: but hadst thou not crost me,   1704
Euermore crost and crost, nothing but crost.   2306
CROW = *1
Kate. No Cocke of mine, you crow too like a crauen   1104
CROWNES = 7
Crownes in my purse I haue, and goods at home,   623
And in possession twentie thousand Crownes.   987
In Iuory cofers I haue stuft my crownes: 1232
Hort. Content, what's the wager? | *Luc.* Twentie crownes.   2613
Petr. Twentie crownes, | Ile venture so much of my Hawke or Hound,   2615
Vnto their losses twentie thousand crownes,   2668
Hath cost me fiue hundred crownes since supper time.   2684
CRUELL = 1
Luc. Ah *Tranio*, what a cruell Fathers he: 488
CRUPPER = *2
*times peec'd, and a womans Crupper of velure, which   1447
*bridle was burst: how I lost my crupper, with manie   1712
CUFFE = 1*2
Pet. I sweare Ile cuffe you, if you strike againe.   1097
*This mad-brain'd bridegroome tooke him such a cuffe,   1547
*Cuffe was but to knocke at your eare, and beseech list-|ning: 1698
CUFFES = 1
With Ruffes and Cuffes, and Fardingales, and things: 2038
CULLION = 1
And makes a God of such a Cullion;   1868
CUM = *1
*counterfeit assurance: take you assurance of her, *Cum*   2278
CUNNING = 5*1
Wherein your cunning can assist me much.   102
Preferre them hither: for to cunning men,   401
To get her cunning Schoolemasters to instruct her.   490

CUNNING *cont.*

Cunning in Musicke, and the Mathematickes,	917
Beene long studying at *Rhemes*, as cunning	943
*A childe shall get a sire, if I faile not of my cunning. *Exit.*	1293

CUP = *1

*1.*Ser.* Wilt please your Lord drink a cup of sacke?	154

CUPS = 1

There, take it to you, trenchers, cups, and all:	1797

CUR = 14*4

CURBE = 1

And thus Ile curbe her mad and headstrong humor:	1843

CURE = *1

*past cure of the Fiues, starke spoyl'd with the	1441

CURIOUS = 1

For curious I cannot be with you	2218

CURIOUSLY = 1

Gru. I confesse two sleeues.	*Tai.* The sleeues curiously cut.	2125

CURRE = 1

Brach *Meriman*, the poore Curre is imbost,	20

CURRISH = 1

Petr. A good swift simile, but something currish.	2597

CURSE = 1

Gre. I doubt it not sir. But you will curse	937

CURST = 9*1

Her elder sister is so curst and shrew'd,	483
As old as *Sibell*, and as curst and shrow'd	636
Is, that she is intollerable curst,	655
Til *Katherine* the Curst, haue got a husband.	693
Gru. Katherine the curst,	A title for a maide, of all titles the worst.	694
Will vndertake to woo curst *Katherine*,	749
And bony *Kate*, and sometimes *Kate* the curst:	1057
If she be curst, it is for pollicie,	1172
That she shall still be curst in company.	1185
Horten. Now goe thy wayes, thou hast tam'd a curst	Shrow.	2748

CURSTER = 1

Tra. Curster then she, why 'tis impossible.	1538

CURSTEST = 1

A meacocke wretch can make the curstest shrew:	1193

CURT = 1

CURTESIE = 1

With soft lowe tongue, and lowly curtesie,	125

CURTIS see also *Cur., Curt.* = 5*3

will take cold: Holla, hoa *Curtis.*	1649
Enter Curtis.	1650
*greater a run but my head and my necke. A fire good	*Curtis.*	1654
**Gru.* Oh I *Curtis* I, and therefore fire, fire, cast on no	water.	1657
**Gru.* She was good *Curtis* before this frost: but thou	1660
*hath tam'd my old master, and my new mistris, and my	selfe fellow	
Curtis.	1662
**Gru.* A cold world *Curtis* in euery office but thine, z	1672
Enter Curtis a Seruant.	1815

CURTSIE = *1

*knit, let them curtsie with their left legges, and not	1721

CUSHIONS = 1

Fine Linnen, Turky cushions bost with pearle,	1235

CUSTARD = 1

A custard coffen, a bauble, a silken pie,	2067

CUSTOME = 1
For you shall hop without my custome sir: 2084
CUT = 5*2
   And to cut off all strife: heere sit we downe,   1316
   Heers snip, and nip, and cut, and slish and slash,   2075
   Tail. But did you not request to haue it cut?   2107
   *vnto thee, I bid thy Master cut out the gowne, but I did   2112
   not bid him cut it to peeces. Ergo thou liest.   2113
   Gru. I confesse two sleeues. | *Tai*. The sleeues curiously cut. 2125
   *the sleeues should be cut out, and sow'd vp againe, and   2129
CYPRES = 1
In Cypres chests my arras counterpoints,   1233
D = 1
D sol re, one Cliffe, two notes haue I,   1370
DAGGER = 1
And *Walters* dagger was not come from sheathing: ·   1762
DAIGNE = 1
Will daigne to sip, or touch one drop of it.   2703
DAINTIE = 1
Kate of *Kate*-hall, my super-daintie *Kate*,   1059
DAINTIES = 1
For dainties are all *Kates*, and therefore *Kate*   1060
DAINTY = 1
Basons and ewers to laue her dainty hands: 1230
DALLIE = 1
Tran. Dallie not with the gods, but get thee gone.   2252
DAM = *1
Gre. You may go to the diuels dam: your guifts are   410
DAME = *1
Bap. Why how now Dame, whence grov·es this in-|solence?   879
DAMME = 1
Tra. Why she's a deuill, a deuill, the deuils damme.   1540
DAMNED = 1
Vin. Where is that damned villaine *Tranio*,   2500
DANCE = 2
   (As wealth is burthen of my woing dance)   634
   I must dance bare-foot on her wedding day,   891
DAPHNE = *1
*3.*Man*. Or *Daphne* roming through a thornie wood,   209
DARE = 4*1
   And heere she stands, touch her who euer dare,   1619
   Gru. No, no forsooth I dare not for my life.   1979
   Kate. I dare assure you sir, 'tis almost two,   2172
   *in this businesse: I dare sweare this is the right | *Vincentio*. 2477
   Gre. Naie, I dare not sweare it.   2480
DARKEST = 1
And as the Sunne breakes through the darkest clouds,   2156
DARST = 1
Ped. Sweare if thou dar'st.   2479
DART = 1
And dart not scornefull glances from those eies,   2695
DAUGHTER = 28*6
   That is, not to bestow my yongest daughter,   352
   Baptistas eldest daughter to a husband, wee set his   440
   Such as the daughter of *Agenor* had,   471
   *that *Lucentio* indeede had *Baptistas* yongest daugh-|ter.   548
   His yongest daughter, beautiful *Bianca*,   685

DAUGHTER *cont.*

And were his daughter fairer then she is,	814
Faire *Laedaes* daughter had a thousand wooers,	816
Did you yet euer see *Baptistas* daughter? | *Tra.* No sir, but heare I do	
that he hath two:	824
The yongest daughter whom you hearken for,	832
*Pet. And you good sir: pray haue you not a daugh- | ter, cal'd *Katerina*,	
faire and vertuous.	903
Bap. I haue a daughter sir, cal'd *Katerina*.	905
But for my daughter *Katerine*, this I know,	923
Do make my selfe a sutor to your daughter,	953
*Bap. What, will my daughter proue a good Musiti- | an?	1011
Proceed in practise with my yonger daughter,	1032
Or shall I send my daughter *Kate* to you. | *Exit. Manet Petruchio.*	1035
*Bap. Now Signior *Petruchio*, how speed you with my | (daughter?	1161
*Bap. Why how now daughter *Katherine*, in your | (dumps?	1164
Kat. Call you me daughter? now I promise you	1165
But now *Baptista*, to your yonger daughter,	1213
That can assure my daughter greatest dower, | Shall haue my *Biancas*	
loue.	1225
If I may haue your daughter to my wife,	1247
On sonday next, you know | My daughter *Katherine* is to be married:	1275
'Twixt me, and one *Baptistas* daughter heere:	1974
Of loue betweene your daughter and himselfe:	2209
And for the loue he beareth to your daughter,	2211
Doth loue my daughter, and she loueth him,	2223
And passe my daughter a sufficient dower,	2227
Your sonne shall haue my daughter with consent.	2229
Send for your daughter by your seruant here,	2240
*Biond. His daughter is to be brought by you to the | supper. | *Luc.* And	
then.	2271
That haue by marriage made thy daughter mine,	2497
daughter without asking my good will?	2514
Another dowrie to another daughter,	2669

DAUGHTERS = 3*2

*Enter Baptista with his two daughters, Katerina & Bianca,	347
*Bion. He that ha's the two faire daughters: ist he you | meane?	790
And toward the education of your daughters:	961
Sirrah, leade these Gentlemen | To my daughters, and tell them both	973
Then tell me, if I get your daughters loue,	984

DAUNT = 1

Thinke you, a little dinne can daunt mine eares?	766

DAY = 23

And twice to day pick'd out the dullest sent,	27
3.*Ser.* What raiment wil your honor weare to day.	157
I must dance bare-foot on her wedding day,	891
And euerie day I cannot come to woo,	980
If she denie to wed, Ile craue the day	1048
That vpon sonday is the wedding day.	1178
To buy apparell 'gainst the wedding day;	1195
Now is the day we long haue looked for,	1214
You know to morrow is the wedding day.	1378
Bap. Signior *Lucentio*, this is the pointed day	1389
Hee'll wooe a thousand, point the day of marriage,	1403
Bap. Why sir, you know this is your wedding day:	1480
I know you thinke to dine with me to day,	1567
Pet. I must away to day before night come,	1572

DAY *cont.*
 Kate. Nay then, | Doe what thou canst, I will not goe to day,   1593
 She eate no meate to day, nor none shall eate.   1831
 That shalbe woo'd, and wedded in a day.   1901
 My father is heere look'd for euerie day,   1972
 I will not goe to day, and ere I doe,   2177
 And that you look't for him this day in *Padua*,   2197
 But bid *Bianca* farewell for euer and a day.   2282
 Faire louely Maide, once more good day to thee: 2331
 To watch the night in stormes, the day in cold,   2708
DAYES = 2
 And I do hope, good dayes and long, to see.   758
 Ere three dayes passe, which hath as long lou'd me,   1886
DEAD = 1*1
 Lord. What's heere? One dead, or drunke? See doth | he breath?   34
 My father dead, my fortune liues for me,   757
DEADLY = 1
 'Twere deadly sicknesse, or else present death.   1992
DEALE = 1
 That like a Father you will deale with him,   2226
DEARE = 1
 Gre. Yongling thou canst not loue so deare as I.   1218
DEATH = 5*1
 Grim death, how foule and loathsome is thine image: 39
 Bap. After my death, the one halfe of my Lands,   986
 Master and mistris are almost frozen to death.   1674
 Tra. 'Tis death for any one in Mantua   1937
 'Twere deadly sicknesse, or else present death.   1992
 *me in the skirts of it, and beate me to death with a bot-|tome of
 browne thred: I said a gowne.   2119
DEBT = 1
 Too little payment for so great a debt.   2712
DEBTS = 1
 To gather in some debts, my son *Lucentio*   2207
DECEASED = 1
 And he knew my deceased father well: 668
DECEAST = 1
 Antonio my father is deceast,   620
DECEITFULL = 1
 deceiuing Father of a deceitfull sonne. | *Luc.* And what of him?   2269
DECEIUD = 2
 And watch withall, for but I be deceiu'd,   1355
 Tail. Your worship is deceiu'd, the gowne is made   2101
DECEIUE = *1
 Gre. Here's packing with a witnesse to deceiue vs all.   2499
DECEIUED = 1
 Ped. I what else, and but I be deceiued,   2182
DECEIUING = 1
 deceiuing Father of a deceitfull sonne. | *Luc.* And what of him?   2269
DECKE = 2
 To decke his fortune with his vertuous deedes: 315
 To decke thy bodie with his ruffling treasure.   2042
DECLINING = 1
 And with declining head into his bosome   130
DECREAST = 1
 Which I haue bettered rather then decreast,   983

DEEDE = 1
As liuelie painted, as the deede was done.   208
DEEDES = 1
To decke his fortune with his vertuous deedes: 315
DEEDS = 2
Gre. Beloued of me, and that my deeds shal proue.   742
'Tis deeds must win the prize, and he of both   1224
DEEPE = 1
A shallow plash, to plunge him in the deepe,   322
DEEPELY = 2
Yet not so deepely as to thee belongs,   1064
Or both dissemble deepely their affections: 2224
DEEPER = *1
Gru. Oh sir, the conceit is deeper then you think for: 2144
DEEPE-MOUTHD = 1
And couple *Clowder* with the deepe-mouth'd brach,   21
DEERE = 3*1
That art to me as secret and as deere   456
Luc. While you sweet deere proue Mistresse of my | heart.   1857
Bian. Pardon deere father.   2493
'Tis thought your Deere does hold you at a baie.   2599
DEFECTS = 1
For those defects I haue before rehearst,   689
DEGREES = 1
Tra. That by degrees we meane to looke into,   1526
DEIGNE *see* daigne
DELICIOUS = 1
A most delicious banquet by his bed,   43
DELIGHT = 1
And for I know she taketh most delight   396
DELIGHTS = 1
wherein she delights, I will wish him to her father.   416
DELIUER = 2
Hor. From all such diuels, good Lord deliuer vs. | *Gre.* And me too,
good Lord.   369
From Florence, and must heere deliuer them.   1946
DELUDING = 1
Kate. Go get thee gone, thou false deluding slaue, | *Beats him.*   2009
DEMI = 1
Whats this? a sleeue? 'tis like demi cannon,   2073
DENIALL = 1
Heere comes your father, neuer make deniall,   1159
DENIE = 2*1
If she denie to wed, Ile craue the day   1048
Bion. Oh we are spoil'd, and yonder he is, denie him,   2488
Petr. Goe fetch them hither, if they denie to come,   2658
DENIERE = *1
Beg. No, not a deniere: go by S.(aint) *Ieronimie,* goe to thy | cold bed,
and warme thee.   11
DEPTH = *1
Bap. And I to sound the depth of this knauerie. *Exit.*   2517
DESCENT *see* discent
DESCRIED = 1
I kil'd a man, and feare I was descried: 539
DESIRE = 2
Luc. Tranio, since for the great desire I had   300
Tail. But how did you desire it should be made?   2105

DESPAIRE = 1
 hic staterat priami, take heede he heare vs not, *regia* pre- |sume not,
 Celsa senis, despaire not. 1336
DESPERATE = 1
 And venture madly on a desperate Mart. 1208
DESPIGHT = 1*1
 Shall in despight enforce a waterie eie: 139
 *wil therefore tarrie in despight of the flesh & the blood 281
DESPIGHTFUL = *1
 Tra. Oh despightful Loue, vnconstant womankind, 1862
DESPITE = 1
 Ile keepe mine owne despite of all the world. 1525
DETAIND = 1
 Hath all so long detain'd you from your wife, 1486
DEUICE = 2
 That's your deuice. | *Luc*. It is: May it be done? 498
 That so I may by this deuice at least 700
DEUILL *see also* diuell = 4
 Gre. Why hee's a deuill, a deuill, a very fiend. 1539
 Tra. Why she's a deuill, a deuill, the deuils damme. 1540
DEUILLISH *see* diuellish
DEUILS *see also* diuels = 2
 Tra. Why she's a deuill, a deuill, the deuils damme. 1540
 Why what a deuils name Tailor cal'st thou this? 2077
DEUOTE = 1
 Or so deuote to *Aristotles* checkes 331
DEW = 1
 As morning Roses newly washt with dew: 1042
DIAN = 3
 Pet. Did euer *Dian* so become a Groue 1137
 O be thou *Dian*, and let her be *Kate*, 1139
 And then let *Kate* be chaste, and *Dian* sportfull. 1140
DIAPER = 1
 Another beare the Ewer: the third a Diaper, 61
DID *l*.235 478 824 884 885 1017 1025 1029 1137 1141 *1560 1757 1805
 1981 2047 2081 2082 2105 2107 *2112 2506 2509 2604 = 21*2
DIDST = 3*1
 Lord. 'Tis verie true, thou didst it excellent: 99
 Bion. Why sir, he comes not. | *Bap*. Didst thou not say hee comes? 1460
 Nath. *Peter* didst euer see the like. 1812
 Vinc. What, you notorious villaine, didst thou neuer | see thy Mistris
 father, *Vincentio*? 2430
DIE = 4*2
 And if I die to morrow this is hers, 1243
 If you should die before him, where's her dower? 1271
 Gre. And may not yong men die as well as old? 1273
 Ela mi, show pitty or I die, 1371
 Gre. Went they not quickly, I should die with laugh- |(ing. 1627
 *things of worthy memorie, which now shall die in obli- |uion, 1713
DIGRESSE = 1
 Though in some part inforced to digresse, 1490
DILIGENCE = 1
 As he shall thinke by our true diligence 74
DILIGENT = 1
 Heere Loue, thou seest how diligent I am, 2020
DIN = 1
 That mortal eares might hardly indure the din. 476

DIND = 1
What hast thou din'd? The Tailor staies thy leasure,   2041
DINE = 2
I know you thinke to dine with me to day,   1567
Dine with my father, drinke a health to me,   1578
DINNE = 1
Thinke you, a little dinne can daunt mine eares?   766
DINNER = 5
Gru. I would I were as sure of a good dinner.   785
And then to dinner: you are passing welcome,   977
Tra. Let vs intreat you stay till after dinner.   1580
Kat. Gentlemen, forward to the bridall dinner,   1605
And well we may come there by dinner time.   2171
DIRECTION = 1
Iust as my master had direction: 2102
DIRT *see* durt
DISCENT = 1
Oh that a mightie man of such discent,   167
DISCIPLINE = 1
Onely (good master) while we do admire | This vertue, and this morall
discipline,   328
DISCOMFITED = 1
Bap. Wel go with me, and be not so discomfited.   1031
DISCONTENT = 1
Bian. Sister content you, in my discontent.   383
DISCREETLY = *1
*you vse your manners discreetly in all kind of com- | panies: 550
DISDAINE = 1
That I disdaine: but for these other goods,   858
DISDAINFUL = 1
As I haue lou'd this proud disdainful Haggard,   1887
DISEASE = 1
And that his Ladie mournes at his disease,   66
DISEASES = *1
*tooth in her head, though she haue as manie diseases as   646
DISFIGURE = *1
*he wil throw a figure in her face, and so disfigure hir   679
DISGUISD = 1
And offer me disguis'd in sober robes,   697
DISGUISE = 1
But one that scorne to liue in this disguise,   1866
DISGUISED = 1*1
Enter Gremio and Lucentio disguised.   703
*disguised thus to get your loue, *hic steterat*, and that   1327
DISH = 3
Kate. A dish that I do loue to feede vpon.   2002
Heere take away this dish. | *Kate.* I pray you let it stand.   2025
A Veluet dish: Fie, fie, 'tis lewd and filthy,   2049
DISPATCHD = 1
See this dispatch'd with all the hast thou canst,   140
DISPLEASE = 1
And let it not displease thee good *Bianca*,   379
DISQUIET = 1
Kate. I pray you husband be not so disquiet,   1800
DISSEMBLE = 2
Whom thou lou'st best: see thou dissemble not.   864
Or both dissemble deepely their affections: 2224

DISTILLED = 1
Balme his foule head in warme distilled waters, 52
DISTINGUISHD = 1
Nor can we be distinguish'd by our faces, 506
DIUELL = 1*1
Gre. A husband: a diuell. | *Hor.* I say a husband. 425
Gre. I say, a diuell: Think'st thou *Hortensio*, though 427
DIUELLISH = 2
For shame thou Hilding of a diuellish spirit, 883
When (with a most impatient diuellish spirit) 1019
DIUELS = 1*1
Hor. From all such diuels, good Lord deliuer vs. | *Gre.* And me too,
good Lord. 369
Gre. You may go to the diuels dam: your guifts are 410
DO *l.*70 90 119 124 137 147 185 188 221 222 328 373 455 *558 *560 *589
605 *674 696 758 774 794 811 825 839 843 844 845 850 861 873 916 920
925 953 998 1037 1046 1055 *1673 *1726 1799 1877 1947 1948 1959
1968 2002 2033 2175 2329 *2348 *2457 2737 = 48*8
DOCTORS = 1
For so your doctors hold it very meete, 285
DOE *l.**675 1288 1292 *1311 1594 1602 2175 2177 2192 *2230 2373 *2407
*2513 2640 *2687 2697 = 10*6
DOES *l.**1089 1131 1476 1990 *2576 2599 = 4*2
DOFF = 1
Fie, doff this habit, shame to your estate, 1483
DOGGE = 2
I would not loose the dogge for twentie pound. 24
Trust me, I take him for the better dogge. 28
DOGGES = 1
What dogges are these? Where is the rascall Cooke? 1794
DOGGE-WEARIE = 1
That I am dogge-wearie, but at last I spied 1912
DOING = 1
Pet. Oh, Pardon me signior *Gremio*, I would faine be | doing. 935
DOLE = *1
*Sweet *Bianca*, happy man be his dole: hee that runnes 442
DOMINEERE = 1
Goe to the feast, reuell and domineere, 1610
DONE *l.*118 208 499 564 751 1318 *1499 *1553 *1558 1838 1966 2103
2195 2228 2620 = 12*3
DOORE = 3*2
Yet would you say, ye were beaten out of doore, 238
Pet. Where be these knaues? What no man at doore 1747
Beggers that come vnto my fathers doore, 1982
Petr. Sir heres the doore, this is *Lucentios* house, 2389
*come from *Pisa*, and is here at the doore to speake with | him. 2409
DORE = 1
The dore is open sir, there lies your way, 1596
DOST *l.**195 *201 340 884 1008 1135 = 4*2
DOTARD = 1
Bap. Awaie with the dotard, to the Iaile with him. 2484
DOTH *l.**34 1131 1153 1219 1220 1342 1522 1569 1848 1882 1956 *1957
2053 2223 2238 2611 = 14*2
DOUBLE = *2
Bianc. Why gentlemen, you doe me double wrong, 1311
*With Scarfes, and Fannes, & double change of brau'ry, 2039

DOUBLET = *1
  *Goddes: oh fine villaine, a silken doublet, a vel-|uet   2444
DOUBLETS = *1
  *me what raiment Ile weare, for I haue no more doub-|lets   161
DOUBT = 5*1
  But if it were, doubt not, her care should be,   366
  Gre. I doubt it not sir. But you will curse   937
  Gre. No doubt but he hath got a quiet catch: 1212
  I should be arguing still vpon that doubt,   1348
  Gru. A piece of Ice: if thou doubt it, thou maist   1652
  She will be pleas'd, then wherefore should I doubt: 2291
DOUBTFULL = 1
  But I am doubtfull of your modesties,   104
DOUE = 2
  For shee's not froward, but modest as the Doue,   1173
  Gre. Tut, she's a Lambe, a Doue, a foole to him: 1541
DOUGH = 1*1
  *and fast it fairely out. Our cakes dough on both sides.   413
  Gre. My cake is dough, but Ile in among the rest,   2520
DOWER = 3
  That can assure my daughter greatest dower, | Shall haue my *Biancas*
  loue.   1225
  If you should die before him, where's her dower?   1271
  And passe my daughter a sufficient dower,   2227
DOWN = *2
  *hath two letters for her name, fairely set down in studs,   1448
  Petr. A hundred marks, my *Kate* does put her down.   2576
DOWNE = 6*3
  And to cut off all strife: heere sit we downe,   1316
  *That downe fell Priest and booke, and booke and Priest,   1548
  *now I begin, Inprimis wee came downe a fowle   1699
  Where are those? Sit downe *Kate*,   1768
  Come *Kate* sit downe, I know you haue a stomacke,   1787
  An ancient Angel comming downe the hill, | Wil serue the turne.   1913
  What, vp and downe caru'd like an apple Tart?   2074
  Ped. What's he that knockes as he would beat downe | the gate?   2398
  After our great good cheere: praie you sit downe,   2547
DOWRE = 1
  To passe assurance of a dowre in marriage   1973
DOWRIE = 5*1
  Gre. I cannot tell: but I had as lief take her dowrie   434
  Yea, and to marrie her, if her dowrie please.   750
  What dowrie shall I haue with her to wife.   985
  Pet. And for that dowrie, Ile assure her of   988
  Her dowrie wealthie, and of worthie birth;   2364
  Another dowrie to another daughter,   2669
DOWRY = 1
  That you shall be my wife; your dowry greed on,   1149
DOZEN = 1
  I would esteeme him worth a dozen such: 30
DRANK = *1
  *Lordship: I ne're drank sacke in my life: and if you giue   159
DRAW = 2
  Draw forth thy weapon, we are beset with theeues,   1622
  And then pursue me as you draw your Bow.   2590
DRAWNE = 3
  So workmanlie the blood and teares are drawne.   212

DRAWNE *cont.*
Let specialties be therefore drawne betweene vs,   991
And there it is in writing fairely drawne.   1363
DREAMD = 2
Or do I dreame? Or haue I dream'd till now?   221
Beg. Madame wife, they say that I haue dream'd,   266
DREAME = 2*2
Lord. Euen as a flatt'ring dreame, or worthles fancie.   48
Or do I dreame? Or haue I dream'd till now?   221
These fifteene yeeres you haue bin in a dreame,   232
*to speake, and sits as one new risen from a dreame: A-|way, away, for
he is comming hither.   1819
DREAMES = 2*1
And when he sayes he is, say that he dreames,   68
And banish hence these abiect lowlie dreames: 184
*But I would be loth to fall into my dreames againe: I   280
DRESSE = 2
And helpe to dresse your sisters chamber vp,   1377
To dresse thy meate my selfe, and bring it thee.   2021
DRESSER = 1
How durst you villaines bring it from the dresser   1795
DREST = 2
And see him drest in all suites like a Ladie: 117
Enter Tranio, and the Pedant drest like Vincentio.   2180
DRIED = 1
Pet. I tell thee *Kate*, 'twas burnt and dried away,   1802
DRINK = *1
1.Ser. Wilt please your Lord drink a cup of sacke?   154
DRINKE =3*1
Striue mightily, but eate and drinke as friends.   851
Dine with my father, drinke a health to me,   1578
Tra. Th'art a tall fellow, hold thee that to drinke,   2198
Vin. You shall not choose but drinke before you go,   2392
DRINKES = 1
Drinkes to Hortentio.   2579
DRINKING = *1
*him sops as hee was drinking: This done, hee tooke the   1558
DROOP = *1
2.Man. Oh this is it that makes your seruants droop.   179
DROP = 1
Will daigne to sip, or touch one drop of it.   2703
DRUDG = *1
Pet. You pezant, swain, you horson malt-horse drudg   1756
DRUNKARD = 2*1
Such dutie to the drunkard let him do: 124
I long to heare him call the drunkard husband,   145
*Enter aloft the drunkard with attendants, some with apparel, | Bason and
Ewer, & other appurtenances, & Lord.*   151
DRUNKARDS = 1
That done, conduct him to the drunkards chamber,   118
DRUNKE = *1
Lord. What's heere? One dead, or drunke? See doth | he breath?   34
DRUNKEN = 1
Sirs, I will practise on this drunken man.   40
DRY = 1
And while it is so, none so dry or thirstie   2702

DUCKETS = 2
| Besides, two thousand Duckets by the yeere | 1251 |
| *Gre*. Two thousand Duckets by the yeere of land, | 1254 |

DUKE = 2
| Your ships are staid at Venice, and the Duke | 1939 |
| For priuate quarrel 'twixt your Duke and him, | 1940 |

DUKES = *1
| *hold on him I charge you in the Dukes name: oh my | 2466 |

DULCET = 1
| To make a dulcet and a heauenly sound: | 55 |

DULLEST = 1
| And twice to day pick'd out the dullest sent, | 27 |

DUMPS = 1
| *Bap*. Why how now daughter *Katherine*, in your | (dumps? | 1164 |

DURST = 2
| How durst you villaines bring it from the dresser | 1795 |
| you that durst sweare that your Mistris *Bianca* | 1860 |

DURT = *2
| *Gru*. Out of their saddles into the durt, and thereby | hangs a tale. | 1690 |
| *how she waded through the durt to plucke him off | 1709 |

DUTIE = 13*2
*2.*Player*. So please your Lordshippe to accept our	dutie.	91
Such dutie to the drunkard let him do:	124
May shew her dutie, and make knowne her loue.	128
So shal I no whit be behinde in dutie	740
So well I know my dutie to my elders.	862
*therefore fire: do thy duty, and haue thy dutie, for my	1673
What? no attendance? no regard? no dutie?	1753
Now doe your dutie throughlie I aduise you:	2192
Bian. Fie what a foolish dutie call you this?	2681
Luc. I would your dutie were as foolish too:	2682
The wisdome of your dutie faire *Bianca*,	2683
Bian. The more foole you for laying on my dutie.	2685
*women, what dutie they doe owe their Lords and hus-	bands.	2687
Such dutie as the subiect owes the Prince,	2713
In token of which dutie, if he please,	My hand is readie, may it do him ease.	2736

DUTY = *1
| *therefore fire: do thy duty, and haue thy dutie, for my | 1673 |

DWELLING = 1
| My name is call'd *Vincentio*, my dwelling *Pisa*, | 2353 |

EACH = 3
And each one to his office when he wakes.	*Sound trumpets*.	77
Each in his office readie at thy becke.	186
Let's each one send vnto his wife,	2609

EARD = 1
| *Pet*. A horson beetle-headed flap-ear'd knaue: | 1786 |

EARE = 1*1
| *Gru*. Lend thine eare. | *Cur*. Heere. | *Gru*. There. | 1693 |
| *Cuffe was but to knocke at your eare, and beseech list- | ning: | 1698 |

EARES = 5
That mortal eares might hardly indure the din.	476
Ile trie how you can *Sol*, *Fa*, and sing it.	*He rings him by the eares*	583
Thinke you, a little dinne can daunt mine eares?	766
And if you cannot, best you stop your eares.	2061
Pitchers haue eares, and I haue manie seruants,	2234

EARTH = 1
And fetch shrill ecchoes from the hollow earth.   198
EASE = 1
In token of which dutie, if he please, | My hand is readie, may it do
him ease.   2736
EATE = 9
Striue mightily, but eate and drinke as friends.   851
She eate no meate to day, nor none shall eate.   1831
As who should say, if I should sleepe or eate   1991
Petr. Eate it vp all *Hortensio*, if thou louest mee: 2032
Kate eate apace; and now my honie Loue,   2034
For now we sit to chat as well as eate.   2548
Petr. Nothing but sit and sit, and eate and eate.   2549
EATEN = *1
Gru. I sir, they be ready, the Oates haue eaten the | horses.   1591
ECCHO = 1*1
Lord. Thou art a Foole, if *Eccho* were as fleete,   29
*eccho: and I seeing this, came thence for very shame, and   1561
ECCHOES = 1
And fetch shrill ecchoes from the hollow earth.   198
EDGE = 1
Affections edge in me. Were she is as rough | As are the swelling
Adriaticke seas.   639
EDUCATION = 1*1
*Pedler, by education a Cardmaker, by transmutation a   172
And toward the education of your daughters: 961
EELE = 1
Or is the Adder better then the Eele,   2160
EFFECT = 1*2
*be happie riuals in *Bianca's* loue, to labour and effect | one thing
specially.   421
I found the effect of Loue in idlenesse,   454
Petr. Hortensio peace: thou knowst not golds effect,   659
EFFECTS = 1
Sorrie am I that our good will effects | *Bianca's* greefe.   389
EFFECTUALL = 1
More pleasant, pithy, and effectuall,   1361
EIE = 1
Shall in despight enforce a waterie eie: 139
EIES = 2*1
*with it, that shee shal haue no more eies to see withall | then a Cat:
you know him not sir.   680
Kate. Pardon old father my mistaking eies,   2343
And dart not scornefull glances from those eies,   2695
EINE = 1
While counterfeit supposes bleer'd thine eine.   2498
EITHER = 4
If either of you both loue *Katherina*,   354
Ile tel you newes indifferent good for either.   746
That couenants may be kept on either hand.   992
As shall with either parts agreement stand.   2232
ELA = 1
Ela mi, show pitty or I die,   1371
ELDER = 4
Before I haue a husband for the elder: 353
Her elder sister is so curst and shrew'd,   483
Vntill the elder sister first be wed.   835

ELDER *cont.*
    Atchieue the elder: set the yonger free,   840
ELDERS = 1
    So well I know my dutie to my elders.   862
ELDEST = 2*1
    Since once he plaide a Farmers eldest sonne,   94
    *Baptistas eldest daughter to a husband, wee set his   440
    In the preferment of the eldest sister.   956
ELEUEN = 1
    That teacheth trickes eleuen and twentie long,   1908
ELOQUENCE = 1
    And say she vttereth piercing eloquence: 1045
ELS = 1
    Or els my heart concealing it wil breake,   2063
ELSE = 13*1
    **Lord.* Madam, and nothing else, so Lords cal Ladies   265
    *When I am alone, why then I am *Tranio*: but in | all places else, your
    master *Lucentio*.   551
    Accept of him, or else you do me wrong.   920
    Or else you like not of my companie.   926
    Kate. A witty mother, witlesse else her sonne.   1143
    Shee is your owne, else you must pardon me: 1270
    Hort. I must beleeue my master, else I promise you,   1347
    Will you giue thankes, sweete *Kate*, or else shall I?   1788
    You might haue heard it else proclaim'd about.   1943
    'Twere deadly sicknesse, or else present death.   1992
    Or else you get no beefe of Grumio.   2006
    Ped. I what else, and but I be deceiued,   2182
    Vinc. But is this true, or is it else your pleasure,   2370
    forsweare him, or else we are all vndone.   2489
ELSEWHERE = 1
    If not, elsewhere they meete with charitie: 1984
EM = *1
    *send'em good shipping: but who is here? mine old Ma-|ster   2421
EMBOSSD *see* imbost
EMBRACE *see also* imbrace = 1
    Sweete *Kate* embrace her for her beauties sake.   2332
EMBRACEMENTS = 1
    And then with kinde embracements, tempting kisses,   129
EMPTIE = 1
    My Faulcon now is sharpe, and passing emptie,   1824
ENCOUNTER = 2
    To giue you ouer at this first encounter,   671
    That with your strange encounter much amasde me: 2352
END = 4*2
    Petr. Hortensio, to what end are all these words?   822
    And 'tis my hope to end successefully: 1823
    And bring our horses vnto Long-lane end,   2168
    **Petr.* Preethe *Kate* let's stand aside and see the end of | this
    controuersie.   2438
    **Kate.* Husband let's follow, to see the end of this adoe.   2522
    Petr. The fouler fortune mine, and there an end.   2652
ENDURD *see* indur'd
ENDURE *see also* indure = *1
    *mine to endure her lowd alarums, why man there bee   431
ENE = *1
    **Gre.* E'ne at hand, alighted by this: and therefore be   1744

ENFORCE = 1
    Shall in despight enforce a waterie eie: 139
ENFORST *see also* inforced = 1
    What *Tranio* did, my selfe enforst him to;   2509
ENGENDERS = 1
    For it engenders choller, planteth anger,   1804
ENIOY = 1
    So shall you quietly enioy your hope,   1519
ENOUGH = 5*2
    Beg. Marrie I fare well, for heere is cheere enough.   255
    *them, would take her with all faults, and mony enough.   433
    One rich enough to be *Petruchio's* wife: 633
    *minde is: why giue him Gold enough, and marrie him   644
    With wealth enough, and yong and beautious,   652
    Her onely fault, and that is faults enough,   654
    Tell me her fathers name, and 'tis enough: 660
ENQUIRE = 1
    I promist to enquire carefully | About a schoolemaster for the faire
    Bianca,   731
ENTER = 57*5
    Enter Begger and Hostes, Christophero Sly.   2
    **Winde hornes. Enter a Lord from hunting, with his traine.*   18
    Enter Seruingman.   82
    Enter Players.   86
    **Enter aloft the drunkard with attendants, some with apparel, | Bason and
    Ewer, & other appurtenances, & Lord.*   151
    Enter Lady with Attendants.   252
    Enter a Messenger.   282
    Flourish. Enter Lucentio, and his man Triano.   299
    **Enter Baptista with his two daughters, Katerina & Bianca,*   347
    Enter Biondello.   527
    Enter Petruchio, and his man Grumio.   565
    Enter Hortensio.   587
    Enter Gremio and Lucentio disguised.   703
    Enter Tranio braue, and Biondello.   786
    Enter Katherina and Bianca.   855
    Enter Baptista.   878
    Enter Gremio, Lucentio, in the habit of a meane man,   897
    Enter a Seruant.   972
    Enter Hortensio with his head broke.   1007
    Enter Katerina.   1051
    Enter Baptista, Gremio, Trayno.   1155
    Enter Lucentio, Hortentio, and Bianca.   1295
    Enter a Messenger.   1375
    **Enter Baptista, Gremio, Tranio, Katherine, Bianca, and o-|thers,
    attendants.*   1387
    Enter Biondello.   1419
    Enter Petruchio and Grumio.   1468
    Enter Gremio.   1532
    Enter Petruchio, Kate, Bianca, Hortensio, Baptista.   1565
    Enter Grumio.   1639
    Enter Curtis.   1650
    Enter foure or fiue seruingmen.   1733
    Enter Petruchio and Kate.   1746
    Enter seruants with supper.   1770
    Enter one with water.   1778
    Enter Seruants seuerally.   1811

ENTER *cont.*

ENTERTAINE = 1

And take a Lodging fit to entertaine 343

ENTERTAINMENT = 2

And for an entrance to my entertainment, 915
Haue you so soone forgot the entertainment 1297

ENTERTAINST = 1

But thou with mildnesse entertain'st thy wooers, 1129

ENTIRE = 1

Tra. Signior *Hortensio,* I haue often heard | Of your entire affection to
Bianca, 1870

ENTITLE *see* intitle
ENTRANCE = 1

And for an entrance to my entertainment, 915

ENTREAT *see also* intreat, intreate = 2

Pet. I am content you shall entreat me stay, 1587
But yet not stay, entreat me how you can. 1588

ENTREATED = 1

Yours will not be entreated: Now, where's my wife? 2642

ENTREATIE *see* intreatie
ENUIE = 1

Bian. Is it for him you do enuie me so? 873

ENUIOUS = 1

Like enuious flouds ore-run her louely face, 217

ERE = 13*1

Luc. What ere I reade to her, Ile pleade for you, 720
Hor. Sir, a word ere you go: 798
I loue her ten times more then ere I did, 1029
And twice as much what ere thou offrest next. 1262
His Lecture will be done ere you haue tun'd. 1318

ERE *cont.*

To put on better ere he goe to Church.	1509
I am to get a man what ere he be,	1514
Gre. As willingly as ere I came from schoole.	1534
*mouth, my heart in my belly, ere I should come by a fire	1646
Ere three dayes passe, which hath as long lou'd me,	1886
And 'twill be supper time ere you come there.	2173
Pet. It shall be seuen ere I go to horse:	2174
I will not goe to day, and ere I doe,	2177
Or ere I iourney to your Fathers house:	2304

ERGO = 1

not bid him cut it to peeces. Ergo thou liest.	2113

ERRAND = 1

Tra. But hast thou done thy errand to *Baptista.*	2195

ERROR = *2

Gru. Error i'th bill sir, error i'th bill? I commanded	2128

ESCAPE *see also* scape = 1

And I for my escape haue put on his:	537

ESCAPES *see* scapes

EST *l.**1322 *1326 *1335 = *3

ESTATE = 1

Fie, doff this habit, shame to your estate,	1483

ESTEEME = 3

I would esteeme him worth a dozen such:	30
Of such possessions, and so high esteeme	168
Nor be not grieued, she is of good esteeme,	2363

ESTEEMED = 1

Who for this seuen yeares hath esteemed him	133

EUEN *see also* e'ne = 7*2

Lord. Euen as a flatt'ring dreame, or worthles fancie.	48
Euen as the wauing sedges play with winde.	205
Tra. Euen he *Biondello.*	792
Pet. Good sooth euen thus: therefore ha done with | (words,	1499
Euen to the vttermost as I please in words.	2065
Euen in these honest meane habiliments:	2153
And the Moone changes euen as your minde:	2317
What you will haue it nam'd, euen that it is,	2318
Euen such a woman oweth to her husband:	2714

EUENT = 1

Bap. Ile after him, and see the euent of this. *Exit.*	1510

EUER = 13*5

And twentie more such names and men as these, | Which neuer were,	
nor no man euer saw.	248
That euer *Katherina* wil be woo'd:	690
Did you yet euer see *Baptistas* daughter? | *Tra.* No sir, but heare I do	
that he hath two:	824
Bap. Was euer Gentleman thus greeu'd as I? | But who comes heere.	895
Pet. Did euer *Dian* so become a Groue	1137
Gre. Was euer match clapt vp so sodainly?	1206
What euer fortune stayes him from his word,	1411
And heere she stands, touch her who euer dare,	1619
*all foule waies: was euer man so beaten? was euer man	1641
*so raide? was euer man so weary? I am sent before to	1642
Nath. Peter didst euer see the like.	1812
Forsweare *Bianca*, and her loue for euer.	1874
First tell me, haue you euer beene at Pisa?	1949
Ped. Oh sir I do, and wil repute you euer	1968

EUER *cont.*

*Gru. Master, if euer I said loose-bodied gowne, sow	2118
But bid *Bianca* farewell for euer and a day.	2282
*brought him vp euer since he was three yeeres old, and	2460

EUERIE = 3*2

And giue them friendly welcome euerie one,	113
*with this condition; To be whipt at the hie crosse euerie | morning.	435
And euerie day I cannot come to woo,	980
*the Gils faire without, the Carpets laide, and euerie | thing in order?	1685
My father is heere look'd for euerie day,	1972

EUERMORE = 1

Euermore crost and crost, nothing but crost.	2306

EUERY = 4*2

Hearing thy mildnesse prais'd in euery Towne,	1062
To cast thy wandring eyes on euery stale:	1384
*Gru. A cold world *Curtis* in euery office but thine, z	1672
*in their new fustian, the white stockings, and euery offi-|cer	1683
Go hop me ouer euery kennell home,	2083
That euery thing I looke on seemeth greene:	2345

EUERYTHING *see* euery

EWER = 2

Another beare the Ewer: the third a Diaper,	61
*Enter aloft the drunkard with attendants, some with apparel, | Bason and Ewer, & other appurtenances, & Lord.	151

EWERS = 1

Basons and ewers to laue her dainty hands:	1230

EX = *1

*Pet. Go rascals, go, and fetch my supper in. *Ex. Ser.*	1766

EXCELLENT = 2*2

It wil be pastime passing excellent,	71
Lord. 'Tis verie true, thou didst it excellent:	99
*Beg. 'Tis a verie excellent peece of worke, Madame	563
*Gru. Bion. Oh excellent motion: fellowes let's be gon.	852

EXCHANGE = 2

For I haue bils for monie by exchange	1945
Made me exchange my state with *Tranio,*	2505

EXCUSE = 2

I hope this reason stands for my excuse.	278
Which at more leysure I will so excuse,	1491

EXECUTE = 1

One thing more rests, that thy selfe execute,	554

EXEUNT = 11

Exeunt ambo. Manet Tranio and Lucentio	448
Exeunt. The Presenters aboue speakes.	557
Petruchio, I shal be your *Been venuto. Exeunt.*	854
Ile buckler thee against a Million. *Exeunt. P. Ka.*	1625
Bap. She shall *Lucentio*: come gentlemen lets goe. | *Exeunt.*	1638
Come I wil bring thee to thy Bridall chamber. *Exeunt.*	1810
Go with me to cloath you as becomes you. *Exeunt.*	1976
Bap. I follow you. *Exeunt.*	2257
For our first merriment hath made thee iealous. *Exeunt.*	2375
*Luc. Looke not pale *Bianca,* thy father will not frown. | *Exeunt.*	2518
Better once then neuer, for neuer to late. *Exeunt.*	2532

EXIT = 27*2

Let them want nothing that my house affoords.| *Exit one with the Players.*	114
Anon Ile giue thee more instructions. | *Exit a seruingman.*	141

EXIT *cont.*

For I haue more to commune with *Bianca. Exit.*	405
(Belike) I knew not what to take, | And what to leaue? Ha. *Exit*	408
Bap. What in my sight? *Bianca* get thee in. *Exit.*	888
Or shall I send my daughter *Kate* to you. | *Exit. Manet Petruchio.*	1035
And kisse me *Kate*, we will be married a sonday. | *Exit Petruchio and Katherine.*	1204
And so I take my leaue, and thanke you both. *Exit.*	1280
An olde Italian foxe is not so kinde my boy. *Exit.*	1285
*A childe shall get a sire, if I faile not of my cunning. *Exit.*	1293
Hortensio will be quit with thee by changing. *Exit.*	1386
Kate. Would *Katherine* had neuer seen him though. | *Exit weeping.*	1414
And seale the title with a louely kisse. *Exit.*	1506
Bap. Ile after him, and see the euent of this. *Exit.*	1510
Now let him speake, 'tis charity to shew. *Exit*	1845
Away I say, commend me to thy master. *Exit Tail.*	2151
Biond. I praie the gods she may withall my heart. | *Exit.*	2250
*the Priest be readie to come against you come with your | appendix. *Exit.*	2288
It shall goe hard if *Cambio* goe without her. *Exit.*	2293
Then hast thou taught *Hortentio* to be vntoward. *Exit.*	2378
thee at home, therefore leaue vs. *Exit.*	2383
Exit Biondello, Tranio and Pedant as fast as may be.	2490
but I will in to be reueng'd for this villanie. *Exit.*	2516
Bap. And I to sound the depth of this knauerie. *Exit.*	2517
You are welcome all. *Exit Bianca.*	2591
Goe *Biondello*, bid your Mistris come to me. | *Bio.* I goe. *Exit.*	2623
come to me forthwith. *Exit. Bion.*	2637
Say I command her come to me. *Exit.*	2648
And being a winner, God giue you good night. | *Exit Petruchio*	2746

EXPECT = *1

Luc. And what of all this. | *Bion.* I cannot tell, expect they are busied about a	2276

EXPERIENCE = 1

Where small experience growes but in a few.	618

EXPOUND = *1

*to expound the meaning or morrall of his signes and to- |kens.	2265

EXPRESSE = 1

Very gratefull, I am sure of it, to expresse	939

EXPRESSELY = 2

For your Physitians haue expressely charg'd,	275
And I expressely am forbid to touch it:	1803

EXTEMPORE = 1

Petr. It is *extempore*, from my mother wit.	1142

EXTERNALL = 1

Should well agree with our externall parts?	2726

EXTREAMES = 1

Which otherwise would grow into extreames.	150

EXTREME = 1*1

Yet extreme gusts will blow out fire and all:	1000
Gru. Why therefore fire, for I haue caught extreme	1680

EXTREMITIE = 1

Tra. To saue your life in this extremitie,	1958

EYE *see also* eie = 3*1

Kate. A pretty peate, it is best put finger in the eye, | and she knew why.	381
Whose sodaine sight hath thral'd my wounded eye.	526

EYE *cont.*

Within your house, to make mine eye the witnesse	913
Because his painted skin contents the eye.	2161

EYES *see also* eies = 4

Tra. But youth in Ladies eyes that florisheth.	1222
To cast thy wandring eyes on euery stale:	1384
And since mine eyes are witnesse of her lightnesse,	1872
As those two eyes become that heauenly face?	2330

EYE-SORE = 1

An eye-sore to our solemne festiuall.	1484

EYING = 1

Least (ouer-eying of his odde behauiour,	105

FA = 1

Ile trie how you can *Sol, Fa*, and sing it. | *He rings him by the eares*	583

FACD = 3*1

Yet I haue fac'd it with a card of ten:	1287
Gru. Thou hast fac'd many things. | *Tail*. I haue.	2108
*braue not me; I will neither bee fac'd nor brau'd. I say	2111
That fac'd and braued me in this matter so?	2501

FACE = 8*3

Like enuious flouds ore-run her louely face,	217
And paint your face, and vse you like a foole.	368
Luc. Oh yes, I saw sweet beautie in her face,	470
*he wil throw a figure in her face, and so disfigure hir	679
I neuer yet beheld that speciall face,	866
Pet. What, you meane my face.	1113
That thinkes with oathes to face the matter out.	1169
*all in the Sextons face: hauing no other reason, but that	1556
Gru. Why she hath a face of her owne.	1728
Gru. Face not mee: thou hast brau'd manie men,	2110
As those two eyes become that heauenly face?	2330

FACES = 1

Nor can we be distinguish'd by our faces,	506

FADED = 1

This is a man old, wrinckled, faded, withered,	2341

FAILE = *1

*A childe shall get a sire, if I faile not of my cunning. *Exit.*	1293

FAINE = *1

Pet. Oh, Pardon me signior *Gremio*, I would faine be | doing.	935

FAIRE = 17*6

To see faire *Padua*, nurserie of Arts,	301
*we may yet againe haue accesse to our faire Mistris, and	420
I promist to enquire carefully | About a schoolemaster for the faire	
Bianca,	731
To faire *Bianca*, so beloued of me.	741
Listen to me, and if you speake me faire,	745
Bion. He that ha's the two faire daughters: ist he you | meane?	790
Faire *Laedaes* daughter had a thousand wooers,	816
Then well one more may faire *Bianca* haue;	817
You wil haue *Gremio* to keepe you faire.	872
Pet. And you good sir: pray haue you not a daugh-|ter, cal'd *Katerina*,	
faire and vertuous.	903
Vnto *Bianca*, faire and vertuous:	954
*his wedding garment on? Be the Iackes faire with-|in,	1684
*the Gils faire without, the Carpets laide, and euerie | thing in order?	1685
I tel you sir, she beares me faire in hand.	1849
Faire louely Maide, once more good day to thee:	2331

FAIRE *cont.*
  Kate. Yong budding Virgin, faire, and fresh, & sweet,   2335
  Happy the Parents of so faire a childe;   2337
  Vin. Faire Sir, and you my merry Mistris,   2351
  My faire *Bianca* bid my father welcome,   2541
  Bap. Now faire befall thee good *Petruchio*;   2666
  The wisdome of your dutie faire *Bianca*,   2683
  *Confounds thy fame, as whirlewinds shake faire budds,   2698
  But loue, faire lookes, and true obedience;   2711
FAIRELY = 2*2
  *and fast it fairely out. Our cakes dough on both sides.   413
  Hearke you sir, Ile haue them verie fairely bound,   711
  And there it is in writing fairely drawne.   1363
  *hath two letters for her name, fairely set down in studs,   1448
FAIRER = 1
  And were his daughter fairer then she is,   814
FAIREST = 2
  Carrie him gently to my fairest Chamber,   50
  She was the fairest creature in the world,   218
FAITH *see also* i'faith, infaith, y'faith = 4*5
  Hor. Faith (as you say) there's small choise in rotten   437
  Tra. So could I 'faith boy, to haue the next wish af-|ter,   547
  Petr. Will it not be? | 'Faith sirrah, and you'l not knocke, Ile ring it,   581
  Bap. Faith Gentlemen now I play a marchants part,   1207
  Luc. Faith Mistresse then I haue no cause to stay.   1380
  Tra. Faith he is gone vnto the taming schoole.   1905
  Hor. Mistris, what cheere? | *Kate.* Faith as cold as can be.   2017
  Biond. Faith nothing: but has left mee here behinde   2264
  Biond. Nay faith, Ile see the Church a your backe,   2384
FALL = 3*1
  *But I would be loth to fall into my dreames againe: I   280
  Fall to them as you finde your stomacke serues you: 337
  That all amaz'd the Priest let fall the booke,   1545
  You horson villaine, will you let it fall?   1784
FALLES = 1
  *him by Law. Ile not budge an inch boy: Let him come, | and kindly.
  Falles asleepe.   16
FALNE = 1
  Gru. First know my horse is tired, my master & mi-|stris falne out.
  Cur. How?   1688
FALSE = 1
  Kate. Go get thee gone, thou false deluding slaue, | *Beats him.*   2009
FAME = *1
  *Confounds thy fame, as whirlewinds shake faire budds,   2698
FAMISH = 1
  What, did he marrie me to famish me?   1981
FAMOUS = 1
  The one, as famous for a scolding tongue,   826
FANCIE = 3*1
  Lord. Euen as a flatt'ring dreame, or worthles fancie.   48
  Which I could fancie, more then any other.   867
  Kate. Oh then belike you fancie riches more,   871
  Doth fancie any other but *Lucentio*,   1848
FANCIES = *1
  *blew lift; an old hat, & the humor of forty fancies prickt   1454
FANNES = *1
  *With Scarfes, and Fannes, & double change of brau'ry,   2039

FARDINGALES = 1
With Ruffes and Cuffes, and Fardingales, and things: 2038
FARE = 1
Beg. Marrie I fare well, for heere is cheere enough.   255
FARES = 1 *1
Lady. How fares my noble Lord?   254
**Petr.* How fares my Kate, what sweeting all a-mort?   2016
FAREWEL = 1
And so farewel signior *Lucentio*,   1888
FAREWELL = 4 *2
And so farewell: *Katherina* you may stay,   404
*Farewell: yet for the loue I beare my sweet *Bianca*, if   414
Kate. Yours if you talke of tales, and so farewell.   1093
**Bian.* Farewell sweet masters both, I must be gone.   1379
For I must hence, and farewell to you all.   1579
But bid *Bianca* farewell for euer and a day.   2282
FARME = 1
To house or house-keeping: then at my farme   1238
FARMERS = 2
Since once he plaide a Farmers eldest sonne,   94
As wil a Chesse-nut in a Farmers fire.   776
FARRE = 7 *1
Thou hast a Ladie farre more Beautifull,   214
*it shall be so farre forth friendly maintain'd, till by hel-|ping   439
Hor. Petruchio, since we are stept thus farre in,   649
That were my state farre worser then it is,   657
Luc. Preposterous Asse that neuer read so farre,   1304
Trauaile you farre on, or are you at the farthest?   1928
But then vp farther, and as farre as Rome,   1930
Kate. Forward I pray, since we haue come so farre,   2308
FARTHER = 3
Bap. Gentlemen, importune me no farther,   350
To seeke their fortunes farther then at home,   617
But then vp farther, and as farre as Rome,   1930
FARTHEST = 2
Trauaile you farre on, or are you at the farthest?   1928
Ped. Sir at the farthest for a weeke or two,   1929
FASHION = 2 *2
Kate. It is my fashion when I see a Crab.   1107
**Tra.* 'Tis some od humor pricks him to this fashion,   1457
According to the fashion, and the time.   2080
**Tail.* Why heere is the note of the fashion to testify. | *Pet.* Reade it. 2114
FASHIOND = 1
Kate. I neuer saw a better fashion'd gowne,   2086
FASHIONS = 1 *1
Old fashions please me best, I am not so nice   1373
*with the Lampasse, infected with the fashions, full   1439
FAST = 4 *1
*and fast it fairely out. Our cakes dough on both sides.   413
Shee vi'd so fast, protesting oath on oath,   1189
And better 'twere that both of vs did fast,   1805
And for this night we'l fast for companie.   1809
Exit Biondello, Tranio and Pedant as fast as may be.   2490
FASTEST = 1
fastest, gets the Ring: How say you signior *Gremio*?   443
FAT = 2 *1
*Aske *Marrian Hacket* the fat Alewife of Wincot, if shee   174

FAT *cont.*

Sixe-score fat Oxen standing in my stalls,	1240
How say you to a fat Tripe finely broyl'd?	1998

FATHER = 47*7

Gaue me my being, and my father first	310
wherein she delights, I will wish him to her father.	416
*her father be verie rich, any man is so verie a foole to be | married to hell?	428
That til the Father rid his hands of her,	484
For so your father charg'd me at our parting:	519
Antonio my father is deceast,	620
Hor. Her father is *Baptista Minola*,	663
Petr. I know her father, though I know not her,	667
And he knew my deceased father well:	668
My father dead, my fortune liues for me,	757
To whom my Father is not all vnknowne,	813
Her father keepes from all accesse of sutors,	833
You knew my father well, and in him me,	981
Pet. Why that is nothing: for I tell you father,	995
Thus in plaine termes: your father hath consented	1148
Heere comes your father, neuer make deniall,	1159
Pet. Father, 'tis thus, your selfe and all the world	1170
Prouide the feast father, and bid the guests,	1196
Pet. Father, and wife, and gentlemen adieu,	1201
Tra. Gremio, 'tis knowne my father hath no lesse	1259
And let your father make her the assurance,	1269
Sirra, yong gamester, your father were a foole	1282
Must get a father, call'd suppos'd *Vincentio*,	1290
Nicke. Mistresse, your father prayes you leaue your | (books,	1376
How does my father? gentles methinkes you frowne,	1476
The narrow prying father *Minola*,	1529
Dine with my father, drinke a health to me,	1578
Father, be quiet, he shall stay my leisure.	1603
In gate and countenance surely like a Father.	1918
Tra. He is my father sir, and sooth to say,	1955
My father is heere look'd for euerie day,	1972
With such austeritie as longeth to a father.	2187
Bion. I told him that your father was at *Venice*,	2196
I pray you stand good father to me now,	2204
That like a Father you will deale with him,	2226
There doth my father lie: and there this night	2238
Lucentios Father is arriued in *Padua*,	2248
deceiuing Father of a deceitfull sonne. | *Luc.* And what of him?	2269
Kate. Pardon old father my mistaking eies,	2343
Now I perceiue thou art a reuerent Father:	2346
I may intitle thee my louing Father,	2360
Hort. I doe assure thee father so it is.	2373
*I pray you tell signior *Lucentio* that his Father is	2408
Ped. Thou liest his Father is come from *Padua*, and	2411
Vin. Art thou his father?	2413
*Vinc. What, you notorious villaine, didst thou neuer | see thy Mistris father, *Vincentio*?	2430
my good Father, I am able to maintaine it.	2454
*Vin. Thy father: oh villaine, he is a Saile-maker in | *Bergamo*.	2455
*the Iaile: father *Baptista*, I charge you see that hee be | forth comming.	2470
Luc. Pardon sweete father. *Kneele.*	2491
Bian. Pardon deere father.	2493

FATHER *cont.*
Then pardon him sweete Father for my sake.	2510
Luc. Looke not pale *Bianca*, thy father will not frown.	*Exeunt.*	2518
My faire *Bianca* bid my father welcome,	2541

FATHERLY = 1
You haue shewd a tender fatherly regard,	1166

FATHERS = 13*1
And by my fathers loue and leaue am arm'd	304
Luc. Ah *Tranio*, what a cruell Fathers he:	488
Tell me her fathers name, and 'tis enough:	660
I am my fathers heyre and onely sonne,	1246
And that's a wonder: fathers commonly	1291
Her fathers liking, which to bring to passe	1512
Beggers that come vnto my fathers doore,	1982
Will we returne vnto thy Fathers house,	2035
Pet. Well, come my *Kate*, we will vnto your fathers,	2152
To feast and sport vs at thy fathers house,	2166
I am content in a good fathers care	2213
Petr. Come on a Gods name, once more toward our	fathers:	2295
Or ere I iourney to your Fathers house:	2304
My Fathers beares more toward the Market-place,	2390

FAULCON = 1
My Faulcon now is sharpe, and passing emptie,	1824

FAULT = 4
At the hedge corner, in the couldest fault,	23
Her onely fault, and that is faults enough,	654
Kate. Patience I pray you, 'twas a fault vnwilling.	1785
As with the meate, some vndeserued fault	1833

FAULTS = 2*1
*them, would take her with all faults, and mony enough.	433
Her onely fault, and that is faults enough,	654
Hortensio, haue you told him all her faults?	752

FAUOR = 1
This fauor wil I do you for his sake,	1959

FAUOUR = 1
And free accesse and fauour as the rest.	960

FAUOURABLE = 1
Happier the man whom fauourable stars	2338

FAUOURD = 1
And wish thee to a shrew'd ill-fauour'd wife?	626

FAUOURS = 1
As one vnworthie all the former fauours	1878

FAY = *1
Beg. These fifteene yeeres, by my fay, a goodly nap,	234

FEARE = 10*2
Plai. Feare not my Lord, we can contain our selues,	110
Kate. I'faith sir, you shall neuer neede to feare,	364
I kil'd a man, and feare I was descried:	539
Tush, tush, feare boyes with bugs.	*Gru.* For he feares none.	777
Hor. For feare I promise you, if I looke pale.	1010
Gre. Adieu good neighbour: now I feare thee not:	1281
Feare not sweet wench, they shall not touch thee *Kate*,	1624
Gru. I feare it is too chollericke a meate.	1997
Gru. I cannot tell, I feare 'tis chollericke.	2000
Tra. Feare you not him: sirra *Biondello*,	2191
Bion. Tut, feare not me.	2194
Vin. Feare not *Baptista*, we will content you, goe to:	2515

FEARES = 2
Tush, tush, feare boyes with bugs. | *Gru.* For he feares none.   777
Pet. Now for my life *Hortentio* feares his Widow.   2553
FEARING = 1
First were we sad, fearing you would not come,   1481
FEAST = 6
Prouide the feast father, and bid the guests,   1196
Goe to the feast, reuell and domineere,   1610
You know there wants no iunkets at the feast: 1634
To feast and sport vs at thy fathers house,   2166
Out of hope of all, but my share of the feast.   2521
Feast with the best, and welcome to my house,   2545
FEATHER = *1
*in't for a feather: a monster, a very monster in apparell,   1455
FEATHERS = 1
Because his feathers are more beautifull.   2159
FED = 1
With oathes kept waking, and with brawling fed,   1988
FEEDE = 2
Then feede it with such ouer-rosted flesh: 1807
Kate. A dish that I do loue to feede vpon.   2002
FEEDES = 1
They do consume the thing that feedes their furie.   998
FEEDST = 1
That feed'st me with the verie name of meate.   2011
FEELE = 2*1
I smel sweet sauours, and I feele soft things: 223
*(she being now at hand) thou shalt soone feele, to thy   1668
Cur. This 'tis to feele a tale, not to heare a tale.   1696
FEET = *1
*no more shooes then feet, nay sometime more feete then   163
FEETE = *1
*no more shooes then feet, nay sometime more feete then   163
FEEZE *see* pheeze
FEL = *1
*thou shouldst haue heard how her horse fel, and she vn-|der   1705
FEL = 1
FELL = *1
*That downe fell Priest and booke, and booke and Priest,   1548
FELLOW = 6*2
Lord. With all my heart. This fellow I remember,   93
*are you? Maister, ha's my fellow *Tranio* stolne your   530
Your fellow *Tranio* heere to saue my life,   535
Luc. Were it not that my fellow schoolemaster   1521
*hath tam'd my old master, and my new mistris, and my | selfe fellow
Curtis.   1662
Ios. What *Grumio*. | *Nick.* Fellow *Grumio*.   1737
Gru. Welcome you: how now you: what you: fel-|low   1740
Tra. Th'art a tall fellow, hold thee that to drinke,   2198
FELLOWES = 1*2
Now fellowes, you are welcome. | *Players.* We thanke your Honor.   88
*good fellowes in the world, and a man could light on   432
Gru. Bion. Oh excellent motion: fellowes let's be gon.   852
FERDINAND = 1
And bid my cozen *Ferdinand* come hither: 1780
FESTIUALL = 1
An eye-sore to our solemne festiuall.   1484

FETCH = 5*3
   Host. I know my remedie, I must go fetch the Head- | borough.   13
   And fetch shrill ecchoes from the hollow earth.   198
   2.M. Dost thou loue pictures? we wil fetch thee strait   201
   Pet. Go rascals, go, and fetch my supper in. *Ex. Ser*.   1766
   Kate. I like it well, good Grumio fetch it me.   1999
   My Boy shall fetch the Scriuener presentlie,   2241
   Goe on, and fetch our horses backe againe,   2305
   Petr. Goe fetch them hither, if they denie to come,   2658
FEW = 2
   Where small experience growes but in a few.   618
   Few words suffice: and therefore, if thou know   632
FIDLER = 2
   While she did call me Rascall, Fidler,   1025
   Luc. Fidler forbeare, you grow too forward Sir,   1296
FIE = 10*4
   Bian. Let's heare, oh fie, the treble iarres.   1332
   Fie, doff this habit, shame to your estate,   1483
   Gru. Fie, fie on all tired Iades, on all mad Masters, z   1640
   Fie on her, see how beastly she doth court him.   1882
   Hor. Signior *Petruchio*, fie you are too blame: 2030
   A Veluet dish: Fie, fie, 'tis lewd and filthy,   2049
   Take vp my Mistris gowne to his masters vse. | Oh fie, fie, fie.   2145
   Bian. Fie what a foolish dutie call you this?   2681
   Kate. Fie, fie, vnknit that threatning vnkinde brow,   2694
FIELD = 3
   Haue I not heard great Ordnance in the field?   770
   My houshold-stuffe, my field, my barne,   1617
   Hort. *Petruchio*, goe thy waies, the field is won.   2320
FIEND = 2
   Gre. Why will you mew her vp | (Signior *Baptista*) for this fiend of hell,   391
   Gre. Why hee's a deuill, a deuill, a very fiend.   1539
FIERY = 1
   Luc. How fiery and forward our Pedant is,   1341
FIFT = *1
   Beg. Third, or fourth, or fift Borough, Ile answere   15
FIFTEENE = 2*1
   These fifteene yeeres you haue bin in a dreame,   232
   Beg. These fifteene yeeres, by my fay, a goodly nap,   234
   And slept aboue some fifteene yeare or more.   267
FIFTIE = *1
   *two and fiftie horses. Why nothing comes amisse, so | monie comes
   withall.   647
FIGURE = *1
   *he wil throw a figure in her face, and so disfigure hir   679
FILL = 1
   Tra. Well said Mr, mum, and gaze your fill.   376
FILTHY = 1
   A Veluet dish: Fie, fie, 'tis lewd and filthy,   2049
FINDE = 10*1
   Fall to them as you finde your stomacke serues you: 337
   Till I can finde occasion of reuenge.   894
   Bap. Mistake me not, I speake but as I finde,   927
   Kate. I, if the foole could finde it where it lies.   1088
   Pet. No, not a whit, I finde you passing gentle: 1121
   And now I finde report a very liar: 1123
   Seize thee that List, if once I finde thee ranging,   1385

FINDE *cont.*
  A grumlling groome, and that the girle shall finde.   1537
  *finde when he comes home. But what talke I of this?   1717
  Ile finde about the making of the bed,   1834
  Me shall you finde readie and willing   2216
FINE = 6*1
  A fine Musitian to instruct our Mistris,   739
  I will be sure my *Katherine* shall be fine.   1197
  We will haue rings, and things, and fine array,   1203
  Fine Linnen, Turky cushions bost with pearle,   1235
  Our fine Musitian groweth amorous.   1356
  There were none fine, but *Adam*, *Rafe*, and *Gregory*,   1763
  *Goddes: oh fine villaine, a silken doublet, a vel-|uet   2444
FINELY = 1
  How say you to a fat Tripe finely broyl'd?   1998
FINGER = *2
  Kate. A pretty peate, it is best put finger in the eye, | and she knew
  why.   381
  *that Ile proue vpon thee, though thy little finger be ar-|med in a
  thimble.   2130
FINGERING = 2
  And bow'd her hand to teach her fingering,   1018
  To learne the order of my fingering,   1358
FINGERS = 1
  Wrap'd in sweet cloathes: Rings put vpon his fingers: 42
FINIS *l.*2751 = 1
FIRE = 4*10
  As wil a Chesse-nut in a Farmers fire.   776
  Though little fire growes great with little winde,   999
  Yet extreme gusts will blow out fire and all: 1000
  *make a fire, and they are comming after to warme them: 1643
  *mouth, my heart in my belly, ere I should come by a fire   1646
  *to thaw me, but I with blowing the fire shall warme my   1647
  *greater a run but my head and my necke. A fire good | *Curtis*.   1654
  Gru. Oh I *Curtis* I, and therefore fire, fire, cast on no | water.   1657
  *and so long am I at the least. But wilt thou make a fire,   1666
  *therefore fire: do thy duty, and haue thy dutie, for my   1673
  Cur. There's fire readie, and therefore good *Grumio* | the newes.   1675
  Gru. Why therefore fire, for I haue caught extreme   1680
  Kate. They sit conferring by the Parler fire.   2657
FIRES = 1
  And where two raging fires meete together,   997
FIRME = 2
  Nor is your firme resolue vnknowne to me,   955
  By your firme promise, *Gremio* is out vied.   1267
FIRMELY = 1
  As firmely as your selfe were still in place,   722
FIRMLY = 2
  For how I firmly am resolu'd you know: 351
  Heere is my hand, and heere I firmly vow   1876
FIRST = 19*3
  Gaue me my being, and my father first   310
  Luc. Tell me thine first.   495
  But I will charme him first to keepe his tongue.   515
  I should knocke you first,   579
  *out? Whom would to God I had well knockt at first,   601
  To giue you ouer at this first encounter,   671

FIRST *cont.*

Vntill the elder sister first be wed.	835
Remoue you hence: I knew you at the first | You were a mouable.	1068
Kate. Ile see thee hang'd on sonday first.	1179
*Gre. Hark *Petruchio*, she saies shee'll see thee hang'd | (first.	1180
I am your neighbour, and was suter first.	1215
Gre. First, as you know, my house within the City	1228
First were we sad, fearing you would not come,	1481
That take it on you at the first so roundly.	1600
*Gru. First know my horse is tired, my master & mi-|stris falne out.	
Cur. How?	1688
*Bian. What Master reade you first, resolue me that?	1854
First tell me, haue you euer beene at Pisa?	1949
For our first merriment hath made thee iealous. *Exeunt.*	2375
Petr. First kisse me *Kate*, and we will.	2523
To come at first when he doth send for her,	2611
Pet. Come on I say, and first begin with her. | *Wid.* She shall not.	2691
Pet. I say she shall, and first begin with her.	2693

FIRSTS = 1

Petr. Sir, sir, the first's for me, let her go by.	828

FIT = 5*2

And take a Lodging fit to entertaine	343
Fit to instruct her youth. If you *Hortensio*,	399
*I can by any meanes light on a fit man to teach her that	415
*sir. Well, was it fit for a seruant to vse his master so,	599
Fit for her turne, well read in Poetrie	735
It skills not much, weele fit him to our turne,	1515
Kate. Ile haue no bigger, this doth fit the time,	2053

FITTED = 1

Was aptly fitted, and naturally perform'd.	97

FIUE = 2

Enter foure or fiue seruingmen.	1733
Hath cost me fiue hundred crownes since supper time.	2684

FIUES = *1

*past cure of the Fiues, starke spoyl'd with the	1441

FLAP-EARD = 1

Pet. A horson beetle-headed flap-ear'd knaue:	1786

FLAT = *1

Petr. Why how now gentleman: why this is flat kna-|uerie	2415

FLATLY = *1

*Gru. Nay looke you sir, hee tels you flatly what his	643

FLATTERD = 1

That I haue fondly flatter'd them withall.	1879

FLATTRING = *1

*Lord. Euen as a flatt'ring dreame, or worthles fancie.	48

FLEA = 1

Thou Flea, thou Nit, thou winter cricket thou:	2095

FLEETE = 1

Lord. Thou art a Foole, if *Eccho* were as fleete,	29

FLEETER = 1

As breathed Stags: I fleeter then the Roe.	200

FLESH = 1*1

*wil therefore tarrie in despight of the flesh & the blood	281·
Then feede it with such ouer-rosted flesh:	1807

FLIE = *1

*Luc. I flie *Biondello*; but they may chance to neede	2382

FLIES = 1
  Kate. Her silence flouts me, and Ile be reueng'd. | *Flies after Bianca*   886
FLING = 1
  And heere Ile fling the pillow, there the boulster,   1835
FLORENCE = 2
  Vincentio's sonne, brought vp in *Florence*,   313
  From Florence, and must heere deliuer them.   1946
FLORENTINE = 1
  I will some other be, some *Florentine*,   510
FLORENTIUS = 1
  Be she as foule as was *Florentius* Loue,   635
FLORISHETH = 1
  Tra. But youth in Ladies eyes that florisheth.   1222
FLOUDS = 1
  Like enuious flouds ore-run her louely face,   217
FLOURISH = 1
  Flourish. Enter Lucentio, and his man Triano.   299
FLOUTS = 1
  Kate. Her silence flouts me, and Ile be reueng'd. | *Flies after Bianca*   886
FLOWERS = 2
  Full of Rose-water, and bestrew'd with Flowers,   60
  But slow in speech: yet sweet as spring-time flowers.   1125
FOLKES = 2*1
  Gru. Heere's no knauerie. See, to beguile the olde- |folkes,   704
  *how the young folkes lay their heads together.   705
  Bap. How likes *Gremio* these quicke witted folkes?   2580
FOLLOW = 1*1
  Bap. I follow you. *Exeunt.*   2257
  Kate. Husband let's follow, to see the end of this adoe.   2522
FOLLOWES = 1
  For man or master: then it followes thus;   507
FOLLOWING = 1
  Now on the sonday following, shall *Bianca*   1277
FONDLY = 1
  That I haue fondly flatter'd them withall.   1879
FOODE *see also* soud = 1
  I care not what, so it be holsome foode.   1994
FOOLE = 11*1
  Lord. Thou art a Foole, if *Eccho* were as fleete,   29
  And paint your face, and vse you like a foole.   368
  *her father be verie rich, any man is so verie a foole to be | married to
hell?   428
  Kate. I, if the foole could finde it where it lies.   1088
  Kate. Go foole, and whom thou keep'st command.   1136
  Sirra, yong gamester, your father were a foole   1282
  I told you I, he was a franticke foole,   1400
  But what a foole am I to chat with you,   1504
  Gre. Tut, she's a Lambe, a Doue, a foole to him: 1541
  I see a woman may be made a foole   1606
  Gru. Away you three inch foole, I am no beast.   1664
  Bian. The more foole you for laying on my dutie.   2685
FOOLISH = 4
  Where is the foolish knaue I sent before?   1754
  Gru. Heere sir, as foolish as I was before.   1755
  Bian. Fie what a foolish dutie call you this?   2681
  Luc. I would your dutie were as foolish too: 2682

FOOT = 2*1
   I must dance bare-foot on her wedding day,   891
   Set foot vnder thy table: tut, a toy,   1284
   Gru. Am I but three inches? Why thy horne is a foot   1665
FOOTE = 4
   Out you rogue, you plucke my foote awrie,   1775
   Gru. What say you to a Neats foote?   1995
   There wil we mount, and thither walke on foote,   2169
   And place your hands below your husbands foote: 2735
FOOT-BOY = *1
   *z not like a Christian foot-boy, or a gentlemans Lacky.   1456
FOR *l.*10 24 28 69 101 106 108 133 137 153 *161 *175 *176 191 *216 237
   242 250 255 273 275 278 285 300 302 309 316 320 351 353 357 362 380
   392 396 401 405 *414 424 *441 460 461 467 493 500 504 507 519 537
   538 546 *549 566 *597 *599 *600 605 627 658 661 666 683 689 695 718
   720 721 732 734 735 746 757 778 781 804 806 807 815 826 827 828 832
   841 858 870 873 883 892 915 922 923 924 *931 988 994 995 1002 1004
   1005 1010 1016 1023 1033 1052 1056 1060 1065 1077 1078 1083 1115
   1124 1151 1152 1156 1172 1173 1175 1176 *1182 1214 1303 1312 1342
   1345 1355 1368 1374 1402 1417 *1448 *1451 *1455 1503 1531 *1551
   *1553 *1561 *1566 1579 1598 1613 1633 *1648 *1661 1669 *1673 *1680
   *1730 *1741 1804 1809 1821 1826 1867 1874 1884 1929 1936 1937 1940
   1944 1945 1951 1959 1972 1979 1987 2084 *2134 2138 2139 *2141 2142
   *2144 *2149 2155 2163 2197 2205 2210 2211 2218 2233 2240 2281 2282
   *2285 2311 2319 2332 2339 2347 2358 2375 2381 *2428 2510 2516 2532
   2548 *2552 2553 *2564 2588 2596 2598 2601 2611 2655 2670 2685 2705
   2706 2712 2720 2721 2730 2734 *2740 = 191*35
FORBEARE = 1
   Luc. Fidler forbeare, you grow too forward Sir,   1296
FORBID = 3
   And I expressely am forbid to touch it: 1803
   Tra. Of *Mantua* Sir, marrie God forbid,   1934
   Kate. No sir, God forbid, but asham'd to kisse.   2526
FOREUER *see* euer
FORGET = 1*1
   Would not the begger then forget himselfe?   45
   Biond. Forgot you, no sir: I could not forget you, for   2428
FORGOT = 2*2
   I haue forgot your name: but sure that part   96
   Haue you so soone forgot the entertainment   1297
   Vin. Come hither you rogue, what haue you forgot | mee?   2426
   Biond. Forgot you, no sir: I could not forget you, for   2428
FORMALL = 2
   Luc. Are you so formall sir, well I must waite   1354
   I know not what, but formall in apparrell,   1917
FORMER = 2
   In perill to incurre your former malady,   276
   As one vnworthie all the former fauours   1878
FORSOOTH = 2
   Kate. No shame but mine, I must forsooth be forst   1396
   Gru. No, no forsooth I dare not for my life.   1979
FORST = 1
   Kate. No shame but mine, I must forsooth be forst   1396
FORSWEARE = 3
   Forsweare *Bianca*, and her loue for euer.   1874
   Neuer to woo her more, but do forsweare her   1877
   forsweare him, or else we are all vndone.   2489

FORSWORN = *1
  Hor. Would all the world but he had quite forsworn   1883
FORSWORNE = 1*1
  And haue forsworne you with *Hortensio*.   1895
  Bian. Tranio you iest, but haue you both forsworne | mee?   1896
FORTH = 7*3
  *it shall be so farre forth friendly maintain'd, till by hel-|ping   439
  Draw forth thy weapon, we are beset with theeues,   1622
  *Call forth *Nathaniel, Ioseph, Nicholas, Phillip, Walter, Su-|gersop*   1718
  Cur. They are. | *Gru*. Call them forth.   1724
  Cur. I call them forth to credit her.   1732
  As he forth walked on his way.   1774
  Lay forth the gowne. What newes with you sir?   2046
  Tra. Call forth an officer: Carrie this mad knaue to   2469
  *the Iaile: father *Baptista*, I charge you see that hee be | forth comming.   2470
  Swinge me them soundly forth vnto their husbands: 2659
FORTHCOMMING *see* comming
FORTHWITH = 2
  And therefore frolicke, we will hence forthwith,   2165
  come to me forthwith. *Exit. Bion.*   2637
FORTUNE = 5
  To decke his fortune with his vertuous deedes: 315
  And by good fortune I haue lighted well   733
  My father dead, my fortune liues for me,   757
  What euer fortune stayes him from his word,   1411
  Petr. The fouler fortune mine, and there an end.   2652
FORTUNES = 2
  To seeke their fortunes farther then at home,   617
  And thinke it not the worst of all your fortunes,   1960
FORTY = *1
  *blew lift; an old hat, & the humor of forty fancies prickt   1454
FORWARD = 7*3
  Luc. Gramercies Lad: Go forward, this contents,   466
  Am bold to shew my selfe a forward guest   912
  *poore petitioners speake too? *Bacare*, you are meruay-|lous forward.   933
  Luc. Fidler forbeare, you grow too forward Sir,   1296
  Luc. How fiery and forward our Pedant is,   1341
  Kat. Gentlemen, forward to the bridall dinner,   1605
  Pet. They shall goe forward *Kate* at thy command,   1608
  Kate. Forward I pray, since we haue come so farre,   2308
  Petr. Well, forward, forward, thus the bowle should | (run,   2321
FOULE = 5*1
  Grim death, how foule and loathsome is thine image: 39
  Balme his foule head in warme distilled waters,   52
  Should be infused with so foule a spirit.   169
  Be she as foule as was *Florentius* Loue,   635
  *all foule waies: was euer man so beaten? was euer man   1641
  What is she but a foule contending Rebell,   2717
FOULER = 1
  Petr. The fouler fortune mine, and there an end.   2652
FOUND = 2
  Luc. Oh *Tranio*, till I found it to be true,   451
  I found the effect of Loue in idlenesse,   454
FOUNTAINE = 1
  A woman mou'd, is like a fountaine troubled,   2700
FOURE = 2
  Ile leaue her houses three or foure as good   1248

FOURE *cont.*

Enter foure or fiue seruingmen.   1733
FOURTEENE-PENCE *see* xiiii.d.
FOURTH = *1
   Beg. Third, or fourth, or fift Borough, Ile answere   15
FOWLE = *1
   *now I begin, Inprimis wee came downe a fowle   1699
FOXE = 1
   An olde Italian foxe is not so kinde my boy. *Exit.*   1285
FRAME = 2
   And frame your minde to mirth and merriment,   289
   And therefore frame your manners to the time   534
FRANTICKE = 1
   I told you I, he was a franticke foole,   1400
FRAY = *1
   Petr. Signior *Hortensio*, come you to part the fray?   591
FREE = 5*1
   *yongest free for a husband, and then haue too't afresh: 441
   Tra. Why sir, I pray are not the streets as free | For me, as for you?   803
   The yonger then is free, and not before.   836
   Atchieue the elder: set the yonger free,   840
   And free accesse and fauour as the rest.   960
   And rather then it shall, I will be free,   2064
FREELY = 1
   Freely giue vnto this yong Scholler, that hath   942
FREEZE = 1*1
   Tra. Gray-beard thy loue doth freeze. | *Gre.* But thine doth frie,   1219
   *might freeze to my teeth, my tongue to the roofe of my   1645
FRENZIE = 1
   And melancholly is the Nurse of frenzie,   287
FRESH = *1
   Kate. Yong budding Virgin, faire, and fresh, & sweet,   2335
FRESHER = 1
   Hast thou beheld a fresher Gentlewoman: 2327
FRET = 1
   Nay, looke not big, nor stampe, not stare, nor fret,   1614
FRETS = 2
   I did but tell her she mistooke her frets,   1017
   Frets call you these? (quoth she) Ile fume with them: 1020
FRETTING = 1
   Tra. Twas a commodity lay fretting by you,   1209
FRIAR = 1
   It was the Friar of Orders gray,   1773
FRIE = 1
   Tra. Gray-beard thy loue doth freeze. | *Gre.* But thine doth frie,   1219
FRIEND = 7*2
   My best beloued and approued friend | *Hortensio*: & I trow this is his
   house: 568
   Hor. How now, what's the matter? My olde friend   588
   Grumio, and my good friend *Petruchio*? How do you all | at *Verona*?   589
   And tell me now (sweet friend) what happie gale   614
   And verie rich: but th'art too much my friend,   629
   Hor. Now shal my friend *Petruchio* do me grace,   696
   Gre. No, sayst me so, friend? What Countreyman?   755
   Bap. How now my friend, why dost thou looke so | pale?   1008
   Tra. Is't possible friend *Lisio*, that mistris *Bianca*   1847

FRIENDLY = 2*1
   And giue them friendly welcome euerie one,   113
   *it shall be so farre forth friendly maintain'd, till by hel-|ping   439
   And in my house you shal be friendly lodg'd,   1963
FRIENDS = 6*3
   Such friends (as time) in *Padua* shall beget.   344
   *apples: but come, since this bar in law makes vs friends,   438
   Keepe house, and ply his booke, welcome his friends,   502
   To see my friends in *Padua*; but of all   567
   Petr. Signior *Hortensio*, 'twixt such friends as wee,   631
   Striue mightily, but eate and drinke as friends.   851
   Make friends, inuite, and proclaime the banes, ·   1404
   Petr. Gentlemen & friends, I thank you for your pains,   1566
   Bap. Neighbours and friends, though Bride & Bride-|(groom wants 1632
FRIGHTED = *1
   Bian. I, but not frighted me, therefore Ile sleepe a-|gaine.   2585
FRIUOLOUS = *1
   Padua: doe you heare sir, to leaue friuolous circumstan-|ces,   2407
FROLICKE = 1
   And therefore frolicke, we will hence forthwith,   2165
FROM *l*.*18 120 146 183 198 269 277 369 463 *480 541 615 686 748 833
   1142 1157 *1266 1346 1411 *1445 1486 1493 1533 1534 *1653 1762 1795
   *1819 1946 *2409 *2411 2604 2695 = 26*8
FROST = *1
   Gru. She was good *Curtis* before this frost: but thou   1660
FROSTS = 1
   It blots thy beautie, as frosts doe bite the Meads, · 2697
FROWARD = 7*1
   That wench is starke mad, or wonderfull froward.   372
   And shrow'd, and froward, so beyond all measure,   656
   For shee's not froward, but modest as the Doue,   1173
   Haue to my Widdow, and if she froward,   2377
   See where she comes, and brings your froward Wiues   2675
   And when she is froward, peeuish, sullen, sowre,   2715
   Come, come, you froward and vnable wormes,   2727
   Luc. But a harsh hearing, when women are froward,   2742
FROWN = *1
   Luc. Looke not pale *Bianca*, thy father will not frown. | *Exeunt.* 2518
FROWNE = 5
   Say that she frowne, Ile say she lookes as cleere   1041
   Thou canst not frowne, thou canst not looke a sconce,   1126
   How does my father? gentles methinkes you frowne,   1476
   To bandie word for word, and frowne for frowne;   2730
FROZEN = 1
   Master and mistris are almost frozen to death.   1674
FRUITFULL = 2
   I am arriu'd for fruitfull *Lumbardie*,   302
   Of fruitfull land, all which shall be her ioynter.   1252
FULL = 7*1
   Full of Rose-water, and bestrew'd with Flowers,   60
   Luc. *Basta*, content thee: for I haue it full.   504
   Vnto a mad-braine rudesby, full of spleene,   1398
   *with the Lampasse, infected with the fashions, full   1439
   Carowse full measure to her maiden-head,   1611
   Cur. Come, you are so full of conicatching.   1679
   And til she stoope, she must not be full gorg'd,   1825
   Who will of thy arriuall be full ioyous.   2369

FULLY = 2
To instruct her fully in those sciences,   918
Grumio. Nathaniels coate sir was not fully made,   1759
FUME = 1
Frets call you these? (quoth she) Ile fume with them: 1020
FURIE = 1
They do consume the thing that feedes their furie.   998
FURNISHED = 1
Is richly furnished with plate and gold,   1229
FURNITURE = 1
For this poore furniture, and meane array.   2163
FUSTIAN = *1
*in their new fustian, the white stockings, and euery offi-|cer   1683
GABRELS = 1
And *Gabrels* pumpes were all vnpinkt i'thheele: 1760
GAINE = 2
'Twill bring you gaine, or perish on the seas.   1210
Bap. The gaine I seeke, is quiet me the match.   1211
GAINST = 1
To buy apparell 'gainst the wedding day;   1195
GAIT *see* gate
GALD = 1
Petr. A has a little gald me I confesse: 2603
GALE = 1
And tell me now (sweet friend) what happie gale   614
GALLANT = 1
Hor. Why so this gallant will command the sunne.   2179
GALLANTS = *1
Pet. Come, where be these gallants? who's at home?   1469
GALLIASSES = 1
Then three great Argosies, besides two Galliasses   1260
GALLIES = 1
And twelue tite Gallies, these I will assure her,   1261
GAMBOLD = 1
a Christmas gambold, or a tumbling tricke?   292
GAMESOME = 1
For thou art pleasant, gamesome, passing courteous,   1124
GAMESTER = 1
Sirra, yong gamester, your father were a foole   1282
GAMOTH = 1
To teach you gamoth in a briefer sort,   1360
GAMOUTH = 4
Bian. Why, I am past my gamouth long agoe.   1364
Hor. Yet read the gamouth of *Hortentio.*   1365
Bian. Gamouth I am, the ground of all accord: 1366
Call you this gamouth? tut I like it not,   1372
GARDEN = 1*1
The pleasant garden of great *Italy,*   303
*afternoone as shee went to the Garden for Parseley to   2285
GARMENT = *1
*his wedding garment on? Be the Iackes faire with-|in,   1684
GARMENTS = 1
Our purses shall be proud, our garments poore: 2154
GARTERS = *1
*their blew coats brush'd, and their garters of an indiffe-|rent   1720
GARTRED = *1
*a kersey boot-hose on the other, gartred with a red and   1453

GATE = 7*1

Voice, gate, and action of a Gentlewoman:	144
Petr. Villaine I say, knocke me at this gate,	576
I bad the rascall knocke vpon your gate,	604
Gru. Knocke at the gate? O heauens: spake you not	606
come you now with knocking at the gate?	609
As *Kate* this chamber with her princely gate:	1138
In gate and countenance surely like a Father.	1918
Ped. What's he that knockes as he would beat downe | the gate?	2398

GATHER = 1

To gather in some debts, my son *Lucentio*	2207

GAUE = 4

Gaue me my being, and my father first	310
Grumio gaue order how it should be done.	2103
Gru. I gaue him no order, I gaue him the stuffe.	2104

GAZE = 2

Tra. Well said Mr, mum, and gaze your fill.	376
And wherefore gaze this goodly company,	1477

GENERALLY = 1

To whom we all rest generally beholding.	846

GENOA = 1

Signior *Baptista* may remember me | Neere twentie yeares a goe in *Genoa*.	2183

GENTLE = 10

This do, and do it kindly, gentle sirs,	70
Tra. Me Pardonato, gentle master mine:	324
Welcome good *Cambio*. But gentle sir,	948
Pet. No, not a whit, I finde you passing gentle:	1121
With gentle conference, soft, and affable.	1130
Nay, I haue tane you napping gentle Loue,	1894
Much good do it vnto thy gentle heart:	2033
Pet. When you are gentle, you shall haue one too, | And not till then.	2055
Good morrow gentle Mistris, where away:	2325
Petr. What is his name? | *Vinc. Lucentio* gentle sir.	2356

GENTLEMAN = 16*2

Belike some Noble Gentleman that meanes	80
An affable and courteous Gentleman,	664
Hor. 'Tis well: and I haue met a Gentleman	737
Heere is a Gentleman whom by chance I met	747
Grem. Hortensio hearke: | This Gentleman is happily arriu'd,	779
Baptista is a noble Gentleman,	812
Gre. What, this Gentleman will out-talke vs all.	820
You must as we do, gratifie this Gentleman,	845
Bap. Was euer Gentleman thus greeu'd as I? | But who comes heere.	895
I am a Gentleman of *Verona* sir,	908
Nay, come againe, good *Kate*, I am a Gentleman,	1095
If you strike me, you are no Gentleman,	1099
And if no Gentleman, why then no armes.	1100
For such a one as leaues a Gentleman,	1867
Sir, this is the gentleman I told you of.	2203
Beside, so qualified, as may beseeme | The Spouse of any noble Gentleman:	2365
Petr. Why how now gentleman: why this is flat kna-|uerie	2415
Tra. Sir, you seeme a sober ancient Gentleman by	2451

GENTLEMANS = *1

*z not like a Christian foot-boy, or a gentlemans Lacky.	1456

GENTLEMEN = 11*5
Bap. Gentlemen, importune me no farther,	350
Bap. Gentlemen, that I may soone make good	377
Bap. Gentlemen content ye: I am resolud: | Go in *Bianca*.	394
Tra. Gentlemen God saue you. If I may be bold	787
Tra. Softly my Masters: If you be Gentlemen	810
Bap. Good morrow neighbour *Gremio*: God saue | you Gentlemen.	901
Sirrah, leade these Gentlemen | To my daughters, and tell them both	973
Pet. Be patient gentlemen, I choose her for my selfe,	1182
Pet. Father, and wife, and gentlemen adieu,	1201
Bap. Faith Gentlemen now I play a marchants part,	1207
Bap. Content you gentlemen, I wil co(m)pound this strife	1223
Bap. Well gentlemen, I am thus resolu'd,	1274
Bianc. Why gentlemen, you doe me double wrong,	1311
Petr. Gentlemen & friends, I thank you for your pains,	1566
Kat. Gentlemen, forward to the bridall dinner,	1605
Bap. She shall *Lucentio*: come gentlemen lets goe. | *Exeunt*.	1638

GENTLER = 1
No mates for you, | Vnlesse you were of gentler milder mould.	362

GENTLES = 1
How does my father? gentles methinkes you frowne,	1476

GENTLEWOMAN = 5
'Twas where you woo'd the Gentlewoman so well:	95
Voice, gate, and action of a Gentlewoman:	144
Brought vp as best becomes a Gentlewoman:	653
Hast thou beheld a fresher Gentlewoman:	2327
The sister to my wife, this Gentlewoman,	2361

GENTLEWOMEN = 1
And Gentlewomen weare such caps as these.	2054

GENTLY = 2
Carrie him gently to my fairest Chamber,	50
Lord. Take him vp gently, and to bed with him,	76

GEORGE = 1
Pet. Now by S.(aint) George I am too yong for you.	1115

GET = 15*3
What I haue said, *Bianca* get you in,	378
Gre. What's that I pray? | *Hor*. Marrie sir to get a husband for her Sister.	423
To get her cunning Schoolemasters to instruct her.	490
And could not get him for my heart to do it.	605
Gremio. No: if without more words you will get you | hence.	801
Bap. What in my sight? *Bianca* get thee in. *Exit*.	888
Then tell me, if I get your daughters loue,	984
Must get a father, call'd suppos'd *Vincentio*,	1290
Doe get their children: but in this case of woing,	1292
*A childe shall get a sire, if I faile not of my cunning. *Exit*.	1293
*disguised thus to get your loue, *hic steterat*, and that	1327
I am to get a man what ere he be,	1514
Where's my Spaniel *Troilus*? Sirra, get you hence,	1779
I prethee go, and get me some repast,	1993
Or else you get no beefe of Grumio.	2006
Kate. Go get thee gone, thou false deluding slaue, | *Beats him*.	2009
Go get thee gone, I say.	2014
Tran. Dallie not with the gods, but get thee gone.	2252

GETS = 1
fastest, gets the Ring: How say you signior *Gremio*?	443

GIDDIE = 1*2

    Am staru'd for meate, giddie for lacke of sleepe: 1987
    *Wid. He that is giddie thinks the world turns round. | Petr. Roundlie
    replied.   2558
    *Kat. He that is giddie thinkes the world turnes round,   2566

GIFT see guift

GIFTS see guifts

GILS = *1

    *the Gils faire without, the Carpets laide, and euerie | thing in order?   1685

GIRD = 1

    Luc. I thanke thee for that gird good Tranio.   2601

GIRLE see also gyrle = 2*1

    For I will loue thee nere the lesse my girle.   380
    *Bap. Goe girle, I cannot blame thee now to weepe,   1416
    A grumlling groome, and that the girle shall finde.   1537

GIRTH = *1

    *often burst, and now repaired with knots: one girth sixe   1446

GIUE = 18*7

    And giue them friendly welcome euerie one,   113
    Anon Ile giue thee more instructions. | Exit a seruingman.   141
    *Lordship: I ne're drank sacke in my life: and if you giue   159
    *me any Conserues, giue me conserues of Beefe: nere ask   160
    *minde is: why giue him Gold enough, and marrie him   644
    To giue you ouer at this first encounter,   671
    Luc. Sir giue him head, I know hee'l proue a Iade.   821
    Pet. You wrong me signior Gremio, giue me leaue.   907
    Freely giue vnto this yong Scholler, that hath   942
    If she do bid me packe, Ile giue her thankes,   1046
    Giue me thy hand Kate, I will vnto Venice   1194
    *Bap. I know not what to say, but giue me your ha(n)ds,   1198
    To giue thee all, and in his wayning age   1283
    Then giue me leaue to haue prerogatiue,   1301
    Then giue me leaue to read Philosophy,   1308
    *Hort. You may go walk, and giue me leaue a while,   1352
    To giue my hand oppos'd against my heart   1397
    That haue beheld me giue away my selfe   1576
    Will you giue thankes, sweete Kate, or else shall I?   1788
    Bian. God giue him ioy. | Tra. I, and hee'l tame her.   1902
    And giue assurance to Baptista Minola.   1922
    *Gru. I am for thee straight: take thou the bill, giue   2134
    Giue me Bianca for my patrimony.   2205
    *Kate. Nay, I will giue thee a kisse, now praie thee | Loue staie.   2529
    And being a winner, God giue you good night. | Exit Petruchio   2746

GIUEN = *1

    *Grem. I am agreed, and would I had giuen him the   444

GIUES = 1

    That giues not halfe so great a blow to heare,   775

GLAD = 3

    Glad that you thus continue your resolue,   326
    Bap. I am glad he's come, howsoere he comes.   1459
    Ile make him glad to seeme Vincentio,   1921

GLANCES = 1

    And dart not scornefull glances from those eies,   2695

GLANDERS = *1

    *with the glanders, and like to mose in the chine, trou-|bled   1438

GLASSE = 1

    Kate. Had I a glasse, I would.   1112

GLASSES = *1
*Host. You will not pay for the glasses you haue burst?   10
GLAUNCE = 1
And as the Iest did glaunce awaie from me,   2604
GO = 31 *9
*Beg. No, not a deniere: go by S.(aint) Ieronimie, goe to thy | cold bed,
and warme thee.   11
*Host. I know my remedie, I must go fetch the Head- | borough.   13
Sirrah, go see what Trumpet 'tis that sounds,   79
Lord. Go sirra, take them to the Butterie,   112
Sirra go you to Bartholmew my Page,   116
Bap. Gentlemen content ye: I am resolud: | Go in Bianca.   394
Kate. Why, and I trust I may go too, may I not?   406
*Gre. You may go to the diuels dam: your guifts are   410
Luc. Gramercies Lad: Go forward, this contents,   466
Luc. Tranio let's go: 553
*Gru. I pray you Sir let him go while the humor lasts.   673
Hor. Tarrie Petruchio, I must go with thee,   682
To whom they go to: what wil you reade to her.   719
Hor. Sir, a word ere you go: 798
Petr. Sir, sir, the first's for me, let her go by.   828
Go ply thy Needle, meddle not with her.   882
Talke not to me, I will go sit and weepe,   893
Gre. You are too blunt, go to it orderly.   906
You shall go see your Pupils presently. | Holla, within.   970
We will go walke a little in the Orchard,   976
Bap. Wel go with me, and be not so discomfited.   1031
Signior Petruchio, will you go with vs,   1034
Kate. I chafe you if I tarrie. Let me go.   1120
Kate. Go foole, and whom thou keep'st command.   1136
*Hort. You may go walk, and giue me leaue a while,   1352
*Pet. Go rascals, go, and fetch my supper in. Ex. Ser.   1766
Tra. Then go with me, to make the matter good,   1970
Go with me to cloath you as becomes you. Exeunt.   1976
I prethee go, and get me some repast,   1993
Kate. Go get thee gone, thou false deluding slaue, | Beats him.   2009
Go get thee gone, I say.   2014
Go hop me ouer euery kennell home,   2083
Pet. Go take it vp vnto thy masters vse.   2140
Go take it hence, be gone, and say no more.   2148
Go call my men, and let vs straight to him,   2167
Pet. It shall be seuen ere I go to horse: 2174
*Vin. You shall not choose but drinke before you go,   2392
Gre. Staie officer, he shall not go to prison.   2473
*Luc. Well go thy waies olde Lad for thou shalt ha't.   2740
GOD = 13 *3
*out? Whom would to God I had well knockt at first,   601
Hor. Grumio mum: God saue you signior Gremio.   728
Tra. Gentlemen God saue you. If I may be bold   787
*Bap. Good morrow neighbour Gremio: God saue | you Gentlemen.   901
God send you ioy, Petruchio, 'tis a match.   1199
And makes a God of such a Cullion;   1868
Bian. God giue him ioy. | Tra. I, and hee'l tame her.   1902
Ped. God saue you sir. | Tra. And you sir, you are welcome.   1926
And so to Tripolie, if God lend me life.   1931
Tra. Of Mantua Sir, marrie God forbid,   1934
Oh mercie God, what masking stuffe is heere?   2072

GOD cont.
    Kate. Then God be blest, it is the blessed sun,   2315
    *Bio. I haue seene them in the Church together, God   2420
    Kate. No sir, God forbid, but asham'd to kisse.   2526
    Praie God sir your wife send you not a worse. | *Petr*. I hope better.   2634
    And being a winner, God giue you good night. | *Exit Petruchio*   2746
GODDES = *1
    *Goddes: oh fine villaine, a silken doublet, a vel-|uet   2444
GODNIGHT = *1
    *Tra. Is this your speeding? nay the(n) godnight our part.   1181
GODS *see also* goggs = 4*1
    Beg. For Gods sake a pot of small Ale.   153
    But if you haue a stomacke, too't a Gods name,   760
    Biond. I praie the gods she may withall my heart. | *Exit*.   2250
    Tran. Dallie not with the gods, but get thee gone.   2252
    *Petr. Come on a Gods name, once more toward our | fathers: 2295
GOD-A-MERCIE = *1
    *Hor. God-a-mercie *Grumio*, then hee shall haue no | oddes.   2136
GOE = 21*8
    *Beg. No, not a deniere: go by S.(aint) *Ieronimie*, goe to thy | cold bed,
    and warme thee.   11
    *Bap. Goe girle, I cannot blame thee now to weepe,   1416
    Goe to my chamber, put on clothes of mine.   1496
    To put on better ere he goe to Church.   1509
    You would intreat me rather goe then stay: 1574
    Kate. Nay then, | Doe what thou canst, I will not goe to day,   1593
    *Pet. They shall goe forward *Kate* at thy command,   1608
    Goe to the feast, reuell and domineere,   1610
    Be madde and merry, or goe hang your selues: 1612
    Bap. Nay, let them goe, a couple of quiet ones.   1626
    Bap. She shall *Lucentio*: come gentlemen lets goe. | *Exeunt*.   1638
    I will not goe to day, and ere I doe,   2177
    Signior *Baptista* may remember me | Neere twentie yeares a goe in
    Genoa,   2183
    *Master hath appointed me to goe to Saint *Lukes* to bid   2287
    Hap what hap may, Ile roundly goe about her: 2292
    It shall goe hard if *Cambio* goe without her. *Exit*.   2293
    Goe on, and fetch our horses backe againe,   2305
    Hort. Say as he saies, or we shall neuer goe.   2307
    Hort. Petruchio, goe thy waies, the field is won.   2320
    Petr. Come goe along and see the truth hereof,   2374
    *Bap. Talke not signior *Gremio*: I saie he shall goe to | prison.   2474
    *Vin. Feare not *Baptista*, we will content you, goe to: 2515
    Goe *Biondello*, bid your Mistris come to me. | *Bio*. I goe. *Exit*.   2623
    *Hor. Sirra *Biondello*, goe and intreate my wife to   2636
    Sirra *Grumio*, goe to your Mistris,   2647
    Petr. Goe fetch them hither, if they denie to come,   2658
    *Horten. Now goe thy wayes, thou hast tam'd a curst | Shrow.   2748
GOES = 2*2
    *Master, master, looke about you: Who goes there? ha.   706
    Yet oftentimes he goes but meane apparel'd.   1458
    *Cur. I prethee good *Grumio*, tell me, how goes the | world?   1670
    Ped. My life sir? how I pray? for that goes hard.   1936
GOGGS = 1
    I, by goggs woones quoth he, and swore so loud,   1544
GOING = 1
    Trow you whither I am going? To *Baptista Minola*,   730

GOLD = 4*2

Their harnesse studded all with Gold and Pearle.	194
*minde is: why giue him Gold enough, and marrie him	644
I would not wed her for a mine of Gold.	658
Is richly furnished with plate and gold,	1229
Vallens of Venice gold, in needle worke:	1236
*sir, what cernes it you, if I weare Pearle and gold: I thank	2453

GOLDEN = 1

With silken coats and caps, and golden Rings,	2037

GOLDS = *1

*Petr. Hortensio peace: thou knowst not golds effect,	659

GON = *1

*Gru. Bion. Oh excellent motion: fellowes let's be gon.	852

GONE = 7*1

Petr. Sirra be gone, or talke not I aduise you.	610
*Bian. Farewell sweet masters both, I must be gone.	1379
For me, Ile not be gone till I please my selfe,	1598
Tra. Faith he is gone vnto the taming schoole.	1905
Kate. Go get thee gone, thou false deluding slaue, | Beats him.	2009
Go get thee gone, I say.	2014
Go take it hence, be gone, and say no more.	2148
Tran. Dallie not with the gods, but get thee gone.	2252

GOOD = 60*21

Saw'st thou not boy how Siluer made it good	22
Hunts. Why Belman is as good as he my Lord,	25
Beg. Now Lord be thanked for my good amends. | All. Amen.	250
Therefore they thought it good you heare a play,	288
Lady. No my good Lord, it is more pleasing stuffe.	293
With his good will, and thy good companie.	305
Onely (good master) while we do admire | This vertue, and this morall discipline,	328
Hor. From all such diuels, good Lord deliuer vs. | Gre. And me too, good Lord.	369
*Tra. Husht master, heres some good pastime toward;	371
Bap. Gentlemen, that I may soone make good	377
And let it not displease thee good Bianca,	379
Sorrie am I that our good will effects | Bianca's greefe.	389
To mine owne children, in good bringing vp,	403
*so good heere's none will holde you: Their loue is not	411
*good fellowes in the world, and a man could light on	432
Sufficeth my reasons are both good and waighty.	556
*Beg. Yes by Saint Anne do I, a good matter surely:	560
*Grumio, and my good friend Petruchio? How do you all | at Verona?	589
Petr. A sencelesse villaine: good Hortensio,	603
*thinke scolding would doe little good vpon him. Shee	675
And by good fortune I haue lighted well	733
And other bookes, good ones, I warrant ye.	736
Ile tel you newes indifferent good for either.	746
And I do hope, good dayes and long, to see.	758
My minde presumes for his owne good, and yours.	781
Gru. I would I were as sure of a good dinner.	785
Hor. The motions good indeed, and be it so,	853
*Bian. Good sister wrong me not, nor wrong your self,	856
Gre. Good morrow neighbour Baptista.	900
*Bap. Good morrow neighbour Gremio: God saue | you Gentlemen.	901
*Pet. And you good sir: pray haue you not a daugh-|ter, cal'd Katerina, faire and vertuous.	903

GOOD *cont.*

Bap. Y'are welcome sir, and he for your good sake.	922
Welcome good *Cambio*. But gentle sir,	948
*Bap. What, will my daughter proue a good Musiti-|an?	1011
She's apt to learne, and thankefull for good turnes:	1033
Good morrow *Kate*, for thats your name I heare.	1052
*Kate. Mou'd, in good time, let him that mou'd you | hether	1066
Pet. Alas good *Kate*, I will not burthen thee,	1076
Nay, come againe, good *Kate*, I am a Gentleman,	1095
Ile leaue her houses three or foure as good	1248
Gre. Adieu good neighbour: now I feare thee not:	1281
'Tis in my head to doe my master good:	1288
Good master take it not vnkindly pray	1350
Tra. Patience good *Katherine* and *Baptista* too,	1409
*Pet. Good sooth euen thus: therefore ha done with | (words,	1499
When I should bid good morrow to my Bride?	1505
'Twere good me-thinkes to steale our marriage,	1523
**greater a run but my head and my necke. A fire good | *Curtis.*	1654
*Gru. She was good *Curtis* before this frost: but thou	1660
*Cur. I prethee good *Grumio*, tell me, how goes the | world?	1670
*Cur. There's fire readie, and therefore good *Grumio* | the newes.	1675
Cur. Let's ha't good *Grumio*.	1692
Why when I say? Nay good sweete *Kate* be merrie.	1771
Tra. Then go with me, to make the matter good,	1970
Kate. 'Tis passing good, I prethee let me haue it.	1996
Kate. I like it well, good Grumio fetch it me.	1999
Much good do it vnto thy gentle heart:	2033
Oh no good *Kate*: neither art thou the worse	2162
'Twere good he were school'd.	2190
I pray you stand good father to me now,	2204
And for the good report I heare of you,	2210
I am content in a good fathers care	2213
Good Lord how bright and goodly shines the Moone.	2297
Good morrow gentle Mistris, where away:	2325
Faire louely Maide, once more good day to thee:	2331
*Petr. Do good old grandsire, & withall make known	2348
Nor be not grieued, she is of good esteeme,	2363
**send'em good shipping: but who is here? mine old Ma-|ster	2421
**vndone, I am vndone: while I plaie the good husband	2446
my good Father, I am able to maintaine it.	2454
daughter without asking my good will?	2514
After our great good cheere: praie you sit downe,	2547
*Petr. Verie well mended: kisse him for that good | Widdow.	2564
Petr. A good swift simile, but something currish.	2597
Luc. I thanke thee for that gird good *Tranio*.	2601
Bap. Now in good sadnesse sonne *Petruchio*,	2606
Bap. Now faire befall thee good *Petruchio*;	2666
*Vin. Tis a good hearing, when children are toward.	2741
And being a winner, God giue you good night. | *Exit Petruchio*	2746

GOODLIE = 1

For though you lay heere in this goodlie chamber,	237

GOODLY = 4*1

*Beg. These fifteene yeeres, by my fay, a goodly nap,	234
Kate. Where did you study all this goodly speech?	1141
And wherefore gaze this goodly company,	1477
Good Lord how bright and goodly shines the Moone.	2297
Bion. She saies you haue some goodly Iest in hand,	2643

GOODS = 4

Crownes in my purse I haue, and goods at home,	623
That I disdaine: but for these other goods,	858
Left solie heire to all his Lands and goods,	982
Shee is my goods, my chattels, she is my house,	1616

GOOD-MAN = 1

My men should call me Lord, I am your good-man.	259

GORGD = 1

And til she stoope, she must not be full gorg'd,	1825

GOT = 2

Til *Katherine* the Curst, haue got a husband.	693
Gre. No doubt but he hath got a quiet catch:	1212

GOUERNOUR = 1

To wound thy Lord, thy King, thy Gouernour.	2696

GOWNE = 10*4

Lay forth the gowne. What newes with you sir?	2046
Pet. Thy gowne, why I: come Tailor let vs see't.	2071
Hor. I see shees like to haue neither cap nor gowne.	2078
Kate. I neuer saw a better fashion'd gowne,	2086
I tell thee I, that thou hast marr'd her gowne.	2100
Tail. Your worship is deceiu'd, the gowne is made	2101
*vnto thee, I bid thy Master cut out the gowne, but I did	2112
Tail. Inprimis, a loose bodied gowne.	2117
Gru. Master, if euer I said loose-bodied gowne, sow	2118
*me in the skirts of it, and beate me to death with a bot-|tome of	
browne thred: I said a gowne.	2119
Pet. Well sir in breefe the gowne is not for me.	2138
Gru. Villaine, not for thy life: Take vp my Mistresse | gowne for thy	
masters vse.	2141
Take vp my Mistris gowne to his masters vse. | Oh fie, fie, fie.	2145
Hor. Tailor, Ile pay thee for thy gowne to morrow,	2149

GRA = 1

Pet. It may not be. | *Gra.* Let me intreat you.	1581

GRACE = 3

I know the boy will wel vsurpe the grace,	143
Hor. Now shal my friend *Petruchio* do me grace,	696
Tra. Mistris *Bianca*, blesse you with such grace,	1892

GRACELESSE = 2

Wil not so gracelesse be, to be ingrate.	842
And gracelesse Traitor to her louing Lord?	2718

GRAMERCIES = 2

Luc. Gramercies *Tranio*, well dost thou aduise,	340
Luc. Gramercies Lad: Go forward, this contents,	466

GRANDFATHER = 1

Was *Aiax* cald so from his grandfather.	1346

GRANDSIRE = *1

Petr. Do good old grandsire, & withall make known	2348

GRATEFULL = 1

Very gratefull, I am sure of it, to expresse	939

GRATIFIE = 1

You must as we do, gratifie this Gentleman,	845

GRAUE = 3

Pisa renowned for graue Citizens	309
and thou returne vnexperienc'd to thy graue.	1714
Pisa renowned for graue Citizens.	1951

GRAY = 1

It was the Friar of Orders gray,	1773

GRAY-BEARD = 1
   Tra. Gray-beard thy loue doth freeze. | *Gre.* But thine doth frie,   1219
GRAY-HOUND = 1
   Tri. Oh sir, *Lucentio* slipt me like his Gray-hound,   2595
GRAY-HOUNDS = *1
   *1.Man. Say thou wilt course, thy gray-hounds are as | (swift   199
GRE = 40*12
GREAT = 14*1
   Luc. Tranio, since for the great desire I had   300
   The pleasant garden of great *Italy,*   303
   A Merchant of great Trafficke through the world: 311
   *so great *Hortensio,* but we may blow our nails together,   412
   That made great *Ioue* to humble him to her hand,   472
   Haue I not heard great Ordnance in the field?   770
   That giues not halfe so great a blow to heare,   775
   Gre. Yea, leaue that labour to great *Hercules,*   829
   If you accept them, then their worth is great: 964
   Though little fire growes great with little winde,   999
   Then three great Argosies, besides two Galliasses   1260
   And haue prepar'd great store of wedding cheere,   1568
   After our great good cheere: praie you sit downe,   2547
   Too little payment for so great a debt.   2712
   My heart as great, my reason haplie more,   2729
GREATER = 1*1
   Of greater summes then I haue promised,   1518
   *greater a run but my head and my necke. A fire good | *Curtis.*   1654
GREATEST = 1
   That can assure my daughter greatest dower, | Shall haue my *Biancas*
   loue.   1225
GREECE = 1
   As *Stephen Slie,* and old *Iohn Naps* of Greece, | And *Peter Turph,* and
   Henry Pimpernell,   246
GREED = 2
   That you shall be my wife; your dowry greed on,   1149
   And to conclude, we haue greed so well together,   1177
GREEFE = 2
   Sorrie am I that our good will effects | *Bianca's* greefe.   389
   She is not for your turne, the more my greefe.   924
GREEKE = 2
   In Greeke, Latine, and other Languages,   944
   And this small packet of Greeke and Latine bookes: 963
GREENE = 2
   You may be iogging whiles your bootes are greene: 1597
   That euery thing I looke on seemeth greene: 2345
GREETING = *1
   *you: and thus much for greeting. Now my spruce   1741
GREEUD = 1
   Bap. Was euer Gentleman thus greeu'd as I? | But who comes heere.   895
GREGORY = 2
   Where is *Nathaniel, Gregory, Phillip.*   1749
   There were none fine, but *Adam, Rafe,* and *Gregory,*   1763
GREM = 1*2
GREMIO see also Gre., Grem., Gromio = 24*7
   Gremio a Pantelowne, Hortentio sister to Bianca. | *Lucen. Tranio,* stand
   by.   348
   Or signior *Gremio* you know any such,   400
   Hor. So will I signiour *Gremio*: but a word I pray: 417

GREMIO cont.

*Hor. Tush Gremio: though it passe your patience z	430
fastest, gets the Ring: How say you signior Gremio?	443
Enter Gremio and Lucentio disguised.	703
Hor. Grumio mum: God saue you signior Gremio.	728
Hor. Gremio, 'tis now no time to vent our loue,	744
That she's the choise loue of Signior Gremio.	808
You wil haue Gremio to keepe you faire.	872
Enter Gremio, Lucentio, in the habit of a meane man,	897
*Bap. Good morrow neighbour Gremio: God saue	you Gentlemen.	901
Pet. You wrong me signior Gremio, giue me leaue.	907
*Pet. Oh, Pardon me signior Gremio, I would faine be	doing.	935
Bap. A thousand thankes signior Gremio:	947
Enter Baptista, Gremio, Trayno.	1155
Say signior Gremio, what can you assure her?	1227
Within rich Pisa walls, as any one	Old Signior Gremio has in Padua,	1249
What, haue I pincht you Signior Gremio?	1253
Tra. Gremio, 'tis knowne my father hath no lesse	1259
By your firme promise, Gremio is out vied.	1267
Be Bride to you, if you make this assurance:	If not, to Signior Gremio:	1278
*Enter Baptista, Gremio, Tranio, Katherine, Bianca, and o-	thers,	
attendants.	1387
Wee'll ouer-reach the grey-beard Gremio,	1528
Enter Gremio.	1532
Signior Gremio, came you from the Church?	1533
Besides old Gremio is harkning still,	2235
Enter Biondello, Lucentio and Bianca, Gremio	is out before.	2379
*Bap. Talke not signior Gremio: I saie he shall goe to	prison.	2474
*Enter Baptista, Vincentio, Gremio, the Pedant, Lucentio, and	2534
Bap. How likes Gremio these quicke witted folkes?	2580

GREMIO = 2*1
GREW = *1

*his beard grew thinne and hungerly, and seem'd to aske	1557

GREY see gray
GREY-BEARD = 1

Wee'll ouer-reach the grey-beard Gremio,	1528

GRIEUED = 1

Nor be not grieued, she is of good esteeme,	2363

GRIM = 1

Grim death, how foule and loathsome is thine image:	39

GRISSELL = 1

For patience shee will proue a second Grissell,	1175

GROOME = 3*1

To want the Bride-groome when the Priest attends	1393
*Gre. A bridegroome say you? 'tis a groome indeed,	1536
A grumlling groome, and that the girle shall finde.	1537
'Tis like you'll proue a iolly surly groome,	1599

GROOMES = 1

You logger-headed and vnpollisht groomes:	1752

GROUE = 1

Pet. Did euer Dian so become a Groue	1137

GROUND = 2

Say thou wilt walke: wee wil bestrow the ground.	192
Bian. Gamouth I am, the ground of all accord:	1366

GROW = 2

Which otherwise would grow into extreames.	150
Luc. Fidler forbeare, you grow too forward Sir,	1296

GROWES = 4*1
  If you should smile, he growes impatient. 109
  No profit growes, where is no pleasure tane: 338
  Where small experience growes but in a few. 618
  *Bap. Why how now Dame, whence growes this in-|solence? 879
  Though little fire growes great with little winde, 999
GROWETH = 1
  Our fine Musitian groweth amorous. 1356
GROWNE = 1
  Gru. My Mr is growne quarrelsome: 578
GRU = 29*31
GRUMBLE = 1
  What, do you grumble? Ile be with you straight. 1799
GRUMIO see also Gru. = 24*4
  Enter Petruchio, and his man Grumio. 565
  Heere sirra Grumio, knocke I say. 570
  *Grumio, and my good friend Petruchio? How do you all | at Verona? 589
  Rise Grumio rise, we will compound this quarrell. 595
  then had not Grumio come by the worst. 602
  Your ancient trustie pleasant seruant Grumio: 613
  Hor. Peace Grumio, it is the riuall of my Loue. 707
  Hor. Grumio mum: God saue you signior Gremio. 728
  Enter Petruchio and Grumio. 1468
  Kat. Now if you loue me stay. | Pet. Grumio, my horse. 1589
  That stops my way in Padua: Grumio 1621
  Enter Grumio. 1639
  Cur. Is my master and his wife comming Grumio? 1656
  *Cur. I prethee good Grumio, tell me, how goes the | world? 1670
  *Cur. There's fire readie, and therefore good Grumio | the newes. 1675
  Cur. Let's ha't good Grumio. 1692
  Nat. Welcome home Grumio. | Phil. How now Grumio. 1735
  Ios. What Grumio. | Nick. Fellow Grumio. 1737
  Enter Katherina and Grumio. 1978
  Kate. I like it well, good Grumio fetch it me. 1999
  Or else you get no beefe of Grumio. 2006
  Grumio gaue order how it should be done. 2103
  *Hor. God-a-mercie Grumio, then hee shall haue no | oddes. 2136
  Enter Petruchio, Kate, Vincentio, Grumio | with Attendants. 2387
  Bianca. Tranio, Biondello Grumio, and Widdow: 2535
  Sirra Grumio, goe to your Mistris, 2647
GRUMIO = 3
GRUMIOS = 1
  Hor. Petruchio patience, I am Grumio's pledge: 611
GRUMLLING = 1
  A grumlling groome, and that the girle shall finde. 1537
GUESSE = 1
  Then words can witnesse, or your thoughts can guesse. 1217
GUEST = 1
  Am bold to shew my selfe a forward guest 912
GUESTS = 1
  Prouide the feast father, and bid the guests, 1196
GUIFT = 2
  And if the boy haue not a womans guift 135
  Your wooing neighbors: this is a guift 938
GUIFTS = *1
  *Gre. You may go to the diuels dam: your guifts are 410

GUSTS = 1
Yet extreme gusts will blow out fire and all: 1000
GYRLE = 2
If I atchieue not this yong modest gyrle: 459
Bianca stand aside, poore gyrle she weepes: 881
HA *l*.409 *706 = 1*1, 1*1
Pet. Good sooth euen thus: therefore ha done with | (words,   1499
Petr. Spoke like an Officer: ha to the lad.   2578
HABERDASHER = 1
Enter Haberdasher.   2045
HABILIMENTS = 1
Euen in these honest meane habiliments: 2153
HABIT = 3*1
Enter Gremio, Lucentio, in the habit of a meane man,   897
Fie, doff this habit, shame to your estate,   1483
So honor peereth in the meanest habit.   2157
*your habit: but your words shew you a mad man: why   2452
HACKET = 1*1
*Aske *Marrian Hacket* the fat Alewife of Wincot, if shee   174
Sometimes you would call out for Cicely Hacket.   242
HAD *l*.300 *434 *444 471 516 *548 *601 602 816 1027 1112 *1414 *1554
1607 *1883 2102 *2132 2670 = 10*8
HADST *l.*1704 = *1
HAGGARD = 2
Another way I haue to man my Haggard,   1827
As I haue lou'd this proud disdainful Haggard,   1887
HAILD = *1
Vin. Thus strangers may be haild and abusd: oh mon-|strous villaine.   2486
HAIRE = *1
*presume to touch a haire of my Masters horse-taile, till   1722
HALFE = 6*1
I-wis it is not halfe way to her heart: 365
*may perhaps call him halfe a score Knaues, or so: Why   676
That giues not halfe so great a blow to heare,   775
Bap. After my death, the one halfe of my Lands,   986
To wish me wed to one halfe Lunaticke,   1167
Thou yard three quarters, halfe yard, quarter, naile,   2094
Bap. Sonne, Ile be your halfe, *Bianca* comes.   2625
HALFE-CHEKT = *1
*halfe-chekt Bitte, & a headstall of sheepes leather, which   1444
HALL = 1
Kate of *Kate*-hall, my super-daintie *Kate*,   1059
HALT = 2
Oh let me see thee walke: thou dost not halt.   1135
Petr. And yet I come not well. | *Bap.* And yet you halt not.   1471
HALUES = 1
Luc. Ile haue no halues: Ile beare it all my selfe.   2626
HAND = 13*3
The rather for I haue some sport in hand,   101
That made great *Ioue* to humble him to her hand,   472
Tra. Master, for my hand, | Both our inuentions meet and iumpe in
one.   493
All bookes of Loue, see that at any hand,   712
Petr. Not her that chides sir, at any hand I pray.   795
That couenants may be kept on either hand.   992
And bow'd her hand to teach her fingering,   1018
Giue me thy hand *Kate*, I will vnto *Venice*   1194

96

HAND *cont.*

To giue my hand oppos'd against my heart	1397
*or shall I complaine on thee to our mistris, whose hand	1667
*(she being now at hand) thou shalt soone feele, to thy	1668
*Gre. E'ne at hand, alighted by this: and therefore be	1744
I tel you sir, she beares me faire in hand.	1849
Heere is my hand, and heere I firmly vow	1876
Bion. She saies you haue some goodly Iest in hand,	2643
In token of which dutie, if he please, | My hand is readie, may it do him ease.	2736

HANDS = 9*2

And say wilt please your Lordship coole your hands.	62
2.Man. Wilt please your mightinesse to wash your | hands:	228
That til the Father rid his hands of her,	484
Vnbinde my hands, Ile pull them off my selfe,	859
I prethee sister Kate, vntie my hands.	876
Bap. I know not what to say, but giue me your ha(n)ds,	1198
Basons and ewers to laue her dainty hands:	1230
they kisse their hands. Are they all readie?	1723
Peda. Lay hands on the villaine, I beleeue a meanes	2417
And craues no other tribute at thy hands,	2710
And place your hands below your husbands foote:	2735

HANG = 3

And hang it round with all my wanton pictures:	51
Gru. Wil he woo her? I: or Ile hang her.	764
Be madde and merry, or goe hang your selues:	1612

HANGD = 1*1

Kate. Ile see thee hang'd on sonday first.	1179
Gre. Hark *Petruchio*, she saies shee'll see thee hang'd | (first.	1180

HANGINGS = 1

My hangings all of *tirian* tapestry:	1231

HANGS = 1

Gru. Out of their saddles into the durt, and thereby | hangs a tale.	1690

HAP = 3

For our accesse, whose hap shall be to haue her,	841
Hap what hap may, Ile roundly goe about her:	2292

HAPLIE = 1

My heart as great, my reason haplie more,	2729

HAPLY = 2

Ile in to counsell them: haply my presence	148
Heere let vs breath, and haply institute	307

HAPNED = 1

And if you will tell what hath hapned,	2247

HAPPIE = 3*1

Well you are come to me in happie time,	100
*be happie riuals in *Bianca's* loue, to labour and effect | one thing specially.	421
And tell me now (sweet friend) what happie gale	614
And to be short, what not, that's sweete and happie.	2665

HAPPIER = 2

Happier the man whom fauourable stars	2338
Petr. Happily met, the happier for thy sonne:	2358

HAPPILIE = 3

Tra. Signior *Baptista* you are happilie met:	2202
And happilie we might be interrupted.	2236
And happilie I haue arriued at the last | Vnto the wished hauen of my blisse:	2507

HAPPILY = 4

Happily to wiue and thriue, as best I may:	622
If wealthily, then happily in *Padua*.	642
Grem. Hortensio hearke:	This Gentleman is happily arriu'd,	779
Petr. Happily met, the happier for thy sonne:	2358

HAPPINESSE = 1

| Vertue and that part of Philosophie | Will I applie, that treats of happinesse, | 317 |

HAPPY = 1 *2

*Sweet *Bianca*, happy man be his dole: hee that runnes	442
Bap. Well maist thou woo, and happy be thy speed:	1003
Happy the Parents of so faire a childe;	2337

HARD = 2 *1

Kate. Well haue you heard, but something hard of	hearing:	1053
Ped. My life sir? how I pray? for that goes hard.	1936
It shall goe hard if *Cambio* goe without her. *Exit*.	2293

HARDLY = 2

| *Beg*. I, it stands so that I may hardly tarry so long: | 279 |
| That mortal eares might hardly indure the din. | 476 |

HARK = *1

| *Gre*. Hark *Petruchio*, she saies shee'll see thee hang'd | (first. | 1180 |

HARKE = *4

*Wilt thou haue Musicke? Harke Apollo plaies, *Musick*	187
Luc. Harke *Tranio*, thou maist heare *Minerua* speak.	387
*neuer was before: harke, harke, I heare the min- |strels play. *Musicke playes*.	1563

HARKNING = 1

| Besides old *Gremio* is harkning still, | 2235 |

HARME = 1

| If that be all Masters, I heare no harme. | 754 |

HARMES = 1

| Which barres a thousand harmes, and lengthens life. | 290 |

HARMONY = 2

| *Hort*. But wrangling pedant, this is | The patronesse of heauenly harmony: | 1299 |
| And while I pause, serue in your harmony. | 1309 |

HARNESSE = 1

| Their harnesse studded all with Gold and Pearle. | 194 |

HARSH = 1 *1

| *Petr*. Tedious it were to tell, and harsh to heare, | 1488 |
| *Luc*. But a harsh hearing, when women are froward, | 2742 |

HARTS = 1

| But that our soft conditions, and our harts, | 2725 |

HAS *l*.486 *530 572 *790 1250 2376 2603 = 5*2, *1

| *Biond*. Faith nothing: but has left mee here behinde | 2264 |

HAST *l*.*195 214 1072 1128 1602 2041 2100 2108 *2110 2195 2327 2378 2494 2607 2667 *2748 = 13*3, 2

| See this dispatch'd with all the hast thou canst, | 140 |
| *Hor*. That will not be in hast. | 2057 |

HASTE *see also* hast = 3

Pet. Signior *Baptista*, my businesse asketh haste,	979
Who woo'd in haste, and meanes to wed at leysure:	1399
But so it is, my haste doth call me hence,	1569

HASTIE = 2

| Take no vnkindnesse of his hastie words: | 2150 |
| *Bian*. Head, and but an hastie witted bodie, | 2582 |

HAT = 3*4
  Vncase thee: take my Coulord hat and cloake,   513
  *Bion. Why Petruchio is comming, in a new hat and   1431
  *blew lift; an old hat, & the humor of forty fancies prickt   1454
  Cur. Let's ha't good Grumio.   1692
  There was no Linke to colour Peters hat,   1761
  *hose, a scarlet cloake, and a copataine hat: oh I am   2445
  *Luc. Well go thy waies olde Lad for thou shalt ha't.   2740
HATCHD = 1
  'Tis hatch'd, and shall be so: Tranio at once   512
HATH l.67 122 133 *216 286 526 684 691 738 825 942 1016 1148 1212
  1259 1362 1405 *1445 *1448 1486 1507 *1662 1728 1886 1941 2247
  *2287 2362 2375 *2465 2584 2592 2602 2684 2728 = 29*6
HAUE see also ha, ha't l.*10 96 101 135 *161 *187 189 220 221 232 245
  266 275 320 333 353 356 378 405 *420 *441 464 492 504 505 528 *529
  537 *547 621 623 *646 *680 689 692 693 701 710 711 717 733 737 752
  760 761 767 768 770 772 794 815 817 841 870 872 875 890 *903 905 914
  940 959 983 985 1030 *1053 1160 1166 1171 1177 1203 1214 1226 1232
  1239 1247 1253 1256 1258 1263 1264 1265 1287 1297 1301 1302 1303
  1318 1351 1370 1380 1381 *1433 1518 1568 1576 *1591 *1673 *1680
  *1705 *1706 1782 1787 1822 1827 1850 1870 1879 1887 1894 1895 *1896
  1898 1900 1911 1943 1945 1949 1950 1953 1966 1983 1996 *2005 2052
  2053 2055 2058 2060 2070 *2078 2107 2109 *2136 2214 2217 2220 2229
  2234 2243 2281 2308 2318 2344 2355 2377 *2420 *2426 *2459 2497 2507
  *2511 *2513 *2587 2588 2626 2643 2679 *2689 = 135*28
HAUEN = 1
  And happilie I haue arriued at the last | Vnto the wished hauen of my
  blisse: 2507
HAUING = *2
  *all in the Sextons face: hauing no other reason, but that 1556
  *Ped. Soft son: sir by your leaue, hauing com to Padua 2206
HAWKE = 1
  Petr. Twentie crownes, | Ile venture so much of my Hawke or Hound, 2615
HAWKES = *1
  *Dost thou loue hawking? Thou hast hawkes will soare   195
HAWKING = *1
  *Dost thou loue hawking? Thou hast hawkes will soare   195
HAZLE = 2
  Oh sland'rous world: Kate like the hazle twig   1132
  As hazle nuts, and sweeter then the kernels: 1134
HE see also a = 92*31, 1
  Ile bring mine action on the proudest he   1620
HEAD = 12*2
  *Host. I know my remedie, I must go fetch the Head-|borough. 13
  Balme his foule head in warme distilled waters,   52
  And with declining head into his bosome   130
  *tooth in her head, though she haue as manie diseases as 646
  Luc. Sir giue him head, I know hee'l proue a Iade.   821
  Enter Hortensio with his head broke.   1007
  And with that word she stroke me on the head,   1021
  'Tis in my head to doe my master good: 1288
  Carowse full measure to her maiden-head,   1611
  *greater a run but my head and my necke. A fire good | Curtis. 1654
  Bian. Head, and but an hastie witted bodie,   2582
  Would say your Head and But were head and horne.   2583
  Thy head, thy soueraigne: One that cares for thee,   2705

HEADED = 3
You logger-headed and vnpollisht groomes:	1752
Pet. A horson beetle-headed flap-ear'd knaue:	1786
*Enter Baptista and Lucentio: Pedant booted	and bare headed.*	2200

HEADS = 1*2
*how the young folkes lay their heads together.	705
*and the rest: let their heads bee slickely comb'd,	1719
You heedlesse iolt-heads, and vnmanner'd slaues.	1798

HEADSTALL = *1
*halfe-chekt Bitte, & a headstall of sheepes leather, which	1444

HEADSTRONG = 1
And thus Ile curbe her mad and headstrong humor:	1843

HEAD-STRONG = *1
Pet. *Katherine* I charge thee tell these head-strong	2686

HEALTH = 4*1
To see her noble Lord restor'd to health,	132
And quaffe carowses to our Mistresse health,	849
*ceremonies done, hee calls for wine, a health quoth	1553
Dine with my father, drinke a health to me,	1578
Therefore a health to all that shot and mist.	2594

HEARD = 10*5
For yet his honor neuer heard a play)	106
*Beare-heard, and now by present profession a Tinker.	173
Haue I not in my time heard Lions rore?	767
Haue I not heard the sea, puft vp with windes,	768
Haue I not heard great Ordnance in the field?	770
Haue I not in a pitched battell heard	772
Of that report, which I so oft haue heard,	914
Kate. Well haue you heard, but something hard of	hearing:	1053
Bion. Master, master, newes, and such newes as you	neuer heard of,	1420
Bion. Why, is it not newes to heard of *Petruchio's*	(comming?	1423
*thou shouldst haue heard how her horse fel, and she vn-	der	1705
*her horse: thou shouldst haue heard in how miery a	1706
Tra. Signior *Hortensio*, I haue often heard	Of your entire affection to *Bianca*,	1870
You might haue heard it else proclaim'd about.	1943
Ped. I know him not, but I haue heard of him:	1953

HEARE = 16*7
There is a Lord will heare you play to night;	103
I long to heare him call the drunkard husband,	145
I do not sleepe: I see, I heare, I speake:	222
Therefore they thought it good you heare a play,	288
Luc. Harke *Tranio*, thou maist heare *Minerua* speak.	387
If that be all Masters, I heare no harme.	754
That giues not halfe so great a blow to heare,	775
Do me this right: heare me with patience.	811
Did you yet euer see *Baptistas* daughter?	*Tra.* No sir, but heare I do that he hath two:	824
Good morrow *Kate*, for thats your name I heare.	1052
Pet. Nay heare you *Kate*. Insooth you scape not so.	1119
Bian. Let's heare, oh fie, the treble iarres.	1332
hic staterat priami, take heede he heare vs not, *regia* pre-	sume not, *Celsa senis*, despaire not.	1336
And yet we heare not of our sonne in Law:	1391
Petr. Tedious it were to tell, and harsh to heare,	1488
*neuer was before: harke, harke, I heare the min-	strels play. *Musicke playes.*	1563

HEARE *cont.*
Cur. This 'tis to feele a tale, not to heare a tale.   1696
*Cur. Do you heare ho? you must meete my maister | to countenance
my mistris.   1726
not--- Cockes passion, silence, I heare my master.   1745
And for the good report I heare of you,   2210
Signior *Baptista*, of whom I heare so well.   2219
Padua: doe you heare sir, to leaue friuolous circumstan-|ces,   2407
*Bap. But doe you heare sir, haue you married my   2513
HEARING = 3*3
*Mes. Your Honors Players hearing your amendment,   283
That hearing of her beautie, and her wit,   909
*Kate. Well haue you heard, but something hard of | hearing: 1053
Hearing thy mildnesse prais'd in euery Towne,   1062
*Vin. Tis a good hearing, when children are toward.   2741
*Luc. But a harsh hearing, when women are froward,   2742
HEARKE = 3
Hearke you sir, Ile haue them verie fairely bound,   711
Grem. *Hortensio* hearke: | This Gentleman is happily arriu'd,   779
Gre. Hearke you sir, you meane not her to---   793
HEARKEN = 1
The yongest daughter whom you hearken for,   832
HEARST = 1
Luc. Hear'st thou *Biondello*.   2283
HEART = 12*1
Lord. With all my heart. This fellow I remember,   93
I-wis it is not halfe way to her heart: 365
Affection is not rated from the heart: 463
And could not get him for my heart to do it.   605
To giue my hand oppos'd against my heart   1397
*mouth, my heart in my belly, ere I should come by a fire   1646
*Luc. While you sweet deere proue Mistresse of my | heart.   1857
Much good do it vnto thy gentle heart: 2033
My tongue will tell the anger of my heart,   2062
Or els my heart concealing it wil breake,   2063
Biond. I praie the gods she may withall my heart. | *Exit*.   2250
Hor. Well *Petruchio*, this has put me in heart;   2376
My heart as great, my reason haplie more,   2729
HEARTILY = 1
Come *Kate* and wash, & welcome heartily: 1783
HEARTS *see* harts
HEATH = *1
*Slie, old Slies sonne of Burton-heath, by byrth a   171
HEAUEN = 1*1
*Lord. Heauen cease this idle humor in your Honor.   166
What stars do spangle heauen with such beautie,   2329
HEAUENLY = 3
To make a dulcet and a heauenly sound: 55
Hort. But wrangling pedant, this is | The patronesse of heauenly
harmony: 1299
As those two eyes become that heauenly face?   2330
HEAUENS = 1*1
*Gru. Knocke at the gate? O heauens: spake you not   606
And heauens Artillerie thunder in the skies?   771
HEAUIE = 2
Why this a heauie chance twixt him and you,   612
And yet as heauie as my waight should be.   1079

HEDGE = 1
At the hedge corner, in the couldest fault,   23
HEE *l.*442 *643 1461 *1553 *1558 *1707 *2136 *2404 *2470 = 1*9
HEEDE = *2
   hic staterat priami, take heede he heare vs not, *regia* pre-|sume not,
   Celsa senis, despaire not.   1336
   Gre. Take heede signior *Baptista*, least you be coni-|catcht   2476
HEEDLESSE = 1
You heedlesse iolt-heads, and vnmanner'd slaues.   1798
HEEL *l.*677 821 1900 1903 = 3*1
HEELE *l.*1760 = 1, *1
   *slide from my shoulder to my heele, with no   1653
HEELL = 1
Hee'll wooe a thousand, point the day of marriage,   1403
HEERE = 49*6
   Lord. What's heere? One dead, or drunke? See doth | he breath?   34
   (Trauelling some iourney) to repose him heere.   81
   For though you lay heere in this goodlie chamber,   237
   Beg. Marrie I fare well, for heere is cheere enough.   255
   Where is my wife? | *La*. Heere noble Lord, what is thy will with her?   256
   Heere let vs breath, and haply institute   307
   And be in *Padua* heere *Vincentio's* sonne,   501
   Heere comes the rogue. Sirra, where haue you bin?   528
   Your fellow *Tranio* heere to saue my life,   535
   Heere sirra *Grumio*, knocke I say.   570
   Petr. Villaine I say, knocke me heere soundly.   573
   Gru. Knocke you heere sir? Why sir, what am I sir,   574
   that I should knocke you heere sir.   575
   *these words plaine? Sirra, Knocke me heere: rappe me   607
   *heere: knocke me well, and knocke me soundly? And   608
   Blowes you to *Padua* heere, from old *Verona*?   615
   Heere is a Gentleman whom by chance I met   747
   Kate. Of all thy sutors heere I charge tel   863
   Bian. If you affect him sister, heere I sweare   869
   Bap. Was euer Gentleman thus greeu'd as I? | But who comes heere.   895
   That being a stranger in this Cittie heere,   952
   I heere bestow a simple instrument,   962
   Pet. I pray you do. Ile attend her heere,   1037
   But heere she comes, and now *Petruchio* speake.   1050
   Heere comes your father, neuer make deniall,   1159
   And to cut off all strife: heere sit we downe,   1316
   Luc. Heere Madam: *Hic Ibat Simois, hic est sigeria*   1322
   Bap. When will he be heere? | *Bion*. When he stands where I am, and
   sees you there.   1428
   and heere and there peec'd with packthred.   1449
   And make assurance heere in *Padua*   1517
   And therefore heere I meane to take my leaue.   1570
   And heere she stands, touch her who euer dare,   1619
   Gru. Lend thine eare. | *Cur*. Heere. | *Gru*. There.   1693
   All ser. Heere, heere sir, heere sir.   1750
   Pet. Heere sir, heere sir, heere sir, heere sir.   1751
   Gru. Heere sir, as foolish as I was before.   1755
   Yet as they are, heere are they come to meete you.   1765
   Be merrie *Kate*: Some water heere: what hoa.   1777
   And heere Ile fling the pillow, there the boulster,   1835
   Heere is my hand, and heere I firmly vow   1876
   Tra. And heere I take the like vnfained oath,   1880

HEERE *cont*.

From Florence, and must heere deliuer them.	1946
My father is heere look'd for euerie day,	1972
'Twixt me, and one *Baptistas* daughter heere:	1974
Heere Loue, thou seest how diligent I am,	2020
Heere take away this dish.	*Kate*. I pray you let it stand.	2025
Fel. Heere is the cap your Worship did bespeake.	2047
Oh mercie God, what masking stuffe is heere?	2072
Tail. Why heere is the note of the fashion to testify.	*Pet*. Reade it.	2114

HEERES = *3

*so good heere's none will holde you: Their loue is not	411
Gru. Heere's no knauerie. See, to beguile the olde-|folkes,	704
Pet. Why heere's no crab, and therefore looke not	sowre.	1108

HEERS = 1

Heers snip, and nip, and cut, and slish and slash,	2075

HEES = 1

Gre. Why hee's a deuill, a deuill, a very fiend.	1539

HEIRE = 1*1

Left solie heire to all his Lands and goods,	982
*he is mine onelie sonne and heire to the Lands of me sig-|nior *Vincentio*.	2463

HELL = 3

Gre. Why will you mew her vp	(Signior *Baptista*) for this fiend of hell,	391
*her father be verie rich, any man is so verie a foole to be	married to hell?	428
And for your loue to her, leade Apes in hell.	892

HELPE = 7*3

Gru. Helpe mistris helpe, my master is mad.	585
I can *Petruchio* helpe thee to a wife	651
Hath promist me to helpe one to another,	738
And helpe to dresse your sisters chamber vp,	1377
Bion. Helpe, helpe, helpe, here's a mad man will mur-|der me.	2435
Pedan. Helpe, sonne, helpe signior *Baptista*.	2437

HELPING = *1

*it shall be so farre forth friendly maintain'd, till by hel-|ping	439

HEN = 1

Pet. A comblesse Cocke, so *Kate* will be my Hen.	1103

HENCE = 11*1

Lord. Hence comes it, that your kindred shuns your	(house	180
As beaten hence by your strange Lunacie.	181
And banish hence these abiect lowlie dreames:	184
While I make way from hence to saue my life:	541
Gremio. No: if without more words you will get you	hence.	801
Remoue you hence: I knew you at the first	You were a mouable.	1068
But so it is, my haste doth call me hence,	1569
For I must hence, and farewell to you all.	1579
Where's my Spaniel *Troilus*? Sirra, get you hence,	1779
Ile none of it; hence, make your best of it.	2085
Go take it hence, be gone, and say no more.	2148
And therefore frolicke, we will hence forthwith,	2165

HENCEFORTH = 1

Henceforth I vowe it shall be so for me.	2311

HENRY = 1

As *Stephen Slie*, and old *Iohn Naps* of Greece,	And *Peter Turph*, and *Henry Pimpernell*,	246

HER *see also* hir *l*.128 132 204 210 217 240 257 262 270 356 357 365 366 391 393 399 *415 416 424 *428 *431 *433 *434 *446 447 470 472 477

HER *cont.*
  478 479 *482 483 484 486 490 630 *646 654 658 660 661 663 665 666
  667 669 *679 686 687 701 702 713 719 720 735 750 752 764 784 793 794
  795 828 833 834 841 *877 882 884 886 891 892 909 910 911 918 925 985
  988 989 994 1001 1014 *1015 1017 1018 1029 1030 1037 1038 1039 1044
  1046 1047 1138 1139 1143 1171 1176 *1182 1190 1227 1230 1248 1252
  1261 1269 1271 1298 1408 *1448 1493 1497 1498 1512 *1559 1609 1611
  1619 1630 1636 *1705 *1706 *1707 *1708 *1711 1728 1732 1813 *1816
  *1817 1826 1828 1829 1838 1841 1843 1872 1874 1877 1881 1882 1903
  1909 2091 2100 2217 *2245 *2278 2292 2293 2328 2332 2364 2414 2563
  2574 2575 *2576 2593 2611 *2638 2644 2648 2649 2672 2673 2676 2691
  2693 2714 2718 = 163*28
HERALD = 1
  Pet. A Herald *Kate*? Oh put me in thy bookes.   1101
HERCULES = 1
  Gre. Yea, leaue that labour to great *Hercules*,   829
HERD *see* heard
HERE = 12*3
  Ped. I warrant you: but sir here comes your boy,   2189
  Here comes *Baptista*: set your countenance sir.   2199
  Right true it is your sonne *Lucentio* here   2222
  Send for your daughter by your seruant here,   2240
  Biond. Faith nothing: but has left mee here behinde   2264
  But soft, Company is comming here.   2323
  Thither must I, and here I leaue you sir.   2391
  I thinke I shall command your welcome here;   2393
  *come from *Pisa*, and is here at the doore to speake with | him.   2409
  here looking out at the window.   2412
  *send'em good shipping: but who is here? mine old Ma-|ster   2421
  Petr. She hath preuented me, here signior *Tranio*,   2592
  Hor. Confesse, confesse, hath he not hit you here?   2602
  Bap. Now by my hollidam here comes *Katerina*.   2654
  Luc. Here is a wonder, if you talke of a wonder.   2661
HEREOF = 1
  Petr. Come goe along and see the truth hereof,   2374
HERES = 2*4
  *sheere Ale, score me vp for the lyingst knaue in Christen|dome. What
  I am not bestraught: here's---   176
  Tra. Husht master, heres some good pastime toward;   371
  Petr. Sir heres the doore, this is *Lucentios* house,   2389
  Bion. Helpe, helpe, helpe, here's a mad man will mur-|der me.   2435
  Luc. Here's *Lucentio*, right sonne to the right *Vin-|centio*,   2495
  Gre. Here's packing with a witnesse to deceiue vs all.   2499
HERS = 1
  And if I die to morrow this is hers,   1243
HERSELFE *see* selfe
HES = 3
  Though he be merry, yet withall he's honest.   1413
  Bap. I am glad he's come, howsoere he comes.   1459
  Ped. He's within sir, but not to be spoken withall.   2401
HETHER = 1
  Kate. Mou'd, in good time, let him that mou'd you | hether   1066
HEYRE = 1
  I am my fathers heyre and onely sonne,   1246
HIC = 1*8
  Luc. Heere Madam: *Hic Ibat Simois, hic est sigeria*   1322
  tellus, hic steterat Priami regia Celsa senis.   1323

HIC *cont.*
    *Luc. Hic Ibat, as I told you before, *Simois*, I am Lu-|centio,   1325
    *hic est, sonne vnto Vincentio of Pisa, *Sigeria tel-|lus,*   1326
    *disguised thus to get your loue, *hic steterat*, and that   1327
    *Bian. Now let mee see if I can conster it. *Hic ibat si-|mois,*   1334
    *I know you not, *hic est sigeria tellus*, I trust you not,   1335
    *hic staterat priami, take heede he heare vs not, *regia* pre-|sume not,
    Celsa senis, despaire not.   1336
HID = 1
    And Citherea all in sedges hid,   203
HIDE = 1
    Tra. A vengeance on your crafty withered hide,   1286
HIDING = 1
    Hiding his bitter iests in blunt behauiour,   1401
HIE = *2
    *with this condition; To be whipt at the hie crosse euerie | morning.   435
    Cambio hie you home, and bid *Bianca* make her readie | straight: 2245
HIGH *see also* hie = 1
    Of such possessions, and so high esteeme   168
HILDING = 1
    For shame thou Hilding of a diuellish spirit,   883
HILL = 2
    hill, my Master riding behinde my Mistris.   1700
    An ancient Angel comming downe the hill, | Wil serue the turne.   1913
HILT = *1
    *Towne Armory, with a broken hilt, and chapelesse: with   1435
HIM *l.**16 28 30 44 *47 49 50 59 64 65 67 76 81 108 117 118 119 120 124
    131 133 145 322 416 *444 472 *480 515 540 546 584 *598 605 612 *644
    *673 *674 *675 *676 *678 681 752 794 821 869 870 873 920 *931 968
    981 *1066 1096 1271 1368 1408 1411 1412 *1414 *1445 1450 *1457
    *1464 1508 1510 1515 1541 *1547 *1552 *1558 1631 *1709 1845 1882
    1902 1919 1921 1940 1953 2010 2104 2113 2167 2191 2196 2197 2212
    2214 2223 2226 2270 2334 *2402 2410 *2460 *2466 2484 *2488 2489
    2509 2510 2561 *2564 2737 = 83*29
HIMSELFE = 4
    Would not the begger then forget himselfe?   45
    He beare himselfe with honourable action,   121
    Of loue betweene your daughter and himselfe: 2209
    Which runs himselfe, and catches for his Master.   2596
HIPD = *1
    *two broken points: his horse hip'd with an olde mo-|thy   1436
HIR *l.**474 *679 = *2
HIS *see also* in's *l.**18 42 43 52 65 66 77 105 106 130 186 299 305 315 323
    *347 *440 *442 *445 473 *480 484 502 503 515 *531 537 565 569 *597
    *599 *643 *677 685 743 748 781 783 814 898 921 *931 946 982 1007
    1090 1091 1283 1307 1318 1319 1346 1401 1411 *1436 *1451 *1464 1507
    1543 *1554 *1557 1656 *1684 1774 1851 1959 1962 *1980 2042 2145
    2150 2159 2161 *2265 *2271 2339 2356 *2408 *2411 2413 2414 2458
    *2459 2461 *2462 *2465 2553 2569 2595 2596 2609 2706 2716 = 73*28
HISTORY = 1
    Lady. It is a kinde of history. | *Beg.* Well, we'l see't: 295
HIT = 4
    Pet. Thou hast hit it: come sit on me.   1072
    This bird you aim'd at, though you hit her not,   2593
    Hor. Confesse, confesse, hath he not hit you here?   2602
    'Twas I wonne the wager, though you hit the white,   2745

HITHER *see also* hether = 10*1

Well, bring our Ladie hither to our sight,	226
Preferre them hither: for to cunning men,	401
Luc. Sirra come hither, 'tis no time to iest,	533
Petr. Why came I hither, but to that intent?	765
And sent you hither so vnlike your selfe?	1487
And bid my cozen *Ferdinand* come hither:	1780
*to speake, and sits as one new risen from a dreame: A- |way, away, for he is comming hither.	1819
Vin. Come hither crackhempe.	2424
*Vin. Come hither you rogue, what haue you forgot | mee?	2426
Petr. Goe fetch them hither, if they denie to come,	2658
Away I say, and bring them hither straight.	2660

HITS = 1

Bap. Oh, oh *Petruchio*, *Tranio* hits you now.	2600

HO = *3

*Gru. Why Iacke boy, ho boy, and as much newes as | wilt thou.	1677
*Cur. Do you heare ho? you must meete my maister | to countenance my mistris.	1726
*Pet. Oh ho, intreate her, nay then shee must needes | come.	2638

HOA = 2

will take cold: Holla, hoa *Curtis*.	1649
Be merrie *Kate*: Some water heere: what hoa.	1777

HOLD = 8*2

For so your doctors hold it very meete,	285
That loue should of a sodaine take such hold.	450
He hath the Iewel of my life in hold,	684
Iron may hold with her, but neuer Lutes.	1014
*Bion. Nay by S.(aint) *Iamy*, I hold you a penny, a horse and	1466
To hold my stirrop, nor to take my horse?	1748
Tis well, and hold your owne in any case	2186
Tra. Th'art a tall fellow, hold thee that to drinke,	2198
*hold on him I charge you in the Dukes name: oh my	2466
'Tis thought your Deere does hold you at a baie.	2599

HOLDE = *1

*so good heere's none will holde you: Their loue is not	411

HOLDS = 1

And her with-holds from me. Other more	686

HOLE = 1

Luc. Spit in the hole man, and tune againe.	1333

HOLLA = 2

You shall go see your Pupils presently. | Holla, within.	970
will take cold: Holla, hoa *Curtis*.	1649

HOLLIDAM = 1

Bap. Now by my hollidam here comes *Katerina*.	2654

HOLLOW = 1

And fetch shrill ecchoes from the hollow earth.	198

HOLSOME = 1

I care not what, so it be holsome foode.	1994

HOMAGE = 1

When they do homage to this simple peasant,	147

HOME = 8*6

Call home thy ancient thoughts from banishment,	183
Master, your Loue must liue a maide at home,	485
To seeke their fortunes farther then at home,	617
Crownes in my purse I haue, and goods at home,	623
*Pet. Come, where be these gallants? who's at home?	1469

HOME *cont.*

*Tra. And is the Bride & Bridegroom coming home?	1535
*finde when he comes home. But what talke I of this?	1717
Nat. Welcome home *Grumio.* | *Phil.* How now *Grumio.*	1735
Go hop me ouer euery kennell home,	2083
*Cambio hie you home, and bid *Bianca* make her readie | straight:	2245
thee at home, therefore leaue vs. *Exit.*	2383
*at home, my sonne and my seruant spend all at the vni- | uersitie.	2447
*Petr. Why then let's home againe: Come Sirra let's | awaie.	2527
Whil'st thou ly'st warme at home, secure and safe,	2709

HONEST = 6

Though he be merry, yet withall he's honest.	1413
And honest company, I thanke you all,	1575
Euen in these honest meane habiliments:	2153
Priest, Clarke, and some sufficient honest witnesses:	2280
And wander we to see thy honest sonne,	2368
And not obedient to his honest will,	2716

HONIE = 1

Kate eate apace; and now my honie Loue,	2034

HONOR = 7*3

Say, what is it your Honor wil command:	58
Ser. An't please your Honor, Players | That offer seruice to your Lordship.	84
Now fellowes, you are welcome. | *Players.* We thanke your Honor.	88
*Sincklo. I thinke 'twas *Soto* that your honor meanes.	98
For yet his honor neuer heard a play)	106
And say: What is't your Honor will command,	126
*2.Ser. Wilt please your Honor taste of these Con- | serues?	155
3.Ser. What raiment wil your honor weare to day.	157
*Lord. Heauen cease this idle humor in your Honor.	166
So honor peereth in the meanest habit.	2157

HONORATA = *1

*Hor. Alla nostra casa bene venuto multo honorata signi- | *or mio Petruchio.*	593

HONORS = *1

*Mes. Your Honors Players hearing your amendment,	283

HONOUR = *1

*Beg. I am *Christophero Sly*, call not mee Honour nor	158

HONOURABLE = 1

He beare himselfe with honourable action,	121

HOOD = 1

Her widdow-hood, be it that she suruiue me	989

HOP = 2

Go hop me ouer euery kennell home,	2083
For you shall hop without my custome sir:	2084

HOPE = 8*1

I hope this reason stands for my excuse.	278
And I do hope, good dayes and long, to see.	758
Though *Paris* came, in hope to speed alone.	819
So shall you quietly enioy your hope,	1519
And 'tis my hope to end successfully:	1823
*Petr. Why how now *Kate*, I hope thou art not mad,	2340
Bion. I hope I may choose Sir.	2425
Out of hope of all, but my share of the feast.	2521
Praie God sir your wife send you not a worse. | *Petr.* I hope better.	2634

HOPES = 1

It shall become to serue all hopes conceiu'd	314

HOR = 45*13
HORNE = 1*1
  *Gru. Am I but three inches? Why thy horne is a foot   1665
  Would say your Head and But were head and horne.   2583
HORNES = *1
  *Winde hornes. Enter a Lord from hunting, with his traine.   18
HORSE = 7*11
  Another tell him of his Hounds and Horse,   65
  *best horse in *Padua* to begin his woing that would tho-|roughly 445
  *two broken points: his horse hip'd with an olde mo-|thy   1436
  *like the horse: with a linnen stock on one leg, and   1452
  *Bion. No sir, I say his horse comes with him on his | (backe. 1464
  *Bion. Nay by S.(aint) *Iamy*, I hold you a penny, a horse and 1466
  Kat. Now if you loue me stay. | *Pet. Grumio*, my horse. 1589
  My horse, my oxe, my asse, my any thing,   1618
  *Gru. First know my horse is tired, my master & mi-|stris falne out.
  Cur. How?   1688
  Cur. Both of one horse?   1701
  Gru. What's that to thee? | *Cur.* Why a horse.   1702
  *thou shouldst haue heard how her horse fel, and she vn-|der 1705
  *her horse: thou shouldst haue heard in how miery a   1706
  *horse vpon her, how he beat me because her horse stum-|bled, 1708
  To hold my stirrop, nor to take my horse?   1748
  *Pet. You pezant, swain, you horson malt-horse drudg   1756
  Pet. It shall be seuen ere I go to horse: 2174
HORSES = 4*2
  Or wilt thou ride? Thy horses shal be trap'd,   193
  *two and fiftie horses. Why nothing comes amisse, so | monie comes
  withall.   647
  *Gru. I sir, they be ready, the Oates haue eaten the | horses. 1591
  *how I cried, how the horses ranne away, how her   1711
  And bring our horses vnto Long-lane end,   2168
  Goe on, and fetch our horses backe againe,   2305
HORSE-TAILE = *1
  *presume to touch a haire of my Masters horse-taile, till 1722
HORSON = 2*1
  *Pet. You pezant, swain, you horson malt-horse drudg   1756
  You horson villaine, will you let it fall?   1784
  Pet. A horson beetle-headed flap-ear'd knaue: 1786
HORT = 10*3
HORTEN = *1
HORTENSIO see also Hor., Hort., Horten. = 24*4
  There, there *Hortensio*, will you any Wife?   358
  Fit to instruct her youth. If you *Hortensio*,   399
  *so great *Hortensio*, but we may blow our nails together, 412
  *Gre. I say, a diuell: Think'st thou *Hortensio*, though   427
  My best beloued and approued friend | *Hortensio*: & I trow this is his
  house: 568
  Enter Hortensio.   587
  *Petr. Signior *Hortensio*, come you to part the fray?   591
  Petr. A sencelesse villaine: good *Hortensio*,   603
  Signior *Hortensio*, thus it stands with me,   619
  Petr. Signior *Hortensio*, 'twixt such friends as wee,   631
  *Petr. Hortensio peace: thou knowst not golds effect,   659
  I wil not sleepe *Hortensio* til I see her,   669
  Gre. And you are wel met, Signior *Hortensio*.   729
  Hortensio, haue you told him all her faults?   752

HORTENSIO cont.

Grem. Hortensio hearke: | This Gentleman is happily arriu'd,	779
Hor. That she's the chosen of signior *Hortensio.*	809
Petr. Hortensio, to what end are all these words?	822
Kate. Minion thou lyest: Is't not *Hortensio?*	868
Enter Hortensio with his head broke.	1007
Hortensio will be quit with thee by changing. *Exit.*	1386
Enter Petruchio, Kate, Bianca, Hortensio, Baptista.	1565
Enter Tranio and Hortensio.	1846
Know sir, that I am cal'd *Hortensio.*	1869
Tra. Signior *Hortensio,* I haue often heard | Of your entire affection to	
Bianca,	1870
And haue forsworne you with *Hortensio.*	1895
Enter Petruchio, and Hortensio with meate.	2015
Petr. Eate it vp all *Hortensio,* if thou louest mee:	2032
Pet. Hortensio, say thou wilt see the Tailor paide:	2147

HORTENSIOS = 2

Are, to plead *Hortensio's* passion:	1367
Petr. Where is your sister, and *Hortensios* wife?	2656

HORTENTIO = 10

Gremio a Pantelowne, Hortentio sister to Bianca. | Lucen. Tranio, stand	
by.	348
Enter Lucentio, Hortentio, and Bianca.	1295
Hor. Yet read the gamouth of *Hortentio.*	1365
Enter Petruchio, Kate, Hortentio	2294
Then hast thou taught *Hortentio* to be vntoward. *Exit.*	2378
Brother *Petruchio,* sister *Katerina,* | And thou *Hortentio* with thy louing	
Widdow:	2543
Pet. Now for my life *Hortentio* feares his Widow.	2553
I meane *Hortentio* is afeard of you.	2557
Petr. Conceiues by me, how likes *Hortentio* that?	2562
Drinkes to Hortentio.	2579

HOSE = *2

*a kersey boot-hose on the other, gartred with a red and	1453
*hose, a scarlet cloake, and a copataine hat: oh I am	2445

HOST = 1*2

HOSTES = 1

Enter Begger and Hostes, Christophero Sly.	2

HOSTESSE *see also Hostes* = 1

And raile vpon the Hostesse of the house,	239

HOT = 4*1

Shee is not hot, but temperate as the morne,	1174
*now were I not a little pot, & soone hot; my very lippes	1644
Cur. Is she so hot a shrew as she's reported.	1659
cold comfort, for being slow in thy hot office.	1669
Gru. I, but the Mustard is too hot a little.	2003

HOUND = 2

Tri. Oh sir, *Lucentio* slipt me like his Gray-hound,	2595
Petr. Twentie crownes, | Ile venture so much of my Hawke or Hound,	2615

HOUNDS = 2*2

Lo. Huntsman I charge thee, tender wel my hounds,	19
Another tell him of his Hounds and Horse,	65
Thy hounds shall make the Welkin answer them	197
1.Man. Say thou wilt course, thy gray-hounds are as | (swift	199

HOURE = 1

And when in Musicke we haue spent an houre,	1302

HOURES = 2
What shall I be appointed houres, as though   407
*Bio. The old Priest at Saint *Lukes* Church is at your | command at all
hours.   2274
HOUSBAND = 1
Wid. Your housband being troubled with a shrew,   2568
HOUSE = 24*2
Let them want nothing that my house affoords. | *Exit one with the*
Players.   114
Lord. Hence comes it, that your kindred shuns your | (house   180
And raile vpon the Hostesse of the house,   239
Beg. I, the womans maide of the house.   243
3.Man. Why sir you know no house, nor no such maid   244
Schoolemasters will I keepe within my house,   398
*woe her, wed her, and bed her, and ridde the | house of her. Come on.   446
Keepe house, and ply his booke, welcome his friends,   502
We haue not yet bin seene in any house,   505
Keepe house, and port, and seruants, as I should,   509
My best beloued and approued friend | *Hortensio*: & I trow this is his
house: 568
To the house of Signior *Baptista Minola*?   789
Within your house, to make mine eye the witnesse   913
Gre. First, as you know, my house within the City   1228
To house or house-keeping: then at my farme   1238
Shee is my goods, my chattels, she is my house,   1616
cold. Where's the Cooke, is supper ready, the house   1681
And in my house you shal be friendly lodg'd,   1963
Will we returne vnto thy Fathers house,   2035
Brau'd in mine owne house with a skeine of thred: 2096
To feast and sport vs at thy fathers house,   2166
Tra. Sirs, this is the house, please it you that I call.   2181
Bap. Not in my house *Lucentio*, for you know   2233
Or ere I iourney to your Fathers house: 2304
Petr. Sir heres the doore, this is *Lucentios* house,   2389
Feast with the best, and welcome to my house,   2545
HOUSES = 1
Ile leaue her houses three or foure as good   1248
HOUSE-KEEPING = 1
To house or house-keeping: then at my farme   1238
HOUSHOLD = 2
Beg. What, houshold stuffe.   294
And bring you from a wilde *Kate* to a *Kate* | Conformable as other
houshold *Kates*:   1157
HOUSHOLD-STUFFE = 1
My houshold-stuffe, my field, my barne,   1617
HOW = 44*28
Saw'st thou not boy how *Siluer* made it good   22
Lord. Oh monstrous beast, how like a swine he lyes.   38
Grim death, how foule and loathsome is thine image: 39
How now? who is it?   83
And how my men will stay themselues from laughter,   146
Looke how thy seruants do attend on thee,   185
And how she was beguiled and surpriz'd,   207
Oh how we ioy to see your wit restor'd,   230
Lady. How fares my noble Lord?   254
For how I firmly am resolu'd you know: 351
Hor. Mates maid, how meane you that?   361

HOW *cont.*

fastest, gets the Ring: How say you signior *Gremio*?	443
Tra. Saw you no more? Mark'd you not how hir sister	474
Bion. Where haue I beene? Nay how now, where	529
Ile trie how you can *Sol, Fa,* and sing it. | *He rings him by the eares*	583
Hor. How now, what's the matter? My olde friend	588
Grumio, and my good friend *Petruchio*? How do you all | at *Verona*?	589
*how the young folkes lay their heads together.	705
Bap. Why how now Dame, whence growes this in- |solence?	879
Bap. How now my friend, why dost thou looke so | pale?	1008
Oh how I long to haue some chat with her.	1030
Bap. Now Signior *Petruchio,* how speed you with my | (daughter?	1161
Pet. How but well sir? how but well?	1162
Bap. Why how now daughter *Katherine,* in your | (dumps?	1164
I tell you 'tis incredible to beleeue | How much she loues me: oh the kindest *Kate,*	1186
How tame when men and women are alone,	1192
Luc. How fiery and forward our Pedant is,	1341
Bap. Is it new and olde too? how may that be?	1422
How does my father? gentles methinkes you frowne,	1476
But yet not stay, entreat me how you can.	1588
Tra. Shall sweet *Bianca* practise how to bride it?	1637
Cur. I prethee good *Grumio,* tell me, how goes the | world?	1670
Gru. First know my horse is tired, my master & mi- |stris falne out.	
Cur. How?	1688
*thou shouldst haue heard how her horse fel, and she vn- |der	1705
*her horse: thou shouldst haue heard in how miery a	1706
*place, how she was bemoil'd, how hee left her with the	1707
*horse vpon her, how he beat me because her horse stum- |bled,	1708
*how she waded through the durt to plucke him off	1709
*me: how he swore, how she prai'd, that neuer prai'd be- |fore:	1710
*how I cried, how the horses ranne away, how her	1711
*bridle was burst: how I lost my crupper, with manie	1712
Nat. Welcome home *Grumio.* | *Phil.* How now *Grumio.*	1735
Nat. How now old lad.	1739
Gru. Welcome you: how now you: what you: fel- |low	1740
Nat. All things is readie, how neere is our master?	1743
How durst you villaines bring it from the dresser	1795
He that knowes better how to tame a shrew,	1844
Hor. See how they kisse and court: Signior *Lucentio,*	1875
Fie on her, see how beastly she doth court him.	1882
Ped. My life sir? how I pray? for that goes hard.	1936
But I, who neuer knew how to intreat,	1985
How say you to a fat Tripe finely broyl'd?	1998
Petr. How fares my Kate, what sweeting all a-mort?	2016
Heere Loue, thou seest how diligent I am,	2020
Grumio gaue order how it should be done.	2103
Tail. But how did you desire it should be made?	2105
And how she's like to be *Lucentios* wife.	2249
Good Lord how bright and goodly shines the Moone.	2297
Petr. Why how now *Kate,* I hope thou art not mad,	2340
Petr. Why how now gentleman: why this is flat kna- |uerie	2415
Tra. How now, what's the matter?	2449
Bap. How hast thou offended, where is *Lucentio*?	2494
Kat. Mistris, how meane you that? | *Wid.* Thus I conceiue by him.	2560
Petr. Conceiues by me, how likes *Hortentio* that?	2562
Bap. How likes *Gremio* these quicke witted folkes?	2580

HOW *cont.*

How now, what newes?	2628
Petr. How? she's busie, and she cannot come: is that | an answere?	2631

HOWRES = 1

Ile not be tied to howres, nor pointed times,	1314

HOWSOERE = 1

Bap. I am glad he's come, howsoere he comes.	1459

HUE = 1

Is straight, and slender, and as browne in hue	1133

HUMBLE = 3

Wherein your Ladie, and your humble wife,	127
That made great *Ioue* to humble him to her hand,	472
Yet if thy thoughts *Bianca* be so humble	1383

HUMBLY = 1

Sir, to your pleasure humbly I subscribe:	384

HUMOR = 2*4

Lord. Heauen cease this idle humor in your Honor.	166
Gru. I pray you Sir let him go while the humor lasts.	673
*blew lift; an old hat, & the humor of forty fancies prickt	1454
Tra. 'Tis some od humor pricks him to this fashion,	1457
Peter. He kils her in her owne humor.	1813
And thus Ile curbe her mad and headstrong humor:	1843

HUMOUR = 1

Much more a shrew of impatient humour.	1418

HUNDRED = 3*3

I haue a hundred milch-kine to the pale,	1239
Vinc. What if a man bring him a hundred pound or | two to make merrie withall.	2402
Ped. Keepe your hundred pounds to your selfe, hee	2404
Petr. A hundred marks, my *Kate* does put her down.	2576
Luc. A hundred then. | *Hor.* Content.	2618
Hath cost me fiue hundred crownes since supper time.	2684

HUNG = 1

Shee hung about my necke, and kisse on kisse	1188

HUNGERLY = *1

*his beard grew thinne and hungerly, and seem'd to aske	1557

HUNT = 2

To morrow I intend to hunt againe. | *Hunts.* I will my Lord.	32
Aboue the morning Larke. Or wilt thou hunt,	196

HUNTED = 1

Tra. 'Tis well sir that you hunted for your selfe:	2598

HUNTING = *1

Winde hornes. Enter a Lord from hunting, with his traine.	18

HUNTS = 2

HUNTSMAN *see also Hunts., 1.Hun., 1.Hunts., 2.H., 2.Hun.* = *1

Lo. Huntsman I charge thee, tender wel my hounds,	19

HURLIE = 1

I, and amid this hurlie I intend,	1837

HUSBAND *see also* housband = 11*7

I long to heare him call the drunkard husband,	145
Beg. Are you my wife, and will not cal me husband?	258
La. My husband and my Lord, my Lord and husband	260
Before I haue a husband for the elder:	353
Gre. What's that I pray? | *Hor.* Marrie sir to get a husband for her Sister.	423
Gre. A husband: a diuell. | *Hor.* I say a husband.	425
Baptistas eldest daughter to a husband, wee set his	440

HUSBAND *cont.*

*yongest free for a husband, and then haue too't afresh:	441
Til *Katherine* the Curst, haue got a husband.	693
She is your treasure, she must haue a husband,	890
Now *Kate*, I am a husband for your turne,	1151
Kate. I pray you husband be not so disquiet,	1800
*vndone, I am vndone: while I plaie the good husband	2446
Kate. Husband let's follow, to see the end of this adoe.	2522
Thy husband is thy Lord, thy life, thy keeper,	2704
Euen such a woman oweth to her husband:	2714

HUSBANDED = 1

If it be husbanded with modestie.	72

HUSBANDS = 3*1

Measures my husbands sorrow by his woe:	2569
Swinge me them soundly forth vnto their husbands:	2659
*women, what dutie they doe owe their Lords and hus-|bands.	2687
And place your hands below your husbands foote:	2735

HUSHT = *1

*Tra. Husht master, heres some good pastime toward;	371

I = 505*113, 26*5

As breathed Stags: I fleeter then the Roe.	200
Beg. I, the womans maide of the house.	243
Lady. I, and the time seeme's thirty vnto me,	268
Beg. I, it stands so that I may hardly tarry so long:	279
Tra. I marry am I sir, and now 'tis plotted.	*Luc.* I haue it *Tranio.*	491
You vnderstand me?	*Bion.* I sir, ne're a whit.	542
Gru. Wil he woo her? I: or Ile hang her.	764
Bap. I, when the speciall thing is well obtain'd,	993
Pet. I to the proofe, as Mountaines are for windes,	1005
Kat. I for a Turtle, as he takes a buzard.	1083
Kate. I, if the foole could finde it where it lies.	1088
Bion. Who, that *Petruchio* came?	*Bap.* I, that *Petruchio* came.	1462
I, by goggs woones quoth he, and swore so loud,	1544
Gru. I sir, they be ready, the Oates haue eaten the	horses.	1591
Gre. I marry sir, now it begins to worke.	1604
Gru. Oh I *Curtis* I, and therefore fire, fire, cast on no	water.	1657
Gru. I, and that thou and the proudest of you all shall	1716
What's this, Mutton?	1.*Ser.* I.	1789
I, and amid this hurlie I intend,	1837
Bian. God giue him ioy.	*Tra.* I, and hee'l tame her.	1902
Tra. I mistris, and *Petruchio* is the master,	1907
Ped. I sir, in Pisa haue I often bin,	1950
Gru. I, but the Mustard is too hot a little.	2003
Pet. Thy gowne, why I: come Tailor let vs see't.	2071
Pet. I there's the villanie.	2127
Ped. I what else, and but I be deceiued,	2182
Ped. I sir, so his mother saies, if I may beleeue her.	2414
Vin. I Mistris Bride, hath that awakened you?	2584
Bian. I, but not frighted me, therefore Ile sleepe a-|gaine.	2585
Gre. I, and a kinde one too:	2633

IACKE = 1*2

*And twangling Iacke, with twentie such vilde tearmes,	1026
A mad-cap ruffian, and a swearing Iacke,	1168
Gru. Why Iacke boy, ho boy, and as much newes as	wilt thou.	1677

IACKES = *1

*his wedding garment on? Be the Iackes faire with-|in,	1684

IADE = 2
   Luc. Sir giue him head, I know hee'l proue a Iade.   821
   Kate. No such Iade as you, if me you meane.   1075
IADES = *1
   *Gru. Fie, fie on all tired Iades, on all mad Masters, z   1640
IAILE = 3*1
   **the Iaile: father *Baptista*, I charge you see that hee be | forth comming.   2470
   Vinc. Carrie me to the Iaile?   2472
   Bap. Awaie with the dotard, to the Iaile with him.   2484
   *Vin. Ile slit the villaines nose that would haue sent | me to the Iaile.   2511
IAMY = *1
   *Bion. Nay by S.(aint) *Iamy*, I hold you a penny, a horse and   1466
IARRES = 1
   Bian. Let's heare, oh fie, the treble iarres.   1332
IARRING = 1
   Luc. At last, though long, our iarring notes agree,   2538
IARS = *1
   *Hort. The base is right, 'tis the base knaue that iars.   1340
IAY = 1
   What is the Iay more precious then the Larke?   2158
IBAT = *3
   *Luc. Heere Madam: *Hic Ibat Simois, hic est sigeria*   1322
   *Luc. *Hic Ibat*, as I told you before, *Simois*, I am Lu- | centio,   1325
   *Bian. Now let mee see if I can conster it. *Hic ibat si- | mois*,   1334
ICE = 1*1
   And if you breake the ice, and do this seeke,   839
   *Gru. A piece of Ice: if thou doubt it, thou maist   1652
IDELY = 1
   But see, while idely I stood looking on,   453
IDLE = 1*1
   *Lord. Heauen cease this idle humor in your Honor.   166
   1.*Man*. Oh yes my Lord, but verie idle words,   236
IDLENESSE = 1
   I found the effect of Loue in idlenesse,   454
IEALOUS = 1
   For our first merriment hath made thee iealous. *Exeunt*.   2375
IERKIN = *1
   **an old ierkin, a paire of old breeches thrice turn'd; a   1432
IERONIMIE = *1
   *Beg. No, not a deniere: go by S.(aint) *Ieronimie*, goe to thy | cold bed,
   and warme thee.   11
IEST = 8*2
   Then take him vp, and manage well the iest: 49
   Luc. Sirra come hither, 'tis no time to iest,   533
   I will continue that I broach'd in iest,   650
   Nay then you iest, and now I wel perceiue   874
   *Ka. If that be iest, then all the rest was so. *Strikes her*   877
   *Bian. *Tranio* you iest, but haue you both forsworne | mee?   1896
   Like pleasant trauailors to breake a Iest   2371
   Haue at you for a better iest or too.   2588
   And as the Iest did glaunce awaie from me,   2604
   Bion. She saies you haue some goodly Iest in hand,   2643
IESTED = 1
   You haue but iested with me all this while: 875
IESTS = 1
   Hiding his bitter iests in blunt behauiour,   1401

IEWEL = 1
He hath the Iewel of my life in hold, 684
IF *l.*29 41 56 72 109 135 *159 *174 *175 233 274 341 354 366 399 *414 459
464 481 *555 *597 632 642 745 750 754 760 787 800 *801 807 810 837
839 869 *877 964 984 1010 1046 1048 1075 1086 1088 1093 1097 1099
1100 1120 1172 1183 1243 1244 1247 1265 1271 1278 1279 *1293 *1334
1383 1385 1408 1478 1543 1549 *1552 *1554 1573 1589 1607 1623 *1652
1801 1840 1873 1920 1923 1931 1967 1984 1991 2032 2061 2081 2116
*2118 2164 2214 2225 2247 2281 2290 2293 2310 2349 2377 *2402 2414
*2453 *2459 2479 2554 2658 2661 2736 = 89*17
IFAITH *see also* 'faith, infaith, y'faith = 2
Kate. I'faith sir, you shall neuer neede to feare, 364
Tra. I'faith hee'l haue a lustie Widdow now, 1900
IGNORANT = 1
Whereof I know she is not ignorant, 919
ILE *l.*4 *15 *16 141 148 *161 577 582 583 628 630 *678 711 716 720 746
764 859 870 886 988 1020 1037 1039 1041 1044 1046 1048 1096 1097
1179 1248 1314 1343 1497 1510 1525 1542 1598 1620 1625 1799 1834
1835 1840 1843 1921 1975 2031 2053 2085 *2130 *2149 2292 *2384
*2511 2520 *2585 2616 2625 2626 = 53*9
ILL = 1
Muddie, ill seeming, thicke, bereft of beautie, 2701
ILL-FAUOURD = 1
And wish thee to a shrew'd ill-fauour'd wife? 626
IMAGE = 1
Grim death, how foule and loathsome is thine image: 39
IMAGINE = 1
Imagine 'twere the right *Vincentio.* 2193
IMBOST = 1
Brach *Meriman*, the poore Curre is imbost, 20
IMBRACE = 1
Let me imbrace with old *Vincentio*, 2367
IMMORTALL = *1
Vinc. What am I sir: nay what are you sir: oh immor-|tall 2443
IMPARTED = 1
As before imparted to your worship, 1513
IMPATIENT = 3
If you should smile, he growes impatient. 109
When (with a most impatient diuellish spirit) 1019
Much more a shrew of impatient humour. 1418
IMPORT = 1
Tra. And tell vs what occasion of import 1485
IMPORTUNE = 1
Bap. Gentlemen, importune me no farther, 350
IMPOSSIBLE = 3
Supposing it a thing impossible, 688
It were impossible I should speed amisse. 1163
Tra. Curster then she, why 'tis impossible. 1538
IMPREMENDUM = *1
preuilegio ad Impremendum solem, to th' Church take the 2279
IN *see also* a, i' = 198*42
INCH = 1*1
*him by Law. Ile not budge an inch boy: Let him come, | and kindly.
Falles asleepe. 16
Gru. Away you three inch foole, I am no beast. 1664
INCHES = *1
Gru. Am I but three inches? Why thy horne is a foot 1665

INCOMPARABLE = 1
A Merchant of incomparable wealth. 1954
INCREDIBLE = 1
I tell you 'tis incredible to beleeue | How much she loues me: oh the
kindest *Kate*, 1186
INCURRE = 1
In perill to incurre your former malady, 276
INDEED = 2*1
Hor. The motions good indeed, and be it so, 853
Gre. A bridegroome say you? 'tis a groome indeed, 1536
That seeming to be most, which we indeed least are. 2733
INDEEDE = 3*1
Vpon my life I am a Lord indeede, 224
*that *Lucentio* indeede had *Baptistas* yongest daugh-|ter. 548
Vin. Ist so indeede. *He beates Biondello.* 2434
Kat. And I am meane indeede, respecting you. 2573
INDIFFERENT = 1*1
Ile tel you newes indifferent good for either. 746
*their blew coats brush'd, and their garters of an indiffe-|rent 1720
INDURD = 2
Your betters haue indur'd me say my minde, 2060
Oh vilde, intollerable, not to be indur'd: 2646
INDURE = 1
That mortal eares might hardly indure the din. 476
INFAITH = 2
Begger. | Ile pheeze you infaith. 3
Pet. You lye infaith, for you are call'd plaine *Kate*, 1056
INFECTED = *1
*with the Lampasse, infected with the fashions, full 1439
INFERIOUR = 1
And yet shee is inferiour to none. 219
INFORCED = 1
Though in some part inforced to digresse, 1490
INFUSED = 1
Should be infused with so foule a spirit. 169
INGENIOUS = 1
A course of Learning, and ingenious studies. 308
INGRATE = 1
Wil not so gracelesse be, to be ingrate. 842
INIURIE = 1
For such an iniurie would vexe a very saint, 1417
INPRIMIS = 1*1
*now I begin, Inprimis wee came downe a fowle 1699
Tail. Inprimis, a loose bodied gowne. 2117
INS = 1
Gru. The note lies in's throate if he say I said so. 2116
INSOLENCE = *1
Bap. Why how now Dame, whence growes this in-|solence? 879
INSOOTH = 1*1
Petr. Sir vnderstand you this of me (insooth) 831
Pet. Nay heare you *Kate.* Insooth you scape not so. 1119
INSTITUTE = 1
Heere let vs breath, and haply institute 307
INSTRUCT = 6
Fit to instruct her youth. If you *Hortensio*, 399
To get her cunning Schoolemasters to instruct her. 490
Well seene in Musicke, to instruct *Bianca*, 699

INSTRUCT *cont.*
   A fine Musitian to instruct our Mistris, 739
   To instruct her fully in those sciences, 918
   In all these circumstances Ile instruct you, 1975
INSTRUCTIONS = 1
   Anon Ile giue thee more instructions. | *Exit a seruingman.* 141
INSTRUMENT = 5
   I heere bestow a simple instrument, 962
   And through the instrument my pate made way, 1022
   Take you your instrument, play you the whiles, 1317
   Luc. That will be neuer, tune your instrument. 1320
   Hor. Madam, before you touch the instrument, 1357
INSTRUMENTS = 3
   My bookes and instruments shall be my companie, 385
   In Musicke, Instruments, and Poetry, 397
   Hort. Madam, my Instrument's in tune. 1331
INT = *1
   *in't for a feather: a monster, a very monster in apparell, 1455
INTEND = 3
   To morrow I intend to hunt againe. | *Hunts.* I will my Lord. 32
   Lord. Do you intend to stay with me to night? 90
   I, and amid this hurlie I intend, 1837
INTENT = 1
   Petr. Why came I hither, but to that intent? 765
INTERRUPTED = 1
   And happilie we might be interrupted. 2236
INTITLE = 1
   I may intitle thee my louing Father, 2360
INTO *l.*107 130 150 *280 545 621 1381 1526 *1690 2503 = 8*2
INTOLLERABLE = 2
   Is, that she is intollerable curst, 655
   Oh vilde, intollerable, not to be indur'd: 2646
INTREAT = 6
   La. Thrice noble Lord, let me intreat of you 272
   You would intreat me rather goe then stay: 1574
   Tra. Let vs intreat you stay till after dinner. 1580
   Pet. It may not be. | *Gra.* Let me intreat you. 1581
   Pet. It cannot be. | *Kat.* Let me intreat you. 1583
   But I, who neuer knew how to intreat, 1985
INTREATE = 2*2
   Neuer to marrie with her, though she would intreate, 1881
   Nor neuer needed that I should intreate, 1986
   Hor. Sirra *Biondello*, goe and intreate my wife to 2636
   Pet. Oh ho, intreate her, nay then shee must needes | come. 2638
INTREATIE = 1
   Vpon intreatie haue a present almes, 1983
INUENTIONS = 2
   Tra. Master, for my hand, | Both our inuentions meet and iumpe in
   one. 493
   To charge true rules for old inuentions. 1374
INUITE = 1
   Make friends, inuite, and proclaime the banes, 1404
IO = 1
   Lord. Wee'l shew thee *Io*, as she was a Maid, 206
IOGGING = 1
   You may be iogging whiles your bootes are greene: 1597

IOHN = 1
As *Stephen Slie*, and old *Iohn Naps* of Greece, | And *Peter Turph*, and
Henry Pimpernell,   246
IOLLY = 1
'Tis like you'll proue a iolly surly groome,   1599
IOLT-HEADS = 1
You heedlesse iolt-heads, and vnmanner'd slaues.   1798
IONE = 1
Beg. Alce Madam, or *Ione* Madam?   264
IOS = 1
IOSEPH see also Ios. = *1
*Call forth *Nathaniel, Ioseph, Nicholas, Phillip, Walter, Su-|gersop*   1718
IOT = 1
Luc. And not a iot of *Tranio* in your mouth,   544
IOUE = 1
That made great *Ioue* to humble him to her hand,   472
IOURNEY = 2
(Trauelling some iourney) to repose him heere.   81
Or ere I iourney to your Fathers house: 2304
IOY = 3
Oh how we ioy to see your wit restor'd,   230
God send you ioy, *Petruchio*, 'tis a match.   1199
Bian. God giue him ioy. | *Tra.* I, and hee'l tame her.   1902
IOYED = 1
Bid him shed teares, as being ouer-ioyed   131
IOYFULL = 1
We shall be ioyfull of thy companie.   2350
IOYND = 1
Pet. Why, what's a mouable? | *Kat.* A ioyn'd stoole.   1070
IOYNTER = 1
Of fruitfull land, all which shall be her ioynter.   1252
IOYOUS = 1
Who will of thy arriuall be full ioyous.   2369
IRKESOME = 1
Petr. I know she is an irkesome brawling scold: 753
IRON = 1
Iron may hold with her, but neuer Lutes.   1014
IS *see also* cakes, counsels, first's, heere's, heer's, here's, hee's, he's,
Instrument's, motions, shees, she's, that's, there's, 'tis, what's, where's,
who's = 220*41
IST = 5*1
And say: What is't your Honor will command,   126
Bion. He that ha's the two faire daughters: ist he you | meane?   790
Kate. Minion thou lyest: Is't not *Hortensio*?   868
Bap. Is't possible you will away to night?   1571
Tra. Is't possible friend *Lisio*, that mistris *Bianca*   1847
Vin. Ist so indeede. *He beates Biondello.*   2434
IT *see also* an't, ha't, in't, is't, let't, morrow't, see't, 't, 'tis, too't,
wilt = 174*22
ITALIAN = 1
An olde Italian foxe is not so kinde my boy. *Exit.*   1285
ITALY = 2
The pleasant garden of great *Italy*,   303
A man well knowne throughout all Italy.   930
ITH = 2*2
And *Gabrels* pumpes were all vnpinkt i'thheele: 1760
Gru. Error i'th bill sir, error i'th bill? I commanded   2128

THE TAMING OF THE SHREW

ITH *cont.*
  Gru. You are i'th right sir, 'tis for my mistris.   2139
ITSELFE *see* selfe
IUGS = 1
  Because she brought stone-Iugs, and no seal'd quarts: 241
IUMPE = 1
  Tra. Master, for my hand, | Both our inuentions meet and iumpe in
one.   493
IUNKETS = 1
  You know there wants no iunkets at the feast: 1634
IUORY = 1
  In Iuory cofers I haue stuft my crownes: 1232
IUST = 1
  Iust as my master had direction: 2102
I-WIS = 1
  I-wis it is not halfe way to her heart: 365
KA = 1
  Ile buckler thee against a Million. *Exeunt. P. Ka.*   1625
KA = *2
KAT = 12*1
KATE = 57*8
  I prethee sister Kate, vntie my hands.   876
  Or shall I send my daughter *Kate* to you. | *Exit. Manet Petruchio.*   1035
  Good morrow *Kate*, for thats your name I heare.   1052
  Pet. You lye infaith, for you are call'd plaine *Kate*,   1056
  And bony *Kate*, and sometimes *Kate* the curst: 1057
  But *Kate*, the prettiest *Kate* in Christendome,   1058
  Kate of *Kate*-hall, my super-daintie *Kate*,   1059
  For dainties are all *Kates*, and therefore *Kate*   1060
  Take this of me, *Kate* of my consolation,   1061
  Pet. Alas good *Kate*, I will not burthen thee,   1076
  Nay, come againe, good *Kate*, I am a Gentleman,   1095
  Pet. A Herald *Kate*? Oh put me in thy bookes.   1101
  Pet. A comblesse Cocke, so *Kate* will be my Hen.   1103
  Pet. Nay come *Kate*, come: you must not looke so | sowre.   1105
  Pet. Nay heare you *Kate*. Insooth you scape not so.   1119
  Why does the world report that *Kate* doth limpe?   1131
  Oh sland'rous world: *Kate* like the hazle twig   1132
  As *Kate* this chamber with her princely gate: 1138
  O be thou *Dian*, and let her be *Kate*,   1139
  And then let *Kate* be chaste, and *Dian* sportfull.   1140
  Now *Kate*, I am a husband for your turne,   1151
  For I am he borne to tame your *Kate*,   1156
  And bring you from a wilde *Kate* to a *Kate* | Conformable as other
houshold *Kates*:   1157
  I tell you 'tis incredible to beleeue | How much she loues me: oh the
kindest *Kate*,   1186
  Giue me thy hand *Kate*, I will vnto *Venice*   1194
  And kisse me *Kate*, we will be married a sonday. | *Exit Petruchio and
Katherine.*   1204
  But where is *Kate*? where is my louely Bride?   1475
  But where is *Kate*? I stay too long from her,   1493
  'Twere well for *Kate*, and better for my selfe.   1503
  Enter Petruchio, Kate, Bianca, Hortensio, Baptista.   1565
  Pet. O *Kate* content thee, prethee be not angry.   1601
  Pet. They shall goe forward *Kate* at thy command,   1608
  But for my bonny *Kate*, she must with me: 1613

119

KATE *cont.*

Feare not sweet wench, they shall not touch thee *Kate*,	1624
Enter Petruchio and Kate.	1746
Where are those? Sit downe *Kate*,	1768
Why when I say? Nay good sweete *Kate* be merrie.	1771
Be merrie *Kate*: Some water heere: what hoa.	1777
One *Kate* you must kisse, and be acquainted with.	1781
Come *Kate* and wash, & welcome heartily:	1783
Come *Kate* sit downe, I know you haue a stomacke,	1787
Will you giue thankes, sweete *Kate*, or else shall I?	1788
Pet. I tell thee *Kate*, 'twas burnt and dried away,	1802
*Petr. How fares my *Kate*, what sweeting all a-mort?	2016
I am sure sweet *Kate*, this kindnesse merites thankes.	2022
Come Mistris Kate, Ile beare you companie.	2031
Kate eate apace; and now my honie Loue,	2034
*Pet. Well, come my *Kate*, we will vnto your fathers,	2152
Oh no good *Kate*: neither art thou the worse	2162
Enter Petruchio, Kate, Hortentio	2294
Tell me sweete *Kate*, and tell me truely too,	2326
Sweete *Kate* embrace her for her beauties sake.	2332
*Petr. Why how now *Kate*, I hope thou art not mad,	2340
Enter Petruchio, Kate, Vincentio, Grumio | with Attendants.	2387
*Petr. Preethe *Kate* let's stand aside and see the end of | this controuersie.	2438
Petr. First kisse me *Kate*, and we will.	2523
Petr. Is not this well? come my sweete *Kate*.	2531
Petr. To her *Kate*. | *Hor.* To her *Widdow*.	2574
*Petr. A hundred marks, my *Kate* does put her down.	2576
Enter Kate, Bianca, and Widdow.	2674
Pet. Come *Kate*, wee'le to bed,	2743

KATE = 57*11
KATED = 1

Gre. I warrant him *Petruchio* is Kated.	1631

KATERINA see also Ka., Kat., Kate. = 6*1

*Enter Baptista with his two daughters, Katerina & Bianca,	347
*Pet. And you good sir: pray haue you not a daugh-|ter, cal'd *Katerina*, faire and vertuous.	903
Bap. I haue a daughter sir, cal'd *Katerina*.	905
Enter Katerina.	1051
Brother *Petruchio*, sister *Katerina*, | And thou *Hortentio* with thy louing *Widdow*:	2543
Enter Katerina.	2653
Bap. Now by my hollidam here comes *Katerina*.	2654

KATERINE = 3

But for my daughter *Katerine*, this I know,	923
They call me *Katerine*, that do talke of me.	1055
Katerine, that Cap of yours becomes you not,	2677

KATES = 2

For dainties are all *Kates*, and therefore *Kate*	1060
And bring you from a wilde *Kate* to a *Kate* | Conformable as other houshold *Kates*:	1157

KATE-HALL = 1

Kate of *Kate*-hall, my super-daintie *Kate*,	1059

KATHERINA = 6

If either of you both loue *Katherina*,	354
And so farewell: *Katherina* you may stay,	404
Her name is *Katherina Minola*,	665

KATHERINA *cont.*
  That euer *Katherina* wil be woo'd: 690
  Enter Katherina and Bianca. 855
  Enter Katherina and Grumio. 1978
KATHERINE *see also Ka.* = 14*4
  Til *Katherine* the Curst, haue got a husband. 693
  Gru. Katherine the curst, | A title for a maide, of all titles the worst. 694
  Will vndertake to woo curst *Katherine,* 749
  Pet. Marry so I meane sweet *Katherine* in thy bed: 1146
  I must, and will haue *Katherine* to my wife. 1160
  **Bap.* Why how now daughter *Katherine,* in your | (dumps? 1164
  I will be sure my *Katherine* shall be fine. 1197
  And kisse me *Kate,* we will be married a sonday. | *Exit Petruchio and*
  Katherine. 1204
  On sonday next, you know | My daughter *Katherine* is to be married: 1275
  Her sister *Katherine* welcom'd you withall. 1298
  **Enter Baptista, Gremio, Tranio, Katherine, Bianca, and o-|thers,*
  attendants. 1387
  That *Katherine* and *Petruchio* should be married, 1390
  Now must the world point at poore *Katherine,* 1406
  Tra. Patience good *Katherine* and *Baptista* too, 1409
  **Kate.* Would *Katherine* had neuer seen him though. | *Exit weeping.* 1414
  Should aske if *Katherine* should be his wife, 1543
  And so it shall be so for *Katherine.* 2319
  **Pet. Katherine* I charge thee tell these head-strong 2686
KEEPE = 11*2
  Schoolemasters will I keepe within my house, 398
  Keepe house, and ply his booke, welcome his friends, 502
  Keepe house, and port, and seruants, as I should, 509
  But I will charme him first to keepe his tongue. 515
  For in *Baptistas* keepe my treasure is: 683
  You wil haue *Gremio* to keepe you faire. 872
  Pet. Am I not wise? | *Kat.* Yes, keepe you warme. 1144
  *being restrain'd to keepe him from stumbling, hath been 1445
  Sufficeth I am come to keepe my word, 1489
  Ile keepe mine owne despite of all the world. 1525
  And with the clamor keepe her stil awake: 1841
  For me, that I may surely keepe mine oath. 1884
  **Ped.* Keepe your hundred pounds to your selfe, hee 2404
KEEPER = 1
  Thy husband is thy Lord, thy life, thy keeper, 2704
KEEPERS = 1
  To make her come, and know her Keepers call: 1828
KEEPES = 1
  Her father keepes from all accesse of sutors, 833
KEEPING = 1
  To house or house-keeping: then at my farme 1238
KEEPST = 1
  Kate. Go foole, and whom thou keep'st command. 1136
KENNELL = 1
  Go hop me ouer euery kennell home, 2083
KEPT = 2
  That couenants may be kept on either hand. 992
  With oathes kept waking, and with brawling fed, 1988
KERNELS = 1
  As hazle nuts, and sweeter then the kernels: 1134

KERSEY = *1
*a kersey boot-hose on the other, gartred with a red and 1453
KIL = 1
This is a way to kil a Wife with kindnesse, 1842
KILD = 1
I kil'd a man, and feare I was descried: 539
KILS = 1
Peter. He kils her in her owne humor. 1813
KIND = *1
*you vse your manners discreetly in all kind of com-|panies: 550
KINDE = 6
And then with kinde embracements, tempting kisses, 129
Lady. It is a kinde of history. | *Beg.* Well, we'l see't: 295
I will be very kinde and liberall, 402
An olde Italian foxe is not so kinde my boy. *Exit.* 1285
Petr. Padua affords nothing but what is kinde. 2551
Gre. I, and a kinde one too: 2633
KINDELY = 1
More kindely beholding to you then any: 941
KINDEST = 1
I tell you 'tis incredible to beleeue | How much she loues me: oh the
kindest *Kate,* 1186
KINDLY = 2
*him by Law. Ile not budge an inch boy: Let him come, | and kindly.
Falles asleepe. 16
This do, and do it kindly, gentle sirs, 70
KINDNESSE = 6
The like kindnesse my selfe, that haue beene 940
This is a way to kil a Wife with kindnesse, 1842
Kindnesse in women, not their beauteous lookes 1889
I am sure sweet Kate, this kindnesse merites thankes. 2022
While I with selfesame kindnesse welcome thine: 2542
Bap. Padua affords this kindnesse, sonne *Petruchio.* 2550
KINDRED = *2
Lord. Hence comes it, that your kindred shuns your | (house 180
*saddle, and stirrops of no kindred: besides possest 1437
KINE = 1
I haue a hundred milch-kine to the pale, 1239
KING = 1
To wound thy Lord, thy King, thy Gouernour. 2696
KISSE = 8*4
Shee hung about my necke, and kisse on kisse 1188
And kisse me *Kate,* we will be married a sonday. | *Exit Petruchio and
Katherine.* 1204
And seale the title with a louely kisse. *Exit.* 1506
they kisse their hands. Are they all readie? 1723
One *Kate* you must kisse, and be acquainted with. 1781
Hor. See how they kisse and court: Signior *Lucentio,* 1875
Petr. First kisse me *Kate,* and we will. 2523
Kate. No sir, God forbid, but asham'd to kisse. 2526
Kate. Nay, I will giue thee a kisse, now praie thee | Loue staie. 2529
Petr. Verie well mended: kisse him for that good | Widdow. 2564
Pet. Why there's a wench: Come on, and kisse mee | *Kate.* 2738
KISSES = 1
And then with kinde embracements, tempting kisses, 129
KIST = 1*1
When with his knees he kist the Cretan strond. 473

KIST *cont.*
*Bride about the necke, and kist her lips with such a cla- | morous   1559
KITES = 1
That is, to watch her, as we watch these Kites,   1829
KNACKE = 1
A knacke, a toy, a tricke, a babies cap: 2051
KNAUE = 3*3
*sheere Ale, score me vp for the lyingst knaue in Christen | dome. What
    I am not bestraught: here's---   176
**Hort.* The base is right, 'tis the base knaue that iars.   1340
Now for my life the knaue doth court my loue,   1342
Where is the foolish knaue I sent before?   1754
Pet. A horson beetle-headed flap-ear'd knaue: 1786
**Tra.* Call forth an officer: Carrie this mad knaue to   2469
KNAUERIE = *3
**Gru.* Heere's no knauerie. See, to beguile the olde- | folkes,   704
**Petr.* Why how now gentleman: why this is flat kna- | uerie   2415
**Bap.* And I to sound the depth of this knauerie. *Exit.*   2517
KNAUES = 2*2
And rap me well, or Ile knocke your knaues pate.   577
*may perhaps call him halfe a score Knaues, or so: Why   676
**Pet.* Where be these knaues? What no man at doore   1747
And bring along these rascal knaues with thee?   1758
KNAURY = 1
With Amber Bracelets, Beades, and all this knau'ry.   2040
KNEELE = 2
Luc. Pardon sweete father. *Kneele.*   2491
To offer warre, where they should kneele for peace: 2720
KNEES = 1
When with his knees he kist the Cretan strond.   473
KNEW = 8*3
Oh that once more you knew but what you are: 231
**Kate.* A pretty peate, it is best put finger in the eye, | and she knew
    why.   381
(Belike) I knew not what to take, | And what to leaue? Ha. *Exit*   408
And he knew my deceased father well: 668
*A my word, and she knew him as wel as I do, she would   674
You knew my father well, and in him me,   981
Remoue you hence: I knew you at the first | You were a mouable.   1068
Make it no wonder: if you knew my businesse,   1573
But I, who neuer knew how to intreat,   1985
**Biond.* I cannot tarry: I knew a wench maried in an   2284
**Vin.* His name, as if I knew not his name: I haue   2459
KNIT = *1
*knit, let them curtsie with their left legges, and not   1721
KNO = 1
Gre. For this reason if you'l kno,   807
KNOCK = 1
And by all likelihood some cheere is toward. *Knock.*   2394
KNOCKE = 9*10
Heere sirra *Grumio*, knocke I say.   570
**Gru.* Knocke sir? whom should I knocke? Is there   571
Petr. Villaine I say, knocke me heere soundly.   573
**Gru.* Knocke you heere sir? Why sir, what am I sir,   574
that I should knocke you heere sir.   575
Petr. Villaine I say, knocke me at this gate,   576
And rap me well, or Ile knocke your knaues pate.   577

KNOCKE *cont.*

I should knocke you first,	579
Petr. Will it not be? | 'Faith sirrah, and you'l not knocke, Ile ring it,	581
Petr. Now knocke when I bid you: sirrah villaine	586
*looke you sir: He bid me knocke him, & rap him sound-|ly	598
I bad the rascall knocke vpon your gate,	604
Gru. Knocke at the gate? O heauens: spake you not	606
*these words plaine? Sirra, Knocke me heere: rappe me	607
*heere: knocke me well, and knocke me soundly? And	608
*Cuffe was but to knocke at your eare, and beseech list-|ning:	1698
Grem. They're busie within, you were best knocke | lowder.	2395

KNOCKES = *1

Ped. What's he that knockes as he would beat downe | the gate?	2398

KNOCKING = 1

come you now with knocking at the gate?	609

KNOCKT = *1

*out? Whom would to God I had well knockt at first,	601

KNOTS = *1

*often burst, and now repaired with knots: one girth sixe	1446

KNOW = 41 *11

Host. I know my remedie, I must go fetch the Head-|borough.	13
I know the boy will wel vsurpe the grace,	143
*know me not: if she say I am not xiiii.d. on the score for	175
3.Man. Why sir you know no house, nor no such maid	244
Beg. I know it well, what must I call her? | *Lord.* Madam.	262
For how I firmly am resolu'd you know:	351
Because I know you well, and loue you well,	355
And for I know she taketh most delight	396
Or signior *Gremio* you know any such,	400
*parle, know now vpon aduice, it toucheth vs both: that	419
Counsaile me *Tranio*, for I know thou canst:	460
Assist me *Tranio*, for I know thou wilt.	461
And then I know after who comes by the worst.	580
Few words suffice: and therefore, if thou know	632
Petr. I know her father, though I know not her,	667
*with it, that shee shal haue no more eies to see withall | then a Cat: you know him not sir.	680
Petr. I know she is an irkesome brawling scold:	753
Luc. Sir giue him head, I know hee'l proue a Iade.	821
So well I know my dutie to my elders.	862
Whereof I know she is not ignorant,	919
But for my daughter *Katerine*, this I know,	923
Bap. I know him well: you are welcome for his sake.	931
*May I be so bold, to know the cause of your comming?	950
I know him well: you are verie welcome sir:	968
Bap. I know not what to say, but giue me your ha(n)ds,	1198
Gre. First, as you know, my house within the City	1228
On sonday next, you know | My daughter *Katherine* is to be married:	1275
To know the cause why musicke was ordain'd:	1305
*I know you not, *hic est sigeria tellus*, I trust you not,	1335
You know to morrow is the wedding day.	1378
Though he be blunt, I know him passing wise,	1412
Bap. Why sir, you know this is your wedding day:	1480
*after mee I know the rout is comming, such a mad mar-|ryage	1562
I know you thinke to dine with me to day,	1567
You know there wants no iunkets at the feast:	1634

KNOW *cont.*

Gru. First know my horse is tired, my master & mi-|stris falne out.	
Cur. How?	1688
Come *Kate* sit downe, I know you haue a stomacke,	1787
To make her come, and know her Keepers call:	1828
Know sir, that I am cal'd *Hortensio.*	1869
I know not what, but formall in apparrell,	1917
To come to Padua, know you not the cause?	1938
Tra. Among them know you one *Vincentio*?	1952
Ped. I know him not, but I haue heard of him:	1953
where thou shouldst know it.	2133
Tra. I thanke you sir, where then doe you know best	2230
Bap. Not in my house *Lucentio*, for you know	2233
Kate. I know it is the Sunne that shines so bright.	2301
Kate. I know it is the Moone.	2313
Gre. Yes, I know thee to be signior *Lucentio*.	2483
And now you know my meaning.	2570
Hor. I know her answere. | *Pet.* What? | *Hor.* She will not.	2649

KNOWES = 2*2

Pet. Who knowes not where a Waspe does weare | his sting? In his	
taile.	1089
Cur. Who knowes not that?	1729
*(poore soule) knowes not which way to stand, to looke,	1818
He that knowes better how to tame a shrew,	1844

KNOWING = 1

For knowing thee to be but yong and light.	1077

KNOWLEDGE = 1

That vpon knowledge of my Parentage,	958

KNOWN = *1

Petr. Do good old grandsire, & withall make known	2348

KNOWNE = 3

May shew her dutie, and make knowne her loue.	128
A man well knowne throughout all Italy.	930
Tra. Gremio, 'tis knowne my father hath no lesse	1259

KNOWST = *2

Petr. Hortensio peace: thou knowst not golds effect,	659
*know'st winter tames man, woman, and beast: for it	1661

LA = 2*1

LABOUR = 2*1

*be happie riuals in *Bianca's* loue, to labour and effect | one thing	
specially.	421
Gre. Yea, leaue that labour to great *Hercules*,	829
To painfull labour, both by sea and land:	2707

LACD = *1

*another lac'd: an olde rusty sword tane out of the	1434

LACKE = 1

Am staru'd for meate, giddie for lacke of sleepe:	1987

LACKEY = *1

Bion. Oh sir, his Lackey, for all the world Capari-|son'd	1451

LACKY = *1

*z not like a Christian foot-boy, or a gentlemans Lacky.	1456

LAD = 3*1

Luc. Gramercies Lad: Go forward, this contents,	466
Nat. How now old lad.	1739
Petr. Spoke like an Officer: ha to the lad.	2578
Luc. Well go thy waies olde Lad for thou shalt ha't.	2740

LADIE = 7*1
And that his Ladie mournes at his disease, 66
And see him drest in all suites like a Ladie: 117
Wherein your Ladie, and your humble wife, 127
*3.*Man.* Oh this it is that makes your Ladie mourne. 178
Thou hast a Ladie farre more Beautifull, 214
Beg. Am I a Lord, and haue I such a Ladie? 220
Well, bring our Ladie hither to our sight, 226
Ladie: would 'twere done. *They sit and marke.* 564
LADIES = 2*1
Such as he hath obseru'd in noble Ladies 122
Lord. Madam, and nothing else, so Lords cal Ladies 265
Tra. But youth in Ladies eyes that florisheth. 1222
LADY see also La. = 1
Enter Lady with Attendants. 252
LADY = 5
LAEDAES = 1
Faire *Laedaes* daughter had a thousand wooers, 816
LAIDE = *1
*the Gils faire without, the Carpets laide, and euerie | thing in order? 1685
LAIE = *1
Ven. Lucentio: oh he hath murdred his Master; laie 2465
LAMBE = 1
Gre. Tut, she's a Lambe, a Doue, a foole to him: 1541
LAMPASSE = *1
*with the Lampasse, infected with the fashions, full 1439
LAND = 4
Of fruitfull land, all which shall be her ioynter. 1252
Gre. Two thousand Duckets by the yeere of land, 1254
My Land amounts not to so much in all: 1255
To painfull labour, both by sea and land: 2707
LANDS = 3*1
Left solie heire to all his Lands and goods, 982
Bap. After my death, the one halfe of my Lands, 986
In all my Lands and Leases whatsoeuer, 990
*he is mine onelie sonne and heire to the Lands of me sig-|nior
Vincentio. 2463
LANE = 1
And bring our horses vnto Long-lane end, 2168
LANGUAGES = 1
In Greeke, Latine, and other Languages, 944
LARGESSE = 1
Ile mend it with a Largesse. Take your paper too, 716
LARKE = 2
Aboue the morning Larke. Or wilt thou hunt, 196
What is the Iay more precious then the Larke? 2158
LARUMS = 1
Loud larums, neighing steeds, & trumpets clangue? 773
LAST = 5
Bian. Where left we last? 1321
Last night she slept not, nor to night she shall not: 1832
That I am dogge-wearie, but at last I spied 1912
And happilie I haue arriued at the last | Vnto the wished hauen of my
blisse: 2507
Luc. At last, though long, our iarring notes agree, 2538
LASTS = *1
Gru. I pray you Sir let him go while the humor lasts. 673

LATE = 2
    Where is the life that late I led?   1767
    Better once then neuer, for neuer to late. *Exeunt.*   2532
LATINE = 2*1
    Gru. Nay 'tis no matter sir, what he leges in Latine.   596
    In Greeke, Latine, and other Languages,   944
    And this small packet of Greeke and Latine bookes: 963
LAUE = 1
    Basons and ewers to laue her dainty hands: 1230
LAUGH = *1
    Biond. You saw my Master winke and laugh vpon | you?   2261
LAUGHING = *1
    Gre. Went they not quickly, I should die with laugh- |(ing.   1627
LAUGHTER = 1
    And how my men will stay themselues from laughter,   146
LAUNCES = 1
    But now I see our Launces are but strawes: 2731
LAW = 3*2
    *him by Law. Ile not budge an inch boy: Let him come, | and kindly.
    Falles asleepe.   16
    *apples: but come, since this bar in law makes vs friends,   438
    And do as aduersaries do in law,   850
    And yet we heare not of our sonne in Law: 1391
    And now by Law, as well as reuerent age,   2359
LAWFULL = *1
    *If this be not a lawfull cause for me to leaue his seruice,   597
LAY = 4*2
    For though you lay heere in this goodlie chamber,   237
    *how the young folkes lay their heads together.   705
    Tra. Twas a commodity lay fretting by you,   1209
    Lay forth the gowne. What newes with you sir?   2046
    If thou accountedst it shame, lay it on me,   2164
    Peda. Lay hands on the villaine, I beleeue a meanes   2417
LAYING = 1
    Bian. The more foole you for laying on my dutie.   2685
LE *l.592* = 1
LEADE = 3
    And for your loue to her, leade Apes in hell.   892
    Sirrah, leade these Gentlemen | To my daughters, and tell them both   973
    Signior *Baptista*, shall I leade the way,   2254
LEARNE = 3
    She's apt to learne, and thankefull for good turnes: 1033
    But learne my Lessons as I please my selfe,   1315
    To learne the order of my fingering,   1358
LEARNING = 3
    A course of Learning, and ingenious studies.   308
    Gre. Oh this learning, what a thing it is.   725
    On this yong man: For learning and behauiour   734
LEASES = 1
    In all my Lands and Leases whatsoeuer,   990
LEAST = 4*2
    Least (ouer-eying of his odde behauiour,   105
    She moues me not, or not remoues at least   638
    That so I may by this deuice at least   700
    *and so long am I at the least. But wilt thou make a fire,   1666
    Gre. Take heede signior *Baptista*, least you be coni- |catcht   2476
    That seeming to be most, which we indeed least are.   2733

LEASURE = 1
What hast thou din'd? The Tailor staies thy leasure,　　　　2041
LEATHER = 1*1
　*shooes, or such shooes as my toes looke through the o-|uer-leather.　164
　*halfe-chekt Bitte, & a headstall of sheepes leather, which　　1444
LEAUE = 18*6
　Beg. 'Tis much, seruants leaue me and her alone:　　　　270
　And by my fathers loue and leaue am arm'd　　　　　304
　Leaue shall you haue to court her at your pleasure.　　　356
　(Belike) I knew not what to take, | And what to leaue? Ha. *Exit*　408
　Petr. Verona, for a while I take my leaue,　　　　　566
　*If this be not a lawfull cause for me to leaue his seruice,　　597
　Haue leaue and leisure to make loue to her,　　　　　701
　Gre. Yea, leaue that labour to great *Hercules*,　　　829
　Pet. You wrong me signior *Gremio*, giue me leaue.　　907
　Ile leaue her houses three or foure as good　　　　　1248
　And so I take my leaue, and thanke you both. *Exit*.　　1280
　Then giue me leaue to haue prerogatiue,　　　　　1301
　Then giue me leaue to read Philosophy,　　　　　1308
　Hort. You'll leaue his Lecture when I am in tune?　　1319
　Hort. You may go walk, and giue me leaue a while,　　1352
　Nicke. Mistresse, your father prayes you leaue your | (books,　1376
　And therefore heere I meane to take my leaue.　　　　1570
　Shal win my loue, and so I take my leaue,　　　　　1890
　Kate. Why sir I trust I may haue leaue to speake,　　2058
　Ped. Soft son: sir by your leaue, hauing com to *Padua*　2206
　thee at home, therefore leaue vs. *Exit*.　　　　　2383
　Thither must I, and here I leaue you sir.　　　　　2391
　Padua: doe you heare sir, to leaue friuolous circumstan-|ces,　2407
　Luc. Tis a wonder, by your leaue, she wil be tam'd so.　2750
LEAUES = 2
　And am to *Padua* come, as he that leaues　　　　　321
　For such a one as leaues a Gentleman,　　　　　　1867
LECTURE = 3
　Your Lecture shall haue leisure for as much.　　　　1303
　His Lecture will be done ere you haue tun'd.　　　　1318
　Hort. You'll leaue his Lecture when I am in tune?　　1319
LECTURES = 1
　And see you reade no other Lectures to her:　　　　713
LED = 1
　Where is the life that late I led?　　　　　　1767
LEETE = 1
　And say you would present her at the Leete,　　　　240
LEFT = 3*3
　Tell me thy minde, for I haue *Pisa* left,　　　　　320
　Left solie heire to all his Lands and goods,　　　　982
　Bian. Where left we last?　　　　　　　1321
　*place, how she was bemoil'd, how hee left her with the　　1707
　*knit, let them curtsie with their left legges, and not　　1721
　Biond. Faith nothing: but has left mee here behinde　　2264
LEG = *1
　*like the horse: with a linnen stock on one leg, and　　1452
LEGD = *1
　*and shoulder-shotten, neere leg'd before, and with a　　1443
LEGES = *1
　Gru. Nay 'tis no matter sir, what he leges in Latine.　　596

128

LEGGD = 1
    To combe your noddle with a three-legg'd stoole,   367
LEGGES = *2
    *then backes: no more stockings then legges: nor   162
    *knit, let them curtsie with their left legges, and not   1721
LEGS = 1
    Scratching her legs, that one shal sweare she bleeds,   210
LEISURE = 3
    Haue leaue and leisure to make loue to her,   701
    Your Lecture shall haue leisure for as much.   1303
    Father, be quiet, he shall stay my leisure.   1603
LEND = 2
    Gru. Lend thine eare. | *Cur*. Heere. | *Gru*. There.   1693
    And so to Tripolie, if God lend me life.   1931
LENGTHENS = 1
    Which barres a thousand harmes, and lengthens life.   290
LESSE = 3
    He is no lesse then what we say he is.   75
    For I will loue thee nere the lesse my girle.   380
    Tra. Gremio, 'tis knowne my father hath no lesse   1259
LESSONS = 2
    But learne my Lessons as I please my selfe,   1315
    My Lessons make no musicke in three parts.   1353
LEST *see* least
LET = 40*9
    *in with *Richard Conqueror*: therefore *Pau-!cas pallabris*, let the world
    slide: Sessa.   8
    *him by Law. Ile not budge an inch boy: Let him come, | and kindly.
    Falles asleepe.   16
    Let one attend him with a siluer Bason   59
    Let them want nothing that my house affoords. | *Exit one with the
    Players*.   114
    Such dutie to the drunkard let him do: 124
    La. Thrice noble Lord, let me intreat of you   272
    Beg. Marrie I will let them play, it is not a Comon-|tie,   291
    And let the world slip, we shall nere be yonger.   298
    Heere let vs breath, and haply institute   307
    And let it not displease thee good *Bianca*,   379
    And let me be a slaue, t'atchieue that maide,   525
    And therefore let me be thus bold with you,   670
    Gru. I pray you Sir let him go while the humor lasts.   673
    And let me haue them verie wel perfum'd;   717
    Hor. Sir, let me be so bold as aske you,   823
    Petr. Sir, sir, the first's for me, let her go by.   828
    And let it be more then *Alcides* twelue.   830
    Gre. Sauing your tale *Petruchio*, I pray let vs that are   932
    Let specialties be therefore drawne betweene vs,   991
    Kate. Mou'd, in good time, let him that mou'd you | hether   1066
    Kate. I chafe you if I tarrie. Let me go.   1120
    Oh let me see thee walke: thou dost not halt.   1135
    O be thou *Dian*, and let her be *Kate*,   1139
    And then let *Kate* be chaste, and *Dian* sportfull.   1140
    And let your father make her the assurance,   1269
    Bian. Now let mee see if I can conster it. *Hic ibat si-|mois*,   1334
    But let it rest, now *Litio* to you: 1349
    Which once perform'd, let all the world say no,   1524
    That all amaz'd the Priest let fall the booke,   1545

LET *cont.*

Tra. Let vs intreat you stay till after dinner.	1580
Pet. It may not be. | *Gra.* Let me intreat you.	1581
Pet. It cannot be. | *Kat.* Let me intreat you.	1583
Bap. Nay, let them goe, a couple of quiet ones.	1626
And let *Bianca* take her sisters roome.	1636
*and the rest: let their heads bee slickely comb'd,	1719
*knit, let them curtsie with their left legges, and not	1721
You horson villaine, will you let it fall?	1784
Now let him speake, 'tis charity to shew. *Exit*	1845
Par. Take me your loue, and then let me alone.	1924
This by the way I let you vnderstand,	1971
Kate. 'Tis passing good, I prethee let me haue it.	1996
Kate. Why then the Beefe, and let the Mustard rest.	2004
Heere take away this dish. | *Kate.* I pray you let it stand.	2025
Come Tailor, let vs see these ornaments.	2044
Away with it, come let me haue a bigger.	2052
Pet. Thy gowne, why I: come Tailor let vs see't.	2071
Go call my men, and let vs straight to him,	2167
Let me imbrace with old *Vincentio*,	2367
Wid. Lord let me neuer haue a cause to sigh,	2679

LETS = 8*5

Let's be no Stoickes, nor no stockes I pray,	330
Luc. Tranio let's go:	553
Tranio. I loue no chiders sir: *Biondello*, let's away.	796
Gru. Bion. Oh excellent motion: fellowes let's be gon.	852
Bian. Let's heare, oh fie, the treble iarres.	1332
Bap. She shall *Lucentio*: come gentlemen lets goe. | *Exeunt.*	1638
Cur. Let's ha't good *Grumio*.	1692
Let's see, I thinke 'tis now some seuen a clocke,	2170
Petr. Preethe *Kate* let's stand aside and see the end of | this controuersie.	2438
Kate. Husband let's follow, to see the end of this adoe.	2522
Petr. Why then let's home againe: Come Sirra let's | awaie.	2527
Let's each one send vnto his wife,	2609

LETT = 1

You are still crossing it, sirs let't alone,	2176

LETTERS = *1

*hath two letters for her name, fairely set down in studs,	1448

LEWD = 1

A Veluet dish: Fie, fie, 'tis lewd and filthy,	2049

LEYSURE = 2

Who woo'd in haste, and meanes to wed at leysure:	1399
Which at more leysure I will so excuse,	1491

LIAR = 1

And now I finde report a very liar:	1123

LIBERALITIE = 1

You vnderstand me. Ouer and beside | Signior *Baptistas* liberalitie,	714

LIBERALL = 1

I will be very kinde and liberall,	402

LIBERTIE = 1

The patron of my life and libertie.	1969

LIBERTY = 1

This liberty is all that I request,	957

LIE *see also* lye = 1

There doth my father lie: and there this night	2238

LIEF = *1
 *Gre. I cannot tell: but I had as lief take her dowrie   434
LIES see also lyes = 3
 Kate. I, if the foole could finde it where it lies.   1088
 The dore is open sir, there lies your way,   1596
 Gru. The note lies in's throate if he say I said so.   2116
LIEST see also lyest, ly'st = 1*1
 not bid him cut it to peeces. Ergo thou liest.   2113
 *Ped. Thou liest his Father is come from Padua, and   2411
LIFE = 17*4
 *Lordship: I ne're drank sacke in my life: and if you giue   159
 Vpon my life I am a Lord indeede,   224
 Which barres a thousand harmes, and lengthens life.   290
 Your fellow Tranio heere to saue my life,   535
 While I make way from hence to saue my life: 541
 He hath the Iewel of my life in hold,   684
 *Gre. Oh sir, such a life with such a wife, were strange: 759
 Now for my life the knaue doth court my loue,   1342
 Vpon my life Petruchio meanes but well,   1410
 Where is the life that late I led?   1767
 And so to Tripolie, if God lend me life.   1931
 And come to Padua carelesse of your life.   1935
 Ped. My life sir? how I pray? for that goes hard.   1936
 Tra. To saue your life in this extremitie,   1958
 The patron of my life and libertie.   1969
 Gru. No, no forsooth I dare not for my life.   1979
 *Gru. Villaine, not for thy life: Take vp my Mistresse | gowne for thy
 masters vse.   2141
 I neuer saw you before in all my life.   2429
 Pet. Now for my life Hortentio feares his Widow.   2553
 *Petr. Marrie peace it boads, and loue, and quiet life,   2663
 Thy husband is thy Lord, thy life, thy keeper,   2704
LIFT = *1
 *blew lift; an old hat, & the humor of forty fancies prickt   1454
LIGHT = 3*2
 *I can by any meanes light on a fit man to teach her that   415
 *good fellowes in the world, and a man could light on   432
 For knowing thee to be but yong and light.   1077
 Kate. Too light for such a swaine as you to catch,   1078
 For by this light, whereby I see thy beauty,   1152
LIGHTED = 1
 And by good fortune I haue lighted well   733
LIGHTNESSE = 1
 And since mine eyes are witnesse of her lightnesse,   1872
LIKE = 35*6
 *Lord. Oh monstrous beast, how like a swine he lyes.   38
 And see him drest in all suites like a Ladie: 117
 Like enuious flouds ore-run her louely face,   217
 And paint your face, and vse you like a foole.   368
 Rage like an angry Boare, chafed with sweat?   769
 Or else you like not of my companie.   926
 The like kindnesse my selfe, that haue beene   940
 Me thinkes you walke like a stranger,   949
 For I am rough, and woo not like a babe.   1002
 Kate. Well tane, and like a buzzard.   1081
 *Kate. No Cocke of mine, you crow too like a crauen   1104
 Oh sland'rous world: Kate like the hazle twig   1132

LIKE *cont.*

Thy beauty that doth make me like thee well,	1153
If you like me, she shall haue me and mine.	1265
Call you this gamouth? tut I like it not,	1372
*with the glanders, and like to mose in the chine, trou- |bled	1438
*like the horse: with a linnen stock on one leg, and	1452
*z not like a Christian foot-boy, or a gentlemans Lacky.	1456
'Tis like you 'll proue a iolly surly groome,	1599
Tra. Of all mad matches neuer was the like.	1628
Nath. Peter didst euer see the like.	1812
Tra. And heere I take the like vnfained oath,	1880
In gate and countenance surely like a Father.	1918
That you are like to Sir *Vincentio.*	1961
Kate. I like it well, good Grumio fetch it me.	1999
Kate. Loue me, or loue me not, I like the cap,	2069
Whats this? a sleeue? 'tis like demi cannon,	2073
What, vp and downe caru'd like an apple Tart?	2074
Like to a Censor in a barbers shoppe:	2076
Hor. I see shees like to haue neither cap nor gowne.	2078
Enter *Tranio, and the Pedant drest like Vincentio.*	2180
To haue him matcht, and if you please to like	2214
That like a Father you will deale with him,	2226
Tra. Then at my lodging, and it like you,	2237
You are like to haue a thin and slender pittance.	2243
And how she's like to be *Lucentios* wife.	2249
Welcome, one messe is like to be your cheere,	2255
Like pleasant trauailors to breake a Iest	2371
Petr. Spoke like an Officer: ha to the lad.	2578
Tri. Oh sir, *Lucentio* slipt me like his Gray-hound,	2595
A woman mou'd, is like a fountaine troubled,	2700

LIKELIHOOD = 1

And by all likelihood some cheere is toward. *Knock.*	2394

LIKELY = 1

I neuer thought it possible or likely.	452

LIKES = 3

Bap. It likes me well:	2244
Petr. Conceiues by me, how likes *Hortentio* that?	2562
Bap. How likes *Gremio* these quicke witted folkes?	2580

LIKING = 2

Vpon agreement from vs to his liking,	748
Her fathers liking, which to bring to passe	1512

LIKST = 1

I loue thee well in that thou lik'st it not.	2068

LIMPE = 1

Why does the world report that *Kate* doth limpe?	1131

LINKE = 1

There was no Linke to colour *Peters* hat,	1761

LINNEN = 1 *1

Fine Linnen, Turky cushions bost with pearle,	1235
*like the horse: with a linnen stock on one leg, and	1452

LIONS = 1

Haue I not in my time heard Lions rore?	767

LIP = 1

Nor bite the lip, as angry wenches will,	1127

LIPPES = *1

*now were I not a little pot, & soone hot; my very lippes	1644

LIPS = 1*1
   Luc. *Tranio*, I saw her corrall lips to moue, 477
   *Bride about the necke, and kist her lips with such a cla-|morous 1559
LISIO = 4
   Tra. Is't possible friend *Lisio*, that mistris *Bianca* 1847
   I tel thee *Lisio* this is wonderfull. 1863
   Hor. Mistake no more, I am not *Lisio*, 1864
   Tra. Mistris we haue. | *Luc.* Then we are rid of *Lisio*. 1898
LIST = 4
   Tra. That only came well in: sir, list to me, 1245
   Seize thee that List, if once I finde thee ranging, 1385
   Now take them vp quoth he, if any list. 1549
   It shall be moone, or starre, or what I list, 2303
LISTEN = 1
   Listen to me, and if you speake me faire, 745
LISTNING = *1
   *Cuffe was but to knocke at your eare, and beseech list-|ning: 1698
LITIO = 3
   His name is *Litio*, borne in *Mantua*. 921
   But let it rest, now *Litio* to you: 1349
   The quaint Musician, amorous *Litio*, 1530
LITLE = *1
   *trickes. Ile tell you what sir, and she stand him but a li-|tle, 678
LITTLE = 8*3
   Thou'dst thanke me but a little for my counsell: 627
   *thinke scolding would doe little good vpon him. Shee 675
   Thinke you, a little dinne can daunt mine eares? 766
   We will go walke a little in the Orchard, 976
   Though little fire growes great with little winde, 999
   *now were I not a little pot, & soone hot; my very lippes 1644
   Gru. I, but the Mustard is too hot a little. 2003
   *that Ile proue vpon thee, though thy little finger be ar-|med in a
   thimble. 2130
   Petr. A has a little gald me I confesse: 2603
   Too little payment for so great a debt. 2712
LIUE = 5
   Master, your Loue must liue a maide at home, 485
   But will you woo this Wilde-cat? | *Petr.* Will I liue? 762
   If whil'st I liue she will be onely mine. 1244
   But one that scorne to liue in this disguise, 1866
   shall neede none so long as I liue. 2405
LIUELIE = 1
   As liuelie painted, as the deede was done. 208
LIUES = 2
   My father dead, my fortune liues for me, 757
   Vin. Liues my sweete sonne? 2492
LIUST = 1
   As thou shalt thinke on prating whil'st thou liu'st: 2099
LO = *1
LOATHSOME = 2
   Grim death, how foule and loathsome is thine image: 39
   No better than a poore and loathsome begger: 134
LODGD = 1
   And in my house you shal be friendly lodg'd, 1963
LODGERS = 1
   Tra. Where we were lodgers, at the *Pegasus*, 2185

LODGICKE = 1
  Balke Lodgicke with acquaintaince that you haue,   333
LODGING = 3
  And burne sweet Wood to make the Lodging sweete: 53
  And take a Lodging fit to entertaine   343
  Tra. Then at my lodging, and it like you,   2237
LOE = 1
  And say, loe, there is mad *Petruchio's* wife   1407
LOGGER-HEADED = 1
  You logger-headed and vnpollisht groomes: 1752
LOMBARDIE *see* Lumbardie
LONG = 16*1
  I long to heare him call the drunkard husband,   145
  Beg. I, it stands so that I may hardly tarry so long: 279
  And I do hope, good dayes and long, to see.   758
  Beene long studying at *Rhemes*, as cunning   943
  Oh how I long to haue some chat with her.   1030
  Now is the day we long haue looked for,   1214
  Bian. Why, I am past my gamouth long agoe.   1364
  Hath all so long detain'd you from your wife,   1486
  But where is *Kate*? I stay too long from her,   1493
  *and so long am I at the least. But wilt thou make a fire,   1666
  Ere three dayes passe, which hath as long lou'd me,   1886
  That teacheth trickes eleuen and twentie long,   1908
  Bion. Oh Master, master I haue watcht so long,   1911
  And she to him: to stay him not too long,   2212
  A sonne of mine, which long I haue not seene.   2355
  shall neede none so long as I liue.   2405
  Luc. At last, though long, our iarring notes agree,   2538
LONGETH = 2
  As longeth to a Louers blessed case: 1893
  With such austeritie as longeth to a father.   2187
LONGLY = 1
  Tra. Master, you look'd so longly on the maide,   468
LONG-LANE = 1
  And bring our horses vnto Long-lane end,   2168
LOOKD = 2
  Tra. Master, you look'd so longly on the maide,   468
  My father is heere look'd for euerie day,   1972
LOOKE = 12*10
  *Rogues. Looke in the Chronicles, we came   7
  But sup them well, and looke vnto them all,   31
  *shooes, or such shooes as my toes looke through the o-|uer-leather.   164
  Looke how thy seruants do attend on thee,   185
  On them to looke, and practise by my selfe.   386
  *looke you sir: He bid me knocke him, & rap him sound-|ly   598
  Gru. Nay looke you sir, hee tels you flatly what his   643
  *Master, master, looke about you: Who goes there? ha.   706
  Bap. How now my friend, why dost thou looke so | pale?   1008
  Hor. For feare I promise you, if I looke pale.   1010
  Pet. Nay come *Kate*, come: you must not looke so | sowre.   1105
  Pet. Why heere's no crab, and therefore looke not | sowre.   1108
  Thou canst not frowne, thou canst not looke a sconce,   1126
  Tra. That by degrees we meane to looke into,   1526
  Nay, looke not big, nor stampe, not stare, nor fret,   1614
  *(poore soule) knowes not which way to stand, to looke,   1818
  Looke that you take vpon you as you should,   1964

LOOKE *cont.*
  *Pet. Plucke vp thy spirits, looke cheerfully vpon me.   2019
  Looke what I speake, or do, or thinke to doe,   2175
  If this be not that you looke for, I haue no more to say,   2281
  That euery thing I looke on seemeth greene: 2345
  *Luc. Looke not pale *Bianca*, thy father will not frown. | *Exeunt.*   2518
LOOKED = 1
  Now is the day we long haue looked for,   1214
LOOKES = 7
  Say that she frowne, Ile say she lookes as cleere   1041
  Methinkes he lookes as though he were in loue: 1382
  For then she neuer lookes vpon her lure.   1826
  Kindnesse in women, not their beauteous lookes   1889
  Pedant lookes out of the window.   2397
  marie sir see where he lookes out of the window.   2433
  But loue, faire lookes, and true obedience;   2711
LOOKING = 3
  But see, while idely I stood looking on,   453
  As on a Pillorie, looking through the Lute,   1024
  here looking out at the window.   2412
LOOKT = 1
  And that you look't for him this day in *Padua*,   2197
LOOSE = 4
  I would not loose the dogge for twentie pound.   24
  Beg. I thanke thee, thou shalt not loose by it.   253
  Kate. So may you loose your armes,   1098
  Tail. Inprimis, a loose bodied gowne.   2117
LOOSE-BODIED = *1
  *Gru. Master, if euer I said loose-bodied gowne, sow   2118
LORD see also Lo. = 27*9
  Winde hornes. Enter a Lord from hunting, with his traine.   18
  Hunts. Why *Belman* is as good as he my Lord,   25
  To morrow I intend to hunt againe. | *Hunts.* I will my Lord.   32
  *2.*Hun.* He breath's my Lord. Were he not warm'd   36
  *1.*Hun.* Beleeue me Lord, I thinke he cannot choose.   46
  For he is nothing but a mightie Lord: 69
  *1.*Hunts.* My Lord I warrant you we wil play our part   73
  There is a Lord will heare you play to night;   103
  *Plai. Feare not my Lord, we can contain our selues,   110
  To see her noble Lord restor'd to health,   132
  Enter aloft the drunkard with attendants, some with apparel, | Bason and
  Ewer, & other appurtenances, & Lord.   151
  *1.*Ser.* Wilt please your Lord drink a cup of sacke?   154
  Oh Noble Lord, bethinke thee of thy birth,   182
  Lord. Thou art a Lord, and nothing but a Lord: 213
  Beg. Am I a Lord, and haue I such a Ladie?   220
  Vpon my life I am a Lord indeede,   224
  1.*Man.* Oh yes my Lord, but verie idle words,   236
  Beg. Now Lord be thanked for my good amends. | *All.* Amen.   250
  Lady. How fares my noble Lord?   254
  Where is my wife? | *La.* Heere noble Lord, what is thy will with her?   256
  My men should call me Lord, I am your good-man.   259
  *La. My husband and my Lord, my Lord and husband   260
  La. Thrice noble Lord, let me intreat of you   272
  Lady. No my good Lord, it is more pleasing stuffe.   293
  Hor. From all such diuels, good Lord deliuer vs. | *Gre.* And me too,
  good Lord.   369

LORD *cont.*

1.Man. My Lord you nod, you do not minde the | play.	558
Lady. My Lord, 'tis but begun.	562
Beeme, Bianca take him for thy Lord	1368
Good Lord how bright and goodly shines the Moone.	2297
Wid. Lord let me neuer haue a cause to sigh,	2679
To wound thy Lord, thy King, thy Gouernour.	2696
Thy husband is thy Lord, thy life, thy keeper,	2704
And gracelesse Traitor to her louing Lord?	2718

LORD = 10*6

LORDS = 1*2

Vnto their Lords, by them accomplished,	123
Lord. Madam, and nothing else, so Lords cal Ladies	265
*women, what dutie they doe owe their Lords and hus-|bands.	2687

LORDSHIP = 2*1

And say wilt please your Lordship coole your hands.	62
Ser. An't please your Honor, Players | That offer seruice to your Lordship.	84
*Lordship: I ne're drank sacke in my life: and if you giue	159

LORDSHIPPE = *1

2.Player. So please your Lordshippe to accept our | dutie.	91

LOSE *see* loose

LOSSE = 1

He cried vpon it at the meerest losse,	26

LOSSES = 1

Vnto their losses twentie thousand crownes,	2668

LOST = *1

*bridle was burst: how I lost my crupper, with manie	1712

LOTH = *1

*But I would be loth to fall into my dreames againe: I	280

LOTS = 1

A lots thee for his louely bedfellow.	2339

LOUD = 6

For I will boord her, though she chide as loud	661
Loud larums, neighing steeds, & trumpets clangue?	773
I, by goggs woones quoth he, and swore so loud,	1544
Lou'd me in the World so wel as *Lucentio*.	1861
Ere three dayes passe, which hath as long lou'd me,	1886
As I haue lou'd this proud disdainful Haggard,	1887

LOUE = 54*8

Tell him from me (as he will win my loue)	120
May shew her dutie, and make knowne her loue.	128
*Dost thou loue hawking? Thou hast hawkes will soare	195
2.M. Dost thou loue pictures? we wil fetch thee strait	201
And by my fathers loue and leaue am arm'd	304
If either of you both loue *Katherina*,	354
Because I know you well, and loue you well,	355
For I will loue thee nere the lesse my girle.	380
*so good heere's none will holde you: Their loue is not	411
*Farewell: yet for the loue I beare my sweet *Bianca*, if	414
*be happie riuals in *Bianca's* loue, to labour and effect | one thing specially.	421
That loue should of a sodaine take such hold.	450
I found the effect of Loue in idlenesse,	454
If loue haue touch'd you, naught remaines but so,	464
I pray awake sir: if you loue the Maide,	481
Master, your Loue must liue a maide at home,	485

LOUE *cont.*

Because so well I loue *Lucentio*.	523
Be she as foule as was *Florentius* Loue,	635
Suters to her, and riuals in my Loue:	687
Haue leaue and leisure to make loue to her,	701
Hor. Peace *Grumio*, it is the riuall of my Loue.	707
All bookes of Loue, see that at any hand,	712
Hor. Gremio, 'tis now no time to vent our loue,	744
Tranio. I loue no chiders sir: *Biondello*, let's away.	796
That she's the choise loue of Signior *Gremio*.	808
And for your loue to her, leade Apes in hell.	892
Then tell me, if I get your daughters loue,	984
That is her loue: for that is all in all.	994
I loue her ten times more then ere I did,	1029
That in a twinke she won me to her loue.	1190
Tra. And I am one that loue *Bianca* more	1216
Gre. Yongling thou canst not loue so deare as I.	1218
Tra. Gray-beard thy loue doth freeze. | *Gre*. But thine doth frie,	1219
That can assure my daughter greatest dower, | Shall haue my *Biancas* loue.	1225
*disguised thus to get your loue, *hic steterat*, and that	1327
Now for my life the knaue doth court my loue,	1342
Methinkes he lookes as though he were in loue:	1382
Tra. But sir, Loue concerneth vs to adde	1511
Kat. Now if you loue me stay. | *Pet. Grumio*, my horse.	1589
And serue it thus to me that loue it not?	1796
Hor. I reade, that I professe the Art to loue.	1855
Tra. Oh despightful Loue, vnconstant womankind,	1862
Forsweare *Bianca*, and her loue for euer.	1874
Shal win my loue, and so I take my leaue,	1890
Nay, I haue tane you napping gentle Loue,	1894
Par. Take me your loue, and then let me alone.	1924
He does it vnder name of perfect loue:	1990
Kate. A dish that I do loue to feede vpon.	2002
Heere Loue, thou seest how diligent I am,	2020
Kate eate apace; and now my honie Loue,	2034
I loue thee well in that thou lik'st it not.	2068
Kate. Loue me, or loue me not, I like the cap,	2069
Of loue betweene your daughter and himselfe:	2209
And for the loue he beareth to your daughter,	2211
Doth loue my daughter, and she loueth him,	2223
Luc. Loue wrought these miracles. *Biancas* loue	2504
Kate. Nay, I will giue thee a kisse, now praie thee | Loue staie.	2529
Petr. Marrie peace it boads, and loue, and quiet life,	2663
But loue, faire lookes, and true obedience;	2711
When they are bound to serue, loue, and obay.	2722

LOUELY = 5

Like enuious flouds ore-run her louely face,	217
But where is *Kate*? where is my louely Bride?	1475
And seale the title with a louely kisse. *Exit*.	1506
Faire louely Maide, once more good day to thee:	2331
A lots thee for his louely bedfellow.	2339

LOUERS = 1

As longeth to a Louers blessed case:	1893

LOUES = 3

Luc. *Tranio* be so, because *Lucentio* loues,	524

LOUES *cont.*

I tell you 'tis incredible to beleeue | How much she loues me: oh the
kindest *Kate*,   1186
Cfaut, that loues with all affection: 1369
LOUEST = 1

Petr. Eate it vp all *Hortensio*, if thou louest mee: 2032
LOUETH = 1

Doth loue my daughter, and she loueth him,   2223
LOUING = 3

I may intitle thee my louing Father,   2360
Brother *Petruchio*, sister *Katerina*, | And thou *Hortentio* with thy louing
Widdow: 2543
And gracelesse Traitor to her louing Lord?   2718
LOUST = 2

Whom thou lou'st best: see thou dissemble not.   864
What, not a word? Nay then, thou lou'st it not: 2023
LOWD = *1

*mine to endure her lowd alarums, why man there bee   431
LOWDER = 1

Grem. They're busie within, you were best knocke | lowder. 2395
LOWE = 2

(And with a lowe submissiue reuerence)   57
With soft lowe tongue, and lowly curtesie,   125
LOWLIE = 1

And banish hence these abiect lowlie dreames: 184
LOWLY = 1

With soft lowe tongue, and lowly curtesie,   125
LUC = 49*10

LUCEN = 1

*Gremio a Pantelowne, Hortentio sister to Bianca. | Lucen. Tranio, stand
by.*   348
LUCEN = 1

LUCENTIO see also Luc., Lucen. = 36*10

Flourish. Enter Lucentio, and his man Triano.   299
Exeunt ambo. Manet Tranio and Lucentio.   448
I am content to bee *Lucentio*,   522
Because so well I loue *Lucentio*.   523
Luc. Tranio be so, because *Lucentio* loues,   524
Tranio is chang'd into *Lucentio*.   545
*that *Lucentio* indeede had *Baptistas* yongest daugh-|ter. 548
*When I am alone, why then I am *Tranio*: but in | all places else, your
master *Lucentio*.   551
Enter Gremio and Lucentio disguised.   703
And so she shall: *Lucentio* shal make one,   818
Enter Gremio, Lucentio, in the habit of a meane man,   897
Bap. Lucentio is your name, of whence I pray.   965
I see no reason but suppos'd *Lucentio*   1289
Enter Lucentio, Hortentio, and Bianca.   1295
Luc. Hic Ibat, as I told you before, *Simois*, I am Lu-|centio, 1325
Lucentio that comes a wooing, *priami*, is my man Tra-|nio, 1328
Bap. Signior *Lucentio*, this is the pointed day   1389
What saies *Lucentio* to this shame of ours?   1395
All for my Masters sake *Lucentio*.   1531
Ile tell you sir *Lucentio*; when the Priest   1542
Lucentio, you shall supply the Bridegroomes place,   1635
Bap. She shall *Lucentio*: come gentlemen lets goe. | *Exeunt.* 1638
Doth fancie any other but *Lucentio*,   1848

LUCENTIO cont.

Lou'd me in the World so wel as *Lucentio*.	1861
Hor. See how they kisse and court: Signior *Lucentio*,	1875
And so farewel signior *Lucentio*,	1888
Enter Baptista and Lucentio: Pedant booted | and bare headed.	2200
To gather in some debts, my son *Lucentio*	2207
Right true it is your sonne *Lucentio* here	2222
Bap. Not in my house *Lucentio*, for you know	2233
Enter Lucentio and Biondello.	2258
Petr. What is his name? | *Vinc. Lucentio* gentle sir.	2356
Enter Biondello, Lucentio and Bianca, Gremio | is out before.	2379
Vin. Is Signior *Lucentio* within sir?	2400
*I pray you tell signior *Lucentio* that his Father is	2408
Ped. Awaie, awaie mad asse, his name is *Lucentio*, and	2462
Ven. Lucentio: oh he hath murdred his Master; laie	2465
*sonne, my sonne: tell me thou villaine, where is my son | *Lucentio*?	2467
Tran. Then thou wert best saie that I am not *Lu-|centio*.	2481
Gre. Yes, I know thee to be signior *Lucentio*.	2483
Enter Biondello, Lucentio and Bianeu.	2485
Bap. How hast thou offended, where is *Lucentio*?	2494
Luc. Here's *Lucentio*, right sonne to the right *Vin-|centio*,	2495
Bian. Cambio is chang'd into *Lucentio*.	2503
Enter Baptista, Vincentio, Gremio, the Pedant, Lucentio, and	2534
Tri. Oh sir, *Lucentio* slipt me like his Gray-hound,	2595

LUCENTIOS = 3

Lucentios Father is arriued in *Padua*,	2248
And how she's like to be *Lucentios* wife.	2249
Petr. Sir heres the doore, this is *Lucentios* house,	2389

LUCRECE = 1

And Romane *Lucrece* for her chastitie:	1176

LUKES = *2

Bio. The old Priest at Saint *Lukes* Church is at your | command at all hources.	2274
*Master hath appointed me to goe to Saint *Lukes* to bid	2287

LUMBARDIE = 1

I am arriu'd for fruitfull *Lumbardie*,	302

LUNACIE = 1

As beaten hence by your strange Lunacie.	181

LUNATICKE = 3

Perswade him that he hath bin Lunaticke,	67
To wish me wed to one halfe Lunaticke,	1167
Bapt. What is the man lunaticke?	2450

LURE = 1

For then she neuer lookes vpon her lure.	1826

LUSTFULL = 1

Softer and sweeter then the lustfull bed	190

LUSTIE = 2

Pet. Now by the world, it is a lustie Wench,	1028
Tra. I'faith hee'l haue a lustie Widdow now,	1900

LUTE = 4*1

Petruchio with Tranio, with his boy | bearing a Lute and Bookes.	898
Take you the Lute, and you the set of bookes,	969
Bap. Why then thou canst not break her to the Lute?	1015
Hor. Why no, for she hath broke the Lute to me:	1016
As on a Pillorie, looking through the Lute,	1024

LUTES = 1

Iron may hold with her, but neuer Lutes.	1014

LYE = 2
  Pet. You lye infaith, for you are call'd plaine *Kate,*   1056
  Petr. Nay then you lye: it is the blessed Sunne.   2314
LYES = *1
  Lord. Oh monstrous beast, how like a swine he lyes.   38
LYEST = 2
  Kate. Minion thou lyest: Is't not *Hortensio?*   868
  Thou lyest, thou thred, thou thimble,   2093
LYING = 1
  That now is lying in Marcellus roade: 1257
LYINGST = *1
  *sheere Ale, score me vp for the lyingst knaue in Christen|dome. What
  I am not bestraught: here's---   176
LYST = 1
  Whil'st thou ly'st warme at home, secure and safe,   2709
MAD = 8*9
  Beg. What would you make me mad? Am not I *Chri-|stopher*   170
  That wench is starke mad, or wonderfull froward.   372
  Gru. Helpe mistris helpe, my master is mad.   585
  And say, loe, there is mad *Petruchio's* wife   1407
  Tra. He hath some meaning in his mad attire,   1507
  *after mee I know the rout is comming, such a mad mar-|ryage   1562
  Tra. Of all mad matches neuer was the like.   1628
  Bian. That being mad her selfe, she's madly mated.   1630
  Gru. Fie, fie on all tired Iades, on all mad Masters, z   1640
  And thus Ile curbe her mad and headstrong humor: 1843
  Hort. A will make the man mad to make the woman | of him.   2333
  Petr. Why how now *Kate,* I hope thou art not mad,   2340
  Pardon I pray thee for my mad mistaking.   2347
  Bion. Helpe, helpe, helpe, here's a mad man will mur-|der me.   2435
  *your habit: but your wordes shew you a mad man: why   2452
  Ped. Awaie, awaie mad asse, his name is *Lucentio,* and   2462
  Tra. Call forth an officer: Carrie this mad knaue to   2469
MADAM = 9*2
  And call him Madam, do him obeisance: 119
  Beg. I know it well, what must I call her? | *Lord.* Madam.   262
  Beg. Alce Madam, or *Ione* Madam?   264
  Lord. Madam, and nothing else, so Lords cal Ladies   265
  Madam vndresse you, and come now to bed.   271
  Come Madam wife sit by my side,   297
  Luc. Heere Madam: *Hic Ibat Simois, hic est sigeria*   1322
  Hort. Madam, my Instrument's in tune.   1331
  Hort. Madam, tis now in tune.   1338
  Hor. Madam, before you touch the instrument,   1357
MADAME = 1*1
  Beg. Madame wife, they say that I haue dream'd,   266
  Beg. 'Tis a verie excellent peece of worke, Madame   563
MADDE = 1
  Be madde and merry, or goe hang your selues: 1612
MADE = 14
  Saw'st thou not boy how *Siluer* made it good   22
  That made great *Ioue* to humble him to her hand,   472
  And through the instrument my pate made way,   1022
  Kate. Asses are made to beare, and so are you.   1073
  Pet. Women are made to beare, and so are you.   1074
  I see a woman may be made a foole   1606
  Grumio. Nathaniels coate sir was not fully made,   1759

MADE *cont.*

Tail. Your worship is deceiu'd, the gowne is made	2101
Tail. But how did you desire it should be made?	2105
Made me acquainted with a waighty cause	2208
The match is made, and all is done,	2228
For our first merriment hath made thee iealous. *Exeunt.*	2375
That haue by marriage made thy daughter mine,	2497
Made me exchange my state with *Tranio,*	2505

MADLY = 2

And venture madly on a desperate Mart.	1208
Bian. That being mad her selfe, she's madly mated.	1630

MAD-BRAIND = *1

*This mad-brain'd bridegroome tooke him such a cuffe,	1547

MAD-BRAINE = 1

Vnto a mad-braine rudesby, full of spleene,	1398

MAD-CAP = 1

A mad-cap ruffian, and a swearing Iacke,	1168

MAID = 4*2

Lord. Wee'l shew thee *Io*, as she was a Maid,	206
3.Man. Why sir you know no house, nor no such maid	244
Hor. Mates maid, how meane you that?	361
And vndertake the teaching of the maid:	497
Are you a sutor to the Maid you talke of, yea or no?	799
Tra. Why then the maid is mine from all the world	1266

MAIDE = 7

Beg. I, the womans maide of the house.	243
Tra. Master, you look'd so longly on the maide,	468
I pray awake sir: if you loue the Maide,	481
Master, your Loue must liue a maide at home,	485
And let me be a slaue, t'atchieue that maide,	525
Gru. Katherine the curst, | A title for a maide, of all titles the worst.	694
Faire louely Maide, once more good day to thee:	2331

MAIDEN = 1

And not a Maiden, as thou saist he is.	2342

MAIDEN-HEAD = 1

Carowse full measure to her maiden-head,	1611

MAIDS = 1

Maids milde behauiour and sobrietie. | Peace *Tranio.*	374

MAIMD = 1

'Tis ten to one it maim'd you too out right	2605

MAINTAIND = *1

*it shall be so farre forth friendly maintain'd, till by hel-|ping	439

MAINTAINE = 1

my good Father, I am able to maintaine it.	2454

MAINTENANCE = 1

And for thy maintenance. Commits his body	2706

MAIST *l.**387 *1003 *1652 = *3

MAISTER = *2

*are you? Maister, ha's my fellow *Tranio* stolne your	530
Cur. Do you heare ho? you must meete my maister | to countenance my mistris.	1726

MAKE = 30*9

And burne sweet Wood to make the Lodging sweete:	53
To make a dulcet and a heauenly sound:	55
May shew her dutie, and make knowne her loue.	128
Beg. What would you make me mad? Am not I *Chri-|stopher*	170
Thy hounds shall make the Welkin answer them	197

MAKE *cont.*

To make a stale of me amongst these mates?	360
Bap. Gentlemen, that I may soone make good	377
And make her beare the pennance of her tongue.	393
While I make way from hence to saue my life:	541
*To make one among these wooers: if thou ask me why,	555
Haue leaue and leisure to make loue to her,	701
And so she shall: *Lucentio* shal make one,	818
To make a bondmaide and a slaue of mee,	857
Within your house, to make mine eye the witnesse	913
Do make my selfe a sutor to your daughter,	953
Thy beauty that doth make me like thee well,	1153
Heere comes your father, neuer make deniall,	1159
A meacocke wretch can make the curstest shrew:	1193
And let your father make her the assurance,	1269
Be Bride to you, if you make this assurance: | If not, to Signior *Gremio*:	1278
My Lessons make no musicke in three parts.	1353
Make friends, inuite, and proclaime the banes,	1404
And make assurance heere in *Padua*	1517
Make it no wonder: if you knew my businesse,	1573
*make a fire, and they are comming after to warme them:	1643
*and so long am I at the least. But wilt thou make a fire,	1666
To make her come, and know her Keepers call:	1828
Ile make him glad to seeme *Vincentio*,	1921
Tra. Then go with me, to make the matter good,	1970
Tai. You bid me make it orderlie and well,	2079
Ile none of it; hence, make your best of it.	2085
Belike you meane to make a puppet of me.	2088
Pet. Why true, he meanes to make a puppet of thee.	2089
Tail. She saies your Worship meanes to make a | puppet of her.	2090
Cambio hie you home, and bid *Bianca* make her readie | straight:	2245
Hort. A will make the man mad to make the woman | of him.	2333
Petr. Do good old grandsire, & withall make known	2348
Vinc. What if a man bring him a hundred pound or | two to make merrie withall.	2402

MAKER = *1

Vin. Thy father: oh villaine, he is a Saile-maker in | *Bergamo*.	2455

MAKES = 2*3

3.Man. Oh this it is that makes your Ladie mourne.	178
2.Man. Oh this is it that makes your seruants droop.	179
*apples: but come, since this bar in law makes vs friends,	438
And makes a God of such a Cullion;	1868
For 'tis the minde that makes the bodie rich.	2155

MAKING = 1*1

Cur. In her chamber, making a sermon of continen-|cie	1816
Ile finde about the making of the bed,	1834

MALADY = 1

In perill to incurre your former malady,	276

MALT-HORSE = *1

Pet. You pezant, swain, you horson malt-horse drudg	1756

MAN = 28*16

Sirs, I will practise on this drunken man.	40
Oh that a mightie man of such discent,	167
And twentie more such names and men as these, | Which neuer were, nor no man euer saw.	248
My men should call me Lord, I am your good-man.	259
Flourish. Enter Lucentio, and his man Triano.	299

MAN *cont.*

*I can by any meanes light on a fit man to teach her that	415
*her father be verie rich, any man is so verie a foole to be | married to	
hell?	428
*mine to endure her lowd alarums, why man there bee	431
*good fellowes in the world, and a man could light on	432
*Sweet *Bianca*, happy man be his dole: hee that runnes	442
For man or master: then it followes thus;	507
Some *Neapolitan*, or meaner man of *Pisa*.	511
I kil'd a man, and feare I was descried:	539
Enter Petruchio, and his man Grumio.	565
any man ha's rebus'd your worship?	572
On this yong man: For learning and behauiour	734
And will not promise her to any man,	834
Tranio. If it be so sir, that you are the man	837
Enter Gremio, Lucentio, in the habit of a meane man,	897
I do present you with a man of mine	916
A man well knowne throughout all Italy.	930
Bap. A mightie man of *Pisa* by report,	967
Thou must be married to no man but me,	1154
Was it not to refresh the minde of man | After his studies, or his vsuall	
paine?	1306
*Lucentio that comes a wooing, *priami*, is my man Tra-|nio,	1328
Luc. Spit in the hole man, and tune againe.	1333
And to be noted for a merry man;	1402
a man is more then one, and yet not many.	1467
I am to get a man what ere he be,	1514
Rescue thy Mistresse if thou be a man:	1623
*all foule waies: was euer man so beaten? was euer man	1641
*so raide? was euer man so weary? I am sent before to	1642
*selfe: for considering the weather, a taller man then I	1648
*know'st winter tames man, woman, and beast: for it	1661
Pet. Where be these knaues? What no man at doore	1747
Another way I haue to man my Haggard,	1827
Hort. A will make the man mad to make the woman | of him.	2333
Happier the man whom fauourable stars	2338
This is a man old, wrinckled, faded, withered,	2341
Vinc. What if a man bring him a hundred pound or | two to make	
merrie withall.	2402
Bion. Helpe, helpe, helpe, here's a mad man will mur-|der me.	2435
Bapt. What is the man lunaticke?	2450
*your habit: but your words shew you a mad man: why	2452

MANAGE = 1

Then take him vp, and manage well the iest:	49

MANET = 2

Exeunt ambo. Manet Tranio and Lucentio	448
Or shall I send my daughter *Kate* to you. | *Exit. Manet Petruchio.*	1035

MANIE = 1 *3

*tooth in her head, though she haue as manie diseases as	646
*bridle was burst: how I lost my crupper, with manie	1712
Gru. Face not mee: thou hast brau'd manie men,	2110
Pitchers haue eares, and I haue manie seruants,	2234

MANNER = 1

Stand by, and marke the manner of his teaching.	1851

MANNERS = 1 *1

And therefore frame your manners to the time	534
*you vse your manners discreetly in all kind of com-|panies:	550

MANS = 1

to take vpon you another mans name. 2416

MANTUA = 4

His name is *Litio*, borne in *Mantua*. 921
Tra. What Countreyman I pray? | *Ped*. Of *Mantua*. 1932
Tra. Of *Mantua* Sir, marrie God forbid, 1934
Tra. 'Tis death for any one in Mantua 1937

MANY = 2*1

a man is more then one, and yet not many. 1467
*swore, as if the Vicar meant to cozen him: but after ma-|ny 1552
Gru. Thou hast fac'd many things. | *Tail*. I haue. 2108

MARCANTANT = 1

Tra. What is he *Biondello*? | *Bio*. Master, a Marcantant, or a pedant, 1915

MARCELLUS = 1

That now is lying in Marcellus roade: 1257

MARCHANTS = *1

**Bap*. Faith Gentlemen now I play a marchants part, 1207

MARIE = 1

marie sir see where he lookes out of the window. 2433

MARIED = *1

**Biond*. I cannot tarry: I knew a wench maried in an 2284

MARKD = 1*1

Perhaps you mark'd not what's the pith of all. 469
Tra. Saw you no more? Mark'd you not how hir sister 474

MARKE = 2

Ladie: would 'twere done. *They sit and marke*. 564
Stand by, and marke the manner of his teaching. 1851

MARKET-PLACE = 1

My Fathers beares more toward the Market-place, 2390

MARKS = *1

**Petr*. A hundred marks, my *Kate* does put her down. 2576

MARRD = 1

I tell thee I, that thou hast marr'd her gowne. 2100

MARRE = 1

I did not bid you marre it to the time. 2082

MARRIAGE = 5

To speake the ceremoniall rites of marriage? 1394
Hee'll wooe a thousand, point the day of marriage,* 1403
'Twere good me-thinkes to steale our marriage, 1523
To passe assurance of a dowre in marriage 1973
That haue by marriage made thy daughter mine, 2497

MARRIAN = *1

*Aske *Marrian Hacket* the fat Alewife of Wincot, if shee 174

MARRIE = 8*3

Beg. Marrie I fare well, for heere is cheere enough. 255
**Beg*. Marrie I will let them play, it is not a Comon-|tie, 291
Gre. What's that I pray? | *Hor*. Marrie sir to get a husband for her
Sister. 423
*minde is: why giue him Gold enough, and marrie him 644
Yea, and to marrie her, if her dowrie please. 750
Neuer to marrie with her, though she would intreate, 1881
Tra. Of *Mantua* Sir, marrie God forbid, 1934
What, did he marrie me to famish me? 1981
Pet. Marrie and did: but if you be remembred, 2081
Gru. Marrie sir with needle and thred. 2106
**Petr*. Marrie peace it boads, and loue, and quiet life, 2663

MARRIED = 10*1

*her father be verie rich, any man is so verie a foole to be | married to hell? 428
When I shall aske the banes, and when be married. 1049
Thou must be married to no man but me, 1154
And kisse me *Kate*, we will be married a sonday. | *Exit Petruchio and Katherine*. 1204
On sonday next, you know | My daughter *Katherine* is to be married: 1275
That *Katherine* and *Petruchio* should be married, 1390
To me she's married, not vnto my cloathes: 1500
I wil be married to a wealthy Widdow, 1885
Thy Sonne by this hath married: wonder not, 2362
Bap. But doe you heare sir, haue you married my 2513
We three are married, but you two are sped. 2744

MARRY = 7*1

Tra. I marry am I sir, and now 'tis plotted. | *Luc*. I haue it *Tranio*. 491
Pet. Marry so I meane sweet *Katherine* in thy bed: 1146
And will you, nill you, I will marry you. 1150
If it would please him come and marry her. 1408
Bap. But thus I trust you will not marry her. 1498
And marry sweet *Bianca* with consent. 1520
Gre. I marry sir, now it begins to worke. 1604
Hor. Quicke proceeders marry, now tel me I pray, 1859

MARRYAGE = *1

*after mee I know the rout is comming, such a mad mar-|ryage 1562

MART = 1

And venture madly on a desperate Mart. 1208

MARUAILE *see also* meruaile = 1

Gre. I maruaile *Cambio* comes not all this while. 2386

MARUAYLOUS *see* meruaylous

MASKING = 1

Oh mercie God, what masking stuffe is heere? 2072

MASTER *see also* Mr., maister = 30*16

Tra. Me Pardonato, gentle master mine: 324
Onely (good master) while we do admire | This vertue, and this morall discipline, 328
Tra. Master some shew to welcome vs to Towne. 346
Tra. Husht master, heres some good pastime toward; 371
Tra. Master, it is no time to chide you now, 462
Tra. Master, you look'd so longly on the maide, 468
Master, your Loue must liue a maide at home, 485
Tra. Master, for my hand, | Both our inuentions meet and iumpe in one. 493
Tra. You will be schoole-master, 496
For man or master: then it followes thus; 507
Thou shalt be master, *Tranio* in my sted: 508
*When I am alone, why then I am *Tranio*: but in | all places else, your master *Lucentio*. 551
Gru. Helpe mistris helpe, my master is mad. 585
sir. Well, was it fit for a seruant to vse his master so, 599
To old *Baptista* as a schoole-master 698
*Master, master, looke about you: Who goes there? ha. 706
'Tis in my head to doe my master good: 1288
Hort. I must beleeue my master, else I promise you, 1347
Good master take it not vnkindly pray 1350
Bion. Master, master, newes, and such newes as you | neuer heard of, 1420
I will be master of what is mine owne, 1615

MASTER *cont.*

Cur. Is my master and his wife comming *Grumio*?	1656
*hath tam'd my old master, and my new mistris, and my | selfe fellow	
Curtis.	1662
Master and mistris are almost frozen to death.	1674
**Gru.* First know my horse is tired, my master & mi-|stris falne out.	
Cur. How?	1688
hill, my Master riding behinde my Mistris.	1700
Nat. All things is readie, how neere is our master?	1743
not--- Cockes passion, silence, I heare my master.	1745
**Bian.* What Master reade you first, resolue me that?	1854
Bian. And may you proue sir Master of your Art.	1856
Tra. I mistris, and *Petruchio* is the master,	1907
Bion. Oh Master, master I haue watcht so long,	1911
Tra. What is he *Biondello*? | *Bio.* Master, a Marcantant, or a pedant,	1915
Iust as my master had direction:	2102
*vnto thee, I bid thy Master cut out the gowne, but I did	2112
**Gru.* Master, if euer I said loose-bodied gowne, sow	2118
Away I say, commend me to thy master. *Exit Tail.*	2151
**Biond.* You saw my Master winke and laugh vpon | you?	2261
*Master hath appointed me to goe to Saint *Lukes* to bid	2287
*send'em good shipping: but who is here? mine old Ma-|ster	2421
**Bion.* What my old worshipfull old master? yes	2432
**Ven.* *Lucentio*: oh he hath murdred his Master; laie	2465
Which runs himselfe, and catches for his Master.	2596

MASTERS = 6*4

*But sirra, not for my sake, but your masters, I ad-|uise	549
If that be all Masters, I heare no harme.	754
Tra. Softly my Masters: If you be Gentlemen	810
**Bian.* Farewell sweet masters both, I must be gone.	1379
All for my Masters sake *Lucentio*.	1531
**Gru.* Fie, fie on all tired Iades, on all mad Masters, z	1640
*presume to touch a haire of my Masters horse-taile, till	1722
Pet. Go take it vp vnto thy masters vse.	2140
**Gru.* Villaine, not for thy life: Take vp my Mistresse | gowne for thy	
masters vse.	2141
Take vp my Mistris gowne to his masters vse. | Oh fie, fie, fie.	2145

MATCH = 5

God send you ioy, *Petruchio*, 'tis a match.	1199
Gre. Was euer match clapt vp so sodainly?	1206
Bap. The gaine I seeke, is quiet me the match.	1211
The match is made, and all is done,	2228
Petr. A match, 'tis done.	2620

MATCHES = 1

Tra. Of all mad matches neuer was the like.	1628

MATCHT = 1

To haue him matcht, and if you please to like	2214

MATED = 1

Bian. That being mad her selfe, she's madly mated.	1630

MATES = 3*1

To make a stale of me amongst these mates?	360
Hor. Mates maid, how meane you that?	361
No mates for you, | Vnlesse you were of gentler milder mould.	362
*he, as if he had beene aboord carowsing to his Mates af-|ter	1554

MATHEMATICKES = 3

The Mathematickes, and the Metaphysickes	336
Cunning in Musicke, and the Mathematickes,	917

MATHEMATICKES *cont.*
As the other in Musicke and Mathematickes: 945
MATTER = 4*3
    Beg. Yes by Saint Anne do I, a good matter surely: 560
    Hor. How now, what's the matter? My olde friend 588
    Gru. Nay 'tis no matter sir, what he leges in Latine. 596
    That thinkes with oathes to face the matter out. 1169
    Tra. Then go with me, to make the matter good, 1970
    Tra. How now, what's the matter? 2449
    That fac'd and braued me in this matter so? 2501
MAY *l.*128 149 279 377 404 406 *410 *412 *420 499 592 622 *676 700 787
    815 817 848 928 *950 959 992 1014 1098 1247 1273 1344 *1352 1422
    1581 1597 1606 1856 1884 2058 2171 2183 2250 *2286 2290 2292 2360
    2365 *2382 2414 2425 *2486 2490 2737 = 41*9
MAZE = 1
    And I haue thrust my selfe into this maze, 621
ME *l.*28 *46 54 90 100 102 120 *160 *161 *170 *175 *176 *258 259 268
    270 272 273 277 310 320 324 350 360 370 449 456 460 461 495 519 525
    542 *555 573 576 577 *597 *598 *607 *608 614 619 627 638 639 660 670
    672 686 696 697 714 717 738 741 742 745 755 757 761 774 788 804 811
    815 823 828 831 838 *856 861 865 873 875 886 889 893 907 920 927
    *935 949 951 955 981 984 989 1001 1016 1021 1025 1027 1031 1046 1047
    1055 1061 1072 1075 1099 1101 1111 1120 1122 1135 1153 1154 1165
    1167 1187 1190 1194 *1198 1204 1211 1245 1265 1270 1301 1308 *1311
    *1352 1373 1497 1500 1501 1567 1569 1574 1576 1578 1582 1584 1587
    1588 1589 1598 1613 *1647 *1670 *1704 *1708 *1710 1757 1796 1849
    *1854 *1859 1861 1884 1886 1924 1931 1944 1949 1965 1970 1974 1976
    1981 1989 1993 1996 1999 2011 *2019 2052 2060 2069 2079 2083 2088
    *2111 *2119 2135 2138 2151 2164 2183 2194 2204 2205 2208 2216 2220
    2221 2244 *2287 2311 2326 2352 2367 2376 2437 *2463 *2467 2472 2501
    2502 2505 2512 2523 2525 2554 2562 2567 2581 *2585 2590 2592 2595
    2603 2604 2623 2637 2648 2655 2659 2679 2684 = 200*35
MEACOCKE = 1
    A meacocke wretch can make the curstest shrew: 1193
MEADS = 1
    It blots thy beautie, as frosts doe bite the Meads, 2697
MEANE = 20
    Hor. Mates maid, how meane you that? 361
    Bion. He that ha's the two faire daughters: ist he you | meane? 790
    Gre. Hearke you sir, you meane not her to--- 793
    Enter Gremio, Lucentio, in the habit of a meane man, 897
    Pet. I see you do not meane to part with her, 925
    Kate. No such Iade as you, if me you meane. 1075
    Pet. What, you meane my face. 1113
    Pet. Marry so I meane sweet *Katherine* in thy bed: 1146
    Yet oftentimes he goes but meane apparel'd. 1458
    Tra. That by degrees we meane to looke into, 1526
    And therefore heere I meane to take my leaue. 1570
    Belike you meane to make a puppet of me. 2088
    Euen in these honest meane habiliments: 2153
    For this poore furniture, and meane array. 2163
    I meane *Hortentio* is afeard of you. 2557
    Kat. Mistris, how meane you that? | *Wid.* Thus I conceiue by him. 2560
    Kate. A verie meane meaning. 2571
    Wid. Right, I meane you. 2572
    Kat. And I am meane indeede, respecting you. 2573
    Bian. Am I your Bird, I meane to shift my bush, 2589

MEANER = 1
Some *Neapolitan,* or meaner man of *Pisa.*   511
MEANES = 5*4
  Belike some Noble Gentleman that meanes   80
  **Sincklo.* I thinke 'twas *Soto* that your honor meanes.   98
  *I can by any meanes light on a fit man to teach her that   415
  Who woo'd in haste, and meanes to wed at leysure: 1399
  Yet neuer meanes to wed where he hath woo'd: 1405
  Vpon my life *Petruchio* meanes but well,   1410
  **Pet.* Why true, he meanes to make a puppet of thee.   2089
  Tail. She saies your Worship meanes to make a | puppet of her.   2090
  **Peda.* Lay hands on the villaine, I beleeue a meanes   2417
MEANEST = 1
So honor peereth in the meanest habit.   2157
MEANING = 3*1
  Tra. He hath some meaning in his mad attire,   1507
  *to expound the meaning or morrall of his signes and to-|kens.   2265
  And now you know my meaning.   2570
  Kate. A verie meane meaning.   2571
MEANT = 1*1
  *swore, as if the Vicar meant to cozen him: but after ma-|ny   1552
  I praie you tell me what you meant by that.   2567
MEASURE = 2
  And shrow'd, and froward, so beyond all measure,   656
  Carowse full measure to her maiden-head,   1611
MEASURES = 1
Measures my husbands sorrow by his woe: 2569
MEATE = 10
  Pet. 'Tis burnt, and so is all the meate: 1793
  The meate was well, if you were so contented.   1801
  She eate no meate to day, nor none shall eate.   1831
  As with the meate, some vndeserued fault   1833
  Am staru'd for meate, giddie for lacke of sleepe: 1987
  Gru. I feare it is too chollericke a meate.   1997
  That feed'st me with the verie name of meate.   2011
  Enter Petruchio, and Hortensio with meate.   2015
  To dresse thy meate my selfe, and bring it thee.   2021
  And so shall mine before you touch the meate.   2028
MEAT-YARD = 1
me thy meat-yard, and spare not me.   2135
MEDDLE = 1
Go ply thy Needle, meddle not with her.   882
MEE *l.*158 357 857 *1334 *1562 1897 2032 *2110 *2264 2427 *2738 = 5*6
MEEREST = 1
He cried vpon it at the meerest losse,   26
MEET = 1
  Tra. Master, for my hand, | Both our inuentions meet and iumpe in
  one.   493
MEETE = 6*1
  For so your doctors hold it very meete,   285
  And where two raging fires meete together,   997
  **Cur.* Do you heare ho? you must meete my maister | to countenance
  my mistris.   1726
  Did I not bid thee meete me in the Parke,   1757
  Yet as they are, heere are they come to meete you.   1765
  If not, elsewhere they meete with charitie: 1984
  And in no sence is meete or amiable.   2699

MELANCHOLLY = 1
And melancholly is the Nurse of frenzie, 287
MEMORIE = *1
*things of worthy memorie, which now shall die in obli-|uion, 1713
MEN = 9*1
And how my men will stay themselues from laughter, 146
Nor no such men as you haue reckon'd vp, 245
And twentie more such names and men as these, | Which neuer were,
nor no man euer saw. 248
My men should call me Lord, I am your good-man. 259
Preferre them hither: for to cunning men, 401
Bianca. Beleeue me sister, of all the men aliue, 865
How tame when men and women are alone, 1192
Gre. And may not yong men die as well as old? 1273
**Gru*. Face not mee: thou hast brau'd manie men, 2110
Go call my men, and let vs straight to him, 2167
MEND = 2
Ile mend it with a Largesse. Take your paper too, 716
Take that, and mend the plucking of the other. 1776
MENDED = 1*1
Be patient, to morrow't shalbe mended, 1808
**Petr*. Verie well mended: kisse him for that good | Widdow. 2564
MERCHANT = 2
A Merchant of great Trafficke through the world: 311
A Merchant of incomparable wealth. 1954
MERCHANTS *see* marchants
MERCIE = 1*1
Oh mercie God, what masking stuffe is heere? 2072
**Hor*. God-a-mercie *Grumio*, then hee shall haue no | oddes. 2136
MERIMAN = 1
Brach *Meriman*, the poore Curre is imbost, 20
MERITES = 1
I am sure sweet Kate, this kindnesse merites thankes. 2022
MERRIE = 5
You breake into some merrie passion, 107
May well abate the ouer-merrie spleene, 149
Why when I say? Nay good sweete *Kate* be merrie. 1771
Be merrie *Kate*: Some water heere: what hoa. 1777
**Vinc*. What if a man bring him a hundred pound or | two to make
merrie withall. 2402
MERRIMENT = 2
And frame your minde to mirth and merriment, 289
For our first merriment hath made thee iealous. *Exeunt*. 2375
MERRY = 4
And to be noted for a merry man; 1402
Though he be merry, yet withall he's honest. 1413
Be madde and merry, or goe hang your selues: 1612
Vin. Faire Sir, and you my merry Mistris, 2351
MERUAILE = 1
'Tis meruaile, but that you are but newly come, 1942
MERUAYLOUS = *1
*poore petitioners speake too? *Bacare*, you are meruay-|lous forward. 933
MES = *1
MESSE = 1
Welcome, one messe is like to be your cheere, 2255
MESSENGER see also Mes. = 2
Enter a Messenger. 282

MESSENGER cont.

Enter a Messenger.	1375

MET = 5

Gre. And you are wel met, Signior *Hortensio.*	729
Hor. 'Tis well: and I haue met a Gentleman	737
Heere is a Gentleman whom by chance I met	747
Tra. Signior *Baptista* you are happilie met:	2202
Petr. Happily met, the happier for thy sonne:	2358

METAPHYSICKES = 1

The Mathematickes, and the Metaphysickes	336

METE = 1

Or I shall so be-mete thee with thy yard,	2098

METHINKES *see also* thinkes = 2

Methinkes he lookes as though he were in loue:	1382
How does my father? gentles methinkes you frowne,	1476

MEUD = 1

And therefore has he closely meu'd her vp,	486

MEW = 1

Gre. Why will you mew her vp | (Signior *Baptista*) for this fiend of hell,	391

ME-THINKES = 1

'Twere good me-thinkes to steale our marriage,	1523

MI = 1

Ela mi, show pitty or I die,	1371

MIDST = 1

Kate. What in the midst of the streete?	2524

MIERY = *1

*her horse: thou shouldst haue heard in how miery a	1706

MIGHT *l.*476 *1329 *1645 1943 2236 = 3*2

MIGHTIE = 3

For he is nothing but a mightie Lord:	69
Oh that a mightie man of such discent,	167
Bap. A mightie man of *Pisa* by report,	967

MIGHTILY = 1

Striue mightily, but eate and drinke as friends.	851

MIGHTINESSE = *1

2.Man. Wilt please your mightinesse to wash your | hands:	228

MILCH-KINE = 1

I haue a hundred milch-kine to the pale,	1239

MILDE = 2

Maids milde behauiour and sobrietie. | Peace *Tranio.*	374
Her wondrous qualities, and milde behauiour,	911

MILDER = 1

No mates for you, | Vnlesse you were of gentler milder mould.	362

MILDNESSE = 2

Hearing thy mildnesse prais'd in euery Towne,	1062
But thou with mildnesse entertain'st thy wooers,	1129

MILLION = 1

Ile buckler thee against a Million. *Exeunt. P. Ka.*	1625

MINDE = 8*2

And frame your minde to mirth and merriment,	289
Tell me thy minde, for I haue *Pisa* left,	320
1.Man. My Lord you nod, you do not minde the | play.	558
*minde is: why giue him Gold enough, and marrie him	644
My minde presumes for his owne good, and yours.	781
Was it not to refresh the minde of man | After his studies, or his vsuall paine?	1306
Your betters haue indur'd me say my minde,	2060

MINDE *cont.*
  For 'tis the minde that makes the bodie rich.   2155
  And the Moone changes euen as your minde: 2317
  My minde hath bin as bigge as one of yours,   2728
MINDED = 1
  I am as peremptorie as she proud minded: 996
MINE *l.*324 403 *431 766 913 916 951 *1104 1244 1265 *1266 1396 1496
  1525 1615 1620 1872 1884 2028 2096 2355 *2421 *2463 2497 2652 =
  20*5, 1
  I would not wed her for a mine of Gold.   658
MINERUA = *1
  Luc. Harke *Tranio*, thou maist heare *Minerua* speak.   387
MINIMO = 1
  Redime te captam quam queas minimo.   465
MINION = 1
  Kate. Minion thou lyest: Is't not *Hortensio*?   868
MINOLA = 6
  Hor. Her father is *Baptista Minola*,   663
  Her name is *Katherina Minola*,   665
  Trow you whither I am going? To *Baptista Minola*,   730
  To the house of Signior *Baptista Minola*?   789
  The narrow prying father *Minola*,   1529
  And giue assurance to *Baptista Minola*.   1922
MINSTRELS = *1
  *neuer was before: harke, harke, I heare the min-|strels play. *Musicke
  playes.*   1563
MIO = 1
  *Hor. Alla nostra casa bene venuto multo honorata signi-|or mio
  Petruchio.*   593
MIRACLES = 1
  Luc. Loue wrought these miracles. *Biancas* loue   2504
MIRTH = 1
  And frame your minde to mirth and merriment,   289
MISERY = 1
  That triumph thus vpon my misery: 2013
MISSD *see* mist
MISSE = *1
  Petr. You are verie sencible, and yet you misse my | sence: 2555
MIST = 1
  Therefore a health to all that shot and mist.   2594
MISTAKE = 2*2
  Bap. Mistake me not, I speake but as I finde,   927
  Hor. Mistake no more, I am not *Lisio*,   1864
  Bap. You mistake sir, you mistake sir, praie what do | you thinke is his
  name?   2457
MISTAKING = 2
  Kate. Pardon old father my mistaking eies,   2343
  Pardon I pray thee for my mad mistaking.   2347
MISTOOKE = 1
  I did but tell her she mistooke her frets,   1017
MISTRESSE = 4*3
  And quaffe carowses to our Mistresse health,   849
  Nicke. Mistresse, your father prayes you leaue your | (books,   1376
  Luc. Faith Mistresse then I haue no cause to stay.   1380
  Rescue thy Mistresse if thou be a man: 1623
  Luc. Mistresse, what's your opinion of your sister?   1629
  Luc. While you sweet deere proue Mistresse of my | heart.   1857

MISTRESSE *cont.*

Gru. Villaine, not for thy life: Take vp my Mistresse | gowne for thy
  masters vse. 2141

MISTRIS = 24*4

*we may yet againe haue accesse to our faire Mistris, and 420
Gru. Helpe mistris helpe, my master is mad. 585
A fine Musitian to instruct our Mistris, 739
*hath tam'd my old master, and my new mistris, and my | selfe fellow
  Curtis. 1662
*or shall I complaine on thee to our mistris, whose hand 1667
Master and mistris are almost frozen to death. 1674
Gru. First know my horse is tired, my master & mi-|stris falne out.
Cur. How? 1688
hill, my Master riding behinde my Mistris. 1700
Cur. Do you heare ho? you must meete my maister | to countenance
  my mistris. 1726
Tra. Is't possible friend *Lisio*, that mistris *Bianca* 1847
Hor. Now Mistris, profit you in what you reade? 1853
you that durst sweare that your Mistris *Bianca* 1860
Tra. Mistris *Bianca*, blesse you with such grace, 1892
Tra. Mistris we haue. | *Luc.* Then we are rid of *Lisio.* 1898
Tra. I mistris, and *Petruchio* is the master, 1907
Hor. Mistris, what cheere? | *Kate.* Faith as cold as can be. 2017
Come Mistris Kate, Ile beare you companie. 2031
Gru. You are i'th right sir, 'tis for my mistris. 2139
Take vp my Mistris gowne to his masters vse. | Oh fie, fie, fie. 2145
Good morrow gentle Mistris, where away: 2325
Vin. Faire Sir, and you my merry Mistris, 2351
and then come backe to my mistris as soone as I can. 2385
Vinc. What, you notorious villaine, didst thou neuer | see thy Mistris
  father, *Vincentio*? 2430
Kat. Mistris, how meane you that? | *Wid.* Thus I conceiue by him. 2560
Vin. I Mistris Bride, hath that awakened you? 2584
Goe *Biondello*, bid your Mistris come to me. | *Bio.* I goe. *Exit.* 2623
Bio. Sir, my Mistris sends you word 2629
Sirra *Grumio*, goe to your Mistris, 2647

MISTRUST = 2

In time I may beleeue, yet I mistrust. 1344
Bian. Mistrust it not, for sure *Aeacides* 1345

MISVSE = 1

As had she studied to misvse me so. 1027

MOCKERY = 1

What will be said, what mockery will it be? 1392

MOCKING = *1

Wid. Come, come, your mocking: we will haue no | telling. 2689

MODEST = 2

If I atchieue not this yong modest gyrle: 459
For shee's not froward, but modest as the Doue, 1173

MODESTIE = 3

If it be husbanded with modestie. 72
As is the other, for beauteous modestie. 827
Her affability and bashfull modestie: 910

MODESTIES = 1

But I am doubtfull of your modesties, 104

MONGST = 1

I may haue welcome 'mongst the rest that woo, 959

MONIE = 2
*two and fiftie horses. Why nothing comes amisse, so | monie comes
withall.   647
For I haue bils for monie by exchange   1945
MONSTER = *2
*in't for a feather: a monster, a very monster in apparell,   1455
MONSTROUS = 1*2
*Lord. Oh monstrous beast, how like a swine he lyes.   38
Pet. Oh monstrous arrogance: 2092
*Vin. Thus strangers may be haild and abusd: oh mon-|strous villaine.   2486
MONUMENT = 1
As if they saw some wondrous monument, | Some Commet, or vnusuall
prodigie?   1478
MONY = *1
*them, would take her with all faults, and mony enough.   433
MOONE = 7*1
Good Lord how bright and goodly shines the Moone.   2297
*Kate. The Moone, the Sunne: it is not Moonelight | now.   2298
Pet. I say it is the Moone that shines so bright.   2300
It shall be moone, or starre, or what I list,   2303
And be it moone, or sunne, or what you please: 2309
Petr. I say it is the Moone.   2312
Kate. I know it is the Moone.   2313
And the Moone changes euen as your minde: 2317
MOONELIGHT = *1
*Kate. The Moone, the Sunne: it is not Moonelight | now.   2298
MOOUD = 1
My selfe am moou'd to woo thee for my wife.   1065
MORALIZE = 1
Luc. I pray thee moralize them.   2267
MORALL = 1
Onely (good master) while we do admire | This vertue, and this morall
discipline,   328
MORE = 43*10
Anon Ile giue thee more instructions. | Exit a seruingman.   141
*me what raiment Ile weare, for I haue no more doub-|lets   161
*then backes: no more stockings then legges: nor   162
*no more shooes then feet, nay sometime more feete then   163
Thou hast a Ladie farre more Beautifull,   214
Oh that once more you knew but what you are: 231
And twentie more such names and men as these, | Which neuer were,
nor no man euer saw.   248
And slept aboue some fifteene yeare or more.   267
Lady. No my good Lord, it is more pleasing stuffe.   293
For I haue more to commune with Bianca. Exit.   405
*Tra. Saw you no more? Mark'd you not how hir sister   474
One thing more rests, that thy selfe execute,   554
Comes there any more of it?   561
*with it, that shee shal haue no more eies to see withall | then a Cat:
you know him not sir.   680
And her with-holds from me. Other more   686
Yea and perhaps with more successefull words   723
*Gremio. No: if without more words you will get you | hence.   801
She may more sutors haue, and me for one.   815
Then well one more may faire Bianca haue;   817
And let it be more then Alcides twelue.   830
Which I could fancie, more then any other.   867

MORE *cont.*

Kate. Oh then belike you fancie riches more,	871
She is not for your turne, the more my greefe.	924
More kindely beholding to you then any:	941
I loue her ten times more then ere I did,	1029
Tra. And I am one that loue *Bianca* more	1216
Gre. Nay, I haue offred all, I haue no more,	1263
And she can haue no more then all I haue,	1264
More pleasant, pithy, and effectuall,	1361
Much more a shrew of impatient humour.	1418
a man is more then one, and yet not many.	1467
Which at more leysure I will so excuse,	1491
Cur. By this reckning he is more shrew than she.	1715
Hor. Mistake no more, I am not *Lisio,*	1864
Neuer to woo her more, but do forsweare her	1877
*Ka. The more my wrong, the more his spite appears.	1980
And that which spights me more then all these wants,	1989
More queint, more pleasing, nor more commendable:	2087
Go take it hence, be gone, and say no more.	2148
What is the Iay more precious then the Larke?	2158
Because his feathers are more beautifull.	2159
And therefore if you say no more then this,	2225
If this be not that you looke for, I haue no more to say,	2281
*Petr. Come on a Gods name, once more toward our | fathers:	2295
Faire louely Maide, once more good day to thee:	2331
My Fathers beares more toward the Market-place,	2390
And show more signe of her obedience,	2672
Bian. The more foole you for laying on my dutie.	2685
My heart as great, my reason haplie more,	2729

MORNE = 1

Shee is not hot, but temperate as the morne,	1174

MORNING = 4

Aboue the morning Larke. Or wilt thou hunt,	196
*with this condition; To be whipt at the hie crosse euerie | morning.	435
As morning Roses newly washt with dew:	1042
The morning weares, 'tis time we were at Church.	1494

MORRALL = *1

*to expound the meaning or morrall of his signes and to-|kens.	2265

MORROW = 8*2

To morrow I intend to hunt againe. | *Hunts.* I will my Lord.	32
Gre. Good morrow neighbour *Baptista.*	900
*Bap. Good morrow neighbour *Gremio*: God saue | you Gentlemen.	901
Good morrow *Kate,* for thats your name I heare.	1052
And if I die to morrow this is hers,	1243
You know to morrow is the wedding day.	1378
When I should bid good morrow to my Bride?	1505
No, nor to morrow, not till I please my selfe,	1595
*Hor. Tailor, Ile pay thee for thy gowne to morrow,	2149
Good morrow gentle Mistris, where away:	2325

MORROWT = 1

Be patient, to morrow't shalbe mended,	1808

MORTAL = 1

That mortal eares might hardly indure the din.	476

MOSE = *1

*with the glanders, and like to mose in the chine, trou-|bled	1438

MOST = 7

A most delicious banquet by his bed,	43

MOST *cont.*

In briefe sir, studie what you most affect.	339
And for I know she taketh most delight	396
When (with a most impatient diuellish spirit)	1019
To this most patient, sweet, and vertuous wife,	1577
And he whose wife is most obedient,	2610
That seeming to be most, which we indeed least are.	2733

MOTHER = 3

Petr. It is *extempore*, from my mother wit.	1142
Kate. A witty mother, witlesse else her sonne.	1143
Ped. I sir, so his mother saies, if I may beleeue her.	2414

MOTHERS = *1

Pet. Now by my mothers sonne, and that's my selfe,	2302

MOTHY = *1

*two broken points: his horse hip'd with an olde mo- |thy	1436

MOTION = *1

Gru. Bion. Oh excellent motion: fellowes let's be gon.	852

MOTIONS = 1

Hor. The motions good indeed, and be it so,	853

MOUABLE = 2

Remoue you hence: I knew you at the first | You were a mouable.	1068
Pet. Why, what's a mouable? | *Kat.* A ioyn'd stoole.	1070

MOUD = 1*2

Kate. Mou'd, in good time, let him that mou'd you | hether	1066
A woman mou'd, is like a fountaine troubled,	2700

MOUE = 2

Which seeme to moue and wanton with her breath,	204
Luc. Tranio, I saw her corrall lips to moue,	477

MOUES = 1

She moues me not, or not remoues at least	638

MOULD = 1

No mates for you, | Vnlesse you were of gentler milder mould.	362

MOULDED = 1

Pet. Why this was moulded on a porrenger,	2048

MOUNT = 1

There wil we mount, and thither walke on foote,	2169

MOUNTAINES = 1

Pet. I to the proofe, as Mountaines are for windes,	1005

MOURNE = *1

3.Man. Oh this it is that makes your Ladie mourne.	178

MOURNES = 1

And that his Ladie mournes at his disease,	66

MOUTH = 1*1

Luc. And not a iot of *Tranio* in your mouth,	544
*mouth, my heart in my belly, ere I should come by a fire	1646

MOUTHD = 1

And couple *Clowder* with the deepe-mouth'd brach,	21

MR = 2

Tra. Well said Mr, mum, and gaze your fill.	376
Gru. My Mr is growne quarrelsome:	578

MUCH = 14*3

Wherein your cunning can assist me much.	102
Beg. 'Tis much, seruants leaue me and her alone:	270
Seeing too much sadnesse hath congeal'd your blood,	286
And verie rich: but th'art too much my friend,	629
I tell you 'tis incredible to beleeue | How much she loues me: oh the kindest *Kate*,	1186

MUCH *cont.*

My Land amounts not to so much in all:	1255
And twice as much what ere thou offrest next.	1262
Your Lecture shall haue leisure for as much.	1303
Much more a shrew of impatient humour.	1418
It skills not much, weele fit him to our turne,	1515
Gru. Why Iacke boy, ho boy, and as much newes as | wilt thou.	1677
*you: and thus much for greeting. Now my spruce	1741
Bion. As much as an apple doth an oyster, & all one.	1957
Much good do it vnto thy gentle heart:	2033
That with your strange encounter much amasde me:	2352
Petr. Twentie crownes, | Ile venture so much of my Hawke or Hound,	2615
But twentie times so much vpon my Wife.	2617

MUDDIE = 1

Muddie, ill seeming, thicke, bereft of beautie,	2701

MULTO = *1

Hor. *Alla nostra casa bene venuto multo honorata signi-|or mio Petruchio.*	593

MUM = 2

Tra. Well said Mr, mum, and gaze your fill.	376
Hor. Grumio mum: God saue you signior *Gremio.*	728

MURDER = *1

Bion. Helpe, helpe, helpe, here's a mad man will mur-|der me.	2435

MURDRED = *1

Ven. Lucentio: oh he hath murdred his Master; laie	2465

MUSCADELL = *1

*a storme, quaft off the Muscadell, and threw the sops	1555

MUSICIAN = 1

The quaint Musician, amorous *Litio,*	1530

MUSICK = *1

*Wilt thou haue Musicke? Harke Apollo plaies, *Musick*	187

MUSICKE = 10*1

Procure me Musicke readie when he wakes,	54
*Wilt thou haue Musicke? Harke Apollo plaies, *Musick*	187
Musicke and Poesie vse, to quicken you,	335
In Musicke, Instruments, and Poetry,	397
Well seene in Musicke, to instruct *Bianca,*	699
Cunning in Musicke, and the Mathematickes,	917
As the other in Musicke and Mathematickes:	945
And when in Musicke we haue spent an houre,	1302
To know the cause why musicke was ordain'd:	1305
My Lessons make no musicke in three parts.	1353
*neuer was before: harke, harke, I heare the min-|strels play. *Musicke playes.*	1563

MUSITIAN = 3*1

A fine Musitian to instruct our Mistris,	739
Bap. What, will my daughter proue a good Musiti-|an?	1011
Our fine Musitian groweth amorous.	1356
Nor a Musitian as I seeme to bee,	1865

MUST = 26*5

Host. I know my remedie, I must go fetch the Head-|borough.	13
Beg. I know it well, what must I call her? | *Lord.* Madam.	262
Master, your Loue must liue a maide at home,	485
Hor. Tarrie *Petruchio,* I must go with thee,	682
Must steed vs all, and me amongst the rest:	838
You must as we do, gratifie this Gentleman,	845
She is your treasure, she must haue a husband,	890

MUST *cont.*

I must dance bare-foot on her wedding day,	891
Pet. Nay come *Kate*, come: you must not looke so | sowre.	1105
Thou must be married to no man but me,	1154
I must, and will haue *Katherine* to my wife.	1160
'Tis deeds must win the prize, and he of both	1224
My selfe am strooke in yeeres I must confesse,	1242
Bap. I must confesse your offer is the best,	1268
Shee is your owne, else you must pardon me:	1270
Must get a father, call'd suppos'd *Vincentio*,	1290
Hort. I must beleeue my master, else I promise you,	1347
Luc. Are you so formall sir, well I must waite	1354
I must begin with rudiments of Art,	1359
Bian. Farewell sweet masters both, I must be gone.	1379
Kate. No shame but mine, I must forsooth be forst	1396
Now must the world point at poore *Katherine*,	1406
Pet. I must away to day before night come,	1572
For I must hence, and farewell to you all.	1579
But for my bonny *Kate*, she must with me:	1613
Cur. Do you heare ho? you must meete my maister | to countenance	
my mistris.	1726
One *Kate* you must kisse, and be acquainted with.	1781
And til she stoope, she must not be full gorg'd,	1825
From *Florence*, and must heere deliuer them.	1946
Thither must I, and here I leaue you sir.	2391
Pet. Oh ho, intreate her, nay then shee must needes | come.	2638

MUSTARD = 3*2

What say you to a peece of Beefe and Mustard?	2001
Gru. I, but the Mustard is too hot a little.	2003
Kate. Why then the Beefe, and let the Mustard rest.	2004
Gru. Nay then I wil not, you shal haue the Mustard	2005
Gru. Why then the Mustard without the beefe.	2008

MUTE = 1

Say she be mute, and will not speake a word,	1043

MUTTON = 1

What's this, Mutton? | 1.*Ser.* I.	1789

MY *1.**13 *19 25 33 *36 50 51 *73 93 *110 114 116 120 146 148 *159 *164 224 *234 236 250 254 256 *258 259 *260 278 *280 293 297 304 306 310 352 380 383 385 386 398 *414 493 508 513 520 526 *530 535 536 537 541 *549 556 *558 562 566 567 568 578 585 *588 *589 605 620 621 623 627 629 634 657 668 *674 683 684 687 696 707 721 742 757 767 781 810 813 859 860 862 870 876 888 912 915 923 924 926 929 940 953 958 974 979 981 986 990 1008 *1011 1022 1032 1035 1059 1061 1065 1079 1086 1087 1094 1103 1107 1113 1142 1149 1160 *1161 *1182 1188 1197 1225 1226 1228 1231 1232 1233 1238 1240 1242 1246 1247 1255 1259 1276 1280 1285 1288 *1293 1312 1315 *1328 1329 1331 1342 1347 1353 1358 1362 1364 1397 1410 1475 1476 1489 1496 1500 1503 1505 1521 1531 1569 1570 1573 1576 1578 1590 1595 1598 1603 1613 1616 1617 1618 1621 *1644 *1645 *1646 *1647 *1653 *1654 1656 *1662 *1673 *1688 1700 *1712 *1722 *1726 1727 *1741 1745 1748 *1766 1772 1775 1779 1780 1782 1822 1823 1824 1827 *1857 1876 1890 1920 1936 1955 1963 1969 1972 1979 *1980 1982 2013 *2016 2021 2024 2034 2060 2062 2063 2084 2102 2139 *2141 2145 *2152 2167 2205 2207 2223 2227 2229 2233 2237 2238 2241 2250 *2261 *2286 *2302 2343 2347 2351 2353 2360 2361 2377 2385 2390 *2418 2429 *2432 *2441 *2447 2454 *2466 *2467 2492 2502 2505 2506 2508 2509 2510 *2513 2514 2520 2521 2531 2541 2545

MY *cont.*
   2546 2553 *2555 2563 2569 2570 *2576 2577 2589 2616 2617 2626 2629
   *2636 2642 2654 2671 2685 2728 2729 2737 = 270*69
MYSELFE *see* selfe
NAIE = 1
   Gre. Naie, I dare not sweare it.   2480
NAILE = 1
   Thou yard three quarters, halfe yard, quarter, naile,   2094
NAILS = *1
   *so great *Hortensio*, but we may blow our nails together,   412
NAMD = 1
   What you will haue it nam'd, euen that it is,   2318
NAME = 19*6
   I haue forgot your name: but sure that part   96
   Tell me her fathers name, and 'tis enough: 660
   Her name is *Katherina Minola*,   665
   But if you haue a stomacke, too't a Gods name,   760
   His name is *Litio*, borne in *Mantua*.   921
   Whence are you sir? What may I call your name.   928
   Pet. Petruchio is my name, *Antonio's* sonne,   929
   His name is *Cambio*: pray accept his seruice.   946
   Bap. Lucentio is your name, of whence I pray.   965
   Good morrow *Kate*, for thats your name I heare.   1052
   *hath two letters for her name, fairely set down in studs,   1448
   His name and credite shal you vndertake,   1962
   He does it vnder name of perfect loue: 1990
   That feed'st me with the verie name of meate.   2011
   Why what a deuils name Tailor cal'st thou this?   2077
   *Petr. Come on a Gods name, once more toward our | fathers: 2295
   My name is call'd *Vincentio*, my dwelling *Pisa*,   2353
   Petr. What is his name? | *Vinc. Lucentio* gentle sir.   2356
   to take vpon you another mans name.   2416
   *Bap. You mistake sir, you mistake sir, praie what do | you thinke is his
   name?   2457
   *Vin. His name, as if I knew not his name: I haue   2459
   his name is *Tronio*.   2461
   *Ped. Awaie, awaie mad asse, his name is *Lucentio*, and 2462
   *hold on him I charge you in the Dukes name: oh my   2466
NAMES = 1
   And twentie more such names and men as these, | Which neuer were,
   nor no man euer saw.   248
NAP = *1
   *Beg. These fifteene yeeres, by my fay, a goodly nap,   234
NAPKIN = 1
   Which in a Napkin (being close conuei'd)   138
NAPPING = 1
   Nay, I haue tane you napping gentle Loue,   1894
NAPS = 1
   As *Stephen Slie*, and old *Iohn Naps* of Greece, | And *Peter Turph*, and
   Henry Pimpernell,   246
NARROW = 1
   The narrow prying father *Minola*,   1529
NARROWLY = 1
   Doth watch *Bianca's* steps so narrowly: 1522
NAT = 3
NATH = 1
   Nath. Peter didst euer see the like.   1812

NATHANIEL see also Nat., Nath. = 1*1
   *Call forth Nathaniel, Ioseph, Nicholas, Phillip, Walter, Su- |gersop   1718
   Where is Nathaniel, Gregory, Phillip.   1749
NATHANIELS = 1
   Grumio. Nathaniels coate sir was not fully made,   1759
NATURALLY = 1
   Was aptly fitted, and naturally perform'd.   97
NATURE = *1
   *Though the nature of our quarrell yet neuer brook'd   418
NAUGHT = 1
   If loue haue touch'd you, naught remaines but so,   464
NAY = 12*16
   *no more shooes then feet, nay sometime more feete then   163
   *Tra. Nay, then 'tis time to stirre him fro(m) his trance: 480
   *Bion. Where haue I beene? Nay how now, where   529
   *Gru. Nay 'tis no matter sir, what he leges in Latine.   596
   *Gru. Nay looke you sir, hee tels you flatly what his   643
   Nay then you iest, and now I wel perceiue   874
   Kate. What will you not suffer me: Nay now I see   889
   Nay, come againe, good Kate, I am a Gentleman,   1095
   *Pet. Nay come Kate, come: you must not looke so | sowre.   1105
   *Pet. Nay heare you Kate. Insooth you scape not so.   1119
   *Tra. Is this your speeding? nay the(n) godnight our part.   1181
   Gre. Nay, I haue offred all, I haue no more,   1263
   *Bion. Nay by S.(aint) Iamy, I hold you a penny, a horse and   1466
   Kate. Nay then, | Doe what thou canst, I will not goe to day,   1593
   Nay, looke not big, nor stampe, not stare, nor fret,   1614
   Bap. Nay, let them goe, a couple of quiet ones.   1626
   Why when I say? Nay good sweete Kate be merrie.   1771
   Nay, I haue tane you napping gentle Loue,   1894
   *Gru. Nay then I wil not, you shal haue the Mustard   2005
   What, not a word? Nay then, thou lou'st it not: 2023
   Petr. Nay then you lye: it is the blessed Sunne.   2314
   *Biond. Nay faith, Ile see the Church a your backe,   2384
   *Petr. Nay, I told you your sonne was well beloued in   2406
   *Vinc. What am I sir: nay what are you sir: oh immor- |tall   2443
   *Kate. Nay, I will giue thee a kisse, now praie thee | Loue staie.   2529
   *Petr. Nay that you shall not since you haue begun: 2587
   *Pet. Oh ho, intreate her, nay then shee must needes | come.   2638
   Petr. Nay, I will win my wager better yet,   2671
NEAPOLITAN = 1
   Some Neapolitan, or meaner man of Pisa.   511
NEATE = 1
   companions, is all readie, and all things neate?   1742
NEATS = 1
   Gru. What say you to a Neats foote?   1995
NECKE = 1*2
   Shee hung about my necke, and kisse on kisse   1188
   *Bride about the necke, and kist her lips with such a cla- |morous   1559
   *greater a run but my head and my necke. A fire good | Curtis.   1654
NEEDE = 3*1
   Kate. I'faith sir, you shall neuer neede to feare,   364
   Tra. So had you neede: 516
   *Luc. I flie Biondello; but they may chance to neede   2382
   shall neede none so long as I liue.   2405
NEEDED = 1
   Nor neuer needed that I should intreate,   1986

NEEDES = *1
  Pet. Oh ho, intreate her, nay then shee must needes | come.   2638
NEEDLE = 3
  Go ply thy Needle, meddle not with her.   882
  Vallens of Venice gold, in needle worke: 1236
  Gru. Marrie sir with needle and thred.   2106
NEERE = 4*1
  And braue attendants neere him when he wakes,   44
  Lord. Bid them come neere: 87
  *and shoulder-shotten, neere leg'd before, and with a   1443
  Nat. All things is readie, how neere is our master?   1743
  Signior *Baptista* may remember me | Neere twentie yeares a goe in
  Genoa.   2183
NEIGHBORS = 1
  Your wooing neighbors: this is a guift   938
NEIGHBOUR = 3*1
  Gre. Good morrow neighbour *Baptista*.   900
  Bap. Good morrow neighbour *Gremio*: God saue | you Gentlemen.   901
  I am your neighbour, and was suter first.   1215
  Gre. Adieu good neighbour: now I feare thee not: 1281
NEIGHBOURS = *1
  Bap. Neighbours and friends, though Bride & Bride-|(groom wants   1632
NEIGHING = 1
  Loud larums, neighing steeds, & trumpets clangue?   773
NEITHER = 1*2
  Hor. I see shees like to haue neither cap nor gowne.   2078
  *braue not me; I will neither bee fac'd nor brau'd. I say   2111
  Oh no good *Kate*: neither art thou the worse   2162
NERE = 4*3
  *Lordship: I ne're drank sacke in my life: and if you giue   159
  *me any Conserues, giue me conserues of Beefe: nere ask   160
  And let the world slip, we shall nere be yonger.   298
  For I will loue thee nere the lesse my girle.   380
  You vnderstand me? | *Bion*. I sir, ne're a whit.   542
  *to a Puppet or an Aglet babie, or an old trot with ne're a   645
  Why dost thou wrong her, that did nere wrong thee?   884
NEUER *see also* ne're = 26*5
  For yet his honor neuer heard a play)   106
  But did I neuer speake of all that time.   235
  And twentie more such names and men as these, | Which neuer were,
  nor no man euer saw.   248
  Kate. I'faith sir, you shall neuer neede to feare,   364
  *Though the nature of our quarrell yet neuer brook'd   418
  I neuer thought it possible or likely.   452
  I neuer yet beheld that speciall face,   866
  Iron may hold with her, but neuer Lutes.   1014
  Heere comes your father, neuer make deniall,   1159
  Luc. Preposterous Asse that neuer read so farre,   1304
  Luc. That will be neuer, tune your instrument.   1320
  Yet neuer meanes to wed where he hath woo'd: 1405
  Kate. Would *Katherine* had neuer seen him though. | *Exit weeping*.   1414
  Bion. Master, master, newes, and such newes as you | neuer heard of,   1420
  *neuer was before: harke, harke, I heare the min-|strels play. *Musicke*
  playes.   1563
  Tra. Of all mad matches neuer was the like.   1628
  *me: how he swore, how she prai'd, that neuer prai'd be-|fore: 1710
  For then she neuer lookes vpon her lure.   1826

NEUER *cont.*

Neuer to woo her more, but do forsweare her	1877
Neuer to marrie with her, though she would intreate,	1881
But I, who neuer knew how to intreat,	1985
Nor neuer needed that I should intreate,	1986
Kate. I neuer saw a better fashion'd gowne,	2086
Hort. Say as he saies, or we shall neuer goe.	2307
I neuer saw you before in all my life.	2429
Vinc. What, you notorious villaine, didst thou neuer | see thy Mistris father, *Vincentio?*	2430
Better once then neuer, for neuer to late. *Exeunt.*	2532
Wid. Then neuer trust me if I be affeard.	2554
For she is chang'd as she had neuer bin.	2670
Wid. Lord let me neuer haue a cause to sigh,	2679

NEW = 2*4

Bap. Is it new and olde too? how may that be?	1422
Bion. Why *Petruchio* is comming, in a new hat and	1431
*hath tam'd my old master, and my new mistris, and my | selfe fellow *Curtis.*	1662
*in their new fustian, the white stockings, and euery offi-|cer	1683
*to speake, and sits as one new risen from a dreame: A-|way, away, for he is comming hither.	1819
Her new built vertue and obedience.	2673

NEWES = 7*4

*cloathes, or you stolne his, or both? Pray what's the | newes?	531
Ile tel you newes indifferent good for either.	746
Bion. Master, master, newes, and such newes as you | neuer heard of,	1420
Bion. Why, is it not newes to heard of *Petruchio's* | (comming?	1423
Tra. But say, what to thine olde newes?	1430
Cur. There's fire readie, and therefore good *Grumio* | the newes.	1675
Gru. Why Iacke boy, ho boy, and as much newes as | wilt thou.	1677
Cur. All readie: and therefore I pray thee newes.	1687
Lay forth the gowne. What newes with you sir?	2046
How now, what newes?	2628

NEWLY = 2

As morning Roses newly washt with dew:	1042
'Tis meruaile, but that you are but newly come,	1942

NEXT = 2*1

Tra. So could I 'faith boy, to haue the next wish af-|ter,	547
And twice as much what ere thou offrest next.	1262
On sonday next, you know | My daughter *Katherine* is to be married:	1275

NICE = 1

Old fashions please me best, I am not so nice	1373

NICHOLAS see also Nick., Nicke. = *1

*Call forth *Nathaniel, Ioseph, Nicholas, Phillip, Walter, Su-|gersop	1718

NICK = 1

NICKE = *1

NIGHT = 12

Lord. Do you intend to stay with me to night?	90
There is a Lord will heare you play to night;	103
To pardon me yet for a night or two:	273
Bap. Is't possible you will away to night?	1571
Pet. I must away to day before night come,	1572
And for this night we'l fast for companie.	1809
Last night she slept not, nor to night she shall not:	1832
And in conclusion, she shal watch all night,	1839
There doth my father lie: and there this night	2238

NIGHT *cont.*

To watch the night in stormes, the day in cold, 2708
And being a winner, God giue you good night. | *Exit Petruchio* 2746
NIGHTINGALES = 1
And twentie caged Nightingales do sing. 188
NIGHTINGHALE = 1
She sings as sweetly as a Nightinghale: 1040
NILL = 1
And will you, nill you, I will marry you. 1150
NIP = 1
Heers snip, and nip, and cut, and slish and slash, 2075
NIT = 1
Thou Flea, thou Nit, thou winter cricket thou: 2095
NO *l.**6 *11 75 134 *161 *162 *163 241 *244 245 249 293 330 338 350 362
462 *474 533 *596 *680 *704 713 740 744 754 755 796 799 *801 825
1016 1075 1099 1100 *1104 *1108 1121 1154 1212 1259 1263 1264 1289
1313 1353 1380 1396 1425 *1437 *1464 1524 *1556 1573 1595 1634
*1653 *1657 1664 *1747 1753 1761 1831 1864 1979 2006 2024 2053 2059
2104 *2136 2148 2150 2162 2215 2225 2281 *2428 2526 2608 2626 *2689
2699 2710 2734 = 70*23
NOBLE = 9
Belike some Noble Gentleman that meanes 80
Such as he hath obseru'd in noble Ladies 122
To see her noble Lord restor'd to health, 132
Oh Noble Lord, bethinke thee of thy birth, 182
Lady. How fares my noble Lord? 254
Where is my wife? | *La.* Heere noble Lord, what is thy will with her? 256
La. Thrice noble Lord, let me intreat of you 272
Baptista is a noble Gentleman, 812
Beside, so qualified, as may beseeme | The Spouse of any noble
Gentleman: 2365
NOD = 1*1
*1.*Man.* My Lord you nod, you do not minde the | play. 558
And if she chance to nod, Ile raile and brawle, 1840
NODDLE = 1
To combe your noddle with a three-legg'd stoole, 367
NONE = 9*1
And yet shee is inferiour to none. 219
*so good heere's none will holde you: Their loue is not 411
That none shal haue accesse vnto *Bianca*, 692
Tush, tush, feare boyes with bugs. | *Gru.* For he feares none. 777
There were none fine, but *Adam*, *Rafe*, and *Gregory*, 1763
She eate no meate to day, nor none shall eate. 1831
And it I will haue, or I will haue none. 2070
Ile none of it; hence, make your best of it. 2085
shall neede none so long as I liue. 2405
And while it is so, none so dry or thirstie 2702
NOR *l.**158 *162 225 *244 245 249 330 506 *856 955 1127 1128 1314 1595
1614 1748 1831 1832 1865 1986 *2078 2087 *2111 2363 = 19*6
NOSE = *1
**Vin.* Ile slit the villaines nose that would haue sent | me to the Iaile. 2511
NOSTRA = *1
**Hor. Alla nostra casa bene venuto multo honorata signi-* | *or mio*
Petruchio. 593
NOT *l.**10 *11 *16 22 24 *36 45 *110 135 *158 *170 *175 177 222 225 253
*258 274 *291 352 365 366 379 406 408 *411 459 463 469 *474 487 489
500 505 544 *549 *558 581 582 *597 602 605 *606 610 630 638 658 *659

NOT *cont.*

667 669 681 767 768 770 772 775 793 795 803 805 813 834 836 842 847
*856 864 868 882 889 893 *903 919 924 925 926 927 937 1002 1006
*1015 1031 1043 1064 1076 *1089 *1105 *1108 1118 *1119 1121 1126
1135 1144 1173 1174 *1198 1218 1255 1273 1279 1281 1285 *1293 1306
1310 1314 *1335 *1336 1338 1345 1350 1372 1373 1391 *1423 *1456
1460 1461 1467 1471 1472 1473 1481 1495 1497 1498 1500 1515 1521
1581 1588 1594 1595 1598 1601 1607 1614 1624 *1627 *1644 1696 *1704
*1721 1729 1745 1757 1759 1762 1796 1800 *1818 1825 1830 1832 1864
1889 1917 1938 1953 1960 1979 1984 1994 *2005 2023 2056 2057 2068
2069 2082 2107 *2110 *2111 2113 2135 2138 *2141 2177 2191 2194 2212
2233 2252 2281 *2298 2316 2322 *2340 2342 2355 2362 2363 2386 *2392
2401 *2428 *2459 2473 *2474 2480 *2481 2502 *2515 *2518 2531 *2585
*2587 2593 2602 2634 2642 2644 2645 2646 2651 2665 2677 2692 2695
2716 = 179*53

NOTE = 2*1

Gremio. O very well, I haue perus'd the note:	710
Tail. Why heere is the note of the fashion to testify. | *Pet.* Reade it.	2114
Gru. The note lies in's throate if he say I said so.	2116

NOTED = 1

And to be noted for a merry man;	1402

NOTES = 2

D sol re, one Cliffe, two notes haue I,	1370
Luc. At last, though long, our iarring notes agree,	2538

NOTHING = 8*5

For he is nothing but a mightie Lord:	69
Let them want nothing that my house affoords. | *Exit one with the Players*.	114
Lord. Thou art a Lord, and nothing but a Lord:	213
Lord. Madam, and nothing else, so Lords cal Ladies	265
*two and fiftie horses. Why nothing comes amisse, so | monie comes withall.	647
*that's nothing; and he begin once, hee'l raile in his rope	677
Pet. Why that is nothing: for I tell you father,	995
Gru. Why she comes to borrow nothing of them.	1734
Biond. Faith nothing: but has left mee here behinde	2264
Euermore crost and crost, nothing but crost.	2306
Vincentio: now wee are vndone and brought to no-|thing.	2422
Petr. Nothing but sit and sit, and eate and eate.	2549
Petr. Padua affords nothing but what is kinde.	2551

NOTORIOUS = *1

Vinc. What, you notorious villaine, didst thou neuer | see thy Mistris father, *Vincentio*?	2430

NOUICES = 1

Oh you are nouices, 'tis a world to see	1191

NOURISHETH = 1

Skipper stand backe, 'tis age that nourisheth.	1221

NOW = 59*24

How now? who is it?	83
Now fellowes, you are welcome. | *Players.* We thanke your Honor.	88
*Beare-heard, and now by present profession a Tinker.	173
Or do I dreame? Or haue I dream'd till now?	221
Beg. Now Lord be thanked for my good amends. | *All.* Amen.	250
Madam vndresse you, and come now to bed.	271
*parle, know now vpon aduice, it toucheth vs both: that	419
And now in plainnesse do confesse to thee	455
Tra. Master, it is no time to chide you now,	462

NOW *cont.*

Tra. I marry am I sir, and now 'tis plotted. | *Luc.* I haue it *Tranio.*	491
Bion. Where haue I beene? Nay how now, where	529
Petr. Now knocke when I bid you: sirrah villaine	586
Hor. How now, what's the matter? My olde friend	588
come you now with knocking at the gate?	609
And tell me now (sweet friend) what happie gale	614
Hor. Now shal my friend *Petruchio* do me grace,	696
Hor. Gremio, 'tis now no time to vent our loue,	744
Nay then you iest, and now I wel perceiue	874
Bap. Why how now Dame, whence growes this in-|solence?	879
Kate. What will you not suffer me: Nay now I see	889
Bap. How now my friend, why dost thou looke so | pale?	1008
Pet. Now by the world, it is a lustie Wench,	1028
But heere she comes, and now *Petruchio* speake.	1050
Pet. Now by S.(aint) George I am too yong for you.	1115
And now I finde report a very liar:	1123
Now *Kate,* I am a husband for your turne,	1151
Bap. Now Signior *Petruchio,* how speed you with my | (daughter?	1161
Bap. Why how now daughter *Katherine,* in your | (dumps?	1164
Kat. Call you me daughter? now I promise you	1165
Bap. Faith Gentlemen now I play a marchants part,	1207
But now *Baptista,* to your yonger daughter,	1213
Now is the day we long haue looked for,	1214
That now is lying in Marcellus roade:	1257
Now on the sonday following, shall *Bianca*	1277
Gre. Adieu good neighbour: now I feare thee not:	1281
Bian. Now let mee see if I can conster it. *Hic ibat si-|mois,*	1334
Hort. Madam, tis now in tune.	1338
Now for my life the knaue doth court my loue,	1342
But let it rest, now *Litio* to you:	1349
Now must the world point at poore *Katherine,*	1406
Bap. Goe girle, I cannot blame thee now to weepe,	1416
*often burst, and now repaired with knots: one girth sixe	1446
Now sadder that you come so vnprouided:	1482
Now take them vp quoth he, if any list.	1549
Kat. Now if you loue me stay. | *Pet. Grumio,* my horse.	1589
Gre. I marry sir, now it begins to worke.	1604
*now were I not a little pot, & soone hot; my very lippes	1644
*(she being now at hand) thou shalt soone feele, to thy	1668
*now I begin, Inprimis wee came downe a fowle	1699
*things of worthy memorie, which now shall die in obli-|uion,	1713
Nat. Welcome home *Grumio.* | *Phil.* How now *Grumio.*	1735
Nat. How now old lad.	1739
Gru. Welcome you: how now you: what you: fel-|low	1740
*you: and thus much for greeting. Now my spruce	1741
My Faulcon now is sharpe, and passing emptie,	1824
Now let him speake, 'tis charity to shew. *Exit*	1845
Hor. Now Mistris, profit you in what you reade?	1853
Hor. Quicke proceeders marry, now tel me I pray,	1859
Tra. I'faith hee'l haue a lustie Widdow now,	1900
Kate eate apace; and now my honie Loue,	2034
Let's see, I thinke 'tis now some seuen a clocke,	2170
Now doe your dutie throughlie I aduise you:	2192
I pray you stand good father to me now,	2204
Kate. The Moone, the Sunne: it is not Moonelight | now.	2298
Pet. Now by my mothers sonne, and that's my selfe,	2302

NOW *cont.*

Petr. Why how now *Kate*, I hope thou art not mad,	2340
Now I perceiue thou art a reuerent Father:	2346
And now by Law, as well as reuerent age,	2359
Petr. Why how now gentleman: why this is flat kna- | uerie	2415
Vincentio: now wee are vndone and brought to no- | thing.	2422
Tra. How now, what's the matter?	2449
Kate. Nay, I will giue thee a kisse, now praie thee | Loue staie.	2529
For now we sit to chat as well as eate.	2548
Pet. Now for my life *Hortentio* feares his Widow.	2553
And now you know my meaning.	2570
Bap. Oh, oh *Petruchio*, *Tranio* hits you now.	2600
Bap. Now in good sadnesse sonne *Petruchio*,	2606
How now, what newes?	2628
Yours will not be entreated: Now, where's my wife?	2642
Bap. Now by my hollidam here comes *Katerina*.	2654
Bap. Now faire befall thee good *Petruchio*;	2666
But now I see our Launces are but strawes:	2731
Horten. Now goe thy wayes, thou hast tam'd a curst | Shrow.	2748

NURSE = 1

And melancholly is the Nurse of frenzie,	287

NURSERIE = 1

To see faire *Padua*, nurserie of Arts,	301

NUT = 1

As wil a Chesse-nut in a Farmers fire.	776

NUTS = 1

As hazle nuts, and sweeter then the kernels:	1134

O *l.**606 710 1139 1601 = 3*1

OATES = *1

Gru. I sir, they be ready, the Oates haue eaten the | horses.	1591

OATH = 4

Shee vi'd so fast, protesting oath on oath,	1189
Tra. And heere I take the like vnfained oath,	1880
For me, that I may surely keepe mine oath.	1884

OATHES = 2

That thinkes with oathes to face the matter out.	1169
With oathes kept waking, and with brawling fed,	1988

OBAY = 1

When they are bound to serue, loue, and obay.	2722

OBEDIENCE = 4

I am your wife in all obedience.	261
And show more signe of her obedience,	2672
Her new built vertue and obedience.	2673
But loue, faire lookes, and true obedience;	2711

OBEDIENT = 4

And I am tyed to be obedient,	518
That baite, and beate, and will not be obedient:	1830
And he whose wife is most obedient,	2610
And not obedient to his honest will,	2716

OBEISANCE = 1

And call him Madam, do him obeisance:	119

OBEY = 1

Obey the Bride you that attend on her.	1609

OBLIUION = *1

*things of worthy memorie, which now shall die in obli- | uion,	1713

OBSERUD = 1

Such as he hath obseru'd in noble Ladies	122

OBTAIND = 1
Bap. I, when the speciall thing is well obtain'd,   993
OCCASION = 2
Till I can finde occasion of reuenge.   894
Tra. And tell vs what occasion of import   1485
OCLOCKE *see* clocke
OD = *1
Tra. 'Tis some od humor pricks him to this fashion,   1457
ODDE = 1
Least (ouer-eying of his odde behauiour,   105
ODDES = 1
Hor. God-a-mercie *Grumio*, then hee shall haue no | oddes.   2136
OF *see also* o' = 203*44
OFF *l.*859 1316 *1555 *1709 1772 2678 = 4*2
OFFENCE = 1
Tra. And if I be sir, is it any offence?   800
OFFEND = 1
And so offend him: for I tell you sirs,   108
OFFENDED = 1
Bap. How hast thou offended, where is *Lucentio*?   2494
OFFER = 4*1
Ser. An't please your Honor, Players | That offer seruice to your
Lordship.   84
And offer me disguis'd in sober robes,   697
Bap. I must confesse your offer is the best,   1268
Tra. Sir, what are you that offer to beate my ser- | uant?   2441
To offer warre, where they should kneele for peace: 2720
OFFICE = 4*1
And each one to his office when he wakes. | *Sound trumpets.*   77
Each in his office readie at thy becke.   186
cold comfort, for being slow in thy hot office.   1669
Gru. A cold world *Curtis* in euery office but thine, z   1672
Hor. That's my office   2577
OFFICER = 2*2
*in their new fustian, the white stockings, and euery offi- | cer   1683
Tra. Call forth an officer: Carrie this mad knaue to   2469
Gre. Staie officer, he shall not go to prison.   2473
Petr. Spoke like an Officer: ha to the lad.   2578
OFFRED = 1
Gre. Nay, I haue offred all, I haue no more,   1263
OFFREST = 1
And twice as much what ere thou offrest next.   1262
OFT = 1
Of that report, which I so oft haue heard,   914
OFTEN = 2*1
*often burst, and now repaired with knots: one girth sixe   1446
Tra. Signior *Hortensio*, I haue often heard | Of your entire affection to
Bianca,   1870
Ped. I sir, in Pisa haue I often bin,   1950
OFTENTIMES = 1
Yet oftentimes he goes but meane apparel'd.   1458
OH *see also* O *l.**38 167 *178 *179 182 230 231 236 451 470 725 726 *759
*852 871 *935 1030 *1082 1101 1132 1135 1187 1191 1332 *1451 *1657
*1862 1911 1968 2072 2092 *2144 2146 2162 *2443 *2444 *2445 *2455
*2465 *2466 *2486 *2488 2595 2600 *2638 2646 = 27*20
OLD = 16*12
Slie, old Slies sonne of Burton-heath, by byrth a   171

OLD *cont.*
As *Stephen Slie*, and old *Iohn Naps* of Greece, | And *Peter Turph*, and
Henry Pimpernell,   246
Blowes you to *Padua* heere, from old *Verona*?   615
As old as *Sibell*, and as curst and shrow'd   636
*to a Puppet or an Aglet babie, or an old trot with ne're a   645
To old *Baptista* as a schoole-master   698
Petr. Borne in *Verona*, old *Butonios* sonne: 756
Within rich *Pisa* walls, as any one | Old Signior *Gremio* has in *Padua*,   1249
Gre. And may not yong men die as well as old?   1273
regia, bearing my port, *celsa senis* that we might be-|guile the old
Pantalowne.   1329
Old fashions please me best, I am not so nice   1373
To charge true rules for old inuentions.   1374
*an old ierkin, a paire of old breeches thrice turn'd; a   1432
*blew lift; an old hat, & the humor of forty fancies prickt   1454
*hath tam'd my old master, and my new mistris, and my | selfe fellow
Curtis.   1662
Nat. How now old lad.   1739
The rest were ragged, old, and beggerly,   1764
Besides old *Gremio* is harkning still,   2235
Bio. The old Priest at Saint *Lukes* Church is at your | command at all
houres.   2274
This is a man old, wrinckled, faded, withered,   2341
Kate. Pardon old father my mistaking eies,   2343
Petr. Do good old grandsire, & withall make known   2348
Let me imbrace with old *Vincentio,*   2367
*send'em good shipping: but who is here? mine old Ma-|ster   2421
Bion. What my old worshipfull old master? yes   2432
*brought him vp euer since he was three yeeres old, and   2460
OLDE = 5*4
Hor. How now, what's the matter? My olde friend   588
Gru. Heere's no knauerie. See, to beguile the olde-|folkes,   704
Tra. That's but a cauill: he is olde, I young.   1272
An olde Italian foxe is not so kinde my boy. *Exit.*   1285
Bap. Is it new and olde too? how may that be?   1422
Tra. But say, what to thine olde newes?   1430
*another lac'd: an olde rusty sword tane out of the   1434
*two broken points: his horse hip'd with an olde mo-|thy   1436
Luc. Well go thy waies olde Lad for thou shalt ha't.   2740
ON *see also* a = 44*16
ONCE = 9*2
Since once he plaide a Farmers eldest sonne,   94
And once againe a pot o'th smallest Ale.   227
Oh that once more you knew but what you are: 231
We could at once put vs in readinesse,   342
'Tis hatch'd, and shall be so: *Tranio* at once   512
*that's nothing; and he begin once, hee'l raile in his rope   677
Seize thee that List, if once I finde thee ranging,   1385
Which once perform'd, let all the world say no,   1524
Petr. Come on a Gods name, once more toward our | fathers: 2295
Faire louely Maide, once more good day to thee: 2331
Better once then neuer, for neuer to late. *Exeunt.*   2532
ONE = 42*7
Lord. What's heere? One dead, or drunke? See doth | he breath?   34
Let one attend him with a siluer Bason   59
Some one be readie with a costly suite,   63

ONE *cont.*

And each one to his office when he wakes. | *Sound trumpets.*	77
And giue them friendly welcome euerie one,	113
Let them want nothing that my house affoords. | *Exit one with the Players.*	114
Scratching her legs, that one shal sweare she bleeds,	210
*be happie riuals in *Bianca's* loue, to labour and effect | one thing specially.	421
Tra. Master, for my hand, | Both our inuentions meet and iumpe in one.	493
One thing more rests, that thy selfe execute,	554
*To make one among these wooers: if thou ask me why,	555
One rich enough to be *Petruchio's* wife:	633
Hath promist me to helpe one to another,	738
She may more sutors haue, and me for one.	815
Then well one more may faire *Bianca* haue;	817
And so she shall: *Lucentio* shal make one,	818
The one, as famous for a scolding tongue,	826
Bap. After my death, the one halfe of my Lands,	986
Kate. Well aym'd of such a yong one.	1114
To wish me wed to one halfe Lunaticke,	1167
Tra. And I am one that loue *Bianca* more	1216
Within rich *Pisa* walls, as any one | Old Signior *Gremio* has in *Padua*,	1249
D sol re, one Cliffe, two notes haue I,	1370
*paire of bootes that haue beene candle-cases, one buck-|led,	1433
*often burst, and now repaired with knots: one girth sixe	1446
*like the horse: with a linnen stock on one leg, and	1452
Bap. Why that's all one.	1465
a man is more then one, and yet not many.	1467
Cur. Both of one horse?	1701
Enter one with water.	1778
One *Kate* you must kisse, and be acquainted with.	1781
*to speake, and sits as one new risen from a dreame: A-|way, away, for he is comming hither.	1819
But one that scorne to liue in this disguise,	1866
For such a one as leaues a Gentleman,	1867
As one vnworthie all the former fauours	1878
Tra. 'Tis death for any one in Mantua	1937
Tra. Among them know you one *Vincentio*?	1952
Bion. As much as an apple doth an oyster, & all one.	1957
'Twixt me, and one *Baptistas* daughter heere:	1974
Kate. Then both or one, or any thing thou wilt.	2007
Pet. When you are gentle, you shall haue one too, | And not till then.	2055
With one consent to haue her so bestowed:	2217
Welcome, one messe is like to be your cheere,	2255
'Tis ten to one it maim'd you too out right	2605
Let's each one send vnto his wife,	2609
Gre. I, and a kinde one too:	2633
Will daigne to sip, or touch one drop of it.	2703
Thy head, thy soueraigne: One that cares for thee,	2705
My minde hath bin as bigge as one of yours,	2728

ONELIE = *1

*he is mine onelie sonne and heire to the Lands of me sig-|nior *Vincentio*.	2463

ONELY = 4

Onely (good master) while we do admire | This vertue, and this morall discipline,	328

ONELY *cont.*
    Her onely fault, and that is faults enough,   654
    If whil'st I liue she will be onely mine.   1244
    I am my fathers heyre and onely sonne,   1246
ONES = 2
    And other bookes, good ones, I warrant ye.   736
    Bap. Nay, let them goe, a couple of quiet ones.   1626
ONION = 1
    An Onion wil do well for such a shift,   137
ONLY = 1
    Tra. That only came well in: sir, list to me,   1245
OPEN = 1
    The dore is open sir, there lies your way,   1596
OPENLY = 1
    Hath publish'd and proclaim'd it openly: 1941
OPINION = 1
    Luc. Mistresse, what's your opinion of your sister?   1629
OPPOSD = 1
    To giue my hand oppos'd against my heart   1397
OR *l.**15 *34 *48 *164 189 193 196 *209 221 233 264 267 273 274 292 331
    372 400 452 507 511 *531 577 610 637 638 *645 *676 764 799 861 920
    926 1035 1210 1217 1238 1248 1307 1371 *1456 1479 1612 *1667 1733
    1788 1916 1928 1929 1991 1992 2006 2007 2050 2063 2069 2070 2098
    2160 2175 2224 *2265 2303 2304 2307 2309 2336 2370 *2402 2489 2588
    2616 2699 2702 2703 2721 = 69*15
ORCHARD = 1
    We will go walke a little in the Orchard,   976
ORDAIND = 1
    To know the cause why musicke was ordain'd: 1305
ORDER = 5
    Therefore this order hath *Baptista* tane,   691
    To learne the order of my fingering,   1358
    *the Gils faire without, the Carpets laide, and euerie | thing in order?   1685
    Grumio gaue order how it should be done.   2103
    Gru. I gaue him no order, I gaue him the stuffe.   2104
ORDERLIE = 1
    Tai. You bid me make it orderlie and well,   2079
ORDERLY = 1
    Gre. You are too blunt, go to it orderly.   906
ORDERS = 1
    It was the Friar of Orders gray,   1773
ORDNANCE = 1
    Haue I not heard great Ordnance in the field?   770
ORE-RUN = 1
    Like enuious flouds ore-run her louely face,   217
ORNAMENTS = 1
    Come Tailor, let vs see these ornaments.   2044
OTH = 1
    And once againe a pot o'th smallest Ale.   227
OTHER = 14*2
    *Enter aloft the drunkard with attendants, some with apparel, | Bason and
    Ewer, & other appurtenances, & Lord.*   151
    I will some other be, some *Florentine*,   510
    And her with-holds from me. Other more   686
    And see you reade no other Lectures to her: 713
    And other bookes, good ones, I warrant ye.   736
    As is the other, for beauteous modestie.   827

OTHER *cont.*
That I disdaine: but for these other goods,	858
Which I could fancie, more then any other.	867
In Greeke, Latine, and other Languages,	944
As the other in Musicke and Mathematickes:	945
And bring you from a wilde *Kate* to a *Kate* | Conformable as other houshold *Kates*:	1157
*a kersey boot-hose on the other, gartred with a red and	1453
*all in the Sextons face: hauing no other reason, but that	1556
Take that, and mend the plucking of the other.	1776
Doth fancie any other but *Lucentio*,	1848
And craues no other tribute at thy hands,	2710

OTHERS = 1*1
Lucen. But in the others silence do I see,	373
Enter Baptista, Gremio, Tranio, Katherine, Bianca, and o-|thers, attendants.	1387

OTHERWISE = 1
Which otherwise would grow into extreames.	150

OUER *see also* ore = 3
To giue you ouer at this first encounter,	671
You vnderstand me. Ouer and beside | Signior *Baptistas* liberalitie,	714
Go hop me ouer euery kennell home,	2083

OUERBLOWNE = 1
To smile at scapes and perils ouerblowne:	2540

OUERTAKE = 1
Vpon the companie you ouertake?	2372

OUER-EYING = 1
Least (ouer-eying of his odde behauiour,	105

OUER-IOYED = 1
Bid him shed teares, as being ouer-ioyed	131

OUER-LEATHER = 1
*shooes, or such shooes as my toes looke through the o-|uer-leather.	164

OUER-MERRIE = 1
May well abate the ouer-merrie spleene,	149

OUER-REACH = 1
Wee'll ouer-reach the grey-beard *Gremio*,	1528

OUER-ROSTED = 1
Then feede it with such ouer-rosted flesh:	1807

OUGHT = *1
*being perhaps (for ought I see) two and thirty, a peepe	600

OUID = 1
As *Ouid*; be an out-cast quite abiur'd:	332

OUR *l.*73 74 *91 *110 226 389 *412 *413 *418 *420 494 506 519 739 744 841 849 *1181 1341 1356 1391 1484 1515 1523 1527 *1667 1743 1806 2154 2168 *2295 2305 2375 2538 2546 2547 *2552 2723 2725 2726 2731 2732 = 36*11

OURS = 1
What saies *Lucentio* to this shame of ours?	1395

OURSELUES *see* selues

OUT *l.*27 238 242 *413 *601 1000 1087 1169 1267 *1434 1690 1775 *2112 *2129 2380 2397 2412 2433 2521 2605 = 15*6

OUT-CAST = 1
As *Ouid*; be an out-cast quite abiur'd:	332

OUT-TALKE = 1
Gre. What, this Gentleman will out-talke vs all.	820

OWE = *1
*women, what dutie they doe owe their Lords and hus-|bands.	2687

OWES = 1
Such dutie as the subiect owes the Prince,   2713
OWETH = 1
Euen such a woman oweth to her husband: 2714
OWNE = 10
To mine owne children, in good bringing vp,   403
My minde presumes for his owne good, and yours.   781
Tra. Pardon me sir, the boldnesse is mine owne,   951
Shee is your owne, else you must pardon me: 1270
Ile keepe mine owne despite of all the world.   1525
I will be master of what is mine owne,   1615
Gru. Why she hath a face of her owne.   1728
Peter. He kils her in her owne humor.   1813
Brau'd in mine owne house with a skeine of thred: 2096
Tis well, and hold your owne in any case   2186
OXE = 1
My horse, my oxe, my asse, my any thing,   1618
OXEN = 1
Sixe-score fat Oxen standing in my stalls,   1240
OYSTER = *1
Bion. As much as an apple doth an oyster, & all one.   1957
P = 1
Ile buckler thee against a Million. *Exeunt. P. Ka.*   1625
PACKE = 2
If she do bid me packe, Ile giue her thankes,   1046
Sorrow on thee, and all the packe of you   2012
PACKET = 1
And this small packet of Greeke and Latine bookes: 963
PACKING = *1
Gre. Here's packing with a witnesse to deceiue vs all.   2499
PACKTHRED = 1
and heere and there peec'd with packthred.   1449
PADUA = 19*4
To see faire *Padua*, nurserie of Arts,   301
And am to *Padua* come, as he that leaues   321
Such friends (as time) in *Padua* shall beget.   344
*best horse in *Padua* to begin his woing that would tho-|roughly   445
And be in *Padua* heere *Vincentio's* sonne,   501
To see my friends in *Padua*; but of all   567
Blowes you to *Padua* heere, from old *Verona*?   615
I come to wiue it wealthily in *Padua*:   641
If wealthily, then happily in *Padua*.   642
Renown'd in *Padua* for her scolding tongue.   666
Within rich *Pisa* walls, as any one | Old Signior *Gremio* has in *Padua*,   1249
And make assurance heere in *Padua*   1517
That stops my way in *Padua*: *Grumio*   1621
And come to Padua carelesse of your life.   1935
To come to Padua, know you not the cause?   1938
And that you look't for him this day in *Padua*,   2197
Ped. Soft son: sir by your leaue, hauing com to *Padua*   2206
Lucentios Father is arriued in *Padua*,   2248
And bound I am to *Padua*, there to visite   2354
Padua: doe you heare sir, to leaue friuolous circumstan-|ces,   2407
Ped. Thou liest his Father is come from *Padua*, and   2411
Bap. Padua affords this kindnesse, sonne *Petruchio*.   2550
Petr. Padua affords nothing but what is kinde.   2551

PAGE = 1
Sirra go you to Bartholmew my Page,   116
PAIDE = 1
Pet. Hortensio, say thou wilt see the Tailor paide: 2147
PAINE = 1
Was it not to refresh the minde of man | After his studies, or his vsuall
paine?   1306
PAINES = 1
And all my paines is sorted to no proofe.   2024
PAINFULL = 1
To painfull labour, both by sea and land: 2707
PAINS = *1
Petr. Gentlemen & friends, I thank you for your pains,   1566
PAINT = 1
And paint your face, and vse you like a foole.   368
PAINTED = 3
Adonis painted by a running brooke,   202
As liuelie painted, as the deede was done.   208
Because his painted skin contents the eye.   2161
PAIRE = 1*2
Host. A paire of stockes you rogue.   5
*an old ierkin, a paire of old breeches thrice turn'd; a   1432
*paire of bootes that haue beene candle-cases, one buck-|led,   1433
PALE = 3*1
Bap. How now my friend, why dost thou looke so | pale?   1008
Hor. For feare I promise you, if I looke pale.   1010
I haue a hundred milch-kine to the pale,   1239
Luc. Looke not pale *Bianca*, thy father will not frown. | *Exeunt.*   2518
PALLABRIS = 1
*in with *Richard Conqueror*: therefore *Pau-!cas pallabris*, let the world
slide: Sessa.   8
PALTRIE = 1
Pet. Why thou saist true, it is paltrie cap,   2066
PANTALOWNE = 1
regia, bearing my port, *celsa senis* that we might be-|guile the old
Pantalowne.   1329
PANTELOWNE = 1
Gremio a Pantelowne, *Hortentio* sister to *Bianca*. | *Lucen. Tranio, stand
by.*   348
PAPER = 1
Ile mend it with a Largesse. Take your paper too,   716
PAR = 1
Par. Take me your loue, and then let me alone.   1924
PARDON = 9*1
To pardon me yet for a night or two: 273
Pet. Oh, Pardon me signior *Gremio*, I would faine be | doing.   935
Tra. Pardon me sir, the boldnesse is mine owne,   951
Shee is your owne, else you must pardon me: 1270
Bap. Sir, pardon me in what I haue to say,   2220
Kate. Pardon old father my mistaking eies,   2343
Pardon I pray thee for my mad mistaking.   2347
Luc. Pardon sweete father. *Kneele.*   2491
Bian. Pardon deere father.   2493
Then pardon him sweete Father for my sake.   2510
PARDONATO = 1
Tra. Me Pardonato, gentle master mine: 324

PARENTAGE = 1
  That vpon knowledge of my Parentage,   958
PARENTS = 1
  Happy the Parents of so faire a childe;   '   2337
PARIS = 1
  Though *Paris* came, in hope to speed alone.   819
PARKE = 1
  Did I not bid thee meete me in the Parke,   1757
PARLE = *1
  *parle, know now vpon aduice, it toucheth vs both: that   419
PARLER = 1
  Kate. They sit conferring by the Parler fire.   2657
PARSELEY = *1
  *afternoone as shee went to the Garden for Parseley to   2285
PART = 5*4
  *1.*Hunts*. My Lord I warrant you we wil play our part   73
  I haue forgot your name: but sure that part   96
  Vertue and that part of Philosophie | Will I applie, that treats of
  happinesse,   317
  Tra. Not possible: for who shall beare your part,   500
  **Petr*. Signior *Hortensio*, come you to part the fray?   591
  Pet. I see you do not meane to part with her,   925
  **Tra*. Is this your speeding? nay the(n) godnight our part. 1181
  **Bap*. Faith Gentlemen now I play a marchants part,   1207
  Though in some part inforced to digresse,   1490
PARTING = 1*1
  For so your father charg'd me at our parting: 519
  *smacke, that at the parting all the Church did   1560
PARTS = 3
  My Lessons make no musicke in three parts.   1353
  As shall with either parts agreement stand.   2232
  Should well agree with our externall parts?   2726
PASSE = 6*1
  **Hor*. Tush *Gremio*: though it passe your patience z   430
  Her fathers liking, which to bring to passe   1512
  Ere three dayes passe, which hath as long lou'd me,   1886
  To passe assurance of a dowre in marriage   1973
  And passe my daughter a sufficient dower,   2227
  Weele passe the businesse priuately and well: 2239
  Till I be brought to such a sillie passe.   2680
PASSING = 7
  It wil be pastime passing excellent,   71
  And then to dinner: you are passing welcome,   977
  Pet. No, not a whit, I finde you passing gentle: 1121
  For thou art pleasant, gamesome, passing courteous, 1124
  Though he be blunt, I know him passing wise,   1412
  My Faulcon now is sharpe, and passing emptie,   1824
  Kate. 'Tis passing good, I prethee let me haue it. 1996
PASSION = 3
  You breake into some merrie passion,   107
  Are, to plead *Hortensio's* passion: 1367
  not--- Cockes passion, silence, I heare my master.   1745
PAST = 2*1
  Bian. Why, I am past my gamouth long agoe.   1364
  *past cure of the Fiues, starke spoyl'd with the   1441
  Our strength as weake, our weakenesse past compare, 2732

PASTIME = 1*1
 It wil be pastime passing excellent,   71
 *Tra. Husht master, heres some good pastime toward;   371
PATE = 2
 And rap me well, or Ile knocke your knaues pate.   577
 And through the instrument my pate made way,   1022
PATIENCE = 5*1
 *Hor. Tush Gremio: though it passe your patience z   430
 Hor. Petruchio patience, I am Grumio's pledge: 611
 Do me this right: heare me with patience.   811
 For patience shee will proue a second Grissell,   1175
 Tra. Patience good Katherine and Baptista too,   1409
 Kate. Patience I pray you, 'twas a fault vnwilling.   1785
PATIENT = 2*1
 *Pet. Be patient gentlemen, I choose her for my selfe,   1182
 To this most patient, sweet, and vertuous wife,   1577
 Be patient, to morrow't shalbe mended,   1808
PATRIMONY = 1
 Giue me Bianca for my patrimony.   2205
PATRON = 2
 As for my patron, stand you so assur'd,   721
 The patron of my life and libertie.   1969
PATRONESSE = 1
 Hort. But wrangling pedant, this is | The patronesse of heauenly
 harmony: 1299
PAUCAS = *1
 *in with Richard Conqueror: therefore Pau-!cas pallabris, let the world
 slide: Sessa.   8
PAUSE = 1
 And while I pause, serue in your harmony.   1309
PAY = *2
 *Host. You will not pay for the glasses you haue burst?   10
 *Hor. Tailor, Ile pay thee for thy gowne to morrow,   2149
PAYMENT = 1
 Too little payment for so great a debt.   2712
PEACE = 4*2
 Maids milde behauiour and sobrietie. | Peace Tranio.   374
 *Petr. Hortensio peace: thou knowst not golds effect,   659
 Hor. Peace Grumio, it is the riuall of my Loue.   707
 Gru. Oh this Woodcocke, what an Asse it is. | Petru. Peace sirra.   726
 *Petr. Marrie peace it boads, and loue, and quiet life,   2663
 To offer warre, where they should kneele for peace: •   2720
PEARLE = 2*1
 Their harnesse studded all with Gold and Pearle.   194
 Fine Linnen, Turky cushions bost with pearle,   1235
 *sir, what cernes it you, if I weare Pearle and gold: I thank   2453
PEASANT see also pezant = 1
 When they do homage to this simple peasant,   147
PEATE = *1
 *Kate. A pretty peate, it is best put finger in the eye, | and she knew
 why.   381
PED = 13*5
PEDA = *1
PEDAN = 1
PEDANT see also Ped., Peda., Pedan. = 10*1
 Hort. But wrangling pedant, this is | The patronesse of heauenly
 harmony: 1299

PEDANT cont.

Luc. How fiery and forward our Pedant is,	1341
Hor. But I haue cause to pry into this pedant,	1381
Tra. What is he Biondello? | Bio. Master, a Marcantant, or a pedant,	1915
Enter a Pedant.	1925
Enter Tranio, and the Pedant drest like Vincentio.	2180
Enter Baptista and Lucentio: Pedant booted | and bare headed.	2200
Pedant lookes out of the window.	2397
Enter Pedant with seruants, Baptista, Tranio.	2440
Exit Biondello, Tranio and Pedant as fast as may be.	2490
*Enter Baptista, Vincentio, Gremio, the Pedant, Lucentio, and	2534

PEDASCULE = 1

Pedascule, Ile watch you better yet:	1343

PEDLER = *1

*Pedler, by education a Cardmaker, by transmutation a	172

PEECD = 1*1

*times peec'd, and a womans Crupper of velure, which	1447
and heere and there peec'd with packthred.	1449

PEECE = 1*1

*Beg. 'Tis a verie excellent peece of worke, Madame	563
What say you to a peece of Beefe and Mustard?	2001

PEECES = 1

not bid him cut it to peeces. Ergo thou liest.	2113

PEEPE = *1

*being perhaps (for ought I see) two and thirty, a peepe	600

PEERETH = 1

So honor peereth in the meanest habit.	2157

PEEUISH = 1

And when she is froward, peeuish, sullen, sowre,	2715

PEGASUS = 1

Tra. Where we were lodgers, at the Pegasus,	2185

PENNANCE = 1

And make her beare the pennance of her tongue.	393

PENNY = *1

*Bion. Nay by S.(aint) Iamy, I hold you a penny, a horse and	1466

PERCEIUE = 2

Nay then you iest, and now I wel perceiue	874
Now I perceiue thou art a reuerent Father:	2346

PEREMPTORIE = 1

I am as peremptorie as she proud minded:	996

PERFECT = 1

He does it vnder name of perfect loue:	1990

PERFORMD = 2

Was aptly fitted, and naturally perform'd.	97
Which once perform'd, let all the world say no,	1524

PERFUMD = 1

And let me haue them verie wel perfum'd;	717

PERFUME = 2

And with her breath she did perfume the ayre,	478
For she is sweeter then perfume it selfe	718

PERHAPS = 3*2

Perhaps you mark'd not what's the pith of all.	469
*being perhaps (for ought I see) two and thirty, a peepe	600
*may perhaps call him halfe a score Knaues, or so: Why	676
Yea and perhaps with more successefull words	723
Tra. Perhaps him and her sir, what haue you to do?	794

PERILL = 1
In perill to incurre your former malady, 276
PERILS = 1
To smile at scapes and perils ouerblowne: 2540
PERISH = 2
Tranio I burne, I pine, I perish *Tranio*, 458
'Twill bring you gaine, or perish on the seas. 1210
PERPETUALLY = 1
That shakes not, though they blow perpetually. 1006
PERSWADE = 2
Perswade him that he hath bin Lunaticke, 67
We will perswade him be it possible, 1508
PERSWASION = 1
As prisoners to her womanlie perswasion: 2676
PERUSD = 1
Gremio. O very well, I haue perus'd the note: 710
PET = 67*22
PETER = 3
As *Stephen Slie*, and old *Iohn Naps* of Greece, | And *Peter Turph*, and
Henry Pimpernell, 246
Nath. Peter didst euer see the like. 1812
Enter Peter. 2253
PETER = 2
PETERS = 1
There was no Linke to colour *Peters* hat, 1761
PETITIONERS = *1
*poore petitioners speake too? *Bacare*, you are meruay-|lous forward. 933
PETR = 49*19
PETRU = 1
PETRUCHIO see also P., Pet., Petr., Petru. = 39*5
Enter Petruchio, and his man Grumio. 565
Grumio, and my good friend *Petruchio*? How do you all | at *Verona*? 589
**Hor.* Alla nostra casa bene venuto multo honorata signi-|or mio*
Petruchio. 593
Hor. Petruchio patience, I am *Grumio's* pledge: 611
Hor. Petruchio, shall I then come roundly to thee, 625
Hor. Petruchio, since we are stept thus farre in, 649
I can *Petruchio* helpe thee to a wife 651
Hor. Tarrie *Petruchio*, I must go with thee, 682
Hor. Now shal my friend *Petruchio* do me grace, 696
Petruchio stand by a while. 708
Petruchio, I shal be your *Been venuto. Exeunt.* 854
Petruchio with Tranio, with his boy | bearing a Lute and Bookes. 898
Pet. Petruchio is my name, *Antonio's* sonne, 929
Gre. Sauing your tale *Petruchio*, I pray let vs that are 932
Signior *Petruchio*, will you go with vs, 1034
Or shall I send my daughter *Kate* to you. | *Exit. Manet Petruchio.* 1035
But heere she comes, and now *Petruchio* speake. 1050
Bap. Now Signior *Petruchio*, how speed you with my | (daughter? 1161
Gre. Hark *Petruchio*, she saies shee'll see thee hang'd | (first. 1180
God send you ioy, *Petruchio*, 'tis a match. 1199
And kisse me *Kate*, we will be married a sonday. | *Exit Petruchio and*
Katherine. 1204
That *Katherine* and *Petruchio* should be married, 1390
Vpon my life *Petruchio* meanes but well, 1410
Bion. Why *Petruchio* is comming, in a new hat and 1431
Bion. Who, that *Petruchio* came? | *Bap.* I, that *Petruchio* came. 1462

PETRUCHIO cont.

Enter Petruchio and Grumio.	1468
Enter Petruchio, Kate, Bianca, Hortensio, Baptista.	1565
Gre. I warrant him *Petruchio* is Kated.	1631
Enter Petruchio and Kate.	1746
Enter Petruchio.	1821
Tra. I mistris, and *Petruchio* is the master,	1907
Enter Petruchio, and Hortensio with meate.	2015
Hor. Signior *Petruchio*, fie you are too blame:	2030
Enter Petruchio, Kate, Hortentio	2294
Hort. Petruchio, goe thy waies, the field is won.	2320
Hor. Well *Petruchio*, this has put me in heart;	2376
Enter Petruchio, Kate, Vincentio, Grumio | *with Attendants.*	2387
Brother *Petruchio*, sister *Katerina*, | And thou *Hortentio* with thy louing	
Widdow:	2543
Bap. Padua affords this kindnesse, sonne *Petruchio*.	2550
Bap. Oh, oh *Petruchio*, *Tranio* hits you now.	2600
Bap. Now in good sadnesse sonne *Petruchio*,	2606
Bap. Now faire befall thee good *Petruchio*;	2666
And being a winner, God giue you good night. | *Exit Petruchio*	2746

PETRUCHIOS = 2*1

One rich enough to be *Petruchio's* wife:	633
And say, loe, there is mad *Petruchio's* wife	1407
Bion. Why, is it not newes to heard of *Petruchio's* | (comming?	1423

PETTICOATE = 1

Yea all my raiment, to my petticoate,	860

PEWTER = 1

Pewter and brasse, and all things that belongs	1237

PEZANT = *1

Pet. You pezant, swain, you horson malt-horse drudg	1756

PHEEZE = 1

Begger. | Ile pheeze you infaith.	3

PHIL = 1

PHILLIP see also Phil. = 1*1

*Call forth *Nathaniel, Ioseph, Nicholas, Phillip, Walter, Su-*|*gersop*	1718
Where is *Nathaniel, Gregory, Phillip*.	1749

PHILOSOPHIE = 2

Vertue and that part of Philosophie | Will I applie, that treats of	
happinesse,	317
To sucke the sweets of sweete Philosophie.	327

PHILOSOPHY = 1

Then giue me leaue to read Philosophy,	1308

PHYSITIANS = 1

For your Physitians haue expressely charg'd,	275

PICKD = 1

And twice to day pick'd out the dullest sent,	27

PICTURES = 1*1

And hang it round with all my wanton pictures:	51
*2.*M.* Dost thou loue pictures? we wil fetch thee strait	201

PIE = 1

A custard coffen, a bauble, a silken pie,	2067

PIECD see peec'd

PIECE see also peece = *1

Gru. A piece of Ice: if thou doubt it, thou maist	1652

PIERCING = 1

And say she vttereth piercing eloquence:	1045

PILLORIE = 1
  As on a Pillorie, looking through the Lute,   1024
PILLOW = 1
  And heere Ile fling the pillow, there the boulster,   1835
PIMPERNELL = 1
  As *Stephen Slie*, and old *Iohn Naps* of Greece, | And *Peter Turph*, and
  Henry Pimpernell,   246
PINCHT = 1
  What, haue I pincht you Signior *Gremio*?   1253
PINE = 1
  Tranio I burne, I pine, I perish *Tranio*,   458
PIP *see* peepe
PISA = 12*2
  Pisa renowned for graue Citizens   309
  Tell me thy minde, for I haue *Pisa* left,   320
  Some *Neapolitan*, or meaner man of *Pisa*.   511
  Tra. Of *Pisa* sir, sonne to *Vincentio*.   966
  Bap. A mightie man of *Pisa* by report,   967
  Within rich *Pisa* walls, as any one | Old Signior *Gremio* has in *Padua*,   1249
  hic est, sonne vnto Vincentio of Pisa, *Sigeria tel-*|*lus*,   1326
  And he shall be *Vincentio* of *Pisa*,   1516
  First tell me, haue you euer beene at Pisa?   1949
  Ped. I sir, in Pisa haue I often bin,   1950
  Pisa renowned for graue Citizens.   1951
  Come sir, we will better it in *Pisa*.   2256
  My name is call'd *Vincentio*, my dwelling *Pisa*,   2353
  *come from *Pisa*, and is here at the doore to speake with | him.   2409
PITCHED = 1
  Haue I not in a pitched battell heard   772
PITCHERS = 1
  Pitchers haue eares, and I haue manie seruants,   2234
PITH = 1
  Perhaps you mark'd not what's the pith of all.   469
PITHY = 1
  More pleasant, pithy, and effectuall,   1361
PITTANCE = 1
  You are like to haue a thin and slender pittance.   2243
PITTY = 1
  Ela mi, show pitty or I die,   1371
PLACE = 4*3
  As firmely as your selfe were still in place,   722
  Lucentio, you shall supply the Bridegroomes place,   1635
  *place, how she was bemoil'd, how hee left her with the   1707
  Bian. The taming schoole: what is there such a place?   1906
  Tail. This is true that I say, and I had thee in place   2132
  My Fathers beares more toward the Market-place,   2390
  And place your hands below your husbands foote: 2735
PLACES = 2
  *When I am alone, why then I am *Tranio*: but in | all places else, your
  master *Lucentio*.   551
  For to supply the places at the table,   1633
PLAI = *1
PLAIDE = 1
  Since once he plaide a Farmers eldest sonne,   94
PLAIE = *1
  *vndone, I am vndone: while I plaie the good husband   2446

PLAIES = *1
  *Wilt thou haue Musicke? Harke Apollo plaies, *Musick*   187
PLAINE = 3*1
  *these words plaine? Sirra, Knocke me heere: rappe me   607
  Say that she raile, why then Ile tell her plaine,   1039
  Pet. You lye infaith, for you are call'd plaine *Kate*,   1056
  Thus in plaine termes: your father hath consented   1148
PLAINNESSE = 2
  And now in plainnesse do confesse to thee   455
  Your plainnesse and your shortnesse please me well: 2221
PLANTETH = 1
  For it engenders choller, planteth anger,   1804
PLASH = 1
  A shallow plash, to plunge him in the deepe,   322
PLATE = 1
  Is richly furnished with plate and gold,   1229
PLAY = 8*3
  1.Hunts. My Lord I warrant you we wil play our part   73
  There is a Lord will heare you play to night;   103
  For yet his honor neuer heard a play)   106
  Euen as the wauing sedges play with winde.   205
  Are come to play a pleasant Comedie,   284
  Therefore they thought it good you heare a play,   288
  Beg. Marrie I will let them play, it is not a Comon-|tie, 291
  1.Man. My Lord you nod, you do not minde the | play. 558
  Bap. Faith Gentlemen now I play a marchants part, 1207
  Take you your instrument, play you the whiles,   1317
  *neuer was before: harke, harke, I heare the min-|strels play. *Musicke*
  playes.   1563
PLAYER see *Plai.*, 2.*Player.*
PLAYERS = 3*1
  Ser. An't please your Honor, Players| That offer seruice to your
  Lordship.   84
  Enter Players.   86
  Let them want nothing that my house affoords.| *Exit one with the*
  Players.   114
  Mes. Your Honors Players hearing your amendment,   283
PLAYERS = 1
PLAYES = 1
  *neuer was before: harke, harke, I heare the min-|strels play. *Musicke*
  playes.   1563
PLEAD = 1
  Are, to plead *Hortensio's* passion: 1367
PLEADE = 2
  Luc. What ere I reade to her, Ile pleade for you,   720
  Ile pleade for you my selfe, but you shal haue him.   870
PLEASANT = 7
  Are come to play a pleasant Comedie,   284
  The pleasant garden of great *Italy*,   303
  Your ancient trustie pleasant seruant *Grumio*:   613
  For thou art pleasant, gamesome, passing courteous, 1124
  That I haue beene thus pleasant with you both.   1351
  More pleasant, pithy, and effectuall,   1361
  Like pleasant trauailors to breake a Iest   2371
PLEASD = 2
  If she and I be pleas'd, what's that to you?   1183
  She will be pleas'd, then wherefore should I doubt: 2291

PLEASE = 16*4

And say wilt please your Lordship coole your hands.	62
Ser. An't please your Honor, Players | That offer seruice to your Lordship.	84
2.Player. So please your Lordshippe to accept our | dutie.	91
1.Ser. Wilt please your Lord drink a cup of sacke?	154
2.Ser. Wilt please your Honor taste of these Con- |serues?	155
2.Man. Wilt please your mightinesse to wash your | hands:	228
Yea, and to marrie her, if her dowrie please.	750
Please ye we may contriue this afternoone,	848
But learne my Lessons as I please my selfe,	1315
Old fashions please me best, I am not so nice	1373
If it would please him come and marry her.	1408
No, nor to morrow, not till I please my selfe,	1595
For me, Ile not be gone till I please my selfe,	1598
Euen to the vttermost as I please in words.	2065
Tra. Sirs, this is the house, please it you that I call.	2181
To haue him matcht, and if you please to like	2214
Your plainnesse and your shortnesse please me well:	2221
And be it moone, or sunne, or what you please:	2309
And if you please to call it a rush Candle,	2310
In token of which dutie, if he please, | My hand is readie, may it do him ease.	2736

PLEASING = 2

Lady. No my good Lord, it is more pleasing stuffe.	293
More queint, more pleasing, nor more commendable:	2087

PLEASURE = 6

No profit growes, where is no pleasure tane:	338
Leaue shall you haue to court her at your pleasure.	356
Sir, to your pleasure humbly I subscribe:	384
In breefe Sir, sith it your pleasure is,	517
Nor hast thou pleasure to be crosse in talke:	1128
Vinc. But is this true, or is it else your pleasure,	2370

PLEDGE = 1

Hor. *Petruchio* patience, I am *Grumio's* pledge:	611

PLOTTED = 1

Tra. I marry am I sir, and now 'tis plotted. | *Luc.* I haue it *Tranio.*	491

PLUCKE = 2*2

Pet. My remedy is then to plucke it out.	1087
*how she waded through the durt to plucke him off	1709
Out you rogue, you plucke my foote awrie,	1775
Pet. Plucke vp thy spirits, looke cheerfully vpon me.	2019

PLUCKING = 1

Take that, and mend the plucking of the other.	1776

PLUNGE = 1

A shallow plash, to plunge him in the deepe,	322

PLY = 2

Keepe house, and ply his booke, welcome his friends,	502
Go ply thy Needle, meddle not with her.	882

POESIE = 1

Musicke and Poesie vse, to quicken you,	335

POETRIE = 1

Fit for her turne, well read in Poetrie	735

POETRY = 1

In Musicke, Instruments, and Poetry,	397

POINT = 2

Hee'll wooe a thousand, point the day of marriage,	1403

POINT *cont.*
  Now must the world point at poore *Katherine*,   1406
POINTED = 2
  Ile not be tied to howres, nor pointed times,   1314
  Bap. Signior *Lucentio*, this is the pointed day   1389
POINTS = *1
  *two broken points: his horse hip'd with an olde mo-|thy   1436
POLITICKELY = 1
  Pet. Thus haue I politickely begun my reigne,   1822
POLLICIE = 1
  If she be curst, it is for pollicie,   1172
POORE = 7*2
  Brach *Meriman*, the poore Curre is imbost,   20
  No better than a poore and loathsome begger: 134
  Bianca stand aside, poore gyrle she weepes: 881
  *poore petitioners speake too? *Bacare*, you are meruay-|lous forward.   933
  Now must the world point at poore *Katherine*,   1406
  As I can change these poore accoutrements,   1502
  *(poore soule) knowes not which way to stand, to looke,   1818
  Our purses shall be proud, our garments poore: 2154
  For this poore furniture, and meane array.   2163
POOREST = 1
  Pet. The poorest seruice is repaide with thankes,   2027
PORRENGER = 1
  ' *Pet.* Why this was moulded on a porrenger,   2048
PORT = 1*1
  Keepe house, and port, and seruants, as I should,   509
  regia, bearing my port, *celsa senis* that we might be-|guile the old
  Pantalowne.   1329
PORTION = 1
  And all things answerable to this portion.   1241
POSSESSION = 1
  And in possession twentie thousand Crownes.   987
POSSESSIONS = 1
  Of such possessions, and so high esteeme   168
POSSEST = *1
  *saddle, and stirrops of no kindred: besides possest   1437
POSSIBLE = 6
  Tra. I pray sir tel me, is it possible   449
  I neuer thought it possible or likely.   452
  Tra. Not possible: for who shall beare your part,   500
  We will perswade him be it possible,   1508
  Bap. Is't possible you will away to night?   1571
  Tra. Is't possible friend *Lisio*, that mistris *Bianca*   1847
POT = 2*1
  Beg. For Gods sake a pot of small Ale.   153
  And once againe a pot o'th smallest Ale.   227
  *now were I not a little pot, & soone hot; my very lippes   1644
POUND = 1*1
  I would not loose the dogge for twentie pound.   24
  Vinc. What if a man bring him a hundred pound or | two to make
  merrie withall.   2402
POUNDS = *1
  Ped. Keepe your hundred pounds to your selfe, hee   2404
PRACTISE = 5
  Sirs, I will practise on this drunken man.   40
  And practise Rhetoricke in your common talke,   334

PRACTISE *cont.*

On them to looke, and practise by my selfe.	386
Proceed in practise with my yonger daughter,	1032
Tra. Shall sweet *Bianca* practise how to bride it?	1637

PRAID = *2

*me: how he swore, how she prai'd, that neuer prai'd be-|fore:	1710

PRAIE = 4*2

Biond. I praie the gods she may withall my heart. | *Exit.*	2250
Bap. You mistake sir, you mistake sir, praie what do | you thinke is his name?	2457
Kate. Nay, I will giue thee a kisse, now praie thee | Loue staie.	2529
After our great good cheere: praie you sit downe,	2547
I praie you tell me what you meant by that.	2567
Praie God sir your wife send you not a worse. | *Petr.* I hope better.	2634

PRAISD = 1

Hearing thy mildnesse prais'd in euery Towne,	1062

PRATING = 1

As thou shalt thinke on prating whil'st thou liu'st:	2099

PRAY = 22*7

Let's be no Stoickes, nor no stockes I pray,	330
Kate. I pray you sir, is it your will	359
Hor. So will I signiour *Gremio*: but a word I pray:	417
Gre. What's that I pray? | *Hor.* Marrie sir to get a husband for her Sister.	423
Tra. I pray sir tel me, is it possible	449
I pray awake sir: if you loue the Maide,	481
*cloathes, or you stolne his, or both? Pray what's the | newes?	531
Gru. I pray you Sir let him go while the humor lasts.	673
Petr. Not her that chides sir, at any hand I pray.	795
Tra. Why sir, I pray are not the streets as free | For me, as for you?	803
Pet. And you good sir: pray haue you not a daugh-|ter, cal'd *Katerina*, faire and vertuous.	903
Gre. Sauing your tale *Petruchio*, I pray let vs that are	932
His name is *Cambio*: pray accept his seruice.	946
Bap. Lucentio is your name, of whence I pray.	965
And so I pray you all to thinke your selues.	978
Pet. I pray you do. Ile attend her heere,	1037
Good master take it not vnkindly pray	1350
Cur. All readie: and therefore I pray thee newes.	1687
Kate. Patience I pray you, 'twas a fault vnwilling.	1785
Kate. I pray you husband be not so disquiet,	1800
Hor. Quicke proceeders marry, now tel me I pray,	1859
Tra. What Countreyman I pray? | *Ped.* Of *Mantua*.	1932
Ped. My life sir? how I pray? for that goes hard.	1936
Heere take away this dish. | *Kate.* I pray you let it stand.	2025
I pray you stand good father to me now,	2204
Luc. I pray thee moralize them.	2267
Kate. Forward I pray, since we haue come so farre,	2308
Pardon I pray thee for my mad mistaking.	2347
*I pray you tell signior *Lucentio* that his Father is	2408

PRAYES = *1

Nicke. Mistresse, your father prayes you leaue your | (books,	1376

PRECIOUS = 1

What is the Iay more precious then the Larke?	2158

PREETHE = *1

Petr. Preethe *Kate* let's stand aside and see the end of | this controuersie.	2438

PRIEST *cont.*

That all amaz'd the Priest let fall the booke,   1545
*That downe fell Priest and booke, and booke and Priest,   1548
Bio. The old Priest at Saint *Lukes* Church is at your | command at all
hours.   2274
Priest, Clarke, and some sufficient honest witnesses: 2280
*the Priest be readie to come against you come with your | appendix.
Exit.   2288
Biond. Softly and swiftly sir, for the Priest is ready.   2381
PRIMA *I.*1 1977 = 2
PRIMUS *I.*1 = 1
PRINCE = 1
Such dutie as the subiect owes the Prince,   2713
PRINCELY = 1
As *Kate* this chamber with her princely gate: 1138
PRISON = 2
Gre. Staie officer, he shall not go to prison.   2473
Bap. Talke not signior *Gremio*: I saie he shall goe to | prison.   2474
PRISONERS = 1
As prisoners to her womanlie perswasion: 2676
PRIUATE = 1
For priuate quarrel 'twixt your Duke and him,   1940
PRIUATELY = 1
Weele passe the businesse priuately and well: 2239
PRIZE = 1
'Tis deeds must win the prize, and he of both   1224
PROCEED = 1
Proceed in practise with my yonger daughter,   1032
PROCEEDE = 1
Pet. Proceede. | *Tai.* With a small compast cape.   2121
PROCEEDERS = *1
Hor. Quicke proceeders marry, now tel me I pray,   1859
PROCLAIMD = 2
Hath publish'd and proclaim'd it openly: 1941
You might haue heard it else proclaim'd about.   1943
PROCLAIME = 1
Make friends, inuite, and proclaime the banes,   1404
PROCURE = 1
Procure me Musicke readie when he wakes,   54
PRODIGIE = 1
As if they saw some wondrous monument, | Some Commet, or vnusuall
prodigie?   1478
PROFESSE = 2
And since you do professe to be a sutor,   844
Hor. I reade, that I professe the Art to loue.   1855
PROFESSION = *1
*Beare-heard, and now by present profession a Tinker.   173
PROFIT = 2
No profit growes, where is no pleasure tane: 338
Hor. Now Mistris, profit you in what you reade?   1853
PROMISE = 6
And yet Ile promise thee she shall be rich,   628
And will not promise her to any man,   834
Hor. For feare I promise you, if I looke pale.   1010
Kat. Call you me daughter? now I promise you   1165
By your firme promise, *Gremio* is out vied.   1267
Hort. I must beleeue my master, else I promise you,   1347

PROMISED = 1
    Of greater summes then I haue promised,   1518
PROMIST = 3
    I promist to enquire carefully | About a schoolemaster for the faire
    Bianca,   731
    Hath promist me to helpe one to another,   738
    Hor. I promist we would be Contributors,   782
PROOFE = 2
    Pet. I to the proofe, as Mountaines are for windes,   1005
    And all my paines is sorted to no proofe.   2024
PROPER = 1
    Grumio. A proper stripling, and an amorous.   709
PROPOSE = 1
    Shall win the wager which we will propose.   2612
PROTESTING = 1
    Shee vi'd so fast, protesting oath on oath,   1189
PROUD = 3
    I am as peremptorie as she proud minded: 996
    As I haue lou'd this proud disdainful Haggard,   1887
    Our purses shall be proud, our garments poore: 2154
PROUDEST = 1*1
    Ile bring mine action on the proudest he   1620
    Gru. I, and that thou and the proudest of you all shall   1716
PROUE = 7*3
    Gre. Beloued of me, and that my deeds shal proue.   742
    Gru. And that his bags shal proue.   743
    Luc. Sir giue him head, I know hee'l proue a Iade.   821
    Bap. What, will my daughter proue a good Musiti-|an?   1011
    Hor. I thinke she'l sooner proue a souldier,   1013
    For patience shee will proue a second *Grissell*,   1175
    'Tis like you'll proue a iolly surly groome,   1599
    Bian. And may you proue sir Master of your Art.   1856
    Luc. While you sweet deere proue Mistresse of my | heart.   1857
    *that Ile proue vpon thee, though thy little finger be ar-|med in a
    thimble.   2130
PROUIDE = 1
    Prouide the feast father, and bid the guests,   1196
PROUIDED = 1
    Gremio. And so we wil, prouided that he win her.   784
PRY = 1
    Hor. But I haue cause to pry into this pedant,   1381
PRYING = 1
    The narrow prying father *Minola*,   1529
PUBLISHD = 1
    Hath publish'd and proclaim'd it openly: 1941
PUFT = 1
    Haue I not heard the sea, puft vp with windes,   768
PULL = 1
    Vnbinde my hands, Ile pull them off my selfe,   859
PUMPES = 1
    And *Gabrels* pumpes were all vnpinkt i'thheele: 1760
PUPILS = 1
    You shall go see your Pupils presently. | Holla, within.   970
PUPPET = 2*2
    *to a Puppet or an Aglet babie, or an old trot with ne're a   645
    Belike you meane to make a puppet of me.   2088
    Pet. Why true, he meanes to make a puppet of thee.   2089

PUPPET *cont.*

Tail. She saies your Worship meanes to make a | puppet of her.   2090
PURPOSE = 1

On purpose trim'd vp for Semiramis.   191
PURSE = 1

Crownes in my purse I haue, and goods at home,   623
PURSES = 1

Our purses shall be proud, our garments poore: 2154
PURSUE = 1

And then pursue me as you draw your Bow.   2590
PUT = 7*2

Wrap'd in sweet cloathes: Rings put vpon his fingers: 42
We could at once put vs in readinesse,   342
Kate. A pretty peate, it is best put finger in the eye, | and she knew
why.   381
And I for my escape haue put on his: 537
Pet. A Herald *Kate*? Oh put me in thy bookes.   1101
Goe to my chamber, put on clothes of mine.   1496
To put on better ere he goe to Church.   1509
Hor. Well *Petruchio*, this has put me in heart;   2376
Petr. A hundred marks, my *Kate* does put her down.   2576
PUTS = 1

Puts my apparrell, and my count'nance on,   536
QUAFFE = 1

And quaffe carowses to our Mistresse health,   849
QUAFT = *1

*a storme, quaft off the Muscadell, and threw the sops   1555
QUAINT *see also* queint = 1

The quaint Musician, amorous *Litio*,   1530
QUALIFIED = 1

Beside, so qualified, as may beseeme | The Spouse of any noble
Gentleman: 2365
QUALITIES = 1

Her wondrous qualities, and milde behauiour,   911
QUAM = 1

Redime te captam quam queas minimo.   465
QUANTITIE = 1

Away thou Ragge, thou quantitie, thou remnant,   2097
QUARREL = 1

For priuate quarrel 'twixt your Duke and him,   1940
QUARRELL = 2*1

*Though the nature of our quarrell yet neuer brook'd   418
For in a quarrell since I came a-shore,   538
Rise *Grumio* rise, we will compound this quarrell.   595
QUARRELSOME = 1

Gru. My Mr is growne quarrelsome: 578
QUARTER = 1

Thou yard three quarters, halfe yard, quarter, naile,   2094
QUARTERS = 1

Thou yard three quarters, halfe yard, quarter, naile,   2094
QUARTS = 1

Because she brought stone-Iugs, and no seal'd quarts: 241
QUARTUS *l.*1977 = 1

QUEAS = 1

Redime te captam quam queas minimo.   465
QUEENE = 1

As *Anna* to the Queene of Carthage was: 457

QUEINT = 1
More queint, more pleasing, nor more commendable: 2087
QUENCH = 1
And with sacietie seekes to quench his thirst.   323
QUICKE = 1*1
*Hor. Quicke proceeders marry, now tel me I pray,   1859
Bap. How likes Gremio these quicke witted folkes?   2580
QUICKEN = 1
Musicke and Poesie vse, to quicken you,   335
QUICKLY = *1
*Gre. Went they not quickly, I should die with laugh-|(ing.   1627
QUIET = 4*1
Bap. The gaine I seeke, is quiet me the match.   1211
Gre. No doubt but he hath got a quiet catch: 1212
Father, be quiet, he shall stay my leisure.   1603
Bap. Nay, let them goe, a couple of quiet ones.   1626
*Petr. Marrie peace it boads, and loue, and quiet life,   2663
QUIETLY = 1
So shall you quietly enioy your hope,   1519
QUINTUS l.2533 = 1
QUIT = 1
Hortensio will be quit with thee by changing. Exit.   1386
QUITE = 1*1
As Ouid; be an out-cast quite abiur'd: 332
*Hor. Would all the world but he had quite forsworn   1883
QUOTH = 4*1
Be seruiceable to my sonne (quoth he)   520
Frets call you these? (quoth she) Ile fume with them: 1020
I, by goggs woones quoth he, and swore so loud,   1544
Now take them vp quoth he, if any list.   1549
*ceremonies done, hee calls for wine, a health quoth   1553
RABIT = *1
*stuffe a Rabit, and so may you sir: and so adew sir, my   2286
RAFE = 1
There were none fine, but Adam, Rafe, and Gregory,   1763
RAGE = 1
Rage like an angry Boare, chafed with sweat?   769
RAGGE = 1
Away thou Ragge, thou quantitie, thou remnant,   2097
RAGGED = 1
The rest were ragged, old, and beggerly,   1764
RAGING = 2
And where two raging fires meete together,   997
And time it is when raging warre is come,   2539
RAIDE = *1
*so raide? was euer man so weary? I am sent before to   1642
RAIED = *1
*of Windegalls, sped with Spauins, raied with the Yel-|lowes,   1440
RAILE = 3*1
And raile vpon the Hostesse of the house,   239
*that's nothing; and he begin once, hee'l raile in his rope   677
Say that she raile, why then Ile tell her plaine,   1039
And if she chance to nod, Ile raile and brawle,   1840
RAILES = *1
*to her, and railes, and sweares, and rates, that shee   1817
RAIMENT = 2*1
3.Ser. What raiment wil your honor weare to day.   157

RAIMENT *cont.*

*me what raiment Ile weare, for I haue no more doub-|lets	161
Yea all my raiment, to my petticoate,	860

RAINE = 1

To raine a shower of commanded teares,	136

RAISE = 1

Began to scold, and raise vp such a storme,	475

RANGING = 1

Seize thee that List, if once I finde thee ranging,	1385

RANNE = *1

*how I cried, how the horses ranne away, how her	1711

RAP = 1*1

And rap me well, or Ile knocke your knaues pate.	577
*looke you sir: He bid me knocke him, & rap him sound-|ly	598

RAPPE = *1

*these words plaine? Sirra, Knocke me heere: rappe me	607

RASCAL = 1

And bring along these rascal knaues with thee?	1758

RASCALL = 3

I bad the rascall knocke vpon your gate,	604
While she did call me Rascall, Fidler,	1025
What dogges are these? Where is the rascall Cooke?	1794

RASCALS = *1

*Pet. Go rascals, go, and fetch my supper in. Ex. Ser.	1766

RATED = 1

Affection is not rated from the heart:	463

RATES = *1

*to her, and railes, and sweares, and rates, that shee	1817

RATHER = 5

The rather for I haue some sport in hand,	101
Gre. To cart her rather. She's to rough for mee,	357
Which I haue bettered rather then decreast,	983
You would intreat me rather goe then stay:	1574
And rather then it shall, I will be free,	2064

RE = 1

D sol re, one Cliffe, two notes haue I,	1370

REACH = 1

Wee'll ouer-reach the grey-beard *Gremio*,	1528

READ = 4

Fit for her turne, well read in Poetrie	735
Luc. Preposterous Asse that neuer read so farre,	1304
Then giue me leaue to read Philosophy,	1308
Hor. Yet read the gamouth of *Hortentio*.	1365

READE = 6*1

And see you reade no other Lectures to her:	713
To whom they go to: what wil you reade to her.	719
Luc. What ere I reade to her, Ile pleade for you,	720
Hor. Now Mistris, profit you in what you reade?	1853
Bian. What Master reade you first, resolue me that?	1854
Hor. I reade, that I professe the Art to loue.	1855
Tail. Why heere is the note of the fashion to testify. | *Pet*. Reade it.	2114

READIE = 10*3

Procure me Musicke readie when he wakes,	54
And if he chance to speake, be readie straight	56
Some one be readie with a costly suite,	63
Each in his office readie at thy becke.	186
Cur. There's fire readie, and therefore good *Grumio* | the newes.	1675

READIE *cont.*

Cur. All readie: and therefore I pray thee newes.	1687
they kisse their hands. Are they all readie?	1723
companions, is all readie, and all things neate?	1742
Nat. All things is readie, how neere is our master?	1743
Me shall you finde readie and willing	2216
Cambio hie you home, and bid *Bianca* make her readie | straight:	2245
*the Priest be readie to come against you come with your | appendix. *Exit.*	2288
In token of which dutie, if he please, | My hand is readie, may it do him ease.	2736

READIEST = 1

Tell me I beseech you, which is the readiest way	788

READINESSE = 1

We could at once put vs in readinesse,	342

READY = 1*2

Gru. I sir, they be ready, the Oates haue eaten the | horses.	1591
*cold. Where's the Cooke, is supper ready, the house	1681
Biond. Softly and swiftly sir, for the Priest is ready.	2381

REASON = 5*1

I hope this reason stands for my excuse.	278
Gre. But so is not she. | *Tra.* For what reason I beseech you.	805
Gre. For this reason if you'l kno,	807
I see no reason but suppos'd *Lucentio*	1289
*all in the Sextons face: hauing no other reason, but that	1556
My heart as great, my reason haplie more,	2729

REASONS = 1

Sufficeth my reasons are both good and waighty.	556

REBELL = 1

What is she but a foule contending Rebell,	2717

REBUSD = 1

any man ha's rebus'd your worship?	572

RECKNING = 1

Cur. By this reckning he is more shrew than she.	1715

RECKOND = 1

Nor no such men as you haue reckon'd vp,	245

RED = 1*1

*a kersey boot-hose on the other, gartred with a red and	1453
Such warre of white and red within her cheekes:	2328

REDIME = 1

Redime te captam quam queas minimo.	465

REFRESH = 1

Was it not to refresh the minde of man | After his studies, or his vsuall paine?	1306

REGARD = 2

You haue shewd a tender fatherly regard,	1166
What? no attendance? no regard? no dutie?	1753

REGIA = 1*2

tellus, hic steterat Priami regia Celsa senis.	1323
*regia, bearing my port, celsa senis that we might be-|guile the old Pantalowne.	1329
*hic staterat priami, take heede he heare vs not, regia pre-|sume not, Celsa senis, despaire not.	1336

REHEARST = 1

For those defects I haue before rehearst,	689

REIGNE = 1

Pet. Thus haue I politickely begun my reigne,	1822

REMAINES = 1
If loue haue touch'd you, naught remaines but so,   464
REMEDIE = *1
*Host. I know my remedie, I must go fetch the Head-|borough.   13
REMEDY = 1
Pet. My remedy is then to plucke it out.   1087
REMEMBER = 2
  Lord. With all my heart. This fellow I remember,   93
Signior Baptista may remember me | Neere twentie yeares a goe in
Genoa.   2183
REMEMBRED = 1
Pet. Marrie and did: but if you be remembred,   2081
REMNANT = 1
Away thou Ragge, thou quantitie, thou remnant,   2097
REMOUE = 1
Remoue you hence: I knew you at the first | You were a mouable.   1068
REMOUES = 1
She moues me not, or not remoues at least   638
RENOWND = 1
Renown'd in Padua for her scolding tongue.   666
RENOWNED = 2
Pisa renowned for graue Citizens   309
Pisa renowned for graue Citizens.   1951
REPAIDE = 1
Pet. The poorest seruice is repaide with thankes,   2027
REPAIRE = 1
Could I repaire what she will weare in me,   1501
REPAIRED = *1
*often burst, and now repaired with knots: one girth sixe   1446
REPAST = 1
I prethee go, and get me some repast,   1993
REPLIED = 1
*Wid. He that is giddie thinks the world turns round. | Petr. Roundlie
replied.   2558
REPORT = 5
Of that report, which I so oft haue heard,   914
Bap. A mightie man of Pisa by report,   967
And now I finde report a very liar: 1123
Why does the world report that Kate doth limpe?   1131
And for the good report I heare of you,   2210
REPORTED = 1
Cur. Is she so hot a shrew as she's reported.   1659
REPOSE = 1
(Trauelling some iourney) to repose him heere.   81
REPUTE = 1
Ped. Oh sir I do, and wil repute you euer   1968
REQUEST = 2
This liberty is all that I request,   957
Tail. But did you not request to haue it cut?   2107
RESCUE = 1
Rescue thy Mistresse if thou be a man: 1623
RESEMBLE = 1
In count'nance somewhat doth resemble you.   1956
RESIST = 1
If she had not a spirit to resist.   1607
RESOLUD = 3
For how I firmly am resolu'd you know: 351

RESOLUD *cont.*
  Bap. Gentlemen content ye: I am resolud: | Go in *Bianca.*   394
  Bap. Well gentlemen, I am thus resolu'd,   1274
RESOLUE = 2*1
  Glad that you thus continue your resolue,   326
  Nor is your firme resolue vnknowne to me,   955
  Bian. What Master reade you first, resolue me that?   1854
RESOLUTION = 1
  In resolution, as I swore before.   1891
RESPECTING = 1
  Kat. And I am meane indeede, respecting you.   2573
REST = 8*3
  The rest wil comfort, for thy counsels sound.   467
  Must steed vs all, and me amongst the rest: 838
  To whom we all rest generally beholding.   846
  Ka. If that be iest, then all the rest was so. *Strikes her*   877
  I may haue welcome 'mongst the rest that woo,   959
  And free accesse and fauour as the rest.   960
  But let it rest, now *Litio* to you: 1349
  *and the rest: let their heads bee slickely comb'd,   1719
  The rest were ragged, old, and beggerly,   1764
  Kate. Why then the Beefe, and let the Mustard rest.   2004
  Gre. My cake is dough, but Ile in among the rest,   2520
RESTETH = 1
  To striue for that which resteth in my choice: 1312
RESTORD = 2
  To see her noble Lord restor'd to health,   132
  Oh how we ioy to see your wit restor'd,   230
RESTRAIND = *1
  *being restrain'd to keepe him from stumbling, hath been   1445
RESTS = 1
  One thing more rests, that thy selfe execute,   554
RETURNE = 2
  and thou returne vnexperienc'd to thy graue.   1714
  Will we returne vnto thy Fathers house,   2035
REUELL = 2
  Goe to the feast, reuell and domineere,   1610
  And reuell it as brauely as the best,   2036
REUENGD = 2
  Kate. Her silence flouts me, and Ile be reueng'd. | *Flies after Bianca*   886
  but I will in to be reueng'd for this villanie. *Exit.*   2516
REUENGE = 1
  Till I can finde occasion of reuenge.   894
REUERENCE = 1
  (And with a lowe submissiue reuerence)   57
REUEREND = 1
  That all is done in reuerend care of her,   1838
REUERENT = 2
  Now I perceiue thou art a reuerent Father: 2346
  And now by Law, as well as reuerent age,   2359
RHEMES = 1
  Beene long studying at *Rhemes*, as cunning   943
RHETORICKE = 1
  And practise Rhetoricke in your common talke,   334
RICH = 5*1
  *her father be verie rich, any man is so verie a foole to be | married to
  hell?   428

RICH *cont*.

And yet Ile promise thee she shall be rich,	628
And verie rich: but th'art too much my friend,	629
One rich enough to be *Petruchio's* wife:	633
Within rich *Pisa* walls, as any one | Old Signior *Gremio* has in *Padua*,	1249
For 'tis the minde that makes the bodie rich.	2155

RICHARD = *1

*in with *Richard Conqueror*: therefore *Pau-!cas pallabris*, let the world slide: Sessa.	8

RICHES = 1

Kate. Oh then belike you fancie riches more,	871

RICHLY = 1

Is richly furnished with plate and gold,	1229

RID = 2

That til the Father rid his hands of her,	484
Tra. Mistris we haue. | *Luc*. Then we are rid of *Lisio*.	1898

RIDDE = *1

*woe her, wed her, and bed her, and ridde the | house of her. Come on.	446

RIDE = 1

Or wilt thou ride? Thy horses shal be trap'd,	193

RIDING = 1

hill, my Master riding behinde my Mistris.	1700

RIGHT = 8*4

Do me this right: heare me with patience.	811
Hort. The base is right, 'tis the base knaue that iars.	1340
As if he were the right *Vincentio*.	1923
Gru. You are i'th right sir, 'tis for my mistris.	2139
Imagine 'twere the right *Vincentio*.	2193
Right true it is your sonne *Lucentio* here	2222
*in this businesse: I dare sweare this is the right | *Vincentio*.	2477
Luc. Here's *Lucentio*, right sonne to the right *Vin-|centio*,	2495
Wid. Right, I meane you.	2572
'Tis ten to one it maim'd you too out right	2605
An awfull rule, and right supremicie:	2664

RING = 2

fastest, gets the Ring: How say you signior *Gremio*?	443
Petr. Will it not be? | 'Faith sirrah, and you'l not knocke, Ile ring it,	581

RINGS = 4

Wrap'd in sweet cloathes: Rings put vpon his fingers:	42
Ile trie how you can *Sol*, *Fa*, and sing it. | *He rings him by the eares*	583
We will haue rings, and things, and fine array,	1203
With silken coats and caps, and golden Rings,	2037

RISE = 2

Rise *Grumio* rise, we will compound this quarrell.	595

RISEN = *1

*to speake, and sits as one new risen from a dreame: A-|way, away, for he is comming hither.	1819

RITES = 1

To speake the ceremoniall rites of marriage?	1394

RIUALL = 1

Hor. Peace *Grumio*, it is the riuall of my Loue.	707

RIUALS = 1*1

*be happie riuals in *Bianca's* loue, to labour and effect | one thing specially.	421
Suters to her, and riuals in my Loue:	687

ROADE = 1

That now is lying in Marcellus roade:	1257

ROBES = 2
    And offer me disguis'd in sober robes,   697
    Tra. See not your Bride in these vnreuerent robes,   1495
ROE = 1
    As breathed Stags: I fleeter then the Roe.   200
ROGUE = 3*1
    Host. A paire of stockes you rogue.   5
    Heere comes the rogue. Sirra, where haue you bin?   528
    Out you rogue, you plucke my foote awrie,   1775
    Vin. Come hither you rogue, what haue you forgot | mee?   2426
ROGUES = 1*1
    Rogues. Looke in the Chronicles, we came   7
    Off with my boots, you rogues: you villaines, when?   1772
ROMANE = 1
    And Romane *Lucrece* for her chastitie: 1176
ROME = 1
    But then vp farther, and as farre as Rome,   1930
ROMING = *1
    3.Man. Or *Daphne* roming through a thornie wood,   209
ROOFE = *1
    *might freeze to my teeth, my tongue to the roofe of my   1645
ROOME = 1
    And let *Bianca* take her sisters roome.   1636
ROPE = *1
    *that's nothing; and he begin once, hee'l raile in his rope   677
RORE = 1
    Haue I not in my time heard Lions rore?   767
ROSE = 1
    Tra. What said the wench when he rose againe?   1550
ROSES = 1
    As morning Roses newly washt with dew: 1042
ROSE-WATER = 1
    Full of Rose-water, and bestrew'd with Flowers,   60
ROSTED = 1
    Then feede it with such ouer-rosted flesh: 1807
ROTTEN = *1
    Hor. Faith (as you say) there's small choise in rotten   437
ROUGH = 4
    Gre. To cart her rather. She's to rough for mee,   357
    Affections edge in me. Were she is as rough | As are the swelling
    Adriaticke seas.   639
    For I am rough, and woo not like a babe.   1002
    'Twas told me you were rough, and coy, and sullen,   1122
ROUND = 1*2
    And hang it round with all my wanton pictures: 51
    Wid. He that is giddie thinks the world turns round. | *Petr*. Roundlie
    replied.   2558
    Kat. He that is giddie thinkes the world turnes round,   2566
ROUNDLIE = 1
    Wid. He that is giddie thinks the world turns round. | *Petr*. Roundlie
    replied.   2558
ROUNDLY = 3
    Hor. Petruchio, shall I then come roundly to thee,   625
    That take it on you at the first so roundly.   1600
    Hap what hap may, Ile roundly goe about her: 2292
ROUT = *1
    *after mee I know the rout is comming, such a mad mar-|ryage 1562

RUDESBY = 1
Vnto a mad-braine rudesby, full of spleene, 1398
RUDIMENTS = 1
I must begin with rudiments of Art, 1359
RUFFES = 1
With Ruffes and Cuffes, and Fardingales, and things: 2038
RUFFIAN = 1
A mad-cap ruffian, and a swearing Iacke, 1168
RUFFLING = 1
To decke thy bodie with his ruffling treasure. 2042
RULE = 2
An awfull rule, and right supremicie: 2664
Or seeke for rule, supremacie, and sway, 2721
RULES = 1
To charge true rules for old inuentions. 1374
RUN = 2*1
Like enuious flouds ore-run her louely face, 217
*greater a run but my head and my necke. A fire good | Curtis. 1654
*Petr. Well, forward, forward, thus the bowle should | (run, 2321
RUNNES = *1
*Sweet Bianca, happy man be his dole: hee that runnes 442
RUNNING = 1
Adonis painted by a running brooke, 202
RUNS = 1
Which runs himselfe, and catches for his Master. 2596
RUSH = 2
Petr. Were it better I should rush in thus: 1474
And if you please to call it a rush Candle, 2310
RUSHES = *1
*trim'd, rushes strew'd, cobwebs swept, the seruingmen 1682
RUSTY = *1
*another lac'd: an olde rusty sword tane out of the 1434
SACIETIE = 1
And with sacietie seekes to quench his thirst. 323
SACKE = *2
*1.Ser. Wilt please your Lord drink a cup of sacke? 154
*Lordship: I ne're drank sacke in my life: and if you giue 159
SACRED = 1
Sacred and sweet was all I saw in her. 479
SAD = 2
And at that sight shal sad Apollo weepe, 211
First were we sad, fearing you would not come, 1481
SADDER = 1
Now sadder that you come so vnprouided: 1482
SADDLE = *1
*saddle, and stirrops of no kindred: besides possest 1437
SADDLES = *1
*Gru. Out of their saddles into the durt, and thereby | hangs a tale. 1690
SADNESSE = 2
Seeing too much sadnesse hath congeal'd your blood, 286
Bap. Now in good sadnesse sonne Petruchio, 2606
SAFE = 1*1
*Biond. Then thus: Baptista is safe talking with the 2268
Whil'st thou ly'st warme at home, secure and safe, 2709
SAID = 8*1
Tra. Well said Mr, mum, and gaze your fill. 376
What I haue said, Bianca get you in, 378

SAID *cont.*

Gre. So said, so done, is well:	751
What will be said, what mockery will it be?	1392
Tra. What said the wench when he rose againe?	1550
Luc. Sir, to satisfie you in what I haue said,	1850
Gru. The note lies in's throate if he say I said so.	2116
Gru. Master, if euer I said loose-bodied gowne, sow	2118
*me in the skirts of it, and beate me to death with a bot-|tome of browne thred: I said a gowne.	2119

SAIE = *2

Bap. Talke not signior *Gremio*: I saie he shall goe to | prison.	2474
Tran. Then thou wert best saie that I am not *Lu-|centio*.	2481

SAIES = 6*1

Gre. Hark *Petruchio*, she saies shee'll see thee hang'd | (first.	1180
What saies *Lucentio* to this shame of ours?	1395
Tail. She saies your Worship meanes to make a | puppet of her.	2090
Hort. Say as he saies, or we shall neuer goe.	2307
Ped. I sir, so his mother saies, if I may beleeue her.	2414
Hor. My Widdow saies, thus she conceiues her tale.	2563
Bion. She saies you haue some goodly Iest in hand,	2643

SAILE-MAKER = *1

Vin. Thy father: oh villaine, he is a Saile-maker in | *Bergamo*.	2455

SAINT = 2*5

Beg. No, not a deniere: go by S.(aint) *Ieronimie*, goe to thy | cold bed, and warme thee.	11
Beg. Yes by Saint Anne do I, a good matter surely:	560
Pet. Now by S.(aint) George I am too yong for you.	1115
For such an iniurie would vexe a very saint,	1417
Bion. Nay by S.(aint) *Iamy*, I hold you a penny, a horse and	1466
Bio. The old Priest at Saint *Lukes* Church is at your | command at all houres.	2274
*Master hath appointed me to goe to Saint *Lukes* to bid	2287

SAIST = 3

Pet. Why thou saist true, it is paltrie cap,	2066
Bion. Cambio. | *Luc.* What saist thou *Biondello*.	2259
And not a Maiden, as thou saist he is.	2342

SAKE = 6*2

Beg. For Gods sake a pot of small Ale.	153
*But sirra, not for my sake, but your masters, I ad-|uise	549
Bap. Y'are welcome sir, and he for your good sake.	922
Bap. I know him well: you are welcome for his sake.	931
All for my Masters sake *Lucentio*.	1531
This fauor wil I do you for his sake,	1959
Sweete *Kate* embrace her for her beauties sake.	2332
Then pardon him sweete Father for my sake.	2510

SAKES = *1

Hor. For both our sakes I would that word were true.	2552

SATISFIE = 1

Luc. Sir, to satisfie you in what I haue said,	1850

SATISFIED = 1

As you shall well be satisfied with all.	1492

SAUE = 6*1

Your fellow *Tranio* heere to saue my life,	535
While I make way from hence to saue my life:	541
Hor. Grumio mum: God saue you signior *Gremio*.	728
Tra. Gentlemen God saue you. If I may be bold	787
Bap. Good morrow neighbour *Gremio*: God saue | you Gentlemen.	901

SAUE *cont.*

Ped. God saue you sir.	*Tra.* And you sir, you are welcome.	1926
Tra. To saue your life in this extremitie,	1958

SAUING = *1

Gre. Sauing your tale *Petruchio*, I pray let vs that are	932

SAUOURS = 1

I smel sweet sauours, and I feele soft things:	223

SAW = 7*2

And twentie more such names and men as these,	Which neuer were, nor no man euer saw.	248
Luc. Oh yes, I saw sweet beautie in her face,	470
Tra. Saw you no more? Mark'd you not how hir sister	474
Luc. Tranio, I saw her corrall lips to moue,	477
Sacred and sweet was all I saw in her.	479
As if they saw some wondrous monument,	Some Commet, or vnusuall prodigie?	1478
Kate. I neuer saw a better fashion'd gowne,	2086
Biond. You saw my Master winke and laugh vpon	you?	2261
I neuer saw you before in all my life.	2429

SAWST = 1

Saw'st thou not boy how *Siluer* made it good	22

SAY = 53*9

Say, what is it your Honor wil command:	58
And say wilt please your Lordship coole your hands.	62
And when he sayes he is, say that he dreames,	68
He is no lesse then what we say he is.	75
And say: What is't your Honor will command,	126
*know me not: if she say I am not xiiii.d. on the score for	175
Say thou wilt walke: wee wil bestrow the ground.	192
1.Man. Say thou wilt course, thy gray-hounds are as	(swift	199
Yet would you say, ye were beaten out of doore,	238
And say you would present her at the Leete,	240
Beg. Madame wife, they say that I haue dream'd,	266
Gre. A husband: a diuell.	*Hor.* I say a husband.	425
Gre. I say, a diuell: Think'st thou *Hortensio,* though	427
Hor. Faith (as you say) there's small choise in rotten	437
fastest, gets the Ring: How say you signior *Gremio*?	443
Heere sirra *Grumio,* knocke I say.	570
Petr. Villaine I say, knocke me heere soundly.	573
Petr. Villaine I say, knocke me at this gate,	576
Contutti le core bene trobatto, may I say.	592
Hor. Sir you say wel, and wel you do conceiue,	843
Say that she raile, why then Ile tell her plaine,	1039
Say that she frowne, Ile say she lookes as cleere	1041
Say she be mute, and will not speake a word,	1043
And say she vttereth piercing eloquence:	1045
Bap. I know not what to say, but giue me your ha(n)ds,	1198
Gre. Tra. Amen say we, we will be witnesses.	1200
Say signior *Gremio,* what can you assure her?	1227
And say, loe, there is mad *Petruchio's* wife	1407
Tra. But say, what to thine olde newes?	1430
Bion. Why sir, he comes not.	*Bap.* Didst thou not say hee comes?	1460
Bion. No sir, I say his horse comes with him on his	(backe.	1464
Which once perform'd, let all the world say no,	1524
Gre. A bridegroome say you? 'tis a groome indeed,	1536
Why when I say? Nay good sweete *Kate* be merrie.	1771
Tra. He is my father sir, and sooth to say,	1955

SAY *cont.*

As who should say, if I should sleepe or eate	1991
Gru. What say you to a Neats foote?	1995
How say you to a fat Tripe finely broyl'd?	1998
What say you to a peece of Beefe and Mustard?	2001
Go get thee gone, I say.	2014
Your betters haue indur'd me say my minde,	2060
*braue not me; I will neither bee fac'd nor brau'd. I say	2111
Gru. The note lies in's throate if he say I said so.	2116
Tail. This is true that I say, and I had thee in place	2132
Pet. Hortensio, say thou wilt see the Tailor paide:	2147
Go take it hence, be gone, and say no more.	2148
Away I say, commend me to thy master. *Exit Tail.*	2151
It shall be what a clock I say it is.	2178
Bap. Sir, pardon me in what I haue to say,	2220
And therefore if you say no more then this,	2225
If this be not that you looke for, I haue no more to say,	2281
Pet. I say it is the Moone that shines so bright.	2300
Hort. Say as he saies, or we shall neuer goe.	2307
Petr. I say it is the Moone.	2312
But sunne it is not, when you say it is not.	2316
Would say your Head and But were head and horne.	2583
Petr. Well, I say no: and therefore sir assurance,	2608
Say I command her come to me. *Exit.*	2648
Away I say, and bring them hither straight.	2660
Pet. Come on I say, and first begin with her. | *Wid.* She shall not.	2691
Pet. I say she shall, and first begin with her.	2693

SAYES = 2

And when he sayes he is, say that he dreames,	68
Bianca. He sayes so *Tranio.*	1904

SAYST = 1

Gre. No, sayst me so, friend? What Countreyman?	755

SCAENA *I.*1 = 1

SCAPE = *1

Pet. Nay heare you *Kate.* Insooth you scape not so.	1119

SCAPES = 1

To smile at scapes and perils ouerblowne:	2540

SCARFES = *1

*With Scarfes, and Fannes, & double change of brau'ry,	2039

SCARLET = *1

*hose, a scarlet cloake, and a copataine hat: oh I am	2445

SCATTERS = *1

Petr. Such wind as scatters yongmen throgh y world,	616

SCENA *I.*1977 = 1

SCENT *see* sent

SCHOLLER = 3

Then you; vnlesse you were a scholler sir.	724
Freely giue vnto this yong Scholler, that hath	942
I am no breeching scholler in the schooles,	1313

SCHOOLD = 1

'Twere good he were school'd.	2190

SCHOOLE = 2*1

Gre. As willingly as ere I came from schoole.	1534
Tra. Faith he is gone vnto the taming schoole.	1905
Bian. The taming schoole: what is there such a place?	1906

SCHOOLEMASTER = 2
I promist to enquire carefully | About a schoolemaster for the faire
Bianca, 731
Luc. Were it not that my fellow schoolemaster 1521
SCHOOLEMASTERS = 2
Schoolemasters will I keepe within my house, 398
To get her cunning Schoolemasters to instruct her. 490
SCHOOLES = 1
I am no breeching scholler in the schooles, 1313
SCHOOLE-MASTER = 2
Tra. You will be schoole-master, 496
To old *Baptista* as a schoole-master 698
SCIENCES = 1
To instruct her fully in those sciences, 918
SCOLD = 2
Began to scold, and raise vp such a storme, 475
Petr. I know she is an irkesome brawling scold: 753
SCOLDING = 2*1
Renown'd in *Padua* for her scolding tongue. 666
*think scolding would doe little good vpon him. Shee 675
The one, as famous for a scolding tongue, 826
SCONCE = 1
Thou canst not frowne, thou canst not looke a sconce, 1126
SCORE = 1*3
*know me not: if she say I am not xiiii.d. on the score for 175
*sheere Ale, score me vp for the lyingst knaue in Christen|dome. What
I am not bestraught: here's--- 176
*may perhaps call him halfe a score Knaues, or so: Why 676
Six-score fat Oxen standing in my stalls, 1240
SCORNE = 1
But one that scorne to liue in this disguise, 1866
SCORNEFULL = 1
And dart not scornefull glances from those eies, 2695
SCRATCHING = 1
Scratching her legs, that one shal sweare she bleeds, 210
SCRIUENER = 1
My Boy shall fetch the Scriuener presentlie, 2241
SEA = 2
Haue I not heard the sea, puft vp with windes, 768
To painfull labour, both by sea and land: 2707
SEALD = 1
Because she brought stone-Iugs, and no seal'd quarts: 241
SEALE = 1
And seale the title with a louely kisse. *Exit.* 1506
SEAS = 2
Affections edge in me. Were she is as rough | As are the swelling
Adriaticke seas. 639
'Twill bring you gaine, or perish on the seas. 1210
SECOND = 1
For patience shee will proue a second *Grissell,* 1175
SECRET = 1
That art to me as secret and as deere 456
SECURE = 1
Whil'st thou ly'st warme at home, secure and safe, 2709
SEDGES = 2
And Citherea all in sedges hid, 203
Euen as the wauing sedges play with winde. 205

SEE = 40*12

*Lord. What's heere? One dead, or drunke? See doth | he breath?	34
Sirrah, go see what Trumpet 'tis that sounds,	79
And see him drest in all suites like a Ladie:	117
To see her noble Lord restor'd to health,	132
See this dispatch'd with all the hast thou canst,	140
I do not sleepe: I see, I heare, I speake:	222
Oh how we ioy to see your wit restor'd,	230
To see faire *Padua*, nurserie of Arts,	301
Lucen. But in the others silence do I see,	373
But see, while idely I stood looking on,	453
To see my friends in *Padua*; but of all	567
*being perhaps (for ought I see) two and thirty, a peepe	600
And so am come abroad to see the world.	624
I wil not sleepe *Hortensio* til I see her,	669
*with it, that shee shal haue no more eies to see withall | then a Cat:	
you know him not sir.	680
*Gru. Heere's no knauerie. See, to beguile the olde-|folkes,	704
All bookes of Loue, see that at any hand,	712
And see you reade no other Lectures to her:	713
And I do hope, good dayes and long, to see.	758
Did you yet euer see *Baptistas* daughter? | *Tra*. No sir, but heare I do	
that he hath two:	824
Whom thou lou'st best: see thou dissemble not.	864
Kate. What will you not suffer me: Nay now I see	889
Pet. I see you do not meane to part with her,	925
You shall go see your Pupils presently. | Holla, within.	970
Kate. It is my fashion when I see a Crab.	1107
Oh let me see thee walke: thou dost not halt.	1135
For by this light, whereby I see thy beauty,	1152
Kate. Ile see thee hang'd on sonday first.	1179
*Gre. Hark *Petruchio*, she saies shee'll see thee hang'd | (first.	1180
Oh you are nouices, 'tis a world to see	1191
I see no reason but suppos'd *Lucentio*	1289
*Bian. Now let mee see if I can conster it. *Hic ibat si-|mois*,	1334
Tra. See not your Bride in these vnreuerent robes,	1495
Bap. Ile after him, and see the euent of this. *Exit*.	1510
I see a woman may be made a foole	1606
Nath. Peter didst euer see the like.	1812
*Hor. See how they kisse and court: Signior *Lucentio*,	1875
Fie on her, see how beastly she doth court him.	1882
Come Tailor, let vs see these ornaments.	2044
*Hor. I see shees like to haue neither cap nor gowne.	2078
Pet. Hortensio, say thou wilt see the Tailor paide:	2147
Let's see, I thinke 'tis now some seuen a clocke,	2170
And wander we to see thy honest sonne,	2368
Petr. Come goe along and see the truth hereof,	2374
*Biond. Nay faith, Ile see the Church a your backe,	2384
*Vinc. What, you notorious villaine, didst thou neuer | see thy Mistris	
father, *Vincentio*?	2430
marie sir see where he lookes out of the window.	2433
*Petr. Preethe *Kate* let's stand aside and see the end of | this	
controuersie.	2438
*the Iaile: father *Baptista*, I charge you see that hee be | forth comming.	2470
*Kate. Husband let's follow, to see the end of this adoe.	2522
See where she comes, and brings your froward Wiues	2675
But now I see our Launces are but strawes:	2731

SEEING = 1*1
   Seeing too much sadnesse hath congeal'd your blood,   286
   *eccho: and I seeing this, came thence for very shame, and   1561
SEEKE = 4
   To seeke their fortunes farther then at home,   617
   And if you breake the ice, and do this seeke,   839
   Bap. The gaine I seeke, is quiet me the match.   1211
   Or seeke for rule, supremacie, and sway,   2721
SEEKES = 1
   And with sacietie seekes to quench his thirst.   323
SEEM = *1
   2.H. It would seem strange vnto him when he wak'd   47
SEEMD = *1
   *his beard grew thinne and hungerly, and seem'd to aske   1557
SEEME = 3*1
   Which seeme to moue and wanton with her breath,   204
   Nor a Musitian as I seeme to bee,   1865
   Ile make him glad to seeme *Vincentio*,   1921
   Tra. Sir, you seeme a sober ancient Gentleman by   2451
SEEMES = 1*1
   Lady. I, and the time seeme's thirty vnto me,   268
   Gru. Thou it seemes, that cals for company to coun- |tenance her.   1730
SEEMETH = 1
   That euery thing I looke on seemeth greene: 2345
SEEMING = 2
   Muddie, ill seeming, thicke, bereft of beautie,   2701
   That seeming to be most, which we indeed least are.   2733
SEEN = *1
   Kate. Would *Katherine* had neuer seen him though. | *Exit weeping.*   1414
SEENE = 3*1
   We haue not yet bin seene in any house,   505
   Well seene in Musicke, to instruct *Bianca*,   699
   A sonne of mine, which long I haue not seene.   2355
   Bio. I haue seene them in the Church together, God   2420
SEES = *1
   Bap. When will he be heere? | *Bion.* When he stands where I am, and
   sees you there.   1428
SEEST = 1
   Heere Loue, thou seest how diligent I am,   2020
SEET = 2
   Lady. It is a kinde of history. | *Beg.* Well, we'l see't: 295
   Pet. Thy gowne, why I: come Tailor let vs see't.   2071
SEIZE = 1
   Seize thee that List, if once I finde thee ranging,   1385
SELF = *1
   Bian. Good sister wrong me not, nor wrong your self,   856
SELFE = 27*4
   I am in all affected as your selfe,   325
   On them to looke, and practise by my selfe.   386
   One thing more rests, that thy selfe execute,   554
   And I haue thrust my selfe into this maze,   621
   And vnsuspected court her by her selfe.   702
   For she is sweeter then perfume it selfe   718
   As firmely as your selfe were still in place,   722
   Vnbinde my hands, Ile pull them off my selfe,   859
   Ile pleade for you my selfe, but you shal haue him.   870
   Am bold to shew my selfe a forward guest   912

SELFE *cont.*

The like kindnesse my selfe, that haue beene	940
Do make my selfe a sutor to your daughter,	953
My selfe am moou'd to woo thee for my wife.	1065
Pet. Father, 'tis thus, your selfe and all the world	1170
Pet. Be patient gentlemen, I choose her for my selfe,	1182
My selfe am strooke in yeeres I must confesse,	1242
But learne my Lessons as I please my selfe,	1315
And sent you hither so vnlike your selfe?	1487
'Twere well for *Kate*, and better for my selfe.	1503
That haue beheld me giue away my selfe	1576
No, nor to morrow, not till I please my selfe,	1595
For me, Ile not be gone till I please my selfe,	1598
Bian. That being mad her selfe, she's madly mated.	1630
*selfe: for considering the weather, a taller man then I	1648
*hath tam'd my old master, and my new mistris, and my | selfe fellow	
Curtis.	1662
To dresse thy meate my selfe, and bring it thee.	2021
Pet. Now by my mothers sonne, and that's my selfe,	2302
Ped. Keepe your hundred pounds to your selfe, hee	2404
What *Tranio* did, my selfe enforst him to;	2509
Tra. 'Tis well sir that you hunted for your selfe:	2598
Luc. Ile haue no halues: Ile beare it all my selfe.	2626

SELFESAME = 1

While I with selfesame kindnesse welcome thine:	2542

SELUES = 4*1

Plai. Feare not my Lord, we can contain our selues,	110
And so I pray you all to thinke your selues.	978
Be madde and merry, or goe hang your selues:	1612
Since of our selues, our selues are chollericke,	1806

SEMIRAMIS = 1

On purpose trim'd vp for Semiramis.	191

SENCE = 2

Petr. You are verie sencible, and yet you misse my | sence:	2555
And in no sence is meete or amiable.	2699

SENCELESSE = 1

Petr. A sencelesse villaine: good *Hortensio*,	603

SENCIBLE = *1

Petr. You are verie sencible, and yet you misse my | sence:	2555

SEND = 7*1

Or shall I send my daughter *Kate* to you. | *Exit. Manet Petruchio.*	1035
God send you ioy, *Petruchio*, 'tis a match.	1199
Send for your daughter by your seruant here,	2240
*send 'em good shipping: but who is here? mine old Ma-|ster	2421
Let's each one send vnto his wife,	2609
To come at first when he doth send for her,	2611
Praie God sir your wife send you not a worse. | *Petr.* I hope better.	2634
Kat. What is your will sir, that you send for me?	2655

SENDS = 1

Bio. Sir, my Mistris sends you word	2629

SENIS = 2*1

tellus, hic steterat Priami regia Celsa senis.	1323
regia, bearing my port, *celsa senis* that we might be-|guile the old	
Pantalowne.	1329
hic staterat priami, take heede he heare vs not, *regia* pre-|sume not,	
Celsa senis, despaire not.	1336

SENSE = 1
   Although I thinke 'twas in another sense,   521
SENSIBLE = *1
   Gru. And therefore 'tis cal'd a sensible tale: and this   1697
SENT = 3*2
   And twice to day pick'd out the dullest sent,   27
   And sent you hither so vnlike your selfe?   1487
   *so raide? was euer man so weary? I am sent before to   1642
   Where is the foolish knaue I sent before?   1754
   Vin. Ile slit the villaines nose that would haue sent | me to the Iaile.   2511
SER = *1
   Pet. Go rascals, go, and fetch my supper in. *Ex. Ser.*   1766
SER = 2
SERMON = *1
   Cur. In her chamber, making a sermon of continen-|cie   1816
SERUANT = 5*3
   My trustie seruant well approu'd in all,   306
   *sir. Well, was it fit for a seruant to vse his master so,   599
   Your ancient trustie pleasant seruant *Grumio*:   613
   Enter a Seruant.   972
   Enter Curtis a Seruant.   1815
   Send for your daughter by your seruant here,   2240
   Tra. Sir, what are you that offer to beate my ser-|uant?   2441
   *at home, my sonne and my seruant spend all at the vni-|uersitie.   2447
SERUANTS = 7*1
   2.Man. Oh this is it that makes your seruants droop.   179
   Looke how thy seruants do attend on thee,   185
   Beg. 'Tis much, seruants leaue me and her alone: 270
   Keepe house, and port, and seruants, as I should,   509
   Enter seruants with supper.   1770
   Enter Seruants seuerally.   1811
   Pitchers haue eares, and I haue manie seruants,   2234
   Enter Pedant with seruants, Baptista, Tranio.   2440
SERUE = 5
   It shall become to serue all hopes conceiu'd   314
   And while I pause, serue in your harmony.   1309
   And serue it thus to me that loue it not?   1796
   An ancient Angel comming downe the hill, | Wil serue the turne. 1913
   When they are bound to serue, loue, and obay.   2722
SERUES = 1
   Fall to them as you finde your stomacke serues you: 337
SERUICE = 3*1
   Ser. An't please your Honor, Players | That offer seruice to your
   Lordship.   84
   *If this be not a lawfull cause for me to leaue his seruice, 597
   His name is *Cambio*: pray accept his seruice.   946
   Pet. The poorest seruice is repaide with thankes,   2027
SERUICEABLE = 1
   Be seruiceable to my sonne (quoth he)   520
SERUINGMAN see also Ser., 1.Man., 1.Ser., 2.M., 2.Man., 2.Ser.,
3.Man., 3.Ser. = 2
   Enter Seruingman.   82
   Anon Ile giue thee more instructions. | *Exit a seruingman.* 141
SERUINGMEN see also Ser. = 2*1
   *trim'd, rushes strew'd, cobwebs swept, the seruingmen   1682
   Enter foure or fiue seruingmen.   1733
   The Seruingmen with Tranio bringing | in a Banquet.   2536

SESSA = 1
*in with *Richard Conqueror*: therefore *Pau-!cas pallabris*, let the world
slide: Sessa.   8
SET = 5*2
Or if not so, vntill the Sun be set.   274
Baptistas eldest daughter to a husband, wee set his   440
Atchieue the elder: set the yonger free,   840
Take you the Lute, and you the set of bookes,   969
Set foot vnder thy table: tut, a toy,   1284
*hath two letters for her name, fairely set down in studs,   1448
Here comes *Baptista*: set your countenance sir.   2199
SETTING = 1
And therefore setting all this chat aside,   1147
SEUEN = 3
Who for this seuen yeares hath esteemed him   133
Let's see, I thinke 'tis now some seuen a clocke,   2170
Pet. It shall be seuen ere I go to horse: 2174
SEUERALLY = 1
Enter Seruants seuerally.   1811
SEW *see* sow
SEWD *see* sow'd
SEXTONS = *1
*all in the Sextons face: hauing no other reason, but that   1556
SHAKE = *1
*Confounds thy fame, as whirlewinds shake faire budds,   2698
SHAKES = 1
That shakes not, though they blow perpetually.   1006
SHAL *l.*193 210 211 *680 692 696 740 742 743 761 818 847 854 870 *1082
  1839 1890 1962 1963 1965 *2005 = 18*3
SHALBE = 2
Be patient, to morrow't shalbe mended,   1808
That shalbe woo'd, and wedded in a day.   1901
SHALL *l.*74 139 197 298 314 344 356 364 385 407 *439 500 512 625 628
  818 841 970 985 1035 1049 1149 1185 1197 1226 1252 1256 1265 1277
  *1293 1303 1492 1516 1519 1537 1587 1603 *1608 1624 1635 1637 1638
  *1647 *1667 *1713 *1716 1782 1788 1831 1832 2028 2055 2064 2084
  2098 *2136 2154 2174 2178 2216 2229 2232 2241 2254 2293 2303 2307
  2311 2319 2350 *2392 2393 2405 2473 *2474 *2587 2612 2621 2692
  2693 = 69*11
SHALLOW = 1
A shallow plash, to plunge him in the deepe,   322
SHALT *l.*253 508 *1668 2099 *2740 = 3*2
SHAME = 5*1
For shame thou Hilding of a diuellish spirit,   883
What saies *Lucentio* to this shame of ours?   1395
Kate. No shame but mine, I must forsooth be forst   1396
Fie, doff this habit, shame to your estate,   1483
*eccho: and I seeing this, came thence for very shame, and   1561
If thou accountedst it shame, lay it on me,   2164
SHARE = 1
Out of hope of all, but my share of the feast.   2521
SHARPE = 1
My Faulcon now is sharpe, and passing emptie,   1824
SHE = 104*15
SHEATHING = 1
And *Walters* dagger was not come from sheathing: 1762

SHED = 1*1
Bid him shed teares, as being ouer-ioyed   131
*1.*Man*. And til the teares that she hath shed for thee,   216
SHEE *l.**174 219 *675 *680 1174 1175 1188 1189 1270 1616 *1817 *2285
   *2638 = 7*6
SHEELL = *1
Gre. Hark *Petruchio*, she saies shee'll see thee hang'd | (first.   1180
SHEEPES = *1
*halfe-chekt Bitte, & a headstall of sheepes leather, which   1444
SHEERE = *1
*sheere Ale, score me vp for the lyingst knaue in Christen|dome. What
I am not bestraught: here's---   176
SHEES = 1*1
For shee's not froward, but modest as the Doue,   1173
Hor. I see shees like to haue neither cap nor gowne.   2078
SHEETS = 1
This way the Couerlet, another way the sheets: 1836
SHEL = 1
Hor. I thinke she'l sooner proue a souldier,   1013
SHELL = 1
Why 'tis a cockle or a walnut-shell,   2050
SHES = 10*1
Gre. To cart her rather. She's to rough for mee,   357
That she's the choise loue of Signior *Gremio*.   808
Hor. That she's the chosen of signior *Hortensio*.   809
She's apt to learne, and thankefull for good turnes: 1033
To me she's married, not vnto my cloathes: 1500
Tra. Why she's a deuill, a deuill, the deuils damme.   1540
Gre. Tut, she's a Lambe, a Doue, a foole to him: 1541
Bian. That being mad her selfe, she's madly mated.   1630
Cur. Is she so hot a shrew as she's reported.   1659
And how she's like to be *Lucentios* wife.   2249
Petr. How? she's busie, and she cannot come: is that | an answere?   2631
SHEW = 6*1
May shew her dutie, and make knowne her loue.   128
Lord. Wee'l shew thee *Io*, as she was a Maid,   206
Tra. Master some shew to welcome vs to Towne.   346
Am bold to shew my selfe a forward guest   912
Kate. There is, there is. | *Pet.* Then shew it me.   1110
Now let him speake, 'tis charity to shew. *Exit*   1845
*your habit: but your words shew you a mad man: why   2452
SHEWD = 1
You haue shewd a tender fatherly regard,   1166
SHIFT = 2
An Onion wil do well for such a shift,   137
Bian. Am I your Bird, I meane to shift my bush,   2589
SHINES = 3
Good Lord how bright and goodly shines the Moone.   2297
Pet. I say it is the Moone that shines so bright.   2300
Kate. I know it is the Sunne that shines so bright.   2301
SHIPPING = *1
*send'em good shipping: but who is here? mine old Ma-|ster   2421
SHIPS = 1
Your ships are staid at Venice, and the Duke   1939
SHOLD *l.*1080 = 1
SHOOES = *3
*no more shooes then feet, nay sometime more feete then   163

SHOOES *cont.*
   *shooes, or such shooes as my toes looke through the o-|uer-leather.   164
SHOOKE = *1
   Gre. Trembled and shooke: for why, he stamp'd and   1551
SHOPPE = 1
   Like to a Censor in a barbers shoppe: 2076
SHORE = 1
   For in a quarrell since I came a-shore,   538
SHORT = 1
   And to be short, what not, that's sweete and happie.   2665
SHORTNESSE = 1
   Your plainnesse and your shortnesse please me well: 2221
SHOT = 1
   Therefore a health to all that shot and mist.   2594
SHOTTEN = *1
   *and shoulder-shotten, neere leg'd before, and with a   1443
SHOULD *l*.109 169 259 277 366 450 509 *571 575 579 1079 1080 1163
   1271 1348 1390 1474 1505 1543 *1627 *1646 1964 1986 1991 2103 2105
   *2129 2291 *2321 2720 2726 = 28*5
SHOULDER = *1
   *slide from my shoulder to my heele, with no   1653
SHOULDER-SHOTTEN = *1
   *and shoulder-shotten, neere leg'd before, and with a   1443
SHOULDST *l*.*1705 *1706 2133 = 1*2
SHOW *see also* shew = 2
   Ela mi, show pitty or I die,   1371
   And show more signe of her obedience,   2672
SHOWD *see* shewd
SHOWER = 1
   To raine a shower of commanded teares,   136
SHREW *see also* shrow = 9
   A meacocke wretch can make the curstest shrew: 1193
   Much more a shrew of impatient humour.   1418
   Cur. Is she so hot a shrew as she's reported.   1659
   Cur. By this reckning he is more shrew than she.   1715
   He that knowes better how to tame a shrew,   1844
   To tame a shrew, and charme her chattering tongue.   1909
   Wid. Your housband being troubled with a shrew,   2568
   I thinke thou hast the veriest shrew of all.   2607
   THE | Taming of the Shrew.   2752
SHREWD = 2
   Her elder sister is so curst and shrew'd,   483
   And wish thee to a shrew'd ill-fauour'd wife?   626
SHRILL = 1
   And fetch shrill ecchoes from the hollow earth.   198
SHROW = 1
   Horten. Now goe thy wayes, thou hast tam'd a curst | Shrow.   2748
SHROWD = 2
   As old as *Sibell*, and as curst and shrow'd   636
   And shrow'd, and froward, so beyond all measure,   656
SHUNS = *1
   Lord. Hence comes it, that your kindred shuns your | (house   180
SIBELL = 1
   As old as *Sibell*, and as curst and shrow'd   636
SICKNESSE = 1
   'Twere deadly sicknesse, or else present death.   1992

SIDE = 1
Come Madam wife sit by my side, 297
SIDES = *1
*and fast it fairely out. Our cakes dough on both sides. 413
SIGERIA = *3
*Luc. Heere Madam: *Hic Ibat Simois, hic est sigeria* 1322
hic est, sonne vnto Vincentio of Pisa, *Sigeria tel-|lus*, 1326
*I know you not, *hic est sigeria tellus*, I trust you not, 1335
SIGH = 1
Wid. Lord let me neuer haue a cause to sigh, 2679
SIGHT = 4
And at that sight shal sad Apollo weepe, 211
Well, bring our Ladie hither to our sight, 226
Whose sodaine sight hath thral'd my wounded eye. 526
Bap. What in my sight? *Bianca get thee in. Exit.* 888
SIGNE = 2
Tranio. Sir, I shal not be slacke, in signe whereof, 847
And show more signe of her obedience, 2672
SIGNES = *1
*to expound the meaning or morrall of his signes and to-|kens. 2265
SIGNIOR = 33*9
Hor. Signior *Baptista*, will you be so strange, 388
Gre. Why will you mew her vp | (Signior *Baptista*) for this fiend of hell, 391
Or signior *Gremio* you know any such, 400
fastest, gets the Ring: How say you signior *Gremio*? 443
Petr. Signior *Hortensio*, come you to part the fray? 591
Hor. Alla nostra casa bene venuto multo honorata signi-|or mio
Petruchio. 593
Signior *Hortensio*, thus it stands with me, 619
Petr. Signior *Hortensio*, 'twixt such friends as wee, 631
You vnderstand me. Ouer and beside | Signior *Baptistas* liberalitie, 714
Hor. Grumio mum: God saue you signior *Gremio.* 728
Gre. And you are wel met, Signior *Hortensio.* 729
To the house of Signior *Baptista Minola*? 789
That she's the choise loue of Signior *Gremio.* 808
Hor. That she's the chosen of signior *Hortensio.* 809
Pet. You wrong me signior *Gremio*, giue me leaue. 907
Pet. Oh, Pardon me signior *Gremio*, I would faine be | doing. 935
Bap. A thousand thankes signior *Gremio*: 947
Pet. Signior *Baptista*, my businesse asketh haste, 979
Signior *Petruchio*, will you go with vs, 1034
Bap. Now Signior *Petruchio*, how speed you with my | (daughter? 1161
Say signior *Gremio*, what can you assure her? 1227
Within rich *Pisa* walls, as any one | Old Signior *Gremio* has in *Padua*, 1249
What, haue I pincht you Signior *Gremio*? 1253
Be Bride to you, if you make this assurance: | If not, to Signior *Gremio*: 1278
Bap. Signior *Lucentio*, this is the pointed day 1389
Signior *Gremio*, came you from the Church? 1533
Tra. Signior *Hortensio*, I haue often heard | Of your entire affection to
Bianca, 1870
Hor. See how they kisse and court: Signior *Lucentio*, 1875
And so farewel signior *Lucentio*, 1888
Hor. Signior *Petruchio*, fie you are too blame: 2030
Signior *Baptista* may remember me | Neere twentie yeares a goe in
Genoa. 2183
Tra. Signior *Baptista* you are happilie met: 2202
Signior *Baptista*, of whom I heare so well. 2219

SIGNIOR *cont.*

Signior *Baptista*, shall I leade the way,	2254
Vin. Is Signior *Lucentio* within sir?	2400
*I pray you tell signior *Lucentio* that his Father is	2408
Pedan. Helpe, sonne, helpe signior *Baptista*.	2437
*he is mine onelie sonne and heire to the Lands of me sig-|nior	
Vincentio.	2463
Bap. Talke not signior *Gremio*: I saie he shall goe to | prison.	2474
Gre. Take heede signior *Baptista*, least you be coni-|catcht	2476
Gre. Yes, I know thee to be signior *Lucentio*.	2483
Petr. She hath preuented me, here signior *Tranio*,	2592

SIGNIOUR = *1

Hor. So will I signiour *Gremio*: but a word I pray:	417

SILENCE = 3

Lucen. But in the others silence do I see,	373
Kate. Her silence flouts me, and Ile be reueng'd. | *Flies after Bianca*	886
not--- Cockes passion, silence, I heare my master.	1745

SILKEN = 2*1

With silken coats and caps, and golden Rings,	2037
A custard coffen, a bauble, a silken pie,	2067
*Goddes: oh fine villaine, a silken doublet, a vel-|uet	2444

SILLIE = 1

Till I be brought to such a sillie passe.	2680

SILUER = 2

Saw'st thou not boy how *Siluer* made it good	22
Let one attend him with a siluer Bason	59

SIMILE = 1

Petr. A good swift simile, but something currish.	2597

SIMOIS = *3

Luc. Heere Madam: *Hic Ibat Simois, hic est sigeria*	1322
Luc. Hic Ibat, as I told you before, *Simois*, I am Lu-|centio,	1325
Bian. Now let mee see if I can conster it. *Hic ibat si-|mois*,	1334

SIMPLE = 3

When they do homage to this simple peasant,	147
I heere bestow a simple instrument,	962
I am asham'd that women are so simple,	2719

SINCE = 9*3

Since once he plaide a Farmers eldest sonne,	94
Luc. Tranio, since for the great desire I had	300
*apples: but come, since this bar in law makes vs friends,	438
For in a quarrell since I came a-shore,	538
Hor. Petruchio, since we are stept thus farre in,	649
And since you do professe to be a sutor,	844
Since of our selues, our selues are chollericke,	1806
And since mine eyes are witnesse of her lightnesse,	1872
Kate. Forward I pray, since we haue come so farre,	2308
*brought him vp euer since he was three yeeres old, and	2460
Petr. Nay that you shall not since you haue begun:	2587
Hath cost me fiue hundred crownes since supper time.	2684

SINCKLO = *1

Sincklo. I thinke 'twas *Soto* that your honor meanes.	98

SING = 2

And twentie caged Nightingales do sing.	188
Ile trie how you can *Sol, Fa*, and sing it. | *He rings him by the eares*	583

SINGS = 1

She sings as sweetly as a Nightinghale:	1040

SIP = 1
Will daigne to sip, or touch one drop of it. 2703
SIR l.*244 339 359 364 384 424 449 481 491 517 543 *571 *574 575 *596
*598 *599 *643 *673 *678 681 711 724 *759 793 794 795 796 798 800
803 821 823 825 828 831 837 843 847 *903 905 908 922 928 937 948 951
966 968 1162 1245 1296 1354 1425 *1451 1460 *1464 1470 1480 1511
1542 *1591 1596 1604 1750 1751 1755 1759 1849 1850 1856 1869 1926
1927 1929 1934 1936 1944 1947 1950 1955 1961 1965 1967 1968 2029
2046 2058 2084 2106 *2128 2138 2139 2143 *2144 2172 2189 2199 2203
*2206 2220 *2230 2256 *2286 2351 2357 2381 2389 2391 2400 2401
*2407 2414 2425 *2428 2433 *2441 *2443 *2451 *2453 *2457 *2513 2526
2581 2595 2598 2608 2629 2634 2640 2655 = 109*32
SIRE = *1
*A childe shall get a sire, if I faile not of my cunning. *Exit.* 1293
SIRRA = 12*4
Lord. Go sirra, take them to the Butterie, 112
Sirra go you to Bartholmew my Page, 116
Heere comes the rogue. Sirra, where haue you bin? 528
Luc. Sirra come hither, 'tis no time to iest, 533
*But sirra, not for my sake, but your masters, I ad-|uise 549
Heere sirra *Grumio*, knocke I say. 570
*these words plaine? Sirra, Knocke me heere: rappe me 607
Petr. Sirra be gone, or talke not I aduise you. 610
Gru. Oh this Woodcocke, what an Asse it is. | *Petru.* Peace sirra. 726
Sirra, yong gamester, your father were a foole 1282
Hort. Sirra, I will not beare these braues of thine. 1310
Where's my Spaniel *Troilus*? Sirra, get you hence, 1779
Tra. Feare you not him: sirra *Biondello*, 2191
Petr. Why then let's home againe: Come Sirra let's | awaie. 2527
Hor. Sirra *Biondello*, goe and intreate my wife to 2636
Sirra *Grumio*, goe to your Mistris, 2647
SIRRAH = 4
Sirrah, go see what Trumpet 'tis that sounds, 79
Petr. Will it not be? | 'Faith sirrah, and you'l not knocke, Ile ring it, 581
Petr. Now knocke when I bid you: sirrah villaine 586
Sirrah, leade these Gentlemen | To my daughters, and tell them both 973
SIRS = 5
Sirs, I will practise on this drunken man. 40
This do, and do it kindly, gentle sirs, 70
And so offend him: for I tell you sirs, 108
You are still crossing it, sirs let't alone, 2176
Tra. Sirs, this is the house, please it you that I call. 2181
SISTER = 14*2
Gremio a Pantelowne, Hortentio sister to Bianca. | *Lucen. Tranio, stand
by.* 348
Bian. Sister content you, in my discontent. 383
Gre. What's that I pray? | *Hor.* Marrie sir to get a husband for her
Sister. 423
Tra. Saw you no more? Mark'd you not how hir sister 474
Her elder sister is so curst and shrew'd, 483
Vntill the elder sister first be wed. 835
Bian. Good sister wrong me not, nor wrong your self, 856
Bianca. Beleeue me sister, of all the men aliue, 865
Bian. If you affect him sister, heere I sweare 869
I prethee sister Kate, vntie my hands. 876
In the preferment of the eldest sister. 956
Her sister *Katherine* welcom'd you withall. 1298

SISTER *cont.*
   Luc. Mistresse, what's your opinion of your sister? 1629
   The sister to my wife, this Gentlewoman, 2361
   Brother *Petruchio*, sister *Katerina*, | And thou *Hortentio* with thy louing
   Widdow: 2543
   Petr. Where is your sister, and *Hortensios* wife? 2656
SISTERS = 2
   And helpe to dresse your sisters chamber vp, 1377
   And let *Bianca* take her sisters roome. 1636
SIT = 12
   Come Madam wife sit by my side, 297
   Ladie: would 'twere done. *They sit and marke.* 564
   Talke not to me, I will go sit and weepe, 893
   Pet. Thou hast hit it: come sit on me. 1072
   And to cut off all strife: heere sit we downe, 1316
   Where are those? Sit downe *Kate*, 1768
   Come *Kate* sit downe, I know you haue a stomacke, 1787
   After our great good cheere: praie you sit downe, 2547
   For now we sit to chat as well as eate. 2548
   Petr. Nothing but sit and sit, and eate and eate. 2549
   Kate. They sit conferring by the Parler fire. 2657
SITH = 1
   In breefe Sir, sith it your pleasure is, 517
SITS = *1
   *to speake, and sits as one new risen from a dreame: A-|way, away, for
   he is comming hither. 1819
SIXE = *1
   *often burst, and now repaired with knots: one girth sixe 1446
SIXE-SCORE = 1
   Sixe-score fat Oxen standing in my stalls, 1240
SKEINE = 1
   Brau'd in mine owne house with a skeine of thred: 2096
SKIES = 1
   And heauens Artillerie thunder in the skies? 771
SKILLS = 1
   It skills not much, weele fit him to our turne, 1515
SKIN = 1
   Because his painted skin contents the eye. 2161
SKIPPER = 1
   Skipper stand backe, 'tis age that nourisheth. 1221
SKIRTS = *1
   *me in the skirts of it, and beate me to death with a bot-|tome of
   browne thred: I said a gowne. 2119
SLACKE = 1
   Tranio. Sir, I shal not be slacke, in signe whereof, 847
SLANDROUS = 1
   Oh sland'rous world: *Kate* like the hazle twig 1132
SLASH = 1
   Heers snip, and nip, and cut, and slish and slash, 2075
SLAUE = 3
   And let me be a slaue, t'atchieue that maide, 525
   To make a bondmaide and a slaue of mee, 857
   Kate. Go get thee gone, thou false deluding slaue, | *Beats him.* 2009
SLAUES = 1
   You heedlesse iolt-heads, and vnmanner'd slaues. 1798
SLEEP = 1
   with Ale, this were a bed but cold to sleep so soundly. 37

SLEEPE = 5*1

Or wilt thou sleepe? Wee'l haue thee to a Couch,	189
I do not sleepe: I see, I heare, I speake:	222
I wil not sleepe *Hortensio* til I see her,	669
Am staru'd for meate, giddie for lacke of sleepe:	1987
As who should say, if I should sleepe or eate	1991
Bian. I, but not frighted me, therefore Ile sleepe a-|gaine.	2585

SLEEUE = 2

Whats this? a sleeue? 'tis like demi cannon,	2073
Gru. I confesse the cape. | *Tai*. With a trunke sleeue.	2123

SLEEUES = 2*1

Gru. I confesse two sleeues. | *Tai*. The sleeues curiously cut.	2125
*the sleeues should be cut out, and sow'd vp againe, and	2129

SLENDER = 3

Is straight, and slender, and as browne in hue	1133
The worst is this that at so slender warning,	2242
You are like to haue a thin and slender pittance.	2243

SLEPT = 3

Or when you wak'd, so wak'd as if you slept.	233
And slept aboue some fifteene yeare or more.	267
Last night she slept not, nor to night she shall not:	1832

SLICKELY = *1

*and the rest: let their heads bee slickely comb'd,	1719

SLIDE = 1*1

*in with *Richard Conqueror*: therefore *Pau-!cas pallabris*, let the world slide: Sessa.	8
*slide from my shoulder to my heele, with no	1653

SLIE = 2*1

Slie, old Slies sonne of Burton-heath, by byrth a	171
And not a Tinker, nor Christopher Slie.	225
As *Stephen Slie*, and old *Iohn Naps* of Greece, | And *Peter Turph*, and *Henry Pimpernell*,	246

SLIES = *2

Beg. Y'are a baggage, the *Slies* are no	6
Slie, old Slies sonne of Burton-heath, by byrth a	171

SLIP = 1

And let the world slip, we shall nere be yonger.	298

SLIPPERS = 1

Where are my Slippers? Shall I haue some water?	1782

SLIPT = 1

Tri. Oh sir, *Lucentio* slipt me like his Gray-hound,	2595

SLISH = 1

Heers snip, and nip, and cut, and slish and slash,	2075

SLIT = *1

Vin. Ile slit the villaines nose that would haue sent | me to the Iaile.	2511

SLOW = 2

But slow in speech: yet sweet as spring-time flowers.	1125
cold comfort, for being slow in thy hot office.	1669

SLOW-WINGD = *1

Pet. Oh slow-wing'd Turtle, shal a buzard take thee?	1082

SLY = 1*1

Enter Begger and Hostes, Christophero Sly.	2
Beg. I am *Christophero Sly*, call not mee Honour nor	158

SMACKE = *1

*smacke, that at the parting all the Chutch did	1560

SMALL = 4*1

Beg. For Gods sake a pot of small Ale.	153

SMALL *cont.*
Hor. Faith (as you say) there's small choise in rotten   437
Where small experience growes but in a few.   618
And this small packet of Greeke and Latine bookes: 963
Pet. Proceede. | *Tai.* With a small compast cape.   2121
SMALLEST = 1
And once againe a pot o'th smallest Ale.   227
SMEL = 1
I smel sweet sauours, and I feele soft things: 223
SMILE = 2
If you should smile, he growes impatient.   109
To smile at scapes and perils ouerblowne: 2540
SMOOTH = 1
Why are our bodies soft, and weake, and smooth,   2723
SNIP = 1
Heers snip, and nip, and cut, and slish and slash,   2075
SO *1.*37 *91 95 108 168 169 212 233 *265 274 279 285 331 388 404 *411
*412 *417 *428 *439 464 468 483 512 516 519 523 524 546 *547 *599
624 *647 656 *676 *679 700 721 740 741 751 755 775 784 805 818 823
837 842 853 862 873 *877 914 *950 978 1001 1008 1027 1031 1064 1073
1074 1093 1098 1103 *1105 *1119 1137 1146 1177 1189 1206 1218 1255
1280 1285 1297 1304 1346 1354 1373 1383 1473 1482 1486 1487 1491
1519 1522 1544 1569 1600 *1641 *1642 1651 1659 *1666 1679 1793 1800
1801 1861 1873 1888 1890 1904 1911 1931 1944 1965 1994 2028 2098
2116 2157 2179 2217 2219 2242 *2286 2290 2300 2301 2308 2311 2319
2337 2344 2365 2373 2405 2414 2434 2501 2616 2617 2662 2702 2712
2719 *2750 = 126*23
SOARE = *1
*Dost thou loue hawking? Thou hast hawkes will soare   195
SOBER = 1*1
And offer me disguis'd in sober robes,   697
Tra. Sir, you seeme a sober ancient Gentleman by   2451
SOBRIETIE = 1
Maids milde behauiour and sobrietie. | Peace *Tranio.*   374
SOCRATES = 1
As *Socrates Zentippe*, or a worse: 637
SODAINE = 2
That loue should of a sodaine take such hold.   450
Whose sodaine sight hath thral'd my wounded eye.   526
SODAINLY = 1
Gre. Was euer match clapt vp so sodainly?   1206
SOFT = 6*1
With soft lowe tongue, and lowly curtesie,   125
I smel sweet sauours, and I feele soft things: 223
With gentle conference, soft, and affable.   1130
Ped. Soft son: sir by your leaue, hauing com to *Padua*   2206
But soft, Company is comming here.   2323
Why are our bodies soft, and weake, and smooth,   2723
But that our soft conditions, and our harts,   2725
SOFTER = 1
Softer and sweeter then the lustfull bed   190
SOFTLY = 2
Tra. Softly my Masters: If you be Gentlemen   810
Biond. Softly and swiftly sir, for the Priest is ready.   2381
SOL = 2
Ile trie how you can *Sol, Fa,* and sing it. | *He rings him by the eares* 583
D sol re, one Cliffe, two notes haue I,   1370

SOLEM = *1
*preuilegio ad Impremendum solem, to th' Church take the 2279
SOLEMNE = 1
An eye-sore to our solemne festiuall. 1484
SOLIE = 1
Left solie heire to all his Lands and goods, 982
SOME = 28*4
Some one be readie with a costly suite, 63
Belike some Noble Gentleman that meanes 80
(Trauelling some iourney) to repose him heere. 81
The rather for I haue some sport in hand, 101
You breake into some merrie passion, 107
*Enter aloft the drunkard with attendants, some with apparel, | Bason and
Ewer, & other appurtenances, & Lord. 151
And slept aboue some fifteene yeare or more. 267
Tra. Master some shew to welcome vs to Towne. 346
*Tra. Husht master, heres some good pastime toward; 371
But art thou not aduis'd, he tooke some care 489
I will some other be, some Florentine, 510
Some Neapolitan, or meaner man of Pisa. 511
But be thou arm'd for some vnhappie words. 1004
Oh how I long to haue some chat with her. 1030
And woo her with some spirit when she comes, 1038
*Tra. 'Tis some od humor pricks him to this fashion, 1457
As if they saw some wondrous monument, | Some Commet, or vnusuall
prodigie? 1478
Though in some part inforced to digresse, 1490
Tra. He hath some meaning in his mad attire, 1507
Be merrie Kate: Some water heere: what hoa. 1777
Where are my Slippers? Shall I haue some water? 1782
As with the meate, some vndeserued fault 1833
I prethee go, and get me some repast, 1993
Let's see, I thinke 'tis now some seuen a clocke, 2170
To gather in some debts, my son Lucentio 2207
No worse then I, vpon some agreement 2215
Priest, Clarke, and some sufficient honest witnesses: 2280
And by all likelihood some cheere is toward. Knock. 2394
*to cosen some bodie in this Citie vnder my countenance. 2418
Bion. She saies you haue some goodly Iest in hand, 2643
SOMEBODIE see some
SOMETHING = 1*1
*Kate. Well haue you heard, but something hard of | hearing: 1053
Petr. A good swift simile, but something currish. 2597
SOMETIME = *1
*no more shooes then feet, nay sometime more feete then 163
SOMETIMES = 2
Sometimes you would call out for Cicely Hacket. 242
And bony Kate, and sometimes Kate the curst: 1057
SOMEWHAT = 1
In count'nance somewhat doth resemble you. 1956
SON = 1*2
*Ped. Soft son: sir by your leaue, hauing com to Padua 2206
To gather in some debts, my son Lucentio 2207
*sonne, my sonne: tell me thou villaine, where is my son | Lucentio? 2467
SONDAY = 6
That vpon sonday is the wedding day. 1178
Kate. Ile see thee hang'd on sonday first. 1179

SONDAY *cont.*
I will to *Venice*, sonday comes apace,   1202
And kisse me *Kate*, we will be married a sonday. | *Exit Petruchio and*
Katherine.   1204
On sonday next, you know | My daughter *Katherine* is to be married: 1275
Now on the sonday following, shall *Bianca*   1277
SONNE = 22*9
Since once he plaide a Farmers eldest sonne,   94
Slie, old Slies sonne of Burton-heath, by byrth a   171
Vincentio's sonne, brought vp in *Florence*,   313
And be in *Padua* heere *Vincentio's* sonne,   501
Be seruiceable to my sonne (quoth he)   520
Petr. Borne in *Verona*, old *Butonios* sonne: 756
Pet. *Petruchio* is my name, *Antonio's* sonne,   929
Tra. Of *Pisa* sir, sonne to *Vincentio*.   966
Kate. A witty mother, witlesse else her sonne.   1143
I am my fathers heyre and onely sonne,   1246
hic est, sonne vnto Vincentio of Pisa, *Sigeria tel-|lus*,   1326
And yet we heare not of our sonne in Law: 1391
Right true it is your sonne *Lucentio* here   2222
Your sonne shall haue my daughter with consent.   2229
deceiuing Father of a deceitfull sonne. | *Luc.* And what of him?   2269
Pet. Now by my mothers sonne, and that's my selfe,   2302
A sonne of mine, which long I haue not seene.   2355
Petr. Happily met, the happier for thy sonne: 2358
Thy Sonne by this hath married: wonder not,   2362
And wander we to see thy honest sonne,   2368
Petr. Nay, I told you your sonne was well beloued in   2406
Pedan. Helpe, sonne, helpe signior *Baptista*.   2437
*at home, my sonne and my seruant spend all at the vni-|uersitie.   2447
*he is mine onelie sonne and heire to the Lands of me sig-|nior
Vincentio.   2463
*sonne, my sonne: tell me thou villaine, where is my son | *Lucentio*?   2467
Vin. Liues my sweete sonne?   2492
Luc. Here's *Lucentio*, right sonne to the right *Vin-|centio*,   2495
Bap. *Padua* affords this kindnesse, sonne *Petruchio*.   2550
Bap. Now in good sadnesse sonne *Petruchio*,   2606
Bap. Sonne, Ile be your halfe, *Bianca* comes.   2625
SOONE = 3*2
Bap. Gentlemen, that I may soone make good   377
Haue you so soone forgot the entertainment   1297
*now were I not a little pot, & soone hot; my very lippes   1644
*(she being now at hand) thou shalt soone feele, to thy   1668
and then come backe to my mistris as soone as I can.   2385
SOONER = 1
Hor. I thinke she'l sooner proue a souldier,   1013
SOOTH *see also* insooth = 1*1
Pet. Good sooth euen thus: therefore ha done with | (words,   1499
Tra. He is my father sir, and sooth to say,   1955
SOPS = *2
*a storme, quaft off the Muscadell, and threw the sops   1555
*him sops as hee was drinking: This done, hee tooke the   1558
SORE = 1
An eye-sore to our solemne festiuall.   1484
SORRIE = 1
Sorrie am I that our good will effects | *Bianca's* greefe.   389

SORROW = 2
Sorrow on thee, and all the packe of you   2012
Measures my husbands sorrow by his woe: 2569
SORT = 1
To teach you gamoth in a briefer sort,   1360
SORTED = 1
And all my paines is sorted to no proofe.   2024
SOTO = *1
*Sincklo. I thinke 'twas Soto that your honor meanes.   98
SOUD = 4
And welcome. Soud, soud, soud, soud.   1769
SOUERAIGNE = 1
Thy head, thy soueraigne: One that cares for thee,   2705
SOULDIER = 1
Hor. I thinke she'l sooner proue a souldier,   1013
SOULE = *1
*(poore soule) knowes not which way to stand, to looke,   1818
SOUND = 3*1
To make a dulcet and a heauenly sound: 55
And each one to his office when he wakes. | Sound trumpets.   77
The rest wil comfort, for thy counsels sound.   467
*Bap. And I to sound the depth of this knauerie. Exit.   2517
SOUNDED = 1
Thy vertues spoke of, and thy beautie sounded,   1063
SOUNDLY = 3*2
with Ale, this were a bed but cold to sleep so soundly.   37
Petr. Villaine I say, knocke me heere soundly.   573
*looke you sir: He bid me knocke him, & rap him sound- | ly   598
*heere: knocke me well, and knocke me soundly? And   608
Swinge me them soundly forth vnto their husbands: 2659
SOUNDS = 1
Sirrah, go see what Trumpet 'tis that sounds,   79
SOW = *1
*Gru. Master, if euer I said loose-bodied gowne, sow   2118
SOWD = *1
*the sleeues should be cut out, and sow'd vp againe, and   2129
SOWRE = 3
*Pet. Nay come Kate, come: you must not looke so | sowre.   1105
*Pet. Why heere's no crab, and therefore looke not | sowre.   1108
And when she is froward, peeuish, sullen, sowre,   2715
SPAKE = *1
*Gru. Knocke at the gate? O heauens: spake you not   606
SPANGLE = 1
What stars do spangle heauen with such beautie,   2329
SPANIEL = 1
Where's my Spaniel Troilus? Sirra, get you hence,   1779
SPARE = 1
me thy meat-yard, and spare not me.   2135
SPAUINS = *1
*of Windegalls, sped with Spauins, raied with the Yel- | lowes, 1440
SPEAK = *1
*Luc. Harke Tranio, thou maist heare Minerua speak.   387
SPEAKE = 12*3
And if he chance to speake, be readie straight   56
I do not sleepe: I see, I heare, I speake: 222
But did I neuer speake of all that time.   235
Listen to me, and if you speake me faire,   745

214

SPEAKE *cont.*

Bap. Mistake me not, I speake but as I finde,	927
*poore petitioners speake too? *Bacare*, you are meruay-|lous forward.	933
Say she be mute, and will not speake a word,	1043
But heere she comes, and now *Petruchio* speake.	1050
To speake the ceremoniall rites of marriage?	1394
*to speake, and sits as one new risen from a dreame: A-|way, away, for he is comming hither.	1819
Now let him speake, 'tis charity to shew. *Exit*	1845
Kate. Why sir I trust I may haue leaue to speake,	2058
And speake I will. I am no childe, no babe,	2059
Looke what I speake, or do, or thinke to doe,	2175
*come from *Pisa*, and is here at the doore to speake with | him.	2409

SPEAKES = 1

Exeunt. The Presenters aboue speakes.	557

SPECIALL = 2

I neuer yet beheld that speciall face,	866
Bap. I, when the speciall thing is well obtain'd,	993

SPECIALLY = 2

By vertue specially to be atchieu'd.	319
*be happie riuals in *Bianca's* loue, to labour and effect | one thing specially.	421

SPECIALTIES = 1

Let specialties be therefore drawne betweene vs,	991

SPED = 1*1

*of Windegalls, sped with Spauins, raied with the Yel-|lowes,	1440
We three are married, but you two are sped.	2744

SPEECH = 2

But slow in speech: yet sweet as spring-time flowers.	1125
Kate. Where did you study all this goodly speech?	1141

SPEED = 2*2

Though *Paris* came, in hope to speed alone.	819
Bap. Well maist thou woo, and happy be thy speed:	1003
Bap. Now Signior *Petruchio*, how speed you with my | (daughter?	1161
It were impossible I should speed amisse.	1163

SPEEDING = *1

Tra. Is this your speeding? nay the(n) godnight our part.	1181

SPEND = *1

*at home, my sonne and my seruant spend all at the vni-|uersitie.	2447

SPENT = 1

And when in Musicke we haue spent an houre,	1302

SPIED = 1

That I am dogge-wearie, but at last I spied	1912

SPIGHTS = 1

And that which spights me more then all these wants,	1989

SPIRIT = 5

Should be infused with so foule a spirit.	169
For shame thou Hilding of a diuellish spirit,	883
When (with a most impatient diuellish spirit)	1019
And woo her with some spirit when she comes,	1038
If she had not a spirit to resist.	1607

SPIRITS = *1

Pet. Plucke vp thy spirits, looke cheerfully vpon me.	2019

SPIT = 1

Luc. Spit in the hole man, and tune againe.	1333

SPITE = *1

Ka. The more my wrong, the more his spite appeares.	1980

SPLEENE = 2
  May well abate the ouer-merrie spleene,   149
  Vnto a mad-braine rudesby, full of spleene,   1398
SPOILD = *1
  *Bion. Oh we are spoil'd, and yonder he is, denie him,   2488
SPOKE = 2
  Thy vertues spoke of, and thy beautie sounded,   1063
  Petr. Spoke like an Officer: ha to the lad.   2578
SPOKEN = 1
  Ped. He's within sir, but not to be spoken withall.   2401
SPORT = 2
  The rather for I haue some sport in hand,   101
  To feast and sport vs at thy fathers house,   2166
SPORTFULL = 1
  And then let Kate be chaste, and Dian sportfull.   1140
SPOUSE = 1
  Beside, so qualified, as may beseeme | The Spouse of any noble
  Gentleman: 2365
SPOYLD = *1
  *past cure of the Fiues, starke spoyl'd with the   1441
SPRING-TIME = 1
  But slow in speech: yet sweet as spring-time flowers.   1125
SPRUCE = *1
  *you: and thus much for greeting. Now my spruce   1741
STAGGERS = *1
  *Staggers, begnawne with the Bots, Waid in the backe,   1442
STAGS = 1
  As breathed Stags: I fleeter then the Roe.   200
STAID = 1
  Your ships are staid at Venice, and the Duke   1939
STAIE = 2
  Gre. Staie officer, he shall not go to prison.   2473
  *Kate. Nay, I will giue thee a kisse, now praie thee | Loue staie.   2529
STAIES = 1
  What hast thou din'd? The Tailor staies thy leasure,   2041
STALE = 2
  To make a stale of me amongst these mates?   360
  To cast thy wandring eyes on euery stale: 1384
STALLS = 1
  Sixe-score fat Oxen standing in my stalls,   1240
STAMPD = *1
  *Gre. Trembled and shooke: for why, he stamp'd and   1551
STAMPE = 1
  Nay, looke not big, nor stampe, not stare, nor fret,   1614
STAND = 9*3
  Gremio a Pantelowne, Hortentio sister to Bianca. | Lucen. Tranio, stand
  by.   348
  *trickes. Ile tell you what sir, and she stand him but a li-|tle,   678
  Petruchio stand by a while.   708
  As for my patron, stand you so assur'd,   721
  Bianca stand aside, poore gyrle she weepes: 881
  Skipper stand backe, 'tis age that nourisheth.   1221
  *(poore soule) knowes not which way to stand, to looke,   1818
  Stand by, and marke the manner of his teaching.   1851
  Heere take away this dish. | Kate. I pray you let it stand.   2025
  I pray you stand good father to me now,   2204
  As shall with either parts agreement stand.   2232

STAND *cont.*

*Petr. Preethe *Kate* let's stand aside and see the end of | this
controuersie. 2438
STANDING = 1
Sixe-score fat Oxen standing in my stalls, 1240
STANDS = 4*2
I hope this reason stands for my excuse. 278
Beg. I, it stands so that I may hardly tarry so long: 279
*Bend thoughts and wits to atcheeue her. Thus it stands: 482
Signior *Hortensio,* thus it stands with me, 619
Bap. When will he be heere? | **Bion.* When he stands where I am, and
sees you there. 1428
And heere she stands, touch her who euer dare, 1619
STARE = 1
Nay, looke not big, nor stampe, not stare, nor fret, 1614
STARKE = 1*1
That wench is starke mad, or wonderfull froward. 372
*past cure of the Fiues, starke spoyl'd with the 1441
STARRE = 1
It shall be moone, or starre, or what I list, 2303
STARS = 2
What stars do spangle heauen with such beautie, 2329
Happier the man whom fauourable stars 2338
STARUD = 1
Am staru'd for meate, giddie for lacke of sleepe: 1987
STATE = 2
That were my state farre worser then it is, 657
Made me exchange my state with *Tranio,* 2505
STATERAT = *1
**hic staterat priami,* take heede he heare vs not, *regia* pre- | sume not,
Celsa senis, despaire not. 1336
STAY = 16
Lord. Do you intend to stay with me to night? 90
And how my men will stay themselues from laughter, 146
But stay a while, what companie is this? 345
And so farewell: *Katherina* you may stay, 404
As though she bid me stay by her a weeke: 1047
Luc. Faith Mistresse then I haue no cause to stay. 1380
But where is *Kate*? I stay too long from her, 1493
You would intreat me rather goe then stay: 1574
Tra. Let vs intreat you stay till after dinner. 1580
Pet. I am content. | *Kat.* Are you content to stay? 1585
Pet. I am content you shall entreat me stay, 1587
But yet not stay, entreat me how you can. 1588
Kat. Now if you loue me stay. | *Pet. Grumio,* my horse. 1589
Father, be quiet, he shall stay my leisure. 1603
You vnderstand me sir: so shal you stay 1965
And she to him: to stay him not too long, 2212
STAYES = 1
What euer fortune stayes him from his word, 1411
STEALE = 1
'Twere good me-thinkes to steale our marriage, 1523
STED = 1
Thou shalt be master, *Tranio* in my sted: 508
STEED = 1
Must steed vs all, and me amongst the rest: 838

STEEDS = 1
Loud larums, neighing steeds, & trumpets clangue?   773
STEPHEN = 1
As *Stephen Slie*, and old *Iohn Naps* of Greece, | And *Peter Turph*, and
Henry Pimpernell,   246
STEPS = 1
Doth watch *Bianca's* steps so narrowly: 1522
STEPT = 1
Hor. Petruchio, since we are stept thus farre in,   649
STETERAT = 1*1
tellus, hic steterat Priami regia Celsa senis.   1323
*disguised thus to get your loue, *hic steterat*, and that   1327
STIL = 1
And with the clamor keepe her stil awake: 1841
STILL = 5
As firmely as your selfe were still in place,   722
That she shall still be curst in company.   1185
I should be arguing still vpon that doubt,   1348
You are still crossing it, sirs let't alone,   2176
Besides old *Gremio* is harkning still,   2235
STING = 2
Kate. If I be waspish, best beware my sting.   1086
Pet. Who knowes not where a Waspe does weare | his sting? In his
taile.   1089
STIRRE = *1
Tra. Nay, then 'tis time to stirre him fro(m) his trance: 480
STIRROP = 1
To hold my stirrop, nor to take my horse?   1748
STIRROPS = *1
*saddle, and stirrops of no kindred: besides possest   1437
STOCK = *1
*like the horse: with a linnen stock on one leg, and   1452
STOCKES = 2
Host. A paire of stockes you rogue.   5
Let's be no Stoickes, nor no stockes I pray,   330
STOCKINGS = *2
*then backes: no more stockings then legges: nor   162
*in their new fustian, the white stockings, and euery offi- | cer   1683
STOICKES = 1
Let's be no Stoickes, nor no stockes I pray,   330
STOLNE = *2
*are you? Maister, ha's my fellow *Tranio* stolne your   530
*cloathes, or you stolne his, or both? Pray what's the | newes?   531
STOMACKE = 3
Fall to them as you finde your stomacke serues you: 337
But if you haue a stomacke, too't a Gods name,   760
Come *Kate* sit downe, I know you haue a stomacke,   1787
STOMACKES = 1
Then vale your stomackes, for it is no boote,   2734
STOMAKES = 1
My Banket is to close our stomakes vp   2546
STONE-IUGS = 1
Because she brought stone-Iugs, and no seal'd quarts: 241
STOOD = 2
But see, while idely I stood looking on,   453
And there I stood amazed for a while,   1023

STOOLE = 2
To combe your noddle with a three-legg'd stoole, 367
Pet. Why, what's a mouable? | *Kat*. A ioyn'd stoole. 1070
STOOPD = 1
And as he stoop'd againe to take it vp, 1546
STOOPE = 1
And til she stoope, she must not be full gorg'd, 1825
STOP = 1
And if you cannot, best you stop your eares. 2061
STOPS = 1
That stops my way in *Padua: Grumio* 1621
STORE = 1
And haue prepar'd great store of wedding cheere, 1568
STORME = 1*1
Began to scold, and raise vp such a storme, 475
*a storme, quaft off the Muscadell, and threw the sops 1555
STORMES = 1
To watch the night in stormes, the day in cold, 2708
STRAIGHT = 6*1
And if he chance to speake, be readie straight 56
Is straight, and slender, and as browne in hue 1133
What, do you grumble? Ile be with you straight. 1799
Gru. I am for thee straight: take thou the bill, giue 2134
Go call my men, and let vs straight to him, 2167
Cambio hie you home, and bid *Bianca* make her readie | straight: 2245
Away I say, and bring them hither straight. 2660
STRAIT = *1
*2.*M*. Dost thou loue pictures? we wil fetch thee strait 201
STRANGE = 3*2
*2.*H*. It would seem strange vnto him when he wak'd 47
As beaten hence by your strange Lunacie. 181
Hor. Signior *Baptista*, will you be so strange, 388
Gre. Oh sir, such a life with such a wife, were strange: 759
That with your strange encounter much amasde me: 2352
STRANGER = 2
Me thinkes you walke like a stranger, 949
That being a stranger in this Cittie heere, 952
STRANGERS = *1
Vin. Thus strangers may be haild and abusd: oh mon-|strous villaine. 2486
STRAWES = 1
But now I see our Launces are but strawes: 2731
STREETE = 1
Kate. What in the midst of the streete? 2524
STREETS = 1
Tra. Why sir, I pray are not the streets as free | For me, as for you? 803
STRENGTH = 1
Our strength as weake, our weakenesse past compare, 2732
STREWD = *1
*trim'd, rushes strew'd, cobwebs swept, the seruingmen 1682
STRIFE = 1*1
Bap. Content you gentlemen, I wil co(m)pound this strife 1223
And to cut off all strife: heere sit we downe, 1316
STRIKE = 2
Pet. I sweare Ile cuffe you, if you strike againe. 1097
If you strike me, you are no Gentleman, 1099
STRIKES = 1*1
Ka. If that be iest, then all the rest was so. *Strikes her* 877

STRIKES *cont.*
   Kate. That Ile trie. *she strikes him*   1096
STRIPLING = 1
   Grumio. A proper stripling, and an amorous.   709
STRIUE = 2
   Striue mightily, but eate and drinke as friends.   851
   To striue for that which resteth in my choice: 1312
STROKE = 1
   And with that word she stroke me on the head,   1021
STROND = 1
   When with his knees he kist the Cretan strond.   473
STRONG = *1
   Pet. Katherine I charge thee tell these head-strong   2686
STROOKE = 1
   My selfe am strooke in yeeres I must confesse,   1242
STUDDED = 1
   Their harnesse studded all with Gold and Pearle.   194
STUDIE = 2
   And therefore *Tranio*, for the time I studie,   316
   In briefe sir, studie what you most affect.   339
STUDIED = 1
   As had she studied to misvse me so.   1027
STUDIES = 2
   A course of Learning, and ingenious studies.   308
   Was it not to refresh the minde of man | After his studies, or his vsuall
   paine?   1306
STUDS = *1
   *hath two letters for her name, fairely set down in studs,   1448
STUDY = 1
   Kate. Where did you study all this goodly speech?   1141
STUDYING = 1
   Beene long studying at *Rhemes*, as cunning   943
STUFFE = 5*1
   Lady. No my good Lord, it is more pleasing stuffe.   293
   Beg. What, houshold stuffe.   294
   My houshold-stuffe, my field, my barne,   1617
   Oh mercie God, what masking stuffe is heere?   2072
   Gru. I gaue him no order, I gaue him the stuffe.   2104
   *stuffe a Rabit, and so may you sir: and so adew sir, my   2286
STUFT = 1
   In Iuory cofers I haue stuft my crownes: 1232
STUMBLED = *1
   *horse vpon her, how he beat me because her horse stum-|bled,   1708
STUMBLING = *1
   *being restrain'd to keepe him from stumbling, hath been   1445
SUBIECT = 1
   Such dutie as the subiect owes the Prince,   2713
SUBMISSIUE = 1
   (And with a lowe submissiue reuerence)   57
SUBSCRIBE = 1
   Sir, to your pleasure humbly I subscribe: 384
SUCCESSEFULL = 1
   Yea and perhaps with more successefull words   723
SUCCESSEFULLY = 1
   And 'tis my hope to end successefully: 1823
SUCH = 32*11
   I would esteeme him worth a dozen such: 30

SUCH *cont.*
Such as he hath obseru'd in noble Ladies	122
Such dutie to the drunkard let him do:	124
An Onion wil do well for such a shift,	137
*shooes, or such shooes as my toes looke through the o-|uer-leather.	164
Oh that a mightie man of such discent,	167
Of such possessions, and so high esteeme	168
Beg. Am I a Lord, and haue I such a Ladie?	220
3.Man. Why sir you know no house, nor no such maid	244
Nor no such men as you haue reckon'd vp,	245
And twentie more such names and men as these, | Which neuer were,	
nor no man euer saw.	248
Such friends (as time) in *Padua* shall beget.	344
Hor. From all such diuels, good Lord deliuer vs. | *Gre.* And me too,	
good Lord.	369
Or signior *Gremio* you know any such,	400
That loue should of a sodaine take such hold.	450
Such as the daughter of *Agenor* had,	471
Began to scold, and raise vp such a storme,	475
Petr. Such wind as scatters yongmen throgh y world,	616
Petr. Signior *Hortensio*, 'twixt such friends as wee,	631
Gre. Oh sir, such a life with such a wife, were strange:	759
*And twangling Iacke, with twentie such vilde tearmes,	1026
Kate. No such Iade as you, if me you meane.	1075
Kate. Too light for such a swaine as you to catch,	1078
Kate. Well aym'd of such a yong one.	1114
For such an iniurie would vexe a very saint,	1417
Bion. Master, master, newes, and such newes as you | neuer heard of,	1420
*This mad-brain'd bridegroome tooke him such a cuffe,	1547
*Bride about the necke, and kist her lips with such a cla-|morous	1559
*after mee I know the rout is comming, such a mad mar-|ryage	1562
Then feede it with such ouer-rosted flesh:	1807
For such a one as leaues a Gentleman,	1867
And makes a God of such a Cullion;	1868
Tra. Mistris *Bianca*, blesse you with such grace,	1892
Bian. The taming schoole: what is there such a place?	1906
And Gentlewomen weare such caps as these.	2054
With such austeritie as longeth to a father.	2187
We be affied and such assurance tane,	2231
Such warre of white and red within her cheekes:	2328
What stars do spangle heauen with such beautie,	2329
Till I be brought to such a sillie passe.	2680
Such dutie as the subiect owes the Prince,	2713
Euen such a woman oweth to her husband:	2714

SUCKE = 1
To sucke the sweets of sweete Philosophie.	327

SUDDEN *see* sodaine

SUFFER = 1
Kate. What will you not suffer me: Nay now I see	889

SUFFICE = 1
Few words suffice: and therefore, if thou know	632

SUFFICETH = 2
Sufficeth my reasons are both good and waighty.	556
Sufficeth I am come to keepe my word,	1489

SUFFICIENT = 2
And passe my daughter a sufficient dower,	2227
Priest, Clarke, and some sufficient honest witnesses:	2280

SUGERSOP = *1
   *Call forth *Nathaniel, Ioseph, Nicholas, Phillip, Walter, Su-|gersop*   1718
SUITE = 1
   Some one be readie with a costly suite,   63
SUITES = 1
   And see him drest in all suites like a Ladie: 117
SULLEN = 2
   'Twas told me you were rough, and coy, and sullen,   1122
   And when she is froward, peeuish, sullen, sowre,   2715
SUMMES = 1
   Of greater summes then I haue promised,   1518
SUN = 2
   Or if not so, vntill the Sun be set.   274
   Kate. Then God be blest, it is the blessed sun,   2315
SUNDAY *see* sonday
SUNNE = 7*1
   And as the Sunne breakes through the darkest clouds,   2156
   Hor. Why so this gallant will command the sunne.   2179
   Kate. The Moone, the Sunne: it is not Moonelight | now.   2298
   Kate. I know it is the Sunne that shines so bright.   2301
   And be it moone, or sunne, or what you please: 2309
   Petr. Nay then you lye: it is the blessed Sunne.   2314
   But sunne it is not, when you say it is not.   2316
   That haue bin so bedazled with the sunne,   2344
SUP = 1
   But sup them well, and looke vnto them all,   31
SUPER-DAINTIE = 1
   Kate of *Kate*-hall, my super-daintie *Kate*,   1059
SUPPER = 4*2
   *cold. Where's the Cooke, is supper ready, the house   1681
   Pet. Go rascals, go, and fetch my supper in. *Ex. Ser.*   1766
   Enter seruants with supper.   1770
   And 'twill be supper time ere you come there.   2173
   Biond. His daughter is to be brought by you to the | supper. | *Luc.* And
   then.   2271
   Hath cost me fiue hundred crownes since supper time.   2684
SUPPLY = 2
   For to supply the places at the table,   1633
   Lucentio, you shall supply the Bridegroomes place,   1635
SUPPOSD = 2
   I see no reason but suppos'd *Lucentio*   1289
   Must get a father, call'd suppos'd *Vincentio*,   1290
SUPPOSES = 1
   While counterfeit supposes bleer'd thine eine.   2498
SUPPOSING = 1
   Supposing it a thing impossible,   688
SUPREMACIE = 1
   Or seeke for rule, supremacie, and sway,   2721
SUPREMICIE = 1
   An awfull rule, and right supremicie: 2664
SURE = 6
   I haue forgot your name: but sure that part   96
   Gru. I would I were as sure of a good dinner.   785
   Very gratefull, I am sure of it, to expresse   939
   I will be sure my *Katherine* shall be fine.   1197
   Bian. Mistrust it not, for sure *Aeacides*   1345
   I am sure sweet Kate, this kindnesse merites thankes.   2022

SURELY = 2*1
   *Beg. Yes by Saint Anne do I, a good matter surely: 560
   For me, that I may surely keepe mine oath.   1884
   In gate and countenance surely like a Father.   1918
SURLY = 1
   'Tis like you'll proue a iolly surly groome,   1599
SURPRIZD = 1
   And how she was beguiled and surpriz'd,   207
SURUIUE = 1
   Her widdow-hood, be it that she suruiue me   989
SUTER = 1
   I am your neighbour, and was suter first.   1215
SUTERS = 2
   Because she will not be annoy'd with suters.   487
   Suters to her, and riuals in my Loue: 687
SUTOR = 3
   Are you a sutor to the Maid you talke of, yea or no?   799
   And since you do professe to be a sutor,   844
   Do make my selfe a sutor to your daughter,   953
SUTORS = 3
   She may more sutors haue, and me for one.   815
   Her father keepes from all accesse of sutors,   833
   Kate. Of all thy sutors heere I charge tel   863
SWAIN = *1
   *Pet. You pezant, swain, you horson malt-horse drudg   1756
SWAINE = 1
   Kate. Too light for such a swaine as you to catch,   1078
SWAY = 1
   Or seeke for rule, supremacie, and sway,   2721
SWEARE = 6*1
   Scratching her legs, that one shal sweare she bleeds,   210
   Bian. If you affect him sister, heere I sweare   869
   Pet. I sweare Ile cuffe you, if you strike againe.   1097
   you that durst sweare that your Mistris Bianca   1860
   *in this businesse: I dare sweare this is the right | Vincentio.   2477
   Ped. Sweare if thou dar'st.   2479
   Gre. Naie, I dare not sweare it.   2480
SWEARES = *1
   *to her, and railes, and sweares, and rates, that shee   1817
SWEARING = 1
   A mad-cap ruffian, and a swearing Iacke,   1168
SWEAT = 1
   Rage like an angry Boare, chafed with sweat?   769
SWEET = 13*5
   Wrap'd in sweet cloathes: Rings put vpon his fingers: 42
   And burne sweet Wood to make the Lodging sweete: 53
   I smel sweet sauours, and I feele soft things: 223
   *Farewell: yet for the loue I beare my sweet Bianca, if   414
   *Sweet Bianca, happy man be his dole: hee that runnes   442
   Luc. Oh yes, I saw sweet beautie in her face,   470
   Sacred and sweet was all I saw in her.   479
   And tell me now (sweet friend) what happie gale   614
   But slow in speech: yet sweet as spring-time flowers.   1125
   Pet. Marry so I meane sweet Katherine in thy bed: 1146
   *Bian. Farewell sweet masters both, I must be gone.   1379
   And marry sweet Bianca with consent.   1520
   To this most patient, sweet, and vertuous wife,   1577

SWEET *cont.*

Feare not sweet wench, they shall not touch thee *Kate*,	1624
Tra. Shall sweet *Bianca* practise how to bride it?	1637
*Luc. While you sweet deere proue Mistresse of my | heart.	1857
I am sure sweet Kate, this kindnesse merites thankes.	2022
*Kate. Yong budding Virgin, faire, and fresh, & sweet,	2335

SWEETE = 11

And burne sweet Wood to make the Lodging sweete:	53
To sucke the sweets of sweete Philosophie.	327
Why when I say? Nay good sweete *Kate* be merrie.	1771
Will you giue thankes, sweete *Kate*, or else shall I?	1788
Tell me sweete *Kate*, and tell me truely too,	2326
Sweete *Kate* embrace her for her beauties sake.	2332
Luc. Pardon sweete father. *Kneele.*	2491
Vin. Liues my sweete sonne?	2492
Then pardon him sweete Father for my sake.	2510
Petr. Is not this well? come my sweete *Kate*.	2531
And to be short, what not, that's sweete and happie.	2665

SWEETER = 3

Softer and sweeter then the lustfull bed	190
For she is sweeter then perfume it selfe	718
As hazle nuts, and sweeter then the kernels:	1134

SWEETING = *1

*Petr. How fares my Kate, what sweeting all a-mort?	2016

SWEETLY = 1

She sings as sweetly as a Nightinghale:	1040

SWEETS = 1

To sucke the sweets of sweete Philosophie.	327

SWELLING = 1

Affections edge in me. Were she is as rough | As are the swelling *Adriaticke* seas.	639

SWEPT = *1

**trim'd, rushes strew'd, cobwebs swept, the seruingmen	1682

SWIFT = 2

*\.Man. Say thou wilt course, thy gray-hounds are as | (swift	199
Petr. A good swift simile, but something currish.	2597

SWIFTLY = 1

Biond. Softly and swiftly sir, for the Priest is ready.	2381

SWINE = *1

*Lord. Oh monstrous beast, how like a swine he lyes.	38

SWINGE = 1

Swinge me them soundly forth vnto their husbands:	2659

SWORD = *1

**another lac'd: an olde rusty sword tane out of the	1434

SWORE = 2*2

I, by goggs woones quoth he, and swore so loud,	1544
**swore, as if the Vicar meant to cozen him: but after ma-|ny	1552
**me: how he swore, how she prai'd, that neuer prai'd be-|fore:	1710
In resolution, as I swore before.	1891

T = 1

And let me be a slaue, t'atchieue that maide,	525

TABLE = 2

Set foot vnder thy table: tut, a toy,	1284
For to supply the places at the table,	1633

TAI = 4

TAIL = 1

Away I say, commend me to thy master. *Exit Tail.*	2151

TAIL = 6*2
TAILE = 2*1
  Pet. Who knowes not where a Waspe does weare | his sting? In his
  taile.   1089
  Pet. What with my tongue in your taile.   1094
  *presume to touch a haire of my Masters horse-taile, till   1722
TAILOR see also Tai., Tail. = 6*1
  What hast thou din'd? The Tailor staies thy leasure,   2041
  Enter Tailor.   2043
  Come Tailor, let vs see these ornaments.   2044
  Pet. Thy gowne, why I: come Tailor let vs see't.   2071
  Why what a deuils name Tailor cal'st thou this?   2077
  Pet. Hortensio, say thou wilt see the Tailor paide: 2147
  Hor. Tailor, Ile pay thee for thy gowne to morrow,   2149
TAKE = 35*9
  Trust me, I take him for the better dogge.   28
  Then take him vp, and manage well the iest: 49
  Lord. Take him vp gently, and to bed with him,   76
  Lord. Go sirra, take them to the Butterie,   112
  And take a Lodging fit to entertaine   343
  (Belike) I knew not what to take, | And what to leaue? Ha. *Exit*   408
  *them, would take her with all faults, and mony enough.   433
  Gre. I cannot tell: but I had as lief take her dowrie   434
  That loue should of a sodaine take such hold.   450
  Vncase thee: take my Coulord hat and cloake,   513
  Petr. Verona, for a while I take my leaue,   566
  Ile mend it with a Largesse. Take your paper too,   716
  Take you the Lute, and you the set of bookes,   969
  Take this of me, *Kate* of my consolation,   1061
  Pet. Oh slow-wing'd Turtle, shal a buzard take thee?   1082
  And so I take my leaue, and thanke you both. *Exit*.   1280
  Take you your instrument, play you the whiles,   1317
  **hic staterat priami*, take heede he heare vs not, *regia* pre-|sume not,
  Celsa senis, despaire not.   1336
  Good master take it not vnkindly pray   1350
  Beeme, Bianca take him for thy Lord   1368
  And as he stoop'd againe to take it vp,   1546
  Now take them vp quoth he, if any list.   1549
  And therefore heere I meane to take my leaue.   1570
  That take it on you at the first so roundly.   1600
  And let *Bianca* take her sisters roome.   1636
  will take cold: Holla, hoa *Curtis*.   1649
  To hold my stirrop, nor to take my horse?   1748
  Take that, and mend the plucking of the other.   1776
  There, take it to you, trenchers, cups, and all: 1797
  Tra. And heere I take the like vnfained oath,   1880
  Shal win my loue, and so I take my leaue,   1890
  Par. Take me your loue, and then let me alone.   1924
  Looke that you take vpon you as you should,   1964
  Heere take away this dish. | *Kate*. I pray you let it stand.   2025
  Gre. I am for thee straight: take thou the bill, giue   2134
  Pet. Go take it vp vnto thy masters vse.   2140
  Gru. Villaine, not for thy life: Take vp my Mistresse | gowne for thy
  masters vse.   2141
  Take vp my Mistris gowne to his masters vse. | Oh fie, fie, fie.   2145
  Go take it hence, be gone, and say no more.   2148
  Take no vnkindnesse of his hastie words: 2150

TAKE *cont*.
    *counterfeit assurance: take you assurance of her, *Cum*   2278
    preuilegio ad Impremendum solem, to th' Church take the   2279
    to take vpon you another mans name.   2416
    Gre. Take heede signior *Baptista*, least you be coni- | catcht   2476
TAKEN *see* tane
TAKES = 1
    Kat. I for a Turtle, as he takes a buzard.   1083
TAKETH = 1
    And for I know she taketh most delight   396
TALE = 5 *3
    Gre. Sauing your tale *Petruchio*, I pray let vs that are   932
    Gru. Out of their saddles into the durt, and thereby | hangs a tale.   1690
    Cur. This 'tis to feele a tale, not to heare a tale.   1696
    Gru. And therefore 'tis cal'd a sensible tale: and this   1697
    Gru. Tell thou the tale: but hadst thou not crost me,   1704
    Tra. If he be credulous, and trust my tale,   1920
    Hor. My Widdow saies, thus she conceiues her tale.   2563
TALES = 1
    Kate. Yours if you talke of tales, and so farewell.   1093
TALKD = 2
    That talk'd of her, haue talk'd amisse of her: 1171
TALKE = 9 *2
    And practise Rhetoricke in your common talke,   334
    Petr. Sirra be gone, or talke not I aduise you.   610
    Are you a sutor to the Maid you talke of, yea or no?   799
    Gre. What, this Gentleman will out-talke vs all.   820
    Talke not to me, I will go sit and weepe,   893
    They call me *Katerine*, that do talke of me.   1055
    Kate. Yours if you talke of tales, and so farewell.   1093
    Nor hast thou pleasure to be crosse in talke: 1128
    *finde when he comes home. But what talke I of this?   1717
    Bap. Talke not signior *Gremio*: I saie he shall goe to | prison.   2474
    Luc. Here is a wonder, if you talke of a wonder.   2661
TALKING = *1
    Biond. Then thus: *Baptista* is safe talking with the   2268
TALL = 1
    Tra. Th'art a tall fellow, hold thee that to drinke,   2198
TALLER = *1
    *selfe: for considering the weather, a taller man then I   1648
TAMD = *3
    *hath tam'd my old master, and my new mistris, and my | selfe fellow
    Curtis.   1662
    Horten. Now goe thy wayes, thou hast tam'd a curst | Shrow.   2748
    Luc. Tis a wonder, by your leaue, she wil be tam'd so.   2750
TAME = 5
    For I am he am borne to tame you *Kate*,   1156
    How tame when men and women are alone,   1192
    He that knowes better how to tame a shrew,   1844
    Bian. God giue him ioy. | *Tra*. I, and hee'l tame her.   1902
    To tame a shrew, and charme her chattering tongue.   1909
TAMES = *1
    *know'st winter tames man, woman, and beast: for it   1661
TAMING = 2 *1
    Tra. Faith he is gone vnto the taming schoole.   1905
    Bian. The taming schoole: what is there such a place?   1906
    THE | Taming of the Shrew.   2752

TANE = 5*1
No profit growes, where is no pleasure tane:	338
Therefore this order hath *Baptista* tane,	691
Kate. Well tane, and like a buzzard.	1081
*another lac'd: an olde rusty sword tane out of the	1434
Nay, I haue tane you napping gentle Loue,	1894
We be affied and such assurance tane,	2231

TAPESTRY = 1
My hangings all of *tirian* tapestry:	1231

TARRIE = 2*1
*wil therefore tarrie in despight of the flesh & the blood	281
Hor. Tarrie *Petruchio*, I must go with thee,	682
Kate. I chafe you if I tarrie. Let me go.	1120

TARRY = 1*1
Beg. I, it stands so that I may hardly tarry so long:	279
Biond. I cannot tarry: I knew a wench maried in an	2284

TART = 1
What, vp and downe caru'd like an apple Tart?	2074

TASTE = *1
2.Ser. Wilt please your Honor taste of these Con-|serues?	155

TAUGHT = 2
Then hath beene taught by any of my trade,	1362
Then hast thou taught *Hortentio* to be vntoward. *Exit*.	2378

TE *l*.465 = 1

TEACH = 2*1
*I can by any meanes light on a fit man to teach her that	415
And bow'd her hand to teach her fingering,	1018
To teach you gamoth in a briefer sort,	1360

TEACHETH = 1
That teacheth trickes eleuen and twentie long,	1908

TEACHING = 2
And vndertake the teaching of the maid:	497
Stand by, and marke the manner of his teaching.	1851

TEARES = 3*1
Bid him shed teares, as being ouer-ioyed	131
To raine a shower of commanded teares,	136
So workmanlie the blood and teares are drawne.	212
1.Man. And til the teares that she hath shed for thee,	216

TEARMES = *1
*And twangling Iacke, with twentie such vilde tearmes,	1026

TEDIOUS = 1
Petr. Tedious it were to tell, and harsh to heare,	1488

TEETH = *1
*might freeze to my teeth, my tongue to the roofe of my	1645

TEL = 5*1
Tra. I pray sir tel me, is it possible	449
Ile tel you newes indifferent good for either.	746
Kate. Of all thy sutors heere I charge tel	863
I tel you sir, she beares me faire in hand.	1849
Hor. Quicke proceeders marry, now tel me I pray,	1859
I tel thee *Lisio* this is wonderfull.	1863

TELL = 28*8
Another tell him of his Hounds and Horse,	65
And so offend him: for I tell you sirs,	108
Tell him from me (as he will win my loue)	120
Tell me thy minde, for I haue *Pisa* left,	320
Gre. I cannot tell: but I had as lief take her dowrie	434

TELL *cont.*

Luc. Tell me thine first.	495
And tell me now (sweet friend) what happie gale	614
Tell me her fathers name, and 'tis enough:	660
*trickes. Ile tell you what sir, and she stand him but a li-|tle,	678
And do you tell me of a womans tongue?	774
Tell me I beseech you, which is the readiest way	788
Sirrah, leade these Gentlemen | To my daughters, and tell them both	973
Then tell me, if I get your daughters loue,	984
Pet. Why that is nothing: for I tell you father,	995
I did but tell her she mistooke her frets,	1017
Say that she raile, why then Ile tell her plaine,	1039
I tell you 'tis incredible to beleeue | How much she loues me: oh the kindest *Kate,*	1186
Tra. And tell vs what occasion of import	1485
Petr. Tedious it were to tell, and harsh to heare,	1488
Ile tell you sir *Lucentio*; when the Priest	1542
Cur. I prethee good *Grumio*, tell me, how goes the | world?	1670
Gru. Tell thou the tale: but hadst thou not crost me,	1704
Pet. I tell thee *Kate*, 'twas burnt and dried away,	1802
First tell me, haue you euer beene at Pisa?	1949
Gru. I cannot tell, I feare 'tis chollericke.	2000
My tongue will tell the anger of my heart,	2062
I tell thee I, that thou hast marr'd her gowne.	2100
And if you will tell what hath hapned,	2247
Luc. And what of all this. | *Bion.* I cannot tell, expect they are busied about a	2276
Tell me sweete *Kate*, and tell me truely too,	2326
*I pray you tell signior *Lucentio* that his Father is	2408
*sonne, my sonne: tell me thou villaine, where is my son | *Lucentio*?	2467
Bap. Why, tell me is not this my *Cambio*?	2502
I praie you tell me what you meant by that.	2567
Pet. Katherine I charge thee tell these head-strong	2686

TELLING = 1

Wid. Come, come, your mocking: we will haue no | telling.	2689

TELLUS = 1*2

tellus, hic steterat Priami regia Celsa senis.	1323
hic est, sonne vnto Vincentio of Pisa, *Sigeria tel-|lus,*	1326
*I know you not, *hic est sigeria tellus*, I trust you not,	1335

TELS = *1

Gru. Nay looke you sir, hee tels you flatly what his	643

TEMPERATE = 1

Shee is not hot, but temperate as the morne,	1174

TEMPTING = 1

And then with kinde embracements, tempting kisses,	129

TEN = 3

I loue her ten times more then ere I did,	1029
Yet I haue fac'd it with a card of ten:	1287
'Tis ten to one it maim'd you too out right	2605

TENDER = 1*1

Lo. Huntsman I charge thee, tender wel my hounds,	19
You haue shewd a tender fatherly regard,	1166

TENTS = 1

Costly apparell, tents, and Canopies,	1234

TERMES = 1

Thus in plaine termes: your father hath consented	1148

TERTIA *l.*1294 = 1
TESTIFY = *1
Tail. Why heere is the note of the fashion to testify. | *Pet*. Reade it.   2114
TH *see also* i'th, o'th = *1
preuilegio ad Impremendum solem, to th' Church take the   2279
THAN *see also* then = 2
    No better than a poore and loathsome begger: 134
    Cur. By this reckning he is more shrew than she.   1715
THANK = *2
    Petr. Gentlemen & friends, I thank you for your pains,   1566
    *sir, what cernes it you, if I weare Pearle and gold: I thank   2453
THANKE = 7*1
    Now fellowes, you are welcome. | *Players*. We thanke your Honor.   88
    Beg. I thanke thee, thou shalt not loose by it.   253
    Thou'dst thanke me but a little for my counsell: 627
    And so I take my leaue, and thanke you both. *Exit*.   1280
    And honest company, I thanke you all,   1575
    Kate. I thanke you sir.   2029
    Tra. I thanke you sir, where then doe you know best   2230
    Luc. I thanke thee for that gird good *Tranio*.   2601
THANKED = 1
    Beg. Now Lord be thanked for my good amends. | *All*. Amen.   250
THANKEFULL = 1
    She's apt to learne, and thankefull for good turnes: 1033
THANKES = 5
    Bap. A thousand thankes signior *Gremio*:   947
    If she do bid me packe, Ile giue her thankes,   1046
    Will you giue thankes, sweete *Kate*, or else shall I?   1788
    I am sure sweet Kate, this kindnesse merites thankes.   2022
    Pet. The poorest seruice is repaide with thankes,   2027
THART = 2
    And verie rich: but th'art too much my friend,   629
    Tra. Th'art a tall fellow, hold thee that to drinke,   2198
THAT *l.*66 67 68 79 80 85 96 *98 114 118 167 *178 *179 *180 210 211
    *216 231 235 266 277 279 317 318 321 326 333 352 361 372 377 389
    *415 *419 423 *442 *445 450 456 472 476 484 525 *548 554 575 650 654
    655 657 *680 690 692 700 712 742 743 754 765 775 784 *790 795 808
    809 825 829 837 858 866 *877 884 909 914 *932 940 942 952 957 958
    959 988 989 992 994 995 998 1006 1021 1039 1041 1055 *1066 1096 1131
    1149 1153 1169 1171 1178 1183 1185 1190 1216 1221 1222 1225 1237
    1245 1256 1257 1304 1312 1320 *1327 *1328 *1329 *1340 1348 1351
    1369 1385 1390 1422 *1433 1462 1463 1482 1521 1526 1537 1545 *1548
    *1556 *1560 1576 1600 1609 1621 1630 1651 1702 *1710 *1716 1729
    *1730 1767 1776 1796 1805 *1817 1829 1830 1838 1844 1847 *1854 1855
    1860 1866 1869 1879 1884 1901 1908 1912 1936 1942 1961 1964 1982
    1986 1989 2002 2011 2013 2057 2068 2100 *2130 *2132 2143 2155 2181
    2196 2197 2198 2226 2242 2263 2281 2300 2301 2318 2330 2344 2345
    2352 *2398 *2408 *2441 *2470 *2481 2497 2500 2501 *2511 *2552 *2558
    2560 2562 *2564 *2566 2567 2584 *2587 2594 2598 2601 2622 2630
    *2631 2655 2677 2678 *2694 2705 2719 2725 2733 = 189*43
THATS = 7*2
    That's your deuice. | *Luc*. It is: May it be done?   498
    *that's nothing; and he begin once, hee'l raile in his rope   677
    Good morrow *Kate*, for thats your name I heare.   1052
    Tra. That's but a cauill: he is olde, I young.   1272
    And that's a wonder: fathers commonly   1291
    Bap. Why that's all one.   1465

THATS *cont.*
Pet. Now by my mothers sonne, and that's my selfe,	2302
Hor. That's my office	2577
And to be short, what not, that's sweete and happie.	2665

THAW = *1
*to thaw me, but I with blowing the fire shall warme my	1647

THE *see also* th', y = 373*127, 1
Petr. Spoke like an Officer: ha to the lad.	2578

THEE *see also* the *l.*12 *19 141 182 185 189 *201 206 *216 253 379 380
455 504 513 514 625 626 628 630 651 682 884 885 888 1064 1065 1076
1077 *1082 1135 1153 1179 *1180 1281 1283 1385 1386 *1416 1601 1624
1625 *1667 1687 1702 1757 1758 1802 1810 1863 2009 2012 2014 2021
2068 *2089 2098 2100 *2112 *2130 *2132 *2134 *2149 2198 2252 2267
2331 2339 2347 2360 2373 2375 2383 2483 *2529 2601 2666 *2686
2705 = 65*16

THEEUES = 1
Draw forth thy weapon, we are beset with theeues,	1622

THEIR *l.*123 194 *411 617 *705 964 975 998 1292 *1683 *1690 *1719
*1720 *1721 1723 1889 2224 2659 2668 *2687 = 12*9

THEM *see also* 'em *l.*31 87 112 113 114 123 148 197 *291 337 386 401
*433 503 711 717 859 964 974 975 1020 1324 1549 1626 *1643 *1721
1725 1732 1734 1879 1946 1952 2267 *2420 2658 2659 2660 = 34*5

THEMSELUES = 1
And how my men will stay themselues from laughter,	146

THEN *l.*45 49 75 129 *162 *163 190 200 215 *441 *480 507 *551 580 602
617 625 642 657 681 718 724 814 817 830 836 867 871 874 *877 941 964
977 983 984 *1015 1029 1039 1044 1087 1100 1111 1134 1140 *1181
1217 1238 1260 1264 *1266 1301 1308 1362 1380 1426 1467 1518 1538
1574 1593 *1648 1807 1826 1899 1924 1930 1944 1970 1989 *2004 *2005
2007 2008 2023 2056 2064 *2136 *2144 2158 2160 2215 2225 *2230 2237
*2268 2273 2291 2314 2315 2378 2385 *2481 2510 *2527 2532 2554 2590
2618 *2638 2734 = 81*21

THENCE = *1
*eccho: and I seeing this, came thence for very shame, and	1561

THERE *l.*103 358 *431 561 *571 *706 1023 1110 1363 1407 *1429 1449
1596 1634 1695 1761 1763 1797 1835 *1906 2169 2171 2173 2238 2354
2652 = 24*5

THEREBY = *1
Gru. Out of their saddles into the durt, and thereby | hangs a tale.	1690

THEREFORE = 17*11
*in with *Richard Conqueror*: therefore *Pau-!cas pallabris*, let the world slide: Sessa.	8
*wil therefore tarrie in despight of the flesh & the blood	281
Therefore they thought it good you heare a play,	288
And therefore *Tranio*, for the time I studie,	316
And therefore has he closely meu'd her vp,	486
And therefore frame your manners to the time	534
Few words suffice: and therefore, if thou know	632
And therefore let me be thus bold with you,	670
Therefore this order hath *Baptista* tane,	691
Let specialties be therefore drawne betweene vs,	991
For dainties are all *Kates*, and therefore *Kate*	1060
Pet. Why heere's no crab, and therefore looke not | sowre.	1108
And therefore setting all this chat aside,	1147
Pet. Good sooth euen thus: therefore ha done with | (words,	1499
And therefore heere I meane to take my leaue.	1570
Gru. Oh I *Curtis* I, and therefore fire, fire, cast on no | water.	1657

THEREFORE *cont.*

*therefore fire: do thy duty, and haue thy dutie, for my	1673
Cur. There's fire readie, and therefore good *Grumio* | the newes.	1675
Gru. Why therefore fire, for I haue caught extreme	1680
Cur. All readie: and therefore I pray thee newes.	1687
Gru. And therefore 'tis cal'd a sensible tale: and this	1697
Gre. E'ne at hand, alighted by this: and therefore be	1744
And therefore frolicke, we will hence forthwith,	2165
And therefore if you say no more then this,	2225
thee at home, therefore leaue vs. *Exit*.	2383
Bian. I, but not frighted me, therefore Ile sleepe a-|gaine.	2585
Therefore a health to all that shot and mist.	2594
Petr. Well, I say no: and therefore sir assurance,	2608

THERES = 1 *3

Hor. Faith (as you say) there's small choise in rotten	437
Cur. There's fire readie, and therefore good *Grumio* | the newes.	1675
Pet. I there's the villanie.	2127
Pet. Why there's a wench: Come on, and kisse mee | *Kate*.	2738

THESE *l*.*155 184 232 *234 248 360 *555 *607 822 858 973 975 1020 1261
1310 *1469 1495 1502 *1747 1758 1794 1829 1975 1989 2044 2054 2153
2504 2580 *2686 = 23*7

THEY = 21*8

THEYRE = *1

Grem. They're busie within, you were best knocke | lowder.	2395

THICKE = 1

Muddie, ill seeming, thicke, bereft of beautie,	2701

THIMBLE = 2

Thou lyest, thou thred, thou thimble,	2093
*that Ile proue vpon thee, though thy little finger be ar-|med in a thimble.	2130

THIN = 1

You are like to haue a thin and slender pittance.	2243

THINE = 8*1

Grim death, how foule and loathsome is thine image:	39
Luc. Tell me thine first.	495
Tra. Gray-beard thy loue doth freeze. | *Gre*. But thine doth frie,	1219
Hort. Sirra, I will not beare these braues of thine.	1310
Tra. But say, what to thine olde newes?	1430
Gru. A cold world *Curtis* in euery office but thine, z	1672
Gru. Lend thine eare. | *Cur*. Heere. | *Gru*. There.	1693
While counterfeit supposes bleer'd thine eine.	2498
While I with selfesame kindnesse welcome thine:	2542

THING = 10

*be happie riuals in *Bianca's* loue, to labour and effect | one thing specially.	421
One thing more rests, that thy selfe execute,	554
Supposing it a thing impossible,	688
Gre. Oh this learning, what a thing it is.	725
Bap. I, when the speciall thing is well obtain'd,	993
They do consume the thing that feedes their furie.	998
My horse, my oxe, my asse, my any thing,	1618
*the Gils faire without, the Carpets laide, and euerie | thing in order?	1685
Kate. Then both or one, or any thing thou wilt.	2007
That euery thing I looke on seemeth greene:	2345

THINGS = 8*1

I smel sweet sauours, and I feele soft things:	223
We will haue rings, and things, and fine array,	1203

THINGS *cont.*

Pewter and brasse, and all things that belongs	1237
And all things answerable to this portion.	1241
*things of worthy memorie, which now shall die in obli-|uion,	1713
companions, is all readie, and all things neate?	1742
Nat. All things is readie, how neere is our master?	1743
With Ruffes and Cuffes, and Fardingales, and things:	2038
Gru. Thou hast fac'd many things. | *Tail.* I haue.	2108

THINK = *1

Gru. Oh sir, the conceit is deeper then you think for:	2144

THINKE = 14*3

What thinke you, if he were conuey'd to bed,	41
*1.*Hun.* Beleeue me Lord, I thinke he cannot choose.	46
As he shall thinke by our true diligence	74
Sincklo. I thinke 'twas *Soto* that your honor meanes.	98
Although I thinke 'twas in another sense,	521
*thinke scolding would doe little good vpon him. Shee	675
Thinke you, a little dinne can daunt mine eares?	766
And so I pray you all to thinke your selues.	978
Hor. I thinke she'l sooner proue a souldier,	1013
I know you thinke to dine with me to day,	1567
And thinke it not the worst of all your fortunes,	1960
As thou shalt thinke on prating whil'st thou liu'st:	2099
Let's see, I thinke 'tis now some seuen a clocke,	2170
Looke what I speake, or do, or thinke to doe,	2175
I thinke I shall command your welcome here;	2393
Bap. You mistake sir, you mistake sir, praie what do | you thinke is his name?	2457
I thinke thou hast the veriest shrew of all.	2607

THINKES = 3*1

Me thinkes you walke like a stranger,	949
That thinkes with oathes to face the matter out.	1169
'Twere good me-thinkes to steale our marriage,	1523
Kat. He that is giddie thinkes the world turnes round,	2566

THINKS = *1

Wid. He that is giddie thinks the world turns round. | *Petr.* Roundlie replied.	2558

THINKST = *1

Gre. I say, a diuell: Think'st thou *Hortensio*, though	427

THINNE = *1

*his beard grew thinne and hungerly, and seem'd to aske	1557

THIRD = 1*1

Beg. Third, or fourth, or fift Borough, Ile answere	15
Another beare the Ewer: the third a Diaper,	61

THIRST = 1

And with sacietie seekes to quench his thirst.	323

THIRSTIE = 1

And while it is so, none so dry or thirstie	2702

THIRTY = 1*1

Lady. I, and the time seeme's thirty vnto me,	268
*being perhaps (for ought I see) two and thirty, a peepe	600

THIS *l.*37 40 70 93 133 140 147 *166 *178 *179 215 237 269 278 329 345
392 *435 *438 459 466 569 576 595 *597 621 671 691 700 725 726 734
762 780 807 811 820 831 839 845 848 875 *879 923 938 942 952 957 963
1061 1138 1141 1147 1152 *1181 *1223 1241 1243 1278 1292 1299 1372
1381 1389 1395 *1457 1477 1480 1483 1510 1527 *1547 *1558 *1561
1577 *1660 1696 *1697 1715 *1717 *1744 1789 1809 1836 1837 1842

THIS *cont.*
1863 1866 1887 1948 1958 1959 1967 1971 2022 2025 2040 2048 2053
2073 2077 *2132 2163 2179 2181 2197 2203 2225 2238 2242 2276 2281
2341 2361 2362 2370 2376 2386 2389 *2415 *2418 2439 *2469 *2477
2501 2502 2516 *2517 *2522 2531 2550 2593 2681 = 111*25, 1
Why this a heauie chance twixt him and you,   612
THITHER = 3
Vnlesse you wil accompanie me thither.   672
There wil we mount, and thither walke on foote,   2169
Thither must I, and here I leaue you sir.   2391
THORNIE = *1
*3.*Man.* Or *Daphne* roming through a thornie wood,   209
THOROUGHLY = *1
*best horse in *Padua* to begin his woing that would tho-|roughly   445
THOSE *l.*689 918 1768 2330 2695 = 5
THOU *see also* th'art *l.*22 29 99 140 *187 189 192 193 *195 196 *199 *201
213 214 253 340 341 *387 *427 460 461 489 508 *555 632 *659 864 868
883 884 *1003 1004 1008 *1015 1072 1124 1126 1128 1129 1135 1136
1139 1154 1218 1262 1461 1594 1602 1623 *1652 *1660 *1666 *1668
1678 *1704 *1705 *1706 1714 *1716 *1730 2007 2009 2020 2023 2032
2041 2066 2068 2077 2093 2094 2095 2097 2099 2100 2108 *2110 2113
2133 *2134 2147 2162 2164 2195 2260 2283 2327 *2340 2342 2346 2349
2378 *2411 2413 *2430 *2467 2479 *2481 2494 2525 2544 2607 2667
2709 *2740 *2748 = 88*31
THOUDST = 1
Thou'dst thanke me but a little for my counsell: 627
THOUGH = 16*7
For though you lay heere in this goodlie chamber,   237
What shall I be appointed houres, as though   407
*Though the nature of our quarrell yet neuer brook'd   418
Gre. I say, a diuell: Think'st thou *Hortensio*, though   427
Hor. Tush *Gremio*: though it passe your patience z   430
*tooth in her head, though she haue as manie diseases as   646
For I will boord her, though she chide as loud   661
Petr. I know her father, though I know not her,   667
Though *Paris* came, in hope to speed alone.   819
Though little fire growes great with little winde,   999
That shakes not, though they blow perpetually.   1006
As though she bid me stay by her a weeke: 1047
Methinkes he lookes as though he were in loue: 1382
Though he be blunt, I know him passing wise,   1412
Though he be merry, yet withall he's honest.   1413
Kate. Would *Katherine* had neuer seen him though. | *Exit weeping.*   1414
Though in some part inforced to digresse,   1490
Bap. Neighbours and friends, though Bride & Bride-|(groom wants   1632
Neuer to marrie with her, though she would intreate,   1881
*that Ile proue vpon thee, though thy little finger be ar-|med in a
thimble.   2130
Luc. At last, though long, our iarring notes agree,   2538
This bird you aim'd at, though you hit her not,   2593
'Twas I wonne the wager, though you hit the white,   2745
THOUGHT = 3
Therefore they thought it good you heare a play,   288
I neuer thought it possible or likely.   452
'Tis thought your Deere does hold you at a baie.   2599
THOUGHTS = 3*1
Call home thy ancient thoughts from banishment,   183

THOUGHTS *cont.*

*Bend thoughts and wits to atcheeue her. Thus it stands:	482
Then words can witnesse, or your thoughts can guesse.	1217
Yet if thy thoughts *Bianca* be so humble	1383

THOUSAND = 8

Which barres a thousand harmes, and lengthens life.	290
Faire *Laedaes* daughter had a thousand wooers,	816
Bap. A thousand thankes signior *Gremio*:	947
And in possession twentie thousand Crownes.	987
Besides, two thousand Duckets by the yeere	1251
Gre. Two thousand Duckets by the yeere of land,	1254
Hee'll wooe a thousand, point the day of marriage,	1403
Vnto their losses twentie thousand crownes,	2668

THRALD = 1

Whose sodaine sight hath thral'd my wounded eye.	526

THREATNING = *1

Kate. Fie, fie, vnknit that threatning vnkinde brow,	2694

THRED = 4

Thou lyest, thou thred, thou thimble,	2093
Brau'd in mine owne house with a skeine of thred:	2096
Gru. Marrie sir with needle and thred.	2106
*me in the skirts of it, and beate me to death with a bot-│tome of browne thred: I said a gowne.	2119

THREE = 7*2

Ile leaue her houses three or foure as good	1248
Then three great Argosies, besides two Galliasses	1260
My Lessons make no musicke in three parts.	1353
Gru. Away you three inch foole, I am no beast.	1664
Gru. Am I but three inches? Why thy horne is a foot	1665
Ere three dayes passe, which hath as long lou'd me,	1886
Thou yard three quarters, halfe yard, quarter, naile,	2094
*brought him vp euer since he was three yeeres old, and	2460
We three are married, but you two are sped.	2744

THREE-LEGGD = 1

To combe your noddle with a three-legg'd stoole,	367

THREW = *1

*a storme, quaft off the Muscadell, and threw the sops	1555

THRICE = 1*1

La. Thrice noble Lord, let me intreat of you	272
*an old ierkin, a paire of old breeches thrice turn'd; a	1432

THRIUE = 1

Happily to wiue and thriue, as best I may:	622

THROATE = 1

Gru. The note lies in's throate if he say I said so.	2116

THROGH = *1

Petr. Such wind as scatters yongmen throgh y world,	616

THROUGH = 4*3

*shooes, or such shooes as my toes looke through the o-│uer-leather.	164
*3.*Man.* Or *Daphne* roming through a thornie wood,	209
A Merchant of great Trafficke through the world:	311
And through the instrument my pate made way,	1022
As on a Pillorie, looking through the Lute,	1024
*how she waded through the durt to plucke him off	1709
And as the Sunne breakes through the darkest clouds,	2156

THROUGHLIE = 1

Now doe your dutie throughlie I aduise you:	2192

THROUGHOUT = 1
| A man well knowne throughout all Italy. | 930 |

THROW = 1*1
| *he wil throw a figure in her face, and so disfigure hir | 679 |
| Off with that bable, throw it vnderfoote. | 2678 |

THRUST = 1
| And I haue thrust my selfe into this maze, | 621 |

THUNDER = 2
| As thunder, when the clouds in Autumne cracke. | 662 |
| And heauens Artillerie thunder in the skies? | 771 |

THUS = 19*7
Glad that you thus continue your resolue,	326
*Bend thoughts and wits to atcheeue her. Thus it stands:	482
For man or master: then it followes thus;	507
Signior *Hortensio*, thus it stands with me,	619
Hor. Petruchio, since we are stept thus farre in,	649
And therefore let me be thus bold with you,	670
Bap. Was euer Gentleman thus greeu'd as I? | But who comes heere.	895
Thus in plaine termes: your father hath consented	1148
Pet. Father, 'tis thus, your selfe and all the world	1170
Bap. Well gentlemen, I am thus resolu'd,	1274
*disguised thus to get your loue, *hic steterat*, and that	1327
That I haue beene thus pleasant with you both.	1351
Petr. Were it better I should rush in thus:	1474
Pet. Not I, beleeue me, thus Ile visit her.	1497
Bap. But thus I trust you will not marry her.	1498
Pet. Good sooth euen thus: therefore ha done with | (words,	1499
*you: and thus much for greeting. Now my spruce	1741
And serue it thus to me that loue it not?	1796
Pet. Thus haue I politickely begun my reigne,	1822
And thus Ile curbe her mad and headstrong humor:	1843
That triumph thus vpon my misery:	2013
Biond. Then thus: *Baptista* is safe talking with the	2268
Petr. Well, forward, forward, thus the bowle should | (run,	2321
Vin. Thus strangers may be haild and abusd: oh mon-|strous villaine.	2486
Kat. Mistris, how meane you that? | *Wid.* Thus I conceiue by him.	2560
Hor. My Widdow saies, thus she conceiues her tale.	2563

THY *l.**11   182 183 185 186 193 197 *199 257 305 320 467 554 863 882
*1003 1062 1063 1101 1129 1146 1152 1153 1194 1219 1284 1368 1383
1384 *1608 1622 1623 *1665 *1668 1669 *1673 1714 1810 *2019 2021
2033 2035 2041 2042 2071 2098 *2112 *2130 2135 2140 *2141 2142
*2149 2151 2166 2195 2320 2336 2350 2358 2362 2368 2369 2431 *2455
2497 *2518 2544 2696 2697 *2698 2704 2705 2706 2710 *2740
*2748 = 67*18

THYSELFE *see* selfe
TIED *see also* tyed = 1
| Ile not be tied to howres, nor pointed times, | 1314 |

TIGHT *see* tite

TIL = 5*1
1.Man. And til the teares that she hath shed for thee,	216
That til the Father rid his hands of her,	484
I wil not sleepe *Hortensio* til I see her,	669
Til *Katherine* the Curst, haue got a husband.	693
And til she stoope, she must not be full gorg'd,	1825
Til you haue done your businesse in the Citie:	1966

TILL = 8*2
| Or do I dreame? Or haue I dream'd till now? | 221 |

TILL *cont.*
*it shall be so farre forth friendly maintain'd, till by hel-|ping   439
Luc. Oh *Tranio*, till I found it to be true,   451
Till I can finde occasion of reuenge.   894
Tra. Let vs intreat you stay till after dinner.   1580
No, nor to morrow, not till I please my selfe,   1595
For me, Ile not be gone till I please my selfe,   1598
*presume to touch a haire of my Masters horse-taile, till   1722
Pet. When you are gentle, you shall haue one too, | And not till then.   2055
Till I be brought to such a sillie passe.   2680

TIME = 21*2
Well you are come to me in happie time,   100
But did I neuer speake of all that time.   235
Lady. I, and the time seeme's thirty vnto me,   268
Being all this time abandon'd from your bed.   269
And therefore *Tranio*, for the time I studie,   316
Such friends (as time) in *Padua* shall beget.   344
Tra. Master, it is no time to chide you now,   462
Tra. Nay, then 'tis time to stirre him fro(m) his trance: 480
Luc. Sirra come hither, 'tis no time to iest,   533
And therefore frame your manners to the time   534
Hor. Gremio, 'tis now no time to vent our loue,   744
Haue I not in my time heard Lions rore?   767
Kate. Mou'd, in good time, let him that mou'd you | hether   1066
But slow in speech: yet sweet as spring-time flowers.   1125
In time I may beleeue, yet I mistrust.   1344
The morning weares, 'tis time we were at Church.   1494
Kate. Ile haue no bigger, this doth fit the time,   2053
According to the fashion, and the time.   2080
I did not bid you marre it to the time.   2082
And well we may come there by dinner time.   2171
And 'twill be supper time ere you come there.   2173
And time it is when raging warre is come,   2539
Hath cost me fiue hundred crownes since supper time.   2684

TIMES = 3*1
I loue her ten times more then ere I did,   1029
Ile not be tied to howres, nor pointed times,   1314
*times peec'd, and a womans Crupper of velure, which   1447
But twentie times so much vpon my Wife.   2617

TINKER = 1*1
*Beare-heard, and now by present profession a Tinker.   173
And not a Tinker, nor Christopher Slie.   225

TIRED = *2
Gru. Fie, fie on all tired Iades, on all mad Masters, &   1640
Gru. First know my horse is tired, my master & mi-|stris falne out.
Cur. How?   1688

TIRIAN = 1
My hangings all of *tirian* tapestry: 1231

TIS *l*.79 99 270 *480 491 512 533 562 *563 *596 660 737 744 1117 1170
1184 1186 1191 1199 1221 1224 1259 1288 1338 *1340 *1457 1494 *1536
1538 1599 1696 *1697 1793 1823 1845 1937 1942 1996 2000 2049 2050
2073 2139 2155 2170 2172 2186 2598 2599 2605 2620 *2741
*2750 = 44*9

TITE = 1
And twelue tite Gallies, these I will assure her,   1261

TITLE = 2
Gru. Katherine the curst, | A title for a maide, of all titles the worst.   694

TITLE *cont.*
 And seale the title with a louely kisse. *Exit.*   1506
TITLES = 1
 Gru. Katherine the curst, | A title for a maide, of all titles the worst.   694
TO *see also* t', too, too't = 427*85, 2
 Gre. To cart her rather. She's to rough for mee,   357
 Better once then neuer, for neuer to late. *Exeunt.*   2532
TODAY *see* day
TOES = *1
 *shooes, or such shooes as my toes looke through the o- | uer-leather.   164
TOGETHER = 3*3
 *so great *Hortensio*, but we may blow our nails together,   412
 *how the young folkes lay their heads together.   705
 And where two raging fires meete together,   997
 And to conclude, we haue greed so well together,   1177
 Bio. I haue seene them in the Church together, God   2420
 Gre. Beleeue me sir, they But together well.   2581
TOKEN = 1
 In token of which dutie, if he please, | My hand is readie, may it do
 him ease.   2736
TOKENS = *1
 *to expound the meaning or morrall of his signes and to- | kens.   2265
TOLD = 5*2
 Hortensio, haue you told him all her faults?   752
 'Twas told me you were rough, and coy, and sullen,   1122
 Luc. Hic Ibat, as I told you before, *Simois*, I am Lu- | centio,   1325
 I told you I, he was a franticke foole,   1400
 Bion. I told him that your father was at *Venice*,   2196
 Sir, this is the gentleman I told you of.   2203
 Petr. Nay, I told you your sonne was well beloued in   2406
TOMORROW *see* morrow
TONGUE = 11*1
 With soft lowe tongue, and lowly curtesie,   125
 And make her beare the pennance of her tongue.   393
 But I will charme him first to keepe his tongue.   515
 Renown'd in *Padua* for her scolding tongue,   666
 And do you tell me of a womans tongue?   774
 The one, as famous for a scolding tongue,   826
 Kate. In his tongue? | *Pet.* Whose tongue?   1091
 Pet. What with my tongue in your taile.   1094
 *might freeze to my teeth, my tongue to the roofe of my   1645
 To tame a shrew, and charme her chattering tongue.   1909
 My tongue will tell the anger of my heart,   2062
TONIGHT *see* night
TOO *see also* to = 24*3
 Seeing too much sadnesse hath congeal'd your blood,   286
 Hor. From all such diuels, good Lord deliuer vs. | *Gre.* And me too,
 good Lord.   369
 Kate. Why, and I trust I may go too, may I not?   406
 Bion. The better for him, would I were so too.   546
 And verie rich: but th'art too much my friend,   629
 Ile mend it with a Largesse. Take your paper too,   716
 Gre. You are too blunt, go to it orderly.   906
 *poore petitioners speake too? *Bacare*, you are meruay- | lous forward.   933
 Kate. Too light for such a swaine as you to catch,   1078
 Pet. Come, come you Waspe, y'faith you are too | angrie.   1084
 Kate. No Cocke of mine, you crow too like a crauen   1104

TOO *cont.*

Pet. Now by S.(aint) George I am too yong for you.	1115
Luc. Fidler forbeare, you grow too forward Sir,	1296
Tra. Patience good *Katherine* and *Baptista* too,	1409
Bap. Is it new and olde too? how may that be?	1422
But where is *Kate*? I stay too long from her,	1493
Gru. I feare it is too chollericke a meate.	1997
Gru. I, but the Mustard is too hot a little.	2003
Hor. Signior *Petruchio*, fie you are too blame:	2030
Pet. When you are gentle, you shall haue one too,	And not till then.	2055
And she to him: to stay him not too long,	2212
Tell me sweete *Kate*, and tell me truely too,	2326
Haue at you for a better iest or too.	2588
'Tis ten to one it maim'd you too out right	2605
Gre. I, and a kinde one too:	2633
Luc. I would your dutie were as foolish too:	2682
Too little payment for so great a debt.	2712

TOOKE = 1*2

But art thou not aduis'd, he tooke some care	489
*This mad-brain'd bridegroome tooke him such a cuffe,	1547
*him sops as hee was drinking: This done, hee tooke the	1558

TOOT = 1*1

*yongest free for a husband, and then haue too't afresh:	441
But if you haue a stomacke, too't a Gods name,	760

TOOTH = *1

*tooth in her head, though she haue as manie diseases as	646

TOUCH = 6*1

Hor. Madam, before you touch the instrument,	1357
And heere she stands, touch her who euer dare,	1619
Feare not sweet wench, they shall not touch thee *Kate*,	1624
*presume to touch a haire of my Masters horse-taile, till	1722
And I expressely am forbid to touch it:	1803
And so shall mine before you touch the meate.	2028
Will daigne to sip, or touch one drop of it.	2703

TOUCHD = 1

If loue haue touch'd you, naught remaines but so,	464

TOUCHETH = *1

*parle, know now vpon aduice, it toucheth vs both: that	419

TOWARD = 3*3

Tra. Husht master, heres some good pastime toward;	371
And toward the education of your daughters:	961
Petr. Come on a Gods name, once more toward our	fathers:	2295
My Fathers beares more toward the Market-place,	2390
And by all likelihood some cheere is toward. *Knock.*	2394
Vin. Tis a good hearing, when children are toward.	2741

TOWNE = 3*1

Tra. Master some shew to welcome vs to Towne.	346
Hearing thy mildnesse prais'd in euery Towne,	1062
*Towne Armory, with a broken hilt, and chapelesse: with	1435
While he did beare my countenance in the towne,	2506

TOY = 2

Set foot vnder thy table: tut, a toy,	1284
A knacke, a toy, a tricke, a babies cap:	2051

TOYLE = 1

Vnapt to toyle and trouble in the world,	2724

TRA = 73*13

TRADE = 1
Then hath beene taught by any of my trade,   1362
TRAFFICKE = 1
A Merchant of great Trafficke through the world: 311
TRAINE = *1
*Winde hornes. Enter a Lord from hunting, with his traine.   18
TRAITOR = 1
And gracelesse Traitor to her louing Lord?   2718
TRAN = 1*1
TRANCE = *1
*Tra. Nay, then 'tis time to stirre him fro(m) his trance: 480
TRANIO see also Tra., Tran., Trayno, Triano, Tronio = 37*6
Luc. Tranio, since for the great desire I had   300
And therefore Tranio, for the time I studie,   316
Luc. Gramercies Tranio, well dost thou aduise,   340
Gremio a Pantelowne, Hortentio sister to Bianca. | Lucen. Tranio, stand
by.   348
Maids milde behauiour and sobrietie. | Peace Tranio.   .   374
*Luc. Harke Tranio, thou maist heare Minerua speak.   ·   387
Exeunt ambo. Manet Tranio and Lucentio   448
Luc. Oh Tranio, till I found it to be true,   451
Tranio I burne, I pine, I perish Tranio,   458
Counsaile me Tranio, for I know thou canst: 460
Assist me Tranio, for I know thou wilt.   461
Luc. Tranio, I saw her corrall lips to moue,   477
Luc. Ah Tranio, what a cruell Fathers he: 488
Tra. I marry am I sir, and now 'tis plotted. | Luc. I haue it Tranio.   491
'Tis hatch'd, and shall be so: Tranio at once   512
Luc. Tranio be so, because Lucentio loues,   524
*are you? Maister, ha's my fellow Tranio stolne your   530
Your fellow Tranio heere to saue my life,   535
Luc. And not a iot of Tranio in your mouth,   544
Tranio is chang'd into Lucentio.   545
*When I am alone, why then I am Tranio: but in | all places else, your
master Lucentio.   551
Luc. Tranio let's go: 553
Enter Tranio braue, and Biondello.   786
Luc. Well begun Tranio.   797
Petruchio with Tranio, with his boy | bearing a Lute and Bookes.   898
*Lucentio that comes a wooing, priami, is my man Tra-|nio,   1328
*Enter Baptista, Gremio, Tranio, Katherine, Bianca, and o-|thers,
attendants.   1387
Enter Tranio and Hortensio.   1846
*Bian. Tranio you iest, but haue you both forsworne | mee?   1896
Bianca. He sayes so Tranio.   1904
Luc. And what of him Tranio?   1919
Enter Tranio, and the Pedant drest like Vincentio.   2180
Enter Pedant with seruants, Baptista, Tranio.   2440
Exit Biondello, Tranio and Pedant as fast as may be.   2490
Vin. Where is that damned villaine Tranio,   2500
Made me exchange my state with Tranio,   2505
What Tranio did, my selfe enforst him to;   2509
Bianca. Tranio, Biondello Grumio, and Widdow: 2535
The Seruingmen with Tranio bringing | in a Banquet.   2536
Petr. She hath preuented me, here signior Tranio,   2592
Bap. Oh, oh Petruchio, Tranio hits you now.   2600
Luc. I thanke thee for that gird good Tranio.   2601

TRANIO = 4
TRANSMUTATION = *1
  *Pedler, by education a Cardmaker, by transmutation a   172
TRAPD = 1
  Or wilt thou ride? Thy horses shal be trap'd,   193
TRAUAILE = 1
  Trauaile you farre on, or are you at the farthest?   1928
ΤRAUAILORS = 1
  Like pleasant trauailors to breake a Iest   2371
TRAUELLEST = 1
  Which way thou trauellest, if along with vs,   2349
TRAUELLING = 1
  (Trauelling some iourney) to repose him heere.   81
TRAYNO = 1
  Enter Baptista, Gremio, Trayno.   1155
TREASURE = 3
  For in *Baptistas* keepe my treasure is: 683
  She is your treasure, she must haue a husband,   890
  To decke thy bodie with his ruffling treasure.   2042
TREATS = 1
  Vertue and that part of Philosophie | Will I applie, that treats of happinesse,   317
TREBLE = 1
  Bian. Let's heare, oh fie, the treble iarres.   1332
TREMBLED = *1
  Gre. Trembled and shooke: for why, he stamp'd and   1551
TRENCHERS = 1
  There, take it to you, trenchers, cups, and all: 1797
TRI = 1
  Tri. Oh sir, *Lucentio* slipt me like his Gray-hound,   2595
TRIANO = 1
  Flourish. Enter Lucentio, and his man Triano.   299
TRIBUTE = 1
  And craues no other tribute at thy hands,   2710
TRICKE = 2
  a Christmas gambold, or a tumbling tricke?   292
  A knacke, a toy, a tricke, a babies cap: 2051
TRICKES = 1*1
  *trickes. Ile tell you what sir, and she stand him but a li-|tle,   678
  That teacheth trickes eleuen and twentie long,   1908
TRIE = 2
  Ile trie how you can *Sol, Fa,* and sing it. | *He rings him by the eares*   583
  Kate. That Ile trie. *she strikes him*   1096
TRIMD = 1*1
  On purpose trim'd vp for Semiramis.   191
  *trim'd, rushes strew'd, cobwebs swept, the seruingmen   1682
TRIPE = 1
  How say you to a fat Tripe finely broyl'd?   1998
TRIPOLIE = 1
  And so to Tripolie, if God lend me life.   1931
TRIUMPH = 1
  That triumph thus vpon my misery: 2013
TROBATTO = 1
  Contutti le core bene trobatto, may I say.   592
TROILUS = 1
  Where's my Spaniel *Troilus*? Sirra, get you hence,   1779

TRONIO = 1
his name is *Tronio*.   2461
TROT = *1
*to a Puppet or an Aglet babie, or an old trot with ne're a   645
TROUBLE = 1
Vnapt to toyle and trouble in the world,   2724
TROUBLED = 2*1
*with the glanders, and like to mose in the chine, trou-|bled   1438
Wid. Your housband being troubled with a shrew,   2568
A woman mou'd, is like a fountaine troubled,   2700
TROW = 2
My best beloued and approued friend | *Hortensio*: & I trow this is his
house: 568
Trow you whither I am going? To *Baptista Minola*,   730
TRUE = 8*3
As he shall thinke by our true diligence   74
Lord. 'Tis verie true, thou didst it excellent: 99
Luc. Oh *Tranio*, till I found it to be true,   451
To charge true rules for old inuentions.   1374
Pet. Why thou saist true, it is paltrie cap,   2066
Pet. Why true, he meanes to make a puppet of thee.   2089
Tail. This is true that I say, and I had thee in place   2132
Right true it is your sonne *Lucentio* here   2222
Vinc. But is this true, or is it else your pleasure,   2370
Hor. For both our sakes I would that word were true.   2552
But loue, faire lookes, and true obedience;   2711
TRUELY = 1
Tell me sweete *Kate*, and tell me truely too,   2326
TRUMPET = 1
Sirrah, go see what Trumpet 'tis that sounds,   79
TRUMPETS = 2
And each one to his office when he wakes. | *Sound trumpets*.   77
Loud larums, neighing steeds, & trumpets clangue?   773
TRUNKE = 1
Gru. I confesse the cape. | *Tai*. With a trunke sleeue.   2123
TRUST = 6*1
Trust me, I take him for the better dogge.   28
Kate. Why, and I trust I may go too, may I not?   406
*I know you not, *hic est sigeria tellus*, I trust you not,   1335
Bap. But thus I trust you will not marry her.   1498
Tra. If he be credulous, and trust my tale,   1920
Kate. Why sir I trust I may haue leaue to speake,   2058
Wid. Then neuer trust me if I be affeard.   2554
TRUSTIE = 2
My trustie seruant well approu'd in all,   306
Your ancient trustie pleasant seruant *Grumio*:   613
TRUTH = 1
Petr. Come goe along and see the truth hereof,   2374
TUMBLING = 1
a Christmas gambold, or a tumbling tricke?   292
TUND = 1
His Lecture will be done ere you haue tun'd.   1318
TUNE = 5
Hort. You'll leaue his Lecture when I am in tune?   1319
Luc. That will be neuer, tune your instrument.   1320
Hort. Madam, my Instrument's in tune.   1331
Luc. Spit in the hole man, and tune againe.   1333

TUNE *cont.*
   Hort. Madam, tis now in tune.   1338
TURKY = 1
   Fine Linnen, Turky cushions bost with pearle,   1235
TURND = *1
   *an old ierkin, a paire of old breeches thrice turn'd; a   1432
TURNE = 5
   Fit for her turne, well read in Poetrie   735
   She is not for your turne, the more my greefe.   924
   Now *Kate*, I am a husband for your turne,   1151
   It skills not much, weele fit him to our turne,   1515
   An ancient Angel comming downe the hill, | Wil serue the turne.   1913
TURNES = 1*1
   She's apt to learne, and thankefull for good turnes: 1033
   Kat. He that is giddie thinkes the world turnes round,   2566
TURNS = *1
   Wid. He that is giddie thinks the world turns round. | *Petr.* Roundlie
   replied.   2558
TURPH = 1
   As *Stephen Slie*, and old *Iohn Naps* of Greece, | And *Peter Turph*, and
   Henry Pimpernell,   246
TURTLE = 1*1
   Pet. Oh slow-wing'd Turtle, shal a buzard take thee?   1082
   Kat. I for a Turtle, as he takes a buzard.   1083
TUSH = 2*1
   Hor. Tush *Gremio*: though it passe your patience z   430
   Tush, tush, feare boyes with bugs. | *Gru.* For he feares none.   777
TUT = 4
   Set foot vnder thy table: tut, a toy,   1284
   Call you this gamouth? tut I like it not,   1372
   Gre. Tut, she's a Lambe, a Doue, a foole to him: 1541
   Bion. Tut, feare not me.   2194
TUTORS = 1
   These are their Tutors, bid them vse them well,   975
TUTTI see contutti
TWAINE = 1
   'Tis bargain'd twixt vs twaine being alone,   1184
TWANGLING = *1
   *And twangling Iacke, with twentie such vilde tearmes,   1026
TWAS = 7*1
   'Twas where you woo'd the Gentlewoman so well: 95
   Sincklo. I thinke 'twas *Soto* that your honor meanes.   98
   Although I thinke 'twas in another sense,   521
   'Twas told me you were rough, and coy, and sullen,   1122
   Tra. Twas a commodity lay fretting by you,   1209
   Kate. Patience I pray you, 'twas a fault vnwilling.   1785
   Pet. I tell thee *Kate*, 'twas burnt and dried away,   1802
   'Twas I wonne the wager, though you hit the white,   2745
TWELUE = 2
   And let it be more then *Alcides* twelue.   830
   And twelue tite Gallies, these I will assure her,   1261
TWENTIE = 10*1
   I would not loose the dogge for twentie pound.   24
   And twentie caged Nightingales do sing.   188
   And twentie more such names and men as these, | Which neuer were,
   nor no man euer saw.   248
   And in possession twentie thousand Crownes.   987

TWENTIE cont.
*And twangling Iacke, with twentie such vilde tearmes, 1026
That teacheth trickes eleuen and twentie long, 1908
Signior *Baptista* may remember me | Neere twentie yeares a goe in
Genoa. 2183
Hort. Content, what's the wager? | *Luc.* Twentie crownes. 2613
Petr. Twentie crownes, | Ile venture so much of my Hawke or Hound, 2615
But twentie times so much vpon my Wife. 2617
Vnto their losses twentie thousand crownes, 2668
TWERE = 7
Ladie: would 'twere done. *They sit and marke.* 564
'Twere well for *Kate*, and better for my selfe. 1503
'Twere good me-thinkes to steale our marriage, 1523
And better 'twere that both of vs did fast, 1805
'Twere deadly sicknesse, or else present death. 1992
'Twere good he were school'd. 2190
Imagine 'twere the right *Vincentio.* 2193
TWICE = 2
And twice to day pick'd out the dullest sent, 27
And twice as much what ere thou offrest next. 1262
TWIG = 1
Oh sland'rous world: *Kate* like the hazle twig 1132
TWILL = 2
'Twill bring you gaine, or perish on the seas. 1210
And 'twill be supper time ere you come there. 2173
TWINKE = 1
That in a twinke she won me to her loue. 1190
TWIXT = 5
Why this a heauie chance twixt him and you, 612
Petr. Signior *Hortensio*, 'twixt such friends as wee, 631
'Tis bargain'd twixt vs twaine being alone, 1184
For priuate quarrel 'twixt your Duke and him, 1940
'Twixt me, and one *Baptistas* daughter heere: 1974
TWO *see also* too = 13*6
To pardon me yet for a night or two: 273
Enter Baptista with his two daughters, Katerina & Bianca, 347
*being perhaps (for ought I see) two and thirty, a peepe 600
*two and fiftie horses. Why nothing comes amisse, so | monie comes
withall. 647
Bion. He that ha's the two faire daughters: ist he you | meane? 790
Did you yet euer see *Baptistas* daughter? | *Tra.* No sir, but heare I do
that he hath two: 824
And where two raging fires meete together, 997
Besides, two thousand Duckets by the yeere 1251
Gre. Two thousand Duckets by the yeere of land, 1254
Then three great Argosies, besides two Galliasses 1260
D sol re, one Cliffe, two notes haue I, 1370
*two broken points: his horse hip'd with an olde mo-|thy 1436
*hath two letters for her name, fairely set down in studs, 1448
Ped. Sir at the farthest for a weeke or two, 1929
Gru. I confesse two sleeues. | *Tai.* The sleeues curiously cut. 2125
Kate. I dare assure you sir, 'tis almost two, 2172
As those two eyes become that heauenly face? 2330
Vinc. What if a man bring him a hundred pound or | two to make
merrie withall. 2402
We three are married, but you two are sped. 2744

TYED = 1
And I am tyed to be obedient,   518
VALE = 1
Then vale your stomackes, for it is no boote,   2734
VALLENS = 1
Vallens of Venice gold, in needle worke: 1236
VANTAGE = 1
And watch our vantage in this businesse,   1527
VELUET = 1*1
A Veluet dish: Fie, fie, 'tis lewd and filthy,   2049
*Goddes: oh fine villaine, a silken doublet, a vel-|uet   2444
VELURE = *1
*times peec'd, and a womans Crupper of velure, which   1447
VEN = *1
VENGEANCE = 1
Tra. A vengeance on your crafty withered hide,   1286
VENICE = 5
Giue me thy hand *Kate*, I will vnto *Venice*   1194
I will to *Venice*, sonday comes apace,   1202
Vallens of Venice gold, in needle worke: 1236
Your ships are staid at Venice, and the Duke   1939
Bion. I told him that your father was at *Venice*,   2196
VENT = 1
Hor. Gremio, 'tis now no time to vent our loue,   744
VENTURE = 2
And venture madly on a desperate Mart.   1208
Petr. Twentie crownes, | Ile venture so much of my Hawke or Hound,   2615
VENUTO = 1*1
Hor. Alla nostra casa bene venuto multo honorata signi-|or mio
Petruchio.   593
Petruchio, I shal be your *Been venuto. Exeunt.*   854
VERIE = 8*5
Lord. 'Tis verie true, thou didst it excellent: 99
1.*Man.* Oh yes my Lord, but verie idle words,   236
*her father be verie rich, any man is so verie a foole to be | married to
hell?   428
Beg. 'Tis a verie excellent peece of worke, Madame   563
And verie rich: but th'art too much my friend,   629
Hearke you sir, Ile haue them verie fairely bound,   711
And let me haue them verie wel perfum'd;   717
I know him well: you are verie welcome sir: 968
That feed'st me with the verie name of meate.   2011
Petr. You are verie sencible, and yet you misse my | sence: 2555
Petr. Verie well mended: kisse him for that good | Widdow.   2564
Kate. A verie meane meaning.   2571
VERIEST = 2
Were he the veriest anticke in the world.   111
I thinke thou hast the veriest shrew of all.   2607
VERONA = 5
Petr. Verona, for a while I take my leaue,   566
Grumio, and my good friend *Petruchio*? How do you all | at *Verona*?   589
Blowes you to *Padua* heere, from old *Verona*?   615
Petr. Borne in *Verona,* old *Butonios* sonne: 756
I am a Gentleman of *Verona* sir,   908
VERTUE = 4
Vertue and that part of Philosophie | Will I applie, that treats of
happinesse,   317

VERTUE *cont.*
By vertue specially to be atchieu'd.   319
Onely (good master) while we do admire | This vertue, and this morall
discipline,   328
Her new built vertue and obedience.   2673
VERTUES = 1
Thy vertues spoke of, and thy beautie sounded,   1063
VERTUOUS = 4
To decke his fortune with his vertuous deedes: 315
Pet. And you good sir: pray haue you not a daugh-|ter, cal'd *Katerina,*
faire and vertuous.   903
Vnto *Bianca,* faire and vertuous: 954
To this most patient, sweet, and vertuous wife,   1577
VERY = 7*3
For so your doctors hold it very meete,   285
I will be very kinde and liberall,   402
Gremio. O very well, I haue perus'd the note: 710
Very gratefull, I am sure of it, to expresse   939
And now I finde report a very liar: 1123
For such an iniurie would vexe a very saint,   1417
*in't for a feather: a monster, a very monster in apparell,   1455
Gre. Why hee's a deuill, a deuill, a very fiend.   1539
*eccho: and I seeing this, came thence for very shame, and   1561
*now were I not a little pot, & soone hot; my very lippes   1644
VEXE = 1
For such an iniurie would vexe a very saint,   1417
VICAR = *1
*swore, as if the Vicar meant to cozen him: but after ma-|ny   1552
VID = 1
Shee vi'd so fast, protesting oath on oath,   1189
VIED = 1
By your firme promise, *Gremio* is out vied.   1267
VILDE = 1*1
*And twangling Iacke, with twentie such vilde tearmes,   1026
Oh vilde, intollerable, not to be indur'd: 2646
VILLAINE = 7*6
Petr. Villaine I say, knocke me heere soundly.   573
Petr. Villaine I say, knocke me at this gate,   576
Petr. Now knocke when I bid you: sirrah villaine   586
Petr. A sencelesse villaine: good *Hortensio,*   603
You horson villaine, will you let it fall?   1784
Gru. Villaine, not for thy life: Take vp my Mistresse | gowne for thy
masters vse.   2141
Peda. Lay hands on the villaine, I beleeue a meanes   2417
Vinc. What, you notorious villaine, didst thou neuer | see thy Mistris
father, *Vincentio?*   2430
*Goddes: oh fine villaine, a silken doublet, a vel-|uet   2444
Vin. Thy father: oh villaine, he is a Saile-maker in | *Bergamo.*   2455
*sonne, my sonne: tell me thou villaine, where is my son | *Lucentio?*   2467
Vin. Thus strangers may be haild and abusd: oh mon-|strous villaine.   2486
Vin. Where is that damned villaine *Tranio,*   2500
VILLAINES = 2*1
Off with my boots, you rogues: you villaines, when?   1772
How durst you villaines bring it from the dresser   1795
Vin. Ile slit the villaines nose that would haue sent | me to the Iaile.   2511
VILLANIE = 2
Pet. I there's the villanie.   2127

VILLANIE *cont.*
but I will in to be reueng'd for this villanie. *Exit.*   2516
VIN = 8*8
VINC = 3*3
VINCENTIO see also Vin., Vinc. = 16*4
   Tra. Of *Pisa* sir, sonne to *Vincentio.*   966
   Must get a father, call'd suppos'd *Vincentio,*   1290
   hic est, sonne vnto Vincentio of Pisa, *Sigeria tel-*|*lus,*   1326
   And he shall be *Vincentio* of *Pisa,*   1516
   Ile make him glad to seeme *Vincentio,*   1921
   As if he were the right *Vincentio.*   1923
   Tra. Among them know you one *Vincentio?*   1952
   That you are like to Sir *Vincentio.*   1961
   Enter Tranio, and the Pedant drest like Vincentio.   2180
   Imagine 'twere the right *Vincentio.*   2193
   Enter Vincentio.   2324
   My name is call'd *Vincentio,* my dwelling *Pisa,*   2353
   Let me imbrace with old *Vincentio,*   2367
   Enter Petruchio, Kate, Vincentio, Grumio | with Attendants.   2387
   Vincentio: now wee are vndone and brought to no-|thing.   2422
   Vinc. What, you notorious villaine, didst thou neuer | see thy Mistris
   father, *Vincentio?*   2430
   *he is mine onelie sonne and heire to the Lands of me sig-|nior
   Vincentio.   2463
   *in this businesse: I dare sweare this is the right | Vincentio.   2477
   *Luc. Here's Lucentio, right sonne to the right Vin-|centio,   2495
   *Enter Baptista, Vincentio, Gremio, the Pedant, Lucentio, and   2534
VINCENTIOS = 3
   Vincentio's come of the *Bentiuolij,*   312
   Vincentio's sonne, brought vp in *Florence,*   313
   And be in *Padua* heere *Vincentio's* sonne,   501
VIRGIN = *1
   Kate. Yong budding Virgin, faire, and fresh, & sweet,   2335
VISIT = 2
   Visit his Countrimen, and banquet them?   503
   Pet. Not I, beleeue me, thus Ile visit her.   1497
VISITE = 1
   And bound I am to *Padua,* there to visite   2354
VNABLE = 1
   Come, come, you froward and vnable wormes,   2727
VNAPT = 1
   Vnapt to toyle and trouble in the world,   2724
VNBINDE = 1
   Vnbinde my hands, Ile pull them off my selfe,   859
VNCASE = 1
   Vncase thee: take my Coulord hat and cloake,   513
VNCONSTANT = *1
   Tra. Oh despightful Loue, vnconstant womankind,   1862
VNDER = 2*2
   Set foot vnder thy table: tut, a toy,   1284
   *thou shouldst haue heard how her horse fel, and she vn-|der   1705
   He does it vnder name of perfect loue: 1990
   *to cosen some bodie in this Citie vnder my countenance.   2418
VNDERFOOTE = 1
   Off with that bable, throw it vnderfoote.   2678
VNDERSTAND = 5
   You vnderstand me? | *Bion.* I sir, ne're a whit.   542

VNTIE = 1
I prethee sister Kate, vntie my hands.   876
VNTILL = 2   .
Or if not so, vntill the Sun be set.   274
Vntill the elder sister first be wed.   835
VNTO = 19*4
But sup them well, and looke vnto them all,   31
*2.*H*. It would seem strange vnto him when he wak'd   47
Vnto their Lords, by them accomplished,   123
Lady. I, and the time seeme's thirty vnto me,   268
That none shal haue accesse vnto *Bianca*,   692
Freely giue vnto this yong Scholler, that hath   942
Vnto *Bianca*, faire and vertuous: 954
Giue me thy hand *Kate*, I will vnto *Venice*   1194
hic est, sonne vnto Vincentio of Pisa, *Sigeria tel-*|*lus*,   1326
Vnto a mad-braine rudesby, full of spleene,   1398
To me she's married, not vnto my cloathes: 1500
Tra. Faith he is gone vnto the taming schoole.   1905
Beggers that come vnto my fathers doore,   1982
Much good do it vnto thy gentle heart: 2033
Will we returne vnto thy Fathers house,   2035
*vnto thee, I bid thy Master cut out the gowne, but I did   2112
Pet. Go take it vp vnto thy masters vse.   2140
* *Pet*. Well, come my *Kate*, we will vnto your fathers,   2152
And bring our horses vnto Long-lane end,   2168
And happilie I haue arriued at the last | Vnto the wished hauen of my
blisse: 2507
Let's each one send vnto his wife,   2609
Swinge me them soundly forth vnto their husbands: 2659
Vnto their losses twentie thousand crownes,   2668
VNTOWARD = 1
Then hast thou taught *Hortentio* to be vntoward. *Exit*.   2378
VNUSUALL = 1
As if they saw some wondrous monument, | Some Commet, or vnusuall
prodigie?   1478
VNWILLING = 1
Kate. Patience I pray you, 'twas a fault vnwilling.   1785
VNWORTHIE = 1
As one vnworthie all the former fauours   1878
VOICE = 1
Voice, gate, and action of a Gentlewoman: 144
VOLUBILITY = 1
Then Ile commend her volubility,   1044
VOW = 1
Heere is my hand, and heere I firmly vow   1876
VOWE = 1
Henceforth I vowe it shall be so for me.   2311
VP = 21*5
Then take him vp, and manage well the iest: 49
Lord. Take him vp gently, and to bed with him,   76
*sheere Ale, score me vp for the lyingst knaue in Christen|dome. What
I am not bestraught: here's---   176
On purpose trim'd vp for Semiramis.   191
Nor no such men as you haue reckon'd vp,   245
Vincentio's sonne, brought vp in *Florence*,   313
Gre. Why will you mew her vp | (Signior *Baptista*) for this fiend of hell,   391
To mine owne children, in good bringing vp,   403

VP *cont.*

Began to scold, and raise vp such a storme,	475
And therefore has he closely meu'd her vp,	486
Brought vp as best becomes a Gentlewoman.	653
Haue I not heard the sea, puft vp with windes,	768
Gre. Was euer match clapt vp so sodainly?	1206
And helpe to dresse your sisters chamber vp,	1377
And as he stoop'd againe to take it vp,	1546
Now take them vp quoth he, if any list.	1549
But then vp farther, and as farre as Rome,	1930
Pet. Plucke vp thy spirits, looke cheerfully vpon me.	2019
Petr. Eate it vp all *Hortensio*, if thou louest mee:	2032
What, vp and downe caru'd like an apple Tart?	2074
*the sleeues should be cut out, and sow'd vp againe, and	2129
Pet. Go take it vp vnto thy masters vse.	2140
Gru. Villaine, not for thy life: Take vp my Mistresse | gowne for thy	
masters vse.	2141
Take vp my Mistris gowne to his masters vse. | Oh fie, fie, fie.	2145
*brought him vp euer since he was three yeeres old, and	2460
My Banket is to close our stomakes vp	2546

VPON = 19*6

He cried vpon it at the meerest losse,	26
Wrap'd in sweet cloathes: Rings put vpon his fingers:	42
Vpon my life I am a Lord indeede,	224
And raile vpon the Hostesse of the house,	239
*parle, know now vpon aduice, it toucheth vs both: that	419
I bad the rascall knocke vpon your gate,	604
*thinke scolding would doe little good vpon him. Shee	675
Vpon agreement from vs to his liking,	748
That vpon knowledge of my Parentage,	958
That vpon sonday is the wedding day.	1178
I should be arguing still vpon that doubt,	1348
Vpon my life *Petruchio* meanes but well,	1410
*horse vpon her, how he beat me because her horse stum-|bled,	1708
For then she neuer lookes vpon her lure.	1826
Looke that you take vpon you as you should,	1964
Vpon intreatie haue a present almes,	1983
Kate. A dish that I do loue to feede vpon.	2002
That triumph thus vpon my misery:	2013
Pet. Plucke vp thy spirits, looke cheerfully vpon me.	2019
*that Ile proue vpon thee, though thy little finger be ar-|med in a	
thimble.	2130
No worse then I, vpon some agreement	2215
Biond. You saw my Master winke and laugh vpon | you?	2261
Vpon the companie you ouertake?	2372
to take vpon you another mans name.	2416
But twentie times so much vpon my Wife.	2617

VS *see also* let's *l.*307 342 346 369 *419 *438 748 820 838 *932 991 1034
1184 *1336 1485 1511 1580 1805 2044 2071 2166 2167 2349 2383
*2499 = 20*5

VSE = 6*2

Musicke and Poesie vse, to quicken you,	335
And paint your face, and vse you like a foole.	368
*you vse your manners discreetly in all kind of com-|panies:	550
*sir. Well, was it fit for a seruant to vse his master so,	599
These are their Tutors, bid them vse them well,	975
Pet. Go take it vp vnto thy masters vse.	2140

VSE *cont.*

*Gru. Villaine, not for thy life: Take vp my Mistresse | gowne for thy
masters vse. 2141

Take vp my Mistris gowne to his masters vse. | Oh fie, fie, fie. 2145

VSUALL = 1

Was it not to refresh the minde of man | After his studies, or his vsuall
paine? 1306

VSURPE = 1

I know the boy will wel vsurpe the grace, 143

VTTERETH = 1

And say she vttereth piercing eloquence: 1045

VTTERMOST = 1

Euen to the vttermost as I please in words. 2065

WADED = *1

*how she waded through the durt to plucke him off 1709

WAGER = 5

Shall win the wager which we will propose. 2612

Hort. Content, what's the wager? | *Luc.* Twentie crownes. 2613

The wager thou hast won, and I will adde 2667

Petr. Nay, I will win my wager better yet, 2671

'Twas I wonne the wager, though you hit the white, 2745

WAID = *1

*Staggers, begnawne with the Bots, Waid in the backe, 1442

WAIES = 1*2

*all foule waies: was euer man so beaten? was euer man 1641

Hort. Petruchio, goe thy waies, the field is won. 2320

*Luc. Well go thy waies olde Lad for thou shalt ha't. 2740

WAIGHT = 1

And yet as heauie as my waight should be. 1079

WAIGHTY = 2

Sufficeth my reasons are both good and waighty. 556

Made me acquainted with a waighty cause 2208

WAINING = 1

Then any woman in this waining age. 215

WAITE = 2

Waite you on him, I charge you, as becomes: 540

Luc. Are you so formall sir, well I must waite 1354

WAITES = 1

When *Biondello* comes, he waites on thee, 514

WAKD = 2*1

*2.*H.* It would seem strange vnto him when he wak'd 47

Or when you wak'd, so wak'd as if you slept. 233

WAKES = 3

And braue attendants neere him when he wakes, 44

Procure me Musicke readie when he wakes, 54

And each one to his office when he wakes. | *Sound trumpets.* 77

WAKING = 1

With oathes kept waking, and with brawling fed, 1988

WALK = *1

*Hort. You may go walk, and giue me leaue a while, 1352

WALKE = 5

Say thou wilt walke: wee wil bestrow the ground. 192

Me thinkes you walke like a stranger, 949

We will go walke a little in the Orchard, 976

Oh let me see thee walke: thou dost not halt. 1135

There wil we mount, and thither walke on foote, 2169

WALKED = 1
As he forth walked on his way.   1774
WALLS = 1
Within rich *Pisa* walls, as any one | Old Signior *Gremio* has in *Padua*,   1249
WALNUT-SHELL = 1
Why 'tis a cockle or a walnut-shell,   2050
WALTER = *1
*Call forth *Nathaniel, Ioseph, Nicholas, Phillip, Walter, Su-* |*gersop*   1718
WALTERS = 1
And *Walters* dagger was not come from sheathing: 1762
WANDER = 1
And wander we to see thy honest sonne,   2368
WANDRING = 1
To cast thy wandring eyes on euery stale: 1384
WANT = 2
Let them want nothing that my house affoords. | *Exit one with the*
Players.   114
To want the Bride-groome when the Priest attends   1393
WANTON = 2
And hang it round with all my wanton pictures: 51
Which seeme to moue and wanton with her breath,   204
WANTS = 3
Bap. Neighbours and friends, though Bride & Bride- |(groom wants   1632
You know there wants no iunkets at the feast: 1634
And that which spights me more then all these wants,   1989
WARMD = *1
*2.*Hun*. He breath's my Lord. Were he not warm'd   36
WARME = 4*2
Beg. No, not a deniere: go by S.(aint) *Ieronimie*, goe to thy | cold bed,
and warme thee.   11
Balme his foule head in warme distilled waters,   52
Pet. Am I not wise? | *Kat*. Yes, keepe you warme.   1144
*make a fire, and they are comming after to warme them: 1643
*to thaw me, but I with blowing the fire shall warme my   1647
Whil'st thou ly'st warme at home, secure and safe,   2709
WARNING = 1
The worst is this that at so slender warning,   2242
WARRANT = 3*1
*1.*Hunts*. My Lord I warrant you we wil play our part   73
And other bookes, good ones, I warrant ye.   736
Gre. I warrant him *Petruchio* is Kated.   1631
Ped. I warrant you: but sir here comes your boy,   2189
WARRE = 3
Such warre of white and red within her cheekes: 2328
And time it is when raging warre is come,   2539
To offer warre, where they should kneele for peace: 2720
WAS *see also* 'twas = 25*13
WASH = 1*1
*2.*Man*. Wilt please your mightinesse to wash your | hands: 228
Come *Kate* and wash, & welcome heartily: 1783
WASHT = 1
As morning Roses newly washt with dew: 1042
WASPE = *2
Pet. Come, come you Waspe, y'faith you are too | angrie.   1084
Pet. Who knowes not where a Waspe does weare | his sting? In his
taile.   1089

WASPISH = 1
Kate. If I be waspish, best beware my sting. 1086
WATCH = 8
Pedascule, Ile watch you better yet: 1343
And watch withall, for but I be deceiu'd, 1355
Doth watch *Bianca's* steps so narrowly: 1522
And watch our vantage in this businesse, 1527
That is, to watch her, as we watch these Kites, 1829
And in conclusion, she shal watch all night, 1839
To watch the night in stormes, the day in cold, 2708
WATCHT = 1
Bion. Oh Master, master I haue watcht so long, 1911
WATER = 5
Full of Rose-water, and bestrew'd with Flowers, 60
Gru. Oh I *Curtis* I, and therefore fire, fire, cast on no | water. 1657
Be merrie *Kate*: Some water heere: what hoa. 1777
Enter one with water. 1778
Where are my Slippers? Shall I haue some water? 1782
WATERIE = 1
Shall in despight enforce a waterie eie: 139
WATERS = 1
Balme his foule head in warme distilled waters, 52
WAUING = 1
Euen as the wauing sedges play with winde. 205
WAY = 14*1
I-wis it is not halfe way to her heart: 365
While I make way from hence to saue my life: 541
Tell me I beseech you, which is the readiest way 788
And through the instrument my pate made way, 1022
The dore is open sir, there lies your way, 1596
That stops my way in *Padua: Grumio* 1621
As he forth walked on his way. 1774
*(poore soule) knowes not which way to stand, to looke, 1818
Another way I haue to man my Haggard, 1827
This way the Couerlet, another way the sheets: 1836
This is a way to kil a Wife with kindnesse, 1842
This by the way I let you vnderstand, 1971
Signior *Baptista*, shall I leade the way, 2254
Which way thou trauellest, if along with vs, 2349
WAYES = *1
Horten. Now goe thy wayes, thou hast tam'd a curst | Shrow. 2748
WAYNING = 1
To giue thee all, and in his wayning age 1283
WE = 52*11
WEAKE = 2
Why are our bodies soft, and weake, and smooth, 2723
Our strength as weake, our weakenesse past compare, 2732
WEAKENESSE = 1
Our strength as weake, our weakenesse past compare, 2732
WEALTH = 3
(As wealth is burthen of my woing dance) 634
With wealth enough, and yong and beautious, 652
A Merchant of incomparable wealth. 1954
WEALTHIE = 1
Her dowrie wealthie, and of worthie birth; 2364
WEALTHILY = 2
I come to wiue it wealthily in *Padua*: 641

WEALTHILY *cont.*
   If wealthily, then happily in *Padua*.   642
WEALTHY = 1
   I wil be married to a wealthy Widdow,   1885
WEAPON = 1
   Draw forth thy weapon, we are beset with theeues,   1622
WEARE = 4*3
   And ask him what apparrel he will weare: 64
   3.*Ser.* What raiment wil your honor weare to day.   157
   *me what raiment Ile weare, for I haue no more doub-|lets   161
   Pet. Who knowes not where a Waspe does weare | his sting? In his
   taile.   1089
   Could I repaire what she will weare in me,   1501
   And Gentlewomen weare such caps as these.   2054
   *sir, what cernes it you, if I weare Pearle and gold: I thank   2453
WEARES = 1
   The morning weares, 'tis time we were at Church.   1494
WEARIE = 1
   That I am dogge-wearie, but at last I spied   1912
WEARY = *1
   *so raide? was euer man so weary? I am sent before to   1642
WEATHER = *1
   *selfe: for considering the weather, a taller man then I   1648
WED = 6*1
   *woe her, wed her, and bed her, and ridde the | house of her. Come on.   446
   I would not wed her for a mine of Gold.   658
   Vntill the elder sister first be wed.   835
   If she denie to wed, Ile craue the day   1048
   To wish me wed to one halfe Lunaticke,   1167
   Who woo'd in haste, and meanes to wed at leysure: 1399
   Yet neuer meanes to wed where he hath woo'd: 1405
WEDDED = 1
   That shalbe woo'd, and wedded in a day.   1901
WEDDING = 6*1
   I must dance bare-foot on her wedding day,   891
   That vpon sonday is the wedding day.   1178
   To buy apparell 'gainst the wedding day;   1195
   You know to morrow is the wedding day.   1378
   Bap. Why sir, you know this is your wedding day: 1480
   And haue prepar'd great store of wedding cheere,   1568
   *his wedding garment on? Be the Iackes faire with-|in,   1684
WEE *l.*192 *440 631 *1699 *2422 = 2*3
WEEKE = 2
   As though she bid me stay by her a weeke: 1047
   Ped. Sir at the farthest for a weeke or two,   1929
WEEL = 2
   Or wilt thou sleepe? Wee'l haue thee to a Couch,   189
   Lord. Wee'l shew thee *Io*, as she was a Maid,   206
WEELE = 3
   It skills not much, weele fit him to our turne,   1515
   Weele passe the businesse priuately and well: 2239
   Pet. Come *Kate*, wee'le to bed,   2743
WEELL = 1
   Wee'll ouer-reach the grey-beard *Gremio*,   1528
WEEPE = 2*1
   And at that sight shal sad Apollo weepe,   211
   Talke not to me, I will go sit and weepe,   893

WEEPE *cont.*
*Bap. Goe girle, I cannot blame thee now to weepe,   1416
WEEPES = 1
Bianca stand aside, poore gyrle she weepes: 881
WEEPING = 1
*Kate. Would *Katherine* had neuer seen him though. | *Exit weeping.*   1414
WEIGHT *see* waight
WEIGHTY *see* waighty
WEL = 11*2
*Lo. Huntsman I charge thee, tender wel my hounds,   19
I know the boy will wel vsurpe the grace,   143
Lady. It is a kinde of history. | *Beg.* Well, we'l see't: 295
*A my word, and she knew him as wel as I do, she would   674
And let me haue them verie wel perfum'd;   717
Gre. And you are wel met, Signior *Hortensio.*   729
Hor. Sir you say wel, and wel you do conceiue,   843
Nay then you iest, and now I wel perceiue   874
Bap. Wel go with me, and be not so discomfited.   1031
And for this night we'l fast for companie.   1809
Lou'd me in the World so wel as *Lucentio.*   1861
Tra. Wel sir, to do you courtesie,   1947
WELCOMD = 1
Her sister *Katherine* welcom'd you withall.   1298
WELCOME = 20*2
Now fellowes, you are welcome. | *Players.* We thanke your Honor.   88
And giue them friendly welcome euerie one,   113
Tra. Master some shew to welcome vs to Towne.   346
Keepe house, and ply his booke, welcome his friends,   502
Bap. Y'are welcome sir, and he for your good sake.   922
*Bap. I know him well: you are welcome for his sake.   931
Welcome good *Cambio.* But gentle sir,   948
I may haue welcome 'mongst the rest that woo,   959
I know him well: you are verie welcome sir: 968
And then to dinner: you are passing welcome,   977
Bap. You are welcome sir.   1470
Nat. Welcome home *Grumio.* | *Phil.* How now *Grumio.*   1735
*Gru. Welcome you: how now you: what you: fel-|low   1740
And welcome. Soud, soud, soud, soud.   1769
Come *Kate* and wash, & welcome heartily: 1783
Ped. God saue you sir. | *Tra.* And you sir, you are welcome.   1926
Welcome, one messe is like to be your cheere,   2255
I thinke I shall command your welcome here;   2393
My faire *Bianca* bid my father welcome,   2541
While I with selfesame kindnesse welcome thine: 2542
Feast with the best, and welcome to my house,   2545
You are welcome all. *Exit Bianca.*   2591
WELKIN = 1
Thy hounds shall make the Welkin answer them   197
WELL = 66*11
But sup them well, and looke vnto them all,   31
Then take him vp, and manage well the iest: 49
'Twas where you woo'd the Gentlewoman so well: 95
Well you are come to me in happie time,   100
An Onion wil do well for such a shift,   137
May well abate the ouer-merrie spleene,   149
Well, bring our Ladie hither to our sight,   226
Beg. Marrie I fare well, for heere is cheere enough.   255

WELL *cont.*

Beg. I know it well, what must I call her? | *Lord.* Madam.	262
Lady. It is a kinde of history. | *Beg.* Well, we'l see't:	295
My trustie seruant well approu'd in all,	306
Luc. Gramercies *Tranio*, well dost thou aduise,	340
Because I know you well, and loue you well,	355
Tra. Well said Mr, mum, and gaze your fill.	376
Because so well I loue *Lucentio*.	523
And rap me well, or Ile knocke your knaues pate.	577
*sir. Well, was it fit for a seruant to vse his master so,	599
*out? Whom would to God I had well knockt at first,	601
*heere: knocke me well, and knocke me soundly? And	608
And he knew my deceased father well:	668
Well seene in Musicke, to instruct *Bianca*,	699
Gremio. O very well, I haue perus'd the note:	710
And by good fortune I haue lighted well	733
Fit for her turne, well read in Poetrie	735
Hor. 'Tis well: and I haue met a Gentleman	737
Gre. So said, so done, is well:	751
Luc. Well begun *Tranio*.	797
Then well one more may faire *Bianca* haue;	817
So well I know my dutie to my elders.	862
A man well knowne throughout all Italy.	930
*Bap. I know him well: you are welcome for his sake.	931
I know him well: you are verie welcome sir:	968
These are their Tutors, bid them vse them well,	975
You knew my father well, and in him me,	981
Bap. I, when the speciall thing is well obtain'd,	993
*Bap. Well maist thou woo, and happy be thy speed:	1003
*Kate. Well haue you heard, but something hard of | hearing:	1053
Kate. Well tane, and like a buzzard.	1081
Kate. Well aym'd of such a yong one.	1114
Thy beauty that doth make me like thee well,	1153
Pet. How but well sir? how but well?	1162
And to conclude, we haue greed so well together,	1177
Tra. That only came well in: sir, list to me,	1245
Gre. And may not yong men die as well as old?	1273
Bap. Well gentlemen, I am thus resolu'd,	1274
Luc. Are you so formall sir, well I must waite	1354
Vpon my life *Petruchio* meanes but well,	1410
Petr. And yet I come not well. | *Bap.* And yet you halt not.	1471
Tra. Not so well apparell'd as I wish you were.	1473
As you shall well be satisfied with all.	1492
'Twere well for *Kate*, and better for my selfe.	1503
The meate was well, if you were so contented.	1801
Kate. I like it well, good Grumio fetch it me.	1999
I loue thee well in that thou lik'st it not.	2068
Tai. You bid me make it orderlie and well,	2079
Pet. Well sir in breefe the gowne is not for me.	2138
*Pet. Well, come my *Kate*, we will vnto your fathers,	2152
And well we may come there by dinner time.	2171
Tis well, and hold your owne in any case	2186
Signior *Baptista*, of whom I heare so well.	2219
Your plainnesse and your shortnesse please me well:	2221
Weele passe the businesse priuately and well:	2239
Bap. It likes me well:	2244
*Petr. Well, forward, forward, thus the bowle should | (run,	2321

WHATSOERE = 1
And beare his charge of wooing whatsoere.   783
WHATSOEUER = 1
In all my Lands and Leases whatsoeuer,   990
WHEN *l*.44 *47 54 68 77 147 233 473 514 *551 586 662 885 993 1019 1038
    1049 1107 1192 1302 1319 1393 1428 *1429 1505 1542 1550 *1717 1771
    1772 2055 2316 2539 2611 2715 2722 *2741 *2742 = 33*6
WHENCE = 2*1
    Bap. Why how now Dame, whence growes this in-|solence?   879
    Whence are you sir? What may I call your name.   928
    Bap. Lucentio is your name, of whence I pray.   965
WHERE *l*.95 256 338 528 *529 618 997 1088 *1089 1141 1321 1405 *1429
    *1469 1475 1493 *1747 1749 1754 1767 1768 1782 1794 1814 2133 2185
    *2230 2325 2433 *2467 2494 2500 2656 2675 2720 = 29*8
WHEREBY = 1
For by this light, whereby I see thy beauty,   1152
WHEREFORE = 2
    And wherefore gaze this goodly company,   1477
    She will be pleas'd, then wherefore should I doubt: 2291
WHEREIN = 3
    Wherein your cunning can assist me much.   102
    Wherein your Ladie, and your humble wife,   127
    wherein she delights, I will wish him to her father.   416
WHEREOF = 2
    Tranio. Sir, I shal not be slacke, in signe whereof,   847
    Whereof I know she is not ignorant,   919
WHERES = 3*1
    If you should die before him, where's her dower?   1271
    *cold. Where's the Cooke, is supper ready, the house   1681
    Where's my Spaniel *Troilus*? Sirra, get you hence,   1779
    Yours will not be entreated: Now, where's my wife?   2642
WHETHER = 2
Whether away, or whether is thy aboade?   2336
WHICH *l*.138 150 204 249 290 788 867 914 983 1252 1312 *1444 *1447
    1491 1512 1524 *1713 *1818 1886 1989 2349 2355 2596 2612 2733
    2736 = 22*4
WHILE = 15*4
    Onely (good master) while we do admire | This vertue, and this morall
    discipline,   328
    But stay a while, what companie is this?   345
    But see, while idely I stood looking on,   453
    While I make way from hence to saue my life: 541
    Petr. Verona, for a while I take my leaue,   566
    Gru. I pray you Sir let him go while the humor lasts.   673
    Petruchio stand by a while.   708
    You haue but iested with me all this while: 875
    And there I stood amazed for a while,   1023
    While she did call me Rascall, Fidler,   1025
    And while I pause, serue in your harmony.   1309
    Hort. You may go walk, and giue me leaue a while,   1352
    Luc. While you sweet deere proue Mistresse of my | heart.   1857
    Gre. I maruaile *Cambio* comes not all this while.   2386
    *vndone, I am vndone: while I plaie the good husband   2446
    While counterfeit supposes bleer'd thine eine.   2498
    While he did beare my countenance in the towne,   2506
    While I with selfesame kindnesse welcome thine: 2542
    And while it is so, none so dry or thirstie   2702

WHILES = 2
Take you your instrument, play you the whiles,   1317
You may be iogging whiles your bootes are greene: 1597
WHILST = 3
If whil'st I liue she will be onely mine.   1244
As thou shalt thinke on prating whil'st thou liu'st: 2099
Whil'st thou ly'st warme at home, secure and safe,   2709
WHIPT = *1
*with this condition; To be whipt at the hie crosse euerie | morning.   435
WHIRLEWINDS = *1
*Confounds thy fame, as whirlewinds shake faire budds,   2698
WHIT = 3
You vnderstand me? | *Bion.* I sir, ne're a whit.   542
So shal I no whit be behinde in dutie   740
Pet. No, not a whit, I finde you passing gentle: 1121
WHITE = 2*1
*in their new fustian, the white stockings, and euery offi- | cer   1683
Such warre of white and red within her cheekes: 2328
'Twas I wonne the wager, though you hit the white,   2745
WHITHER *see also* whether = 1
Trow you whither I am going? To *Baptista Minola,*   730
WHO *l.*83 133 500 580 *706 896 *1089 1399 1450 1462 1619 1651 1729
1791 1985 1991 2369 *2421 2621 = 16*3
WHOEUER *see* ouer
WHOLSOME *see* holsome
WHOM *l.*571 *601 719 747 813 832 846 864 1136 2219 2338 = 9*2
WHOS = *1
Pet. Come, where be these gallants? who's at home?   1469
WHOSE = 4*1
Whose sodaine sight hath thral'd my wounded eye.   526
For our accesse, whose hap shall be to haue her,   841
Kate. In his tongue? | *Pet.* Whose tongue.   1091
*or shall I complaine on thee to our mistris, whose hand   1667
And he whose wife is most obedient,   2610
WHY *l.*25 *244 382 391 406 *431 *551 *555 *574 612 *644 *647 *676 765
803 *879 884 995 1008 *1015 1016 1039 1070 1100 *1108 1131 *1164
*1266 1305 *1311 1364 *1423 1425 *1431 1460 1465 1480 1538 1539
1540 *1551 *1665 *1677 *1680 1703 1728 1734 1771 *2004 2008 2048
2050 2058 2066 2071 2077 *2089 *2114 2143 2179 *234) *2415 *2452
2502 *2527 2723 *2738 = 39*29
WID = 6*2
WIDDOW see also Wid. = 9
I wil be married to a wealthy Widdow,   1885
Tra. I'faith hee'l haue a lustie Widdow now,   1900
Haue to my Widdow, and if she froward,   2377
Bianca. Tranio, Biondello Grumio, and Widdow: 2535
Brother *Petruchio,* sister *Katerina,* | And thou *Hortentio* with thy louing
Widdow: 2543
Hor. My Widdow saies, thus she conceiues her tale.   2563
Petr. Verie well mended: kisse him for that good | Widdow.   2564
Petr. To her *Kate.* | *Hor.* To her *Widdow.*   2574
Enter Kate, Bianca, and Widdow.   2674
WIDDOW-HOOD = 1
Her widdow-hood, be it that she suruiue me   989
WIDOW = 1
Pet. Now for my life *Hortentio* feares his Widow.   2553

WIFE = 29*3
WIL *l*.58 71 *73 137 157 192 *201 *281 467 669 672 *679 690 719 764 776
784 842 861 872 *1223 1810 1873 1885 1914 1948 1959 1968 *2005 2063
2169 *2750 = 26*7
WILDE = 1
WILDE-CAT = 1
WILL *see also* hee'l, hee'll, Ile, she'l, 'twill, wee'l, weele, we'l, you'l,
you'll *l*.*10 33 40 64 103 120 126 143 146 *195 *258 *291 318 358 380
388 391 398 402 *411 416 *417 487 496 510 515 581 595 650 661 749
762 763 *801 820 834 861 889 893 937 976 1000 *1011 1034 1043 1076
1103 1127 1150 1160 1175 1194 1197 1200 1202 1203 1204 1244 1261
1310 1318 1320 1386 1392 1428 1491 1498 1501 1508 1571 1594 1602
1615 1649 1784 1788 1830 2035 2057 2059 2062 2064 2070 *2111 *2152
2165 2177 2179 2226 2247 2256 2290 2291 2318 *2333 2369 *2435 *2515
2516 *2518 2523 *2529 2612 2622 2642 2644 2645 2651 2667 2671 *2689
2703 = 99*16, 7

WILL *cont.*

And not obedient to his honest will,	2716

WILLING = 1

Me shall you finde readie and willing	2216

WILLINGLY = 1

Gre. As willingly as ere I came from schoole.	1534

WILT *l.**187 189 192 193 196 *199 461 *1666 1678 2007 2147 = 8*3, 1*3

And say wilt please your Lordship coole your hands.	62
*1.*Ser.* Wilt please your Lord drink a cup of sacke?	154
*2.*Ser.* Wilt please your Honor taste of these Con- | serues?	155
*2.*Man.* Wilt please your mightinesse to wash your | hands:	228

WIN = 6

Tell him from me (as he will win my loue)	120
Gremio. And so we wil, prouided that he win her.	784
'Tis deeds must win the prize, and he of both	1224
Shal win my loue, and so I take my leaue,	1890
Shall win the wager which we will propose.	2612
Petr. Nay, I will win my wager better yet,	2671

WINCOT = *1

*Aske *Marrian Hacket* the fat Alewife of Wincot, if shee	174

WIND = *1

**Petr.* Such wind as scatters yongmen throgh y world,	616

WINDE = 2*1

**Winde hornes. Enter a Lord from hunting, with his traine.*	18
Euen as the wauing sedges play with winde.	205
Though little fire growes great with little winde,	999

WINDEGALLS = *1

*of Windegalls, sped with Spauins, raied with the Yel- |lowes,	1440

WINDES = 2

Haue I not heard the sea, puft vp with windes,	768
Pet. I to the proofe, as Mountaines are for windes,	1005

WINDOW = 3

Pedant lookes out of the window.	2397
here looking out at the window.	2412
marie sir see where he lookes out of the window.	2433

WINE = *1

*ceremonies done, hee calls for wine, a health quoth	1553

WINGD = *1

**Pet.* Oh slow-wing'd Turtle, shal a buzard take thee?	1082

WINKE = *1

**Biond.* You saw my Master winke and laugh vpon | you?	2261

WINNER = 1

And being a winner, God giue you good night. | *Exit Petruchio*	2746

WINTER = 1*1

*know'st winter tames man, woman, and beast: for it	1661
Thou Flea, thou Nit, thou winter cricket thou:	2095

WISDOME = 1

The wisdome of your dutie faire *Bianca*,	2683

WISE = 2

Pet. Am I not wise? | *Kat.* Yes, keepe you warme.	1144
Though he be blunt, I know him passing wise,	1412

WISH = 5*1

wherein she delights, I will wish him to her father.	416
**Tra.* So could I 'faith boy, to haue the next wish af- |ter,	547
And wish thee to a shrew'd ill-fauour'd wife?	626
And Ile not wish thee to her.	630
To wish me wed to one halfe Lunaticke,	1167

WISH *cont.*
Tra. Not so well apparell'd as I wish you were.   1473
WISHED = 1
And happilie I haue arriued at the last | Vnto the wished hauen of my
blisse: 2507
WIT = 3
Oh how we ioy to see your wit restor'd,   230
That hearing of her beautie, and her wit,   909
Petr. It is *extempore*, from my mother wit.   1142
WITH = 147*41
WITHALL = 8*2
*two and fiftie horses. Why nothing comes amisse, so | monie comes
withall.   647
*with it, that shee shal haue no more eies to see withall | then a Cat:
you know him not sir.   680
Her sister *Katherine* welcom'd you withall.   1298
And watch withall, for but I be deceiu'd,   1355
Though he be merry, yet withall he's honest.   1413
That I haue fondly flatter'd them withall.   1879
Biond. I praie the gods she may withall my heart. | *Exit.*   2250
Petr. Do good old grandsire, & withall make known   2348
Ped. He's within sir, but not to be spoken withall.   2401
Vinc. What if a man bring him a hundred pound or | two to make
merrie withall.   2402
WITHERD = 1
Kate. Yet you are wither'd.   1116
WITHERED = 2
Tra. A vengeance on your crafty withered hide,   1286
This is a man old, wrinckled, faded, withered,   2341
WITHIN = 8*2
Schoolemasters will I keepe within my house,   398
Within your house, to make mine eye the witnesse   913
You shall go see your Pupils presently. | Holla, within.   970
Gre. First, as you know, my house within the City   1228
Within rich *Pisa* walls, as any one | Old Signior *Gremio* has in *Padua,*   1249
*his wedding garment on? Be the Iackes faire with-|in,   1684
Such warre of white and red within her cheekes: 2328
Grem. They're busie within, you were best knocke | lowder.   2395
Vin. Is Signior *Lucentio* within sir?   2400
Ped. He's within sir, but not to be spoken withall.   2401
WITHOUT = 4*2
Gremio. No: if without more words you will get you | hence.   801
*the Gils faire without, the Carpets laide, and euerie | thing in order?   1685
Gru. Why then the Mustard without the beefe.   2008
For you shall hop without my custome sir: 2084
It shall goe hard if *Cambio* goe without her. *Exit.*   2293
daughter without asking my good will?   2514
WITH-HOLDS = 1
And her with-holds from me. Other more   686
WITLESSE = 1
Kate. A witty mother, witlesse else her sonne.   1143
WITNESSE = 3*1
Within your house, to make mine eye the witnesse   913
Then words can witnesse, or your thoughts can guesse.   1217
And since mine eyes are witnesse of her lightnesse,   1872
Gre. Here's packing with a witnesse to deceiue vs all.   2499

WITNESSES = 2
   Gre. Tra. Amen say we, we will be witnesses. 1200
   Priest, Clarke, and some sufficient honest witnesses: 2280
WITS = *1
   *Bend thoughts and wits to atcheeue her. Thus it stands: 482
WITTED = 2
   Bap. How likes *Gremio* these quicke witted folkes? 2580
   Bian. Head, and but an hastie witted bodie, 2582
WITTY = 1
   Kate. A witty mother, witlesse else her sonne. 1143
WIUE = 2
   Happily to wiue and thriue, as best I may: 622
   I come to wiue it wealthily in *Padua*: 641
WIUES = 1
   See where she comes, and brings your froward Wiues 2675
WOE = 1*1
   *woe her, wed her, and bed her, and ridde the | house of her. Come on. 446
   Measures my husbands sorrow by his woe: 2569
WOING = 2*1
   *best horse in *Padua* to begin his woing that would tho-|roughly 445
   (As wealth is burthen of my woing dance) 634
   Doe get their children: but in this case of woing, 1292
WOMAN = 4*2
   Then any woman in this waining age. 215
   I see a woman may be made a foole 1606
   *know'st winter tames man, woman, and beast: for it 1661
   Hort. A will make the man mad to make the woman | of him. 2333
   A woman mou'd, is like a fountaine troubled, 2700
   Euen such a woman oweth to her husband: 2714
WOMANKIND = *1
   Tra. Oh despightful Loue, vnconstant womankind, 1862
WOMANLIE = 1
   As prisoners to her womanlie perswasion: 2676
WOMANS = 3*1
   And if the boy haue not a womans guift 135
   Beg. I, the womans maide of the house. 243
   And do you tell me of a womans tongue? 774
   *times peec'd, and a womans Crupper of velure, which 1447
WOMEN = 4*2
   Pet. Women are made to beare, and so are you. 1074
   How tame when men and women are alone, 1192
   Kindnesse in women, not their beauteous lookes 1889
   *women, what dutie they doe owe their Lords and hus-|bands. 2687
   I am asham'd that women are so simple, 2719
   Luc. But a harsh hearing, when women are froward, 2742
WON = 3
   That in a twinke she won me to her loue. 1190
   Hort. Petruchio, goe thy waies, the field is won. 2320
   The wager thou hast won, and I will adde 2667
WONDER = 6*1
   And that's a wonder: fathers commonly 1291
   Make it no wonder: if you knew my businesse, 1573
   Thy Sonne by this hath married: wonder not, 2362
   Luc. Here is a wonder, if you talke of a wonder. 2661
   Hor. And so it is: I wonder what it boads. 2662
   Luc. Tis a wonder, by your leaue, she wil be tam'd so. 2750

WONDERFULL = 2
 That wench is starke mad, or wonderfull froward.   372
 I tel thee *Lisio* this is wonderfull.   1863
WONDROUS = 2
 Her wondrous qualities, and milde behauiour,   911
 As if they saw some wondrous monument, | Some Commet, or vnusuall
 prodigie?   1478
WONNE = 1
 'Twas I wonne the wager, though you hit the white,   2745
WOO *see also* woe = 9*1
 Will vndertake to woo curst *Katherine*,   749
 But will you woo this Wilde-cat? | *Petr.* Will I liue?   762
 Gru. Wil he woo her? I: or Ile hang her.   764
 I may haue welcome 'mongst the rest that woo,   959
 And euerie day I cannot come to woo,   980
 For I am rough, and woo not like a babe.   1002
 Bap. Well maist thou woo, and happy be thy speed: 1003
 And woo her with some spirit when she comes,   1038
 My selfe am moou'd to woo thee for my wife.   1065
 Neuer to woo her more, but do forsweare her   1877
WOOD = 6*1
 And burne sweet Wood to make the Lodging sweete: 53
 'Twas where you woo'd the Gentlewoman so well: 95
 3.Man. Or *Daphne* roming through a thornie wood,   209
 That euer *Katherina* wil be woo'd: 690
 Who woo'd in haste, and meanes to wed at leysure: 1399
 Yet neuer meanes to wed where he hath woo'd: 1405
 That shalbe woo'd, and wedded in a day.   1901
WOODCOCKE = 1
 Gru. Oh this Woodcocke, what an Asse it is. | *Petru.* Peace sirra.   726
WOOE = 1
 Hee'll wooe a thousand, point the day of marriage,   1403
WOOERS = 2*1
 *To make one among these wooers: if thou ask me why,   555
 Faire *Laedaes* daughter had a thousand wooers,   816
 But thou with mildnesse entertain'st thy wooers,   1129
WOOING *see also* woing = 2*1
 And beare his charge of wooing whatsoere.   783
 Your wooing neighbors: this is a guift   938
 *Lucentio that comes a wooing, *priami*, is my man Tra-|nio,   1328
WOONES = 1
 I, by goggs woones quoth he, and swore so loud,   1544
WORD = 10*3
 Hor. So will I signiour *Gremio*: but a word I pray: 417
 *A my word, and she knew him as wel as I do, she would   674
 Hor. Sir, a word ere you go: 798
 When did she crosse thee with a bitter word?   885
 And with that word she stroke me on the head,   1021
 Say she be mute, and will not speake a word,   1043
 What euer fortune stayes him from his word,   1411
 Sufficeth I am come to keepe my word,   1489
 What, not a word? Nay then, thou lou'st it not: 2023
 Hor. For both our sakes I would that word were true.   2552
 Bio. Sir, my Mistris sends you word   2629
 To bandie word for word, and frowne for frowne;   2730
WORDS = 9*3
 1.Man. Oh yes my Lord, but verie idle words,   236

WORDS *cont.*

*these words plaine? Sirra, Knocke me heere: rappe me	607
Few words suffice: and therefore, if thou know	632
Yea and perhaps with more successefull words	723
Gremio. No: if without more words you will get you | hence.	801
Petr. Hortensio, to what end are all these words?	822
But be thou arm'd for some vnhappie words.	1004
Then words can witnesse, or your thoughts can guesse.	1217
Pet. Good sooth euen thus: therefore ha done with | (words,	1499
Euen to the vttermost as I please in words.	2065
Take no vnkindnesse of his hastie words:	2150
*your habit: but your words shew you a mad man: why	2452

WORKE = 2*1

Beg. 'Tis a verie excellent peece of worke, Madame	563
Vallens of Venice gold, in needle worke:	1236
Gre. I marry sir, now it begins to worke.	1604

WORKMANLIE = 1

So workmanlie the blood and teares are drawne.	212

WORLD = 17*8

*in with *Richard Conqueror*: therefore *Pau-!cas pallabris*, let the world slide: Sessa.	8
Were he the veriest anticke in the world.	111
She was the fairest creature in the world,	218
And let the world slip, we shall nere be yonger.	298
A Merchant of great Trafficke through the world:	311
*good fellowes in the world, and a man could light on	432
Petr. Such wind as scatters yongmen throgh y world,	616
And so am come abroad to see the world.	624
Pet. Now by the world, it is a lustie Wench,	1028
Why does the world report that *Kate* doth limpe?	1131
Oh sland'rous world: *Kate* like the hazle twig	1132
Pet. Father, 'tis thus, your selfe and all the world	1170
Oh you are nouices, 'tis a world to see	1191
Tra. Why then the maid is mine from all the world	1266
Now must the world point at poore *Katherine*,	1406
Bion. Oh sir, his Lackey, for all the world Capari-|son'd	1451
Which once perform'd, let all the world say no,	1524
Ile keepe mine owne despite of all the world.	1525
Cur. I prethee good *Grumio*, tell me, how goes the | world?	1670
Gru. A cold world *Curtis* in euery office but thine, z	1672
Lou'd me in the World so wel as *Lucentio*.	1861
Hor. Would all the world but he had quite forsworn	1883
Wid. He that is giddie thinks the world turns round. | *Petr.* Roundlie replied.	2558
Kat. He that is giddie thinkes the world turnes round,	2566
Vnapt to toyle and trouble in the world,	2724

WORMES = 1

Come, come, you froward and vnable wormes,	2727

WORSE = 7

As *Socrates Zentippe*, or a worse:	637
Ped. Alas sir, it is worse for me then so,	1944
Oh no good *Kate*: neither art thou the worse	2162
No worse then I, vpon some agreement	2215
Praie God sir your wife send you not a worse. | *Petr.* I hope better.	2634
Petr. Worse and worse, she will not come:	2645

WORSER = 1

That were my state farre worser then it is,	657

WORSHIP = 5
any man ha's rebus'd your worship?   572
As before imparted to your worship,   1513
Fel. Heere is the cap your Worship did bespeake.   2047
Tail. She saies your Worship meanes to make a | puppet of her.   2090
Tail. Your worship is deceiu'd, the gowne is made   2101
WORSHIPFULL = *1
Bion. What my old worshipfull old master? yes   2432
WORST = 5
And then I know after who comes by the worst.   580
then had not *Grumio* come by the worst.   602
Gru. *Katherine* the curst, | A title for a maide, of all titles the worst.   694
And thinke it not the worst of all your fortunes,   1960
The worst is this that at so slender warning,   2242
WORTH = 2
I would esteeme him worth a dozen such: 30
If you accept them, then their worth is great: 964
WORTHIE = 1
Her dowrie wealthie, and of worthie birth;   2364
WORTHLES = *1
Lord. Euen as a flatt'ring dreame, or worthles fancie.   48
WORTHY = *1
*things of worthy memorie, which now shall die in obli- | uion,   1713
WOULD *l*.24 30 45 *47 150 *170 238 240 242 *280 *433 *444 *445 546
564 *601 658 *674 *675 782 785 *935 1112 1408 *1414 1417 1481 1574
1881 *1883 *2398 *2511 *2552 2583 2682 = 20*15
WOUND = 1
To wound thy Lord, thy King, thy Gouernour.   2696
WOUNDED = 1
Whose sodaine sight hath thral'd my wounded eye.   526
WRANGLING = 1
Hort. But wrangling pedant, this is | The patronesse of heauenly
harmony: 1299
WRAPD = 1
Wrap'd in sweet cloathes: Rings put vpon his fingers: 42
WRETCH = 1
A meacocke wretch can make the curstest shrew: 1193
WRINCKLED = 1
This is a man old, wrinckled, faded, withered,   2341
WRITING = 1
And there it is in writing fairely drawne.   1363
WRONG = 4*4
Bian. Good sister wrong me not, nor wrong your self,   856
Why dost thou wrong her, that did nere wrong thee?   884
Pet. You wrong me signior *Gremio*, giue me leaue.   907
Accept of him, or else you do me wrong.   920
Bianc. Why gentlemen, you doe me double wrong,   1311
Ka. The more my wrong, the more his spite appears.   1980
WROUGHT = 1
Luc. Loue wrought these miracles. *Biancas* loue   2504
XIIIID = *1
*know me not: if she say I am not xiiii.d. on the score for   175
Y = *1
Petr. Such wind as scatters yongmen throgh y world,   616
YARD = 4
Thou yard three quarters, halfe yard, quarter, naile,   2094
Or I shall so be-mete thee with thy yard,   2098

YARD *cont.*
me thy meat-yard, and spare not me.   2135
YARE = 1*1
Beg. Y'are a baggage, the *Slies* are no   6
Bap. Y'are welcome sir, and he for your good sake.   922
YE *l.*238 394 736 848 = 4
YEA = 5
Yea and perhaps with more successefull words   723
Yea, and to marrie her, if her dowrie please.   750
Are you a sutor to the Maid you talke of, yea or no?   799
Gre. Yea, leaue that labour to great *Hercules*,   829
Yea all my raiment, to my petticoate,   860
YEARE = 1
And slept aboue some fifteene yeare or more.   267
YEARES = 2
Who for this seuen yeares hath esteemed him   133
Signior *Baptista* may remember me | Neere twentie yeares a goe in
Genoa.   2183
YEELDS = 1
So I to her, and so she yeelds to me,   1001
YEERE = 2
Besides, two thousand Duckets by the yeere   1251
Gre. Two thousand Duckets by the yeere of land,   1254
YEERES = 2*2
These fifteene yeeres you haue bin in a dreame,   232
Beg. These fifteene yeeres, by my fay, a goodly nap,   234
My selfe am strooke in yeeres I must confesse,   1242
*brought him vp euer since he was three yeeres old, and   2460
YELLOWES = *1
*of Windegalls, sped with Spauins, raied with the Yel-|lowes,   1440
YES = 4*2
1.*Man.* Oh yes my Lord, but verie idle words,   236
Luc. Oh yes, I saw sweet beautie in her face,   470
Beg. Yes by Saint Anne do I, a good matter surely: 560
Pet. Am I not wise? | *Kat.* Yes, keepe you warme.   1144
Bion. What my old worshipfull old master? yes   2432
Gre. Yes, I know thee to be signior *Lucentio*.   2483
YET = 29*4
For yet his honor neuer heard a play)   106
And yet shee is inferiour to none.   219
Yet would you say, ye were beaten out of doore,   238
To pardon me yet for a night or two: 273
That I should yet absent me from your bed: 277
*Farewell: yet for the loue I beare my sweet *Bianca*, if   414
*Though the nature of our quarrell yet neuer brook'd   418
*we may yet againe haue accesse to our faire Mistris, and   420
We haue not yet bin seene in any house,   505
And yet Ile promise thee she shall be rich,   628
Did you yet euer see *Baptistas* daughter? | *Tra*. No sir, but heare I do
that he hath two: 824
I neuer yet beheld that speciall face,   866
Yet extreme gusts will blow out fire and all: 1000
Yet not so deepely as to thee belongs,   1064
And yet as heauie as my waight should be.   1079
Kate. Yet you are wither'd.   1116
But slow in speech: yet sweet as spring-time flowers.   1125
Yet I haue fac'd it with a card of ten: 1287

YET *cont.*

Pedascule, Ile watch you better yet:	1343
In time I may beleeue, yet I mistrust.	1344
Hor. Yet read the gamouth of *Hortentio.*	1365
Yet if thy thoughts *Bianca* be so humble	1383
And yet we heare not of our sonne in Law:	1391
Yet neuer meanes to wed where he hath woo'd:	1405
Though he be merry, yet withall he's honest.	1413
Yet oftentimes he goes but meane apparel'd.	1458
a man is more then one, and yet not many.	1467
Petr. And yet I come not well. | *Bap.* And yet you halt not.	1471
But yet not stay, entreat me how you can.	1588
Yet as they are, heere are they come to meete you.	1765
**Petr.* You are verie sencible, and yet you misse my | sence:	2555
Petr. Nay, I will win my wager better yet,	2671

YFAITH = *1

**Pet.* Come, come you Waspe, y'faith you are too | angrie.	1084

YIELDE *see* yeelde

YONDER = *1

**Bion.* Oh we are spoil'd, and yonder he is, denie him,	2488

YONG = 9*1

If I atchieue not this yong modest gyrle:	459
With wealth enough, and yong and beautious,	652
On this yong man: For learning and behauiour	734
Freely giue vnto this yong Scholler, that hath	942
For knowing thee to be but yong and light.	1077
Kate. Well aym'd of such a yong one.	1114
Pet. Now by S.(aint) George I am too yong for you.	1115
Gre. And may not yong men die as well as old?	1273
Sirra, yong gamester, your father were a foole	1282
**Kate.* Yong budding Virgin, faire, and fresh, & sweet,	2335

YONGER = 5

And let the world slip, we shall nere be yonger.	298
The yonger then is free, and not before.	836
Atchieue the elder: set the yonger free,	840
Proceed in practise with my yonger daughter,	1032
But now *Baptista,* to your yonger daughter,	1213

YONGEST = 3*2

That is, not to bestow my yongest daughter,	352
*yongest free for a husband, and then haue too't afresh:	441
*that *Lucentio* indeede had *Baptistas* yongest daugh-|ter.	548
His yongest daughter, beautiful *Bianca,*	685
The yongest daughter whom you hearken for,	832

YONGLING = 1

Gre. Yongling thou canst not loue so deare as I.	1218

YONGMEN = *1

**Petr.* Such wind as scatters yongmen throgh y world,	616

YOU *see also* y'are = 402*106

YOUL = 2

Petr. Will it not be? | 'Faith sirrah, and you'l not knocke, Ile ring it,	581
Gre. For this reason if you'l kno,	807

YOULL = 2

Hort. You'll leaue his Lecture when I am in tune?	1319
'Tis like you'll proue a iolly surly groome,	1599

YOUNG = 1*1

*how the young folkes lay their heads together.	705
Tra. That's but a cauill: he is olde, I young.	1272

YOUR *l.*58 62 84 85 89 *91 96 *98 102 104 126 127 *154 *155 157 *166 *178 *179 *180 181 *228 230 259 261 269 275 276 277 *283 285 286 289 325 326 334 337 356 359 367 368 376 384 *410 *430 485 498 500 517 519 *530 534 535 544 *549 *550 552 572 577 604 613 716 722 854 *856 890 892 913 922 924 928 *932 938 *950 953 955 961 965 970 978 984 1052 1094 1098 1102 1148 1149 1151 1159 *1164 1170 *1181 *1198 1213 1215 1217 1247 1267 1268 1269 1270 1282 1286 1303 1309 1317 1320 *1327 *1376 1377 1480 1483 1486 1487 1495 1513 1519 *1566 1596 1597 1612 1629 *1698 1856 1860 1871 1924 1935 1939 1940 1958 1960 1966 2047 2060 2061 2085 2090 2101 2143 *2152 2186 2189 2192 2196 2199 *2206 2209 2211 2221 2222 2229 2240 2255 *2274 *2288 2304 2317 2352 2370 *2384 2393 *2404 *2406 *2452 2568 2583 2589 2590 2598 2599 2623 2625 2634 2647 2655 2656 2675 2682 2683 2734 2735 *2750 = 154*40, *1

Wid. Come, come, your mocking: we will haue no | telling.	2689

YOURS = 5

My minde presumes for his owne good, and yours.	781
Kate. Yours if you talke of tales, and so farewell.	1093
Yours will not be entreated: Now, where's my wife?	2642
Katerine, that Cap of yours becomes you not,	2677
My minde hath bin as bigge as one of yours,	2728

YOURSELFE *see* selfe
YOURSELUES *see* selues
YOUTH = 2

Fit to instruct her youth. If you *Hortensio*,	399
Tra. But youth in Ladies eyes that florisheth.	1222

ZENTIPPE = 1

As *Socrates Zentippe*, or a worse:	637

& *l.*152 *281 *347 *430 569 *598 773 *1444 *1454 *1456 *1535 *1566 *1632 *1640 *1644 *1672 *1688 1783 *1957 *2039 *2335 *2348 = 5*18

1HUN = *1
1HUNTS = *1
1MAN = 1*3
1SER = 1*1
2H = *1
2HUN = *1
2M = *1
2MAN = *2
2PLAYER = *1
2SER = *1
3MAN = *3
3SER = 1